HD 30.2 KNO

Knowledge Economy

Knowledge Economy

The Indian Challenge

Edited by

Ashoka Chandra
M.K. Khanijo

Ⓢ**SAGE** Los Angeles • London • New Delhi • Singapore • Washington DC
www.sagepublications.com

First published in 2009 by

SAGE Publications India Pvt Ltd
B1/I-1 Mohan Cooperative Industrial Area
Mathura Road, New Delhi 110 044, India
www.sagepub.in

SAGE Publications Inc
2455 Teller Road
Thousand Oaks, California 91320, USA

SAGE Publications Ltd
1 Oliver's Yard, 55 City Road
London EC1Y 1SP, United Kingdom

SAGE Publications Asia-Pacific Pte Ltd
33 Pekin Street
#02-01 Far East Square
Singapore 048763

Published by Vivek Mehra for SAGE Publications India Pvt Ltd, typeset in 10/12 pt Times Roman by Star Compugraphics Private Limited, Delhi and printed at Chaman Enterprises, New Delhi.

Second Printing 2009

Library of Congress Cataloging-in-Publication Data

Knowledge economy: the Indian challenge/edited by Ashoka Chandra and M.K. Khanijo.
    p. cm.
  Includes bibliographical references and index.
  1. Knowledge management—India.   2. Information resources management—India.   3. Intellectual capital—Economic aspects—India.   I. Chandra, Ashoka.   II. Khanijo, M.K.

HD30.2.K63628	658.4'038—dc22	2009	2008051391

ISBN: 978-81-7829-909-9 (HB)

The SAGE Team: Anjana C. Saproo, Samprati Pani, Gautam Dubey and Trinankur Banerjee

Contents

List of Tables

List of Figures

List of Abbreviations

AA	Arthur Anderson
ADB	Asian Development Bank
AI	Appreciative Inquiry
AIDS	Acquired Immuno Deficiency Syndrome
APO	Asian Productivity Organization
APQC	American Productivity & Quality Center
ASEAN	Association of Southeast Asian Nations
ATI	Administrative Training Institutions
BPO	Business Process Outsourcing
CGIAR	Consultative Group for International Agricultural Research
CoP	Communities of Practice
CRM	Customer Relationship Management
CSIR	Council of Scientific and Industrial Research
CTQ	Critical to Quality
DBE	Digital Business Ecosystem
DE	Digital Ecosystem
DEAL	Digital Ecosystem for Agriculture and Rural Livelihood
DIT	Department of Information Technology, Government of India
DFID	Department for International Development
DoE	Department of Electronics, Government of India
ECIL	Electronics Corporation of India Limited
ELC	Evolutionary Learning Community
ERP	Enterprise Resource Planning
ESP	Extended Sensory Perception
EU	European Union
FDI	Foreign Direct Investment
FSP	Future Search Process
GB	Governing Body
GDLN	Global Development Learning Network
GDP	Gross Domestic Product
GIAN	Gujarat Grassroots Innovation Augmentation Network
GNP	Gross National Product

HCL	Hindustan Computers Limited
HYV	High-Yielding Variety
IBA	Indian Business Academy
IBM	International Business Machines
ICC	International Chamber of Commerce
ICT	Information and Communication Technologies
IDM	International Data Machines
IFFCO	Indian Farmers Fertiliser Cooperative Limited
IIFT	Indian Institute of Foreign Trade
IIM	Indian Institute of Management
IISD	International Institute of Sustainable Development
IIT	Indian Institute of Technology
IIM-A	Indian Institute of Management-Ahmedabad
IIT-B	Indian Institute of Technology-Bombay
IIT-M	Indian Institute of Technology-Madras
IIT-R	Indian Institute of Technology-Roorkee
IMF	International Monetary Fund
IMI	International Management Institute, New Delhi
IMTECH	Institute of Microbial Technology
IMTT	Innovation Management and Technology Transfer
IOP	Industry-Originated Projects
IPN	International Production Network
IPR	Intellectual Property Rights
ISP	Internet Service Provider
ISPIM	International Society for Professional Innovation Management
IT	Information Technology
ITeS	Information Technology-enabled Services
ITI	Industrial Training Institute
IP	Internet Protocol
JIT	Just-in-Time
JICA	Japan International Cooperation Agency
KAM	Knowledge Assessment Methodology
KBCS	Knowledge-Based Computer Systems
KBD	Knowledge-Based Development
KE	Knowledge Economy
KEI	Knowledge Economy Indicator
KIBS	Knowledge-Intensive Business Services
KM	Knowledge Management
KMAT	Knowledge Management Assessment Tool
KPO	Knowledge Process Outsourcing
KVK	Krishi Vigyan Kendra
LGD	Large Group Dynamics
LGIP	Large-Group Interactive Process
MBNQA	Malcolm Baldridge National Quality Award

MC	Management Council
MCA	Ministry of Company Affairs
MCIT	Ministry of Communications and Information Technology, Government of India
MNC	Multi-National Company
MNE	Multi-National Enterprise
NASSCOM	National Association of Software and Services Companies
NEGP	National e-Governance Plan
NEP	Nationally Evolved Projects
NGO	Non-Governmental Organization
NID	National Institute of Design
NIF	National Innovation Foundation
NKC	National Knowledge Commission
NMITLI	New Millennium Indian Technology Leadership Initiative
NPC	National Productivity Council
NPO	National Productivity Organization
NREGP	National Rural Employment Guarantee Programme
NSDP	Net State Domestic Product
OECD	Organisation for Economic Co-operation and Development
OEM	Original Equipment Manufacturer
ORG	Operations Research Group
PAB	Performance Appraisal Board
PBT	Profit Before Tax
PCT	Patent Cooperation Treaty
PDCA	Plan, Do, Check and Action
PPP	Public Private Partnership
PURA	Providing Urban Amenities in Rural Areas
RAC	Research Advisory Council
RC	Research Council
R&D	Research and Development
RPN	Regional Production Network
RTI	Right to Information Act
SAARC	South Asian Association for Regional Cooperation
S&T	Science and Technology
SDP	State Domestic Product
SGD	Small Group Dynamics
SIDA	Swedish International and Development Agency
SIDO	Small Industries Development Organisation
SIRO	Scientific and Industrial Research Organization
SME	Small and Medium Enterprise
SWOT	Strengths, Weaknesses, Opportunities and Threats
TAB	Technology Advisory Board
TCS	Tata Consultancy Services
TNC	Transnational Corporation
ToT	Transfer of Technology

TRIPS	Trade-Related Intellectual Property Rights
UN	United Nations
VLSI	Very Large Scale Integrated Networks
WAN	Wide Area Network
WIPO	World Intellectual Property Organization
WTO	World Trade Organization

Preface

It has been a long journey from an agricultural economy to an industrial economy. The transformation took a few centuries. The increasing pace of change is amply reflected in the next step, that is, development of information technology (IT)-based economy. The IT revolution has witnessed exponential growth of computing power. Moore's Law postulates that the performance of integrated circuits doubles every 18 to 24 months. That is how it has been over the last four decades. Such a record of technological development—30 doublings in computational performance over 40 years—is unprecedented in the history of mankind. While such fast changes throw up immense opportunities, they also present 'emerging systemic risks' resulting from interactions between complex social, technological and economic systems. Social systems have their own inertia and can adjust to slow changes easily. For adjusting to fast changes, proactive policies are needed to expedite changes in society. In the absence of such policies, growth cannot be inclusive. Disparities between the 'haves' and the 'have-nots', manifesting in the rich–poor divide, rural–urban divide, digital divide and the like, are giving rise to serious non-participation in the development process and conflicts within the countries as well as amongst them.

In the globalized knowledge economy as it has emerged till now, corporates use innovation as an integral part of their strategy to deal with competition, diversification of products and services, quality, market share and profits. Innovation at the corporate level is not limited to technology; it extends to marketing, finance, supply chain and management. With the world economy undergoing a process of profound restructuring in the recent times, changes in the economic scene are not confined to production, distribution and delivering value to the customers with the application of information and communication technologies (ICT). A managerial revolution is also under way influencing quality control, team production, supply chain management and customer relations. Yet another development of consequence is the unhindered flow of capital across national boundaries along with diminished role of labour, as understood conventionally, as a factor of production. The emergence of multi-lateral blocs, chief amongst them being the World Trade Organization (WTO), has facilitated harmonization of economic policies across nations and increased the momentum of change.

Human resources have become increasingly more important as conventional labour is being replaced by knowledge workers who can create, utilize and distribute knowledge. The output is shifting more and more towards knowledge goods and knowledge-based services. All of this implies a profound change in the role of labour, and is putting knowledge workers at the centre of all economic and social developments. The main challenge, therefore, is creating a knowledge society where workers would not be mere labour but knowledge workers—producers and users of knowledge.

These developments have been driving the nations in an increasing manner to maintain competitiveness while ensuring the welfare of their people. Changes taking place at the corporate level regarding acquisition, sharing and utilization of knowledge have been having significant implications for public policy at the national level. It has become important to define the public role of knowledge in a knowledge economy. It has also become important to understand the role of public systems in the generation, dissemination and application of knowledge for commercial as well as non-commercial segments of activities.

Thus, national policies, especially in India, have to sharpen the focus on enhancing productivity and growth rate through increased knowledge-intensive economic activities with corresponding emphasis on social development. In the attainment of this objective, India has to utilize the scientific, technological and entrepreneurial talents of its people, which are recognized as being immense. We have to re-orient our management of innovation and knowledge which are important drivers of economic growth and social development. Knowledge management is thus emerging as the key strategy for ensuring competitiveness and social well-being.

Knowledge economy throws up its own challenges, not the least being the fast pace at which it is developing. Since we are still trailing the developed world, we have to run faster if we do not wish to be left behind. We have to map the directions in which the economy is moving and identify changes that must be brought about for the knowledge economy to be competitive. We must prepare the human resource for the knowledge economy by re-orienting the educational and training systems. We must build institutions and institutional linkages, national as well as international, appropriate for knowledge economy. Policies, resources and efforts devoted to building a competitive knowledge economy would be justified only if the benefits accrue to the society, that is, the people of the country.

Precisely with the above considerations in mind, the Ministry of Communications and Information Technology (MCIT) has launched a national initiative for the development of national competitiveness in a knowledge economy. The Ministry awarded a project on this issue to a group of four eminent institutions, namely, the Indian Institutes of Technology at Chennai and Roorkee, the National Productivity Council (NPC) and the International Management Institute (IMI). In late 2006, a national symposium was organized as a part of the project on 'Competitiveness in a Knowledge Economy: Imperatives of Change'. Distinguished experts participated in the symposium and a number of papers were presented and discussed. It was felt that the collection of these papers would form a valuable resource material for those who wish to study the subject and take up further work on it. This volume made use of the papers presented at the symposium and supplemented them with a few more to add value to the endeavour.

We are grateful to MCIT for providing financial assistance for the project that facilitated the organization of the symposium. We wish to thank the contributors of the papers included in this volume. We received the cooperation and support of the four participating institutions of the project and would like to record our appreciation of the same. Many others extended help of various kinds in this task; their assistance is duly acknowledged.

Editors

Overview

ASHOKA CHANDRA AND M.K. KHANIJO

Preamble

Concept of Knowledge

Knowledge is defined as, 'The fact or condition of knowing something with a considerable degree of familiarity through experience, association or contact.' Michael Polanyi (1958/1998) provided an explanation of knowledge upon which models of knowledge creation have been built. He differentiated between explicit, tacit and implicit forms of knowledge. Explicit knowledge is that which is stated in detail and leaves nothing implied. It is termed 'codified' or 'formal' knowledge because it can be recorded. Tacit knowledge is that which is understood, implied and exists without being stated. It is informal, experiential and difficult to capture or share. It is knowledge that cannot be expressed.

Central to Michael Polanyi's thinking was the belief that creative acts (especially acts of discovery) are shot through or charged with strong personal feelings and commitments, and hence the title of his most famous work, *Personal Knowledge.* As Michael Polanyi wrote in *The Tacit Dimension,* we should start from the fact that 'we can know more than we can tell' (Polanyi 1966). He termed this pre-logical phase of knowing as 'tacit knowledge'. Tacit knowledge comprises a range of conceptual and sensory information and images that can be brought to bear in an attempt to make sense of something.

Nonaka and Takeuchi (1995) argue that effective organizational knowledge creation best occurs through the spiral process where knowledge is converted from tacit to explicit in a continuous and dynamic cycle. It is when tacit knowledge and explicit knowledge interact that innovation occurs. Knowledge creation is facilitated by deliberately managing the cycle.

Organizational knowledge creation begins with socialization, where individuals share experience and mental models. It develops into externalization when individuals use metaphors or analogies to articulate hidden tacit knowledge that is otherwise difficult to communicate. It moves into the combination phase for knowledge to be articulated, shared and expounded. Finally, individuals learn by doing and internalizing the new knowledge. The spiral begins again as the experience-based operational knowledge learned in the first cycle provides a larger knowledge base for continuous innovation and growth. It is this model that demonstrates how knowledge comes into action.

Knowledge societies have the characteristic that knowledge constitutes a major input of any activity, particularly economic activities. Economic, social, cultural and all other human activities become dependent on a large volume of knowledge and information. Knowledge, in a knowledge society, becomes a major product as also a significant raw material.

Knowledge management (KM) is about facilitating the process by which knowledge is created, shared and utilized. At the societal level, the aim is to apply the collective knowledge of the entire people to achieve specific societal goals. The knowledge society will investigate knowledge formation and communication processes in organizations from the perspective of the social sciences, investigate group decision-making processes from the perspective of the cognitive sciences to establish information systems that support the creation of knowledge including groupware and attempt to clarify the nature of knowledge through research on complex systems. The knowledge society will provide a fusion of knowledge from the social sciences, humanities, engineering and natural sciences while resourcing knowledge of nature and knowledge available with individuals, organizations and society. It will approach various issues from the perspective of knowledge, a new point of view, without regard to the borders of the traditional disciplines.

Knowledge is emerging as an important parameter in the economic, political and cultural domains. As a result, it is being used to qualify the state of development. The terms 'knowledge economy' and 'knowledge society' reflect the growing significance of knowledge as a measure of advancement of the economy and the society, respectively.

Knowledge presents a promising future because it offers a potential for human and sustainable development and the building of more transparent and democratic societies through the application of new technologies. At the same time, there are some concerns relating to the access to and application of knowledge. For example, within the nations, there is the digital divide. Across the nations, and even within the nation, obstacles appear as intellectual property rights (IPR). These factors could increase the disparities within and across the nations to the disadvantage of the weak.

Context

Economists, administrators, academicians, entrepreneurs, accountants and managers are used to dealing with physical assets and understand their importance and correlations through quantities, wages, prices, profits, and so on. They understand the importance of education, yet they find it difficult to evaluate knowledge, it being abstract and subjective.

Knowledge is an ancient concept. It has been engaging the attention of philosophers and thinkers through the ages. As a result, the concept has been evolving. In particular, its growth, processes of generation, dissemination and areas of application have undergone a radical change. Knowledge can no longer be confined to high-value and high-technology areas. It has to be applied to a variety of situations relating to all human activities. Its benefits have to be made available to the rich and the poor, the industrialist and the worker, the urban and the rural, those who govern as also to those who are governed. Its benefits should be made accessible to all irrespective of their capacity to pay. Therein lies an essential difference between other acquisitions of mankind, such as capital, land, labour and technology, on the one hand, and knowledge on the other.

India was, at some point in the past, at the forefront of knowledge development but centuries of neglect and foreign domination reduced it to a level of relative backwardness. After the country regained freedom in the middle of the last century, it opted for planned socio-economic development to move from an agrarian economy to an industrial economy. While the country was engaged in the process of modernizing its economy and setting up a variety of industries, it witnessed the emergence of information technology (IT). Despite having the disadvantage of being a poor country, India took up the challenge and due to the foresight of its leadership and the talent of its people, it emerged as a global player in IT within a short time. There are now departments of IT in the central government as also in the state governments—India having a federal system with a central government at the federal level and state governments at the state level—for spearheading the IT movement, and evolving policies and strategies for the promotion of IT in the country. The policy framework, infrastructure, educational and research institutions, and industry provided adequate support, and IT professionals rose to the occasion and developed the nation's image as that of a leader moving ahead shoulder to shoulder with the developed nations and competing with them. Information technology is one of the few areas for which the country is known in the outside world.

India may have achieved a great deal in establishing its supremacy in the field of IT, but it has to be striving all the time to make further advances. The subject of knowledge economy is an emerging one and it holds tremendous potential as well as challenges for India. The country's biggest challenge as well as opportunity lies within itself. It has to meet the requirements of its growing masses. Conscious of this responsibility, the Ministry of Communications and Information Technology (MCIT) has developed a 10-point agenda for the development of communications and IT (Office of the Minister for Communications & Information Technology 2006). Among the initiatives in the area of IT that will directly benefit the masses are as follows:

1. Bringing cyber connectivity to every citizen.
2. Providing broadband connectivity to all schools, public healthcare centres and *gram panchayats* by 2010.
3. State-wide area e-governance network over all the states of the country and one lakh community service centres spread over 6,000 blocks.
4. Software tools and fonts for 19 Indian languages by 2007.
5. Information technology and information technology-enabled services (ITeS) sector to provide employment to about 2.2 million software professionals by 2008.

At this juncture, India can see the possibility of widening its horizon to prepare itself for new and emerging challenges of the future. It can foresee that just as IT is the flavour of the present times, biotechnology will emerge as a hot subject over the next couple of decades, and knowledge applications will be the leading thrust area in the remaining part of this century. India is probably among the first few nations in the world which are moving from less-developed status to developing or developed status using knowledge as a differentiator. In addition to IT, some industrial sectors such as pharmaceuticals and biotechnology are already looking at KM as a strategy for dealing with global competition.

Knowledge management is a recently developed area. It is a contribution of the private sector where knowledge as a competitive advantage of the firm is recognized as knowledge capital. More recently, KM has been adopted by the public sector as well. It is now being extended to the functions of the government under the scheme of e-governance. 'There is now persuasive evidence that the information and computer technology (ICT) investment boom of the 1990's has led to significant changes in the absolute and relative productivity performance of firms, sectors and countries' (Hughes and Morton 2005).

The pervasive use of KM has led to the emergence of knowledge worker and knowledge economy.

As a new movement, KM is being initiated by large companies. Most people consider it as more or less the same thing as information management. At the company level, the difference between KM and information management gets blurred because of the extensive use of IT platform for the former. Information overload and a virtual absence of formal training and infrastructure for knowledge managers are posing a challenge for companies globally. Companies need qualified knowledge managers but are finding them hard to come by. The educational system in developed countries is seizing the opportunity and launching programmes for training knowledge managers. Not to be left behind, India is joining the movement and its top-level business and technology institutes are planning to train students in all aspects of KM—data mining and data warehousing, natural language processing, project planning, scheduling and management, information management and security.

Although 'knowledge' is an important concept in considering the direction in which the society should move, the related important issues have not yet been investigated in a scientific manner. For example, questions such as the following need to be answered: What is knowledge in the context of society? Of what practical use is knowledge in delivering services to the people? Or, how can knowledge be created, disseminated and applied with the participation of the people? Many other questions will have to be addressed for developing a future with a focus on 'knowledge'.

An open platform will be useful as a pool of ideas for all companies, educational institutions, government agencies and people's organizations that wish to promote and share knowledge. It can co-operate with education experts, research institutes, universities, business and industry associations, and government and non-government agencies. The aim of such a platform could be to trigger public impulses by means of imaginative ideas and projects and to enlist further institutions and companies for the network. Building up knowledge as a science would imply educating knowledge scientists, training such knowledge creators as project/team leaders, strategic planners, research and development (R&D) managers and those engaged in the production and distribution of goods and services. An institution that meets the above objectives and, in addition, develops pioneers of the knowledge society could be termed as Knowledge School.

The impact of the school's research would manifest in its education, service and outreach activities. The faculty could publish regularly and contribute to scientific literature. Their research work could be of various kinds such as exploratory, conceptual, empirical, policy analysis, diagnostic and evaluatory. In addition, the faculty could, besides offering consultancy services, contribute to the deliberations of various commissions and study committees.

Knowledge schools could soon become preferred destinations for students just as B-schools are at present. There is a growing realization that a country, which aims to become competitive, will need knowledge scientists and managers in large numbers.

Some companies in developed countries are ascertaining how goods can be produced at a lower cost in the developing countries and exploring how to distribute them, again at a lower cost, across their own country. The emerging 'model' has knowledge transfer and KM as a basis for establishing new modes of decentralized and offshore production and distribution. This model has the potential of making drastic changes in the production and consumption patterns in the country. If it can be taken across the world and scaled up, it can make an impact on the global market and significantly alter existing well-set technologies, business models and business paradigms.

While the companies may look at KM in the limited frame of corporate working, those outside, in the government and academia, have to project it over a wider canvas. Their concerns have to be universal encompassing all sectoral activities on the one hand, and all subsystems, on the other. Public policy has to aim at all levels, large, medium and small industries, small-scale and tiny sectors, informal sector and self-employed, manufacturing as well as agriculture, mining, construction, transport and a host of services. Through the development and implementation of appropriate KM policies and strategies, the economy must become competitive, enhance productivity and quality, increase employment and incomes, and improve the delivery of services.

A relatively newer trend in KM is to apply it to the social sectors. In this direction, the possibilities of applying KM techniques to such areas as healthcare and education need to be explored. In countries like India, this is a significant need. The economic sectors are making progress and contributing to the increase in gross domestic product (GDP) growth rate, but the social sector needs greater attention of policy planners for building human capital and providing public welfare. As a process, managing knowledge involves a multi-stage decision framework, starting with investments in R&D to diffusion of knowledge to creation of innovations and finally capturing value through application of inventions and innovations. The whole process is ridden with uncertainties and difficulties in managing the complexities, more so in the social sectors where cost–benefit analysis involves non-commercial parameters.

It is time to rethink the past and focus on policies and programmes for the future suited to the emerging knowledge economy. Various stakeholders may have their concerns. Issues relevant to them should be brought out for conducting an in-depth examination with a view to making recommendations on policies and strategies to be followed for smooth, efficient and fast transformation of the economy.

Objectives

The objectives set for preparing this book are as follows:

1. To present a perspective of changes that are taking place in the economy.
2. To identify the directions that the economy should take for transformation to a knowledge economy.
3. To elicit the concerns of stakeholders regarding the process and consequences of change.
4. To bring out issues that need to be looked into through further research.
5. To provide inputs for the identification of education, training and dissemination of activities.
6. To facilitate the development of research programmes that will lead to recommendations on policies and strategies of change.

Themes

The objectives were translated into themes for the purpose of writing the chapters. Accordingly, authors were requested to focus on the following themes:

1. Mapping the directions of transition from industrial economy to knowledge economy.
2. Anticipating trends and identifying issues for formulating policy initiatives and developing strategies of change management for transformation from industrial age to information age.

3. Identifying new knowledge streams/disciplines that are likely to emerge in the evolving knowledge economy and suggesting specialized courses to help meet manpower requirements of the knowledge economy.
4. Generating deeper understanding, among key stakeholders, of the scope and significance of knowledge, technology, R&D and innovation management for the emerging knowledge economy and developing model course-curricula for adoption by other knowledge institutions.
5. Creating a network of knowledge institutions.
6. Promoting the use of KM as a tool for securing larger good for society.

In all, 27 chapters were prepared. The chapters discuss a variety of issues related to the concerned themes. But the area of each theme is so wide and the amount of work done on KM is so limited that the themes may not be seen to have been covered comprehensively. Besides, it was not the intention to offer solutions through these chapters. The aim was to bring out as many significant issues as possible for deeper study and research.

Directions of Change towards a Knowledge Economy

The transition from industrial economy to knowledge economy will manifest itself at the macro level. However, it must be noted that changes will take place in each of the industrial sectors though at differing pace. These changes also need to be mapped for developing future strategies. Operationally, changes emanate at the organization level and get aggregated at the sector and national levels. It is important to study changes taking place in organizations to get a feel of what is happening at the ground level. As such, for mapping the directions of transition, the entire spectrum will need to be looked at.

Four chapters are grouped under this theme. They are as follows:

1. 'Mapping the Directions of Transition from Industrial Economy to Knowledge Economy' by Vinod Kumar, Harsha Sinvhal and Vinay K. Nangia.
2. 'Conceptual and Assessment Dimensions of Knowledge Management: An Overview' by Vidhu Shekhar Jha, Siddharth Mahajan and Himanshu Joshi.
3. 'Knowledge Management in a Manufacturing Organization' by Ravi Prakash.
4. 'Structure and Behaviour of IT Firms in India' by K. Narayanan and Savita Bhat.

Megatrends

Kumar, Sinvhal and Nangia report in their chapter 'Mapping the Directions of Transition from Industrial Economy to Knowledge Economy' that, according to John Naisbitt, the term 'megatrend' describes a fundamental underlying trend that shapes the future. There are numerous trends, including the shifts from an industrial society to an information society, a national economy to a global economy and hierarchies to networking, but three of them are considered especially important. They are as follows:

1. The increasing power of technology and especially the acceptance of the internet as a key tool of business and commerce.
2. Virtualization—the ability to work and trade over large geographic distances.
3. The emergence of knowledge as a key focus of policy and strategy.

These megatrends can help in visualizing the future, thereby assisting in formulating strategies for taking up the challenges that are likely to emerge in the future. It is, thus, logical to study the megatrends first and then map the transition in a somewhat definitive sense.

The authors have identified the following 13 areas where action is likely to be of great importance:

1. Demography
2. Socio-economic scenario
3. Technology (IT based and non-IT based)
4. Environment
5. Natural resources (renewable and non-renewable)
6. Energy (renewable and non-renewable)
7. Water management
8. Inequalities
9. Health
10. Military
11. Geo-political realities
12. Agriculture
13. Global systems

In each of these areas, the following issues have been brought out for further study.

Demography

1. National and global demography.
2. India versus China.
3. Comparative demography of various continents, namely, Asia, America and Europe.

Socio-economic Scenario

1. Will there be a knowledge divide in times to come?
2. How will knowledge economy change the socio-economic scenario or be governed by it in future? The study may be divided into social, cultural and political scenarios. It may cover regional aspects globally and at the country level. It may also include study of various castes and communities, their role in nation building and Indian diaspora the world over.

Technology

1. Will the role of information and IT continue in the knowledge economy, or will IT in future be used merely as a tool while advances in other non-IT fields overtake IT and once again govern

the economy? The study is expected to see the status of sunset industries and use of technology in such industries.
2. Which are the sunrise industries today and how long are these going to last?
3. Which are the future technologies and industries? What is the likely direction and future of technologies in areas like nanotechnology, material science, bio-sciences and biotechnology?
4. Which new inter-disciplinary subjects and topics will emerge?

Environment

1. In a knowledge economy, will the nations, which are ahead, force nations lagging behind to do the 'dirty' work and produce and take over the 'elite' businesses themselves? What is likely to be the policy framework globally and at the national level?
2. What kind of interventions will be required and what will be the regulatory framework?

Natural Resources

1. What is the possibility of finding new reserves?
2. Shall we change the way we live to be able to manage with decreasing availability of natural resources?
3. Can we find altogether new ways of exploring and/or producing new resources economically?

Energy

1. What are the future energy scenarios for India?
2. Will India, which has climatic advantages, have an edge in the new world order?

Water Management

1. Will there be major international disputes, even wars, over water?
2. How will the country meet fresh water requirements for the growing population with increasing pollution? How will the future water needs be met?
3. Will we supply drinking water which has been condensed from the atmosphere? What will be its effect on climate?
4. Will desalination of the sea water be a practical solution to water availability problems?

Inequalities

1. Which factors will contribute to national, regional and global inequalities?
2. How do we evolve strategies to bridge the gaps? Will knowledge economy widen the divide or bridge it?
3. How can knowledge economy help in making the world a better place with more equitable distribution of resources?
4. How will knowledge economy deal with issues related to equal rights and opportunities, irrespective of colour, race and gender?

Health

1. Will the nature's law of 'survival of the fittest' be challenged? Will advancement in knowledge lead to a less healthy and aged society in which the majority of the old live on the produce of the few?
2. Where will the major health facilities and services reside in the new order? Will access to health-care be available to all sections in all areas?
3. What will be the new health systems and practices in the future? What kinds of new diseases and their cures will emerge? Will there be drastic changes in medicinal systems and practices?

Military

1. What challenges will the knowledge economy pose in relation to the national, regional and world power equations and what will be its effect on economy?
2. What kinds of warfare are expected to take place in future?
3. What shall be the type, kind, style and composition of defence forces of the future? What kinds of military institutions and organizations will evolve in future?

Geo-political Realities

1. What will be the parameter of measuring 'power'? Will the 'military power' or 'currency' or 'monetary' values be replaced by 'knowledge' values?
2. How will the new power equations influence the way people, societies, nations, regions and the world are ruled?

Agriculture

1. Food security.
2. Efficiency and effectiveness of production that covers yield and cropping pattern.
3. Marketing of the agricultural produce at a reasonable price.
4. Storage and distribution.
5. Contribution of agriculture to national economy vis-à-vis the number of persons engaged in or dependent on agriculture.
6. What can be the impact of knowledge economy on the agricultural sector and how will it ensure a better life for a majority of the population?

Global Systems

1. Financial: Will there be international bodies like Bank of International Settlements, or will new systems for global financial order evolve?
2. Trade: Will new bodies and systems evolve in addition to those that exist today, such as the World Trade Organization (WTO) and International Chamber of Commerce (ICC)?

3. Legal: What is going to be the system for global law making and for dispensing justice; will the new bodies and systems come into existence?
4. Global Systems of Cooperation: Will the agencies such as the International Monetary Fund (IMF), United Nations (UN) and World Bank continue to be relevant, or will they change or disappear and be replaced by new ones?

Conceptual Issues at Industry Level

The chapter entitled 'Conceptual and Assessment Dimensions of Knowledge Management: An Overview' by Jha, Mahajan and Joshi discusses, at the industry level, various issues related to knowledge-based assets. These include information about the external business environment, internal business processes and customers. The key is to link the decision makers with the knowledge-based assets that will help them to arrive at good decisions.

In the context of organizations, the authors argue that KM as a business practice is being widely adopted by companies. Knowledge management is the process through which organizations generate value from their knowledge-based assets. Generating value from these assets involves sharing them among employees. Information technology tools enhance the transfer of knowledge-based assets across departmental boundaries within a company. In addition, in order to implement KM, a company needs to consider leadership, culture and measurement issues.

From a survey of literature, the authors identified the following activities through which KM can be pursued in companies:

1. Identify intangible assets.
2. Prioritize the critical knowledge issues.
3. Accelerate learning patterns within the organization.
4. Identify and diffuse best practices.
5. Increase innovation.
6. Increase collaborative activities and a knowledge-sharing culture as a result of increase in awareness of the benefits of KM.

For assessing the implementation of KM within the company, certain methods have been designed. In one of them that incorporates a number of metrics and is used widely for strategy implementation, namely, the Skandia Navigator, measures have been organized into five categories. These are as follows:

1. Financial: includes standard financial measures of performance.
2. Customer: looks at measures of customer satisfaction and retention.
3. Process: focuses on the company's processes and how they are organized to deliver value.
4. Renewal and development: how the organization is preparing for the future, considering such areas as customers, markets and products.
5. Employee related: considers such issues as productivity and values.

In another method, five types of KM metrics, which would help assess the level of KM implementation within a company, have been considered. These are as follows:

1. Technology metrics—number of e-mails, number of online forums, website traffic, number of search queries.
2. Process metrics—response time to queries, meeting international certification Standards.
3. Knowledge metrics—number of employee ideas submitted, best practices created, active CoP.
4. Employee metrics—peer validation, feeling of empowerment.
5. Business metrics—reduced cost, increased market share, improved productivity.

Two knowledge management assessment tools (KMATs) for assessing the level of KM implementation in a company have been referred to. These are (*a*) KMAT developed by American Productivity & Quality Center (APQC) and Arthur Anderson and (*b*) KMAT developed by Maier and Moseley. The tool developed by APQC and Arthur Anderson is divided into five sections: the KM process, leadership, culture, technology and measurement. Within each section four to six questions are used to assess the KM capability within that area. In the KMAT developed by Maier and Moseley, the implementation of KM is assessed in five dimensions: identification and creation, collection and capture, storage and organization, sharing and distribution and application and use. The tool consists of 30 statements on which respondents have to give their response.

The two KMATs together provide a useful way to assess the level of KM implementation in companies. The first tool assesses KM implementation based on the issues of leadership, culture, technology and measurement. The second tool looks at how knowledge in a company is identified, captured, stored, shared and applied. These tools have already been used in companies abroad to assess KM implementation. They could be used in Indian companies too. A review is necessary to see if they need any modifications for use in the Indian situation.

Application of KM in a Specific Industry

Ravi Prakash, in his chapter on 'Knowledge Management in a Manufacturing Organization', has put forward certain issues related to the use of KM in industrial organizations. The importance of KM has become more apparent due to the accelerating pace of change of industrial, political and service environments, staff attrition (especially that resulting from years of downsizing and re-engineering), growth in organizational scope, geographic dispersion associated with globalization of markets, global integration, increase in networked organizations, growing knowledge intensity of goods and services, revolution in IT, and so on. On the increase are complexity of products, services and operations, competition and innovation. On the decrease are staff availability and time required for obtaining skills and expertise. Organizations have to develop systems for generating knowledge, storing it, sharing the same with different teams and making it useful for decision making at all levels.

In the industry, KM draws inputs from a wide range of disciplines and technologies like cognitive science, expert systems, artificial intelligence and knowledge-based management systems, computer-supported collaborative work, library and information science, technical writing, document management, decision support systems, semantic networks, relational and object databases and simulation.

The growth of KM in the manufacturing industry can be attributed to, amongst others, the following needs:

1. Interaction with suppliers, subcontractors and customers.
2. History of previous product runs/projects.
3. Improvement in productivity to deal with shrinking profit margins, shorter life cycles, outsourcing and cost control.
4. Consistent, complete and timely knowledge/information to every entity involved in manufacturing.
5. Re-organization of professional skills due to ever-changing technology.
6. Migration of experts in search of better job opportunities.
7. New recruits taking long time to acquire the required level of skills.
8. Collective learning/capacity for innovation.

The author has suggested the following measures for adopting KM in a manufacturing organization:

1. Pooling of all the information, including work-related files and orders dispatched, etc. Availability of best practices centrally.
2. Capturing of data about customers at the point of sales.
3. Use of R&D to leverage application of the concepts of KM.
4. Creation of greater value from existing intellectual assets.
5. Strategies for focusing on individuals' innovation and knowledge creation.
6. Firm commitment at all the levels of management to a knowledge-focused strategy.

The architecture for KM in a manufacturing industry should be based on integrated system of knowledge manager, enterprise resource planning (ERP) system and process tracker. Enterprise resource planning module consists of production management, production planning, trade promotion, quality control, inventory management, packing and forwarding, purchase, maintenance, personnel and payroll, finance, receipts and payments, and management information system. Process tracker involves capture, transfer and renewal of information as major processes; it is a feedback system in which feedback is sent by the user of process/products to the knowledge manager. Knowledge manager captures this information to modify it and convert it as an input to the knowledge base. Transfer of this knowledge base should be available to user for future reference. Knowledge capturing involves codification, indexing, classification, aggregation and discussion. Transferring is a series of processes by which the organization distributes information and knowledge. By transferring information, the organization permits the user to incorporate, transform and apply the accessible knowledge for turning information into a value-creating process. Renewal of data implies that knowledge has to be adapted, transformed, destroyed and renewed all the time in the process. When all the three entities, namely, ERP system, knowledge manager and process tracker, work in tandem, strategies for KM are accomplished.

The knowledge manager may use a set of tools that could include configurable interface, data integrator, business intelligence, content and document manager, and knowledge enabler.

A manufacturing organization can reap the following benefits after achieving successful implementation of KM:

1. Creation a knowledge base of various batch runs (product category-wise), percentage yield achieved, reasons for improved/reduced yield, process parameters/quality control measures affected, and so on.

2. Tracking production personnel efficiencies and their training/skill needs.
3. Downtime analysis, categorization and breakdown forecast, maintenance scheduling and planning.
4. Production process simulation for a new product or product mix.
5. Capturing of information electronically.
6. Reduced load on personnel.
7. Improvement in the workers' skill profile.
8. Capturing of interactions with quality assurance, production and production planning and control departments.
9. Conservation of energy and materials.
10. Improvement in the final yield.

Emerging Activities

Knowledge management is being introduced in existing activities and organizations. In addition, new types of activities and organizations are emerging which are essentially knowledge based. A typical example of such activities is the IT sector. Narayanan and Bhat examine the structure and behaviour of IT firms in India in their chapter on 'Structure and Behavior of IT Firms in India'. The IT sector has the potential to grow, provide employment and internationalize. It is now recognized that information and communication technologies (ICT) can help in promoting social equity and sustainable development. Further, the drive to use ICT to transform India into a knowledge economy has increased the importance of computer hardware, software and services industry.

The IT industry in India dates back to 1960s. It has many developments as a result of policy changes since then. Major changes could be summarized as follows:

1. Mandatory Indian participation in ownership and control of foreign subsidiaries was introduced in 1970s resulting in the exit of IBM and splitting up of International Computers Limited (ICL).
2. Indian companies such as Tata Consultancy Services (TCS), Electronics Corporation of India Limited (ECIL), Computers Maintenance Corporation (CMC), Hindustan Computers Limited (HCL), DCM Data Products and others came up.
3. During the 1980s, the export of software and computer peripherals was encouraged while permitting import of mainframes and supercomputers.
4. A new computer policy was announced by Department of Electronics (DoE) in 1984 to promote manufacture of latest technology computers at internationally comparable prices. Imports (parts and know-how) were liberalized at low duties to support domestic hardware manufacturers.
5. In 1986, DoE announced a Software Export Development and Training Policy. Duty was cut to 60 per cent, which was subsequently cut to 25 per cent in 1992, and 100 per cent income tax exemption was announced on profits from software export. Most of the regulations were made lenient in this period. The DoE also invested in knowledge-based computer systems (KBCS) programme with five Indian Institutes of Technology (IITs), Indian Institute of Science (IISc) and National Centre for Software Technology (NCST).

6. National Informatics Center set up NICNET, a satellite-based communication network over 439 cities and towns, to computerize government business at all levels.
7. During the 1990s, DoE was reprioritized to promote IT rather than regulate it. Liberalization became more effective.
8. Import duty for software, which was 112 per cent in 1991, fell to 10 per cent by 1995.
9. In 1996, VSNL started internet services. Encouragement in the form of tax incentives, infrastructure, free licensing to Internet Service Providers (ISPs), permission to lay cables or setting up gateways, and so on was given to the industry as value of internet was recognized.
10. Software technology parks were set up in the 1990s to provide duty-free imports of capital goods, high-speed data communication links and tax holidays for 10 years.
11. In the year 2000, the IT Act was enacted. This Act underscores the legal infrastructure for e-commerce and e-governance.

The IT industry in India can be broadly divided into IT services, software products and IT-enabled services and e-businesses.

Recent studies conducted on the IT sector have come up with findings, some of which are as follows:

1. Continuous technological upgradation is an important factor for keeping the industry competitive.
2. Role of transnational corporations (TNCs), especially of tacit knowledge transfer, has been important in the competitive evolution of software segment.
3. Foreign equity participation positively determines export competitiveness of firms in the IT industry.
4. Because of the small product life of computer hardware, know-how technology is especially important for export competitiveness of electrical/electronics (software and services excluded) firms.
5. Multi-national Enterprise (MNE) affiliates in this industry are using only one off arms length technology purchases or tacit technological skills from their foreign equity holder firms, to compete in foreign markets.
6. Established Indian companies are now trying to export more sophisticated, higher value-added software and services that would give them higher margins. However, the relative amount of in-house R&D investment in product R&D in Indian IT software firms is much less as compared to similar-sized firms in other nations.
7. India is still having software and services led growth in the IT sector.

The chapter concludes that the Indian IT sector is enjoying software and service segments led growth. Further, there is a need to encourage the IT industry, especially service firms, to use more sophisticated technologies and to invest in in-house R&D to discover new areas of operation, so that the focus is shifted from low-end routine jobs to high-value-added jobs. Also, around the time when policy makers are trying to reduce concessions offered to the IT industry, there are important policy implications whereby specific concessions like tax holiday could be extended to the new, rather than old firms and the nature of subsidy could shift to promote technological capabilities in general and R&D investments in particular.

Trends and Issues in Formulating Policy Initiatives and Developing Strategies of Change Management

The transformation from industrial economy to knowledge economy will be smoother if a congenial policy environment is created. For developing policies and strategies for change management, it is necessary to project trends in the economy and identify issues that need to be dealt with in the policy framework. Research and analysis should provide the necessary inputs to policy makers. All discussions on change management at the macro level should, therefore, lead to recommendations on policies and strategies.

Five chapters are discussed under this theme. They are as follows:

1. 'India's Transition to Knowledge Economy: Variation across States' by Arindam Banik and Pradip K. Bhaumik.
2. 'An Approach to Developing Knowledge Economy Indicators for Individual States' by Siddharth Mahajan, Ashoka Chandra and Mainak Sarkar.
3. 'Knowledge Management Initiative and Practice for Moving towards Learning Organization and Business Excellence' by Himanshu Joshi, Vidhu Shekhar Jha and Siddharth Mahajan.
4. 'New Approaches to Management Research and Knowledge Building: Division, D-Vision and Direct Vision Approaches and Their Convergence' by Subhash Sharma.
5. 'A Note on Change Management Processes' by M.D.G. Koreth.

Inter-state Variation in Transition to Knowledge Economy

Banik and Bhaumik, in their chapter on 'India's Transition to Knowledge Economy: Variation across States', analyse the performance of the Indian states in terms of their convergence based on select state domestic characteristics. The analysis is carried out within distinctive groups of states to reflect different institutional and economic parameters in the light of the current situation. On the basis of analysis of statistical data, the authors infer as follows:

1. The current structure of the select state economies with the help of broad primary and secondary sectors' contribution to state domestic product (SDP) in 2003–04 indicates that three clear pictures are discernible. One, the contribution of the tertiary sector to the respective SDP appears to be dominating for the southern states. Two, as regards the northern states, the role of the primary sector is distinct. Gujarat, on the other hand, has taken a commanding position with the help of its secondary sector. This postulates the possibility of convergence and divergence across states.
2. Data reveal the beneficial effects of investment in human capital and institutions across states. Quite significantly, the new economy services contributed to net state domestic product (NSDP) in southern states and hence raising their per capita income. West Bengal and Maharashtra have recently encroached in these areas. Basic literacy, on the other hand, has little role to play in raising the per capita income. This implies the need for further investment in human capital. Currently this unskilled population is in the wrong line of work. The cities are now hungrier for skilled

populations. The poor in backward states are less likely to be at school despite the government regulation of education till 16 years of age.

3. The rise of 'knowledge industries' is a new aspect of India's future development. This is the Indian edition of 'leapfrog' where human capital in the high-technology sector has acted as a powerful engine of growth. States (such as Gujarat, Maharashtra) which are relatively well developed due to manufacturing activities have human capital in the low-technology sector, less intervention by the state sector and their geographical closeness to prosperous cities.

4. States which are relatively well developed due to high technology (computers, software) have created human capital from endogenous factors such as proactive policies and other interventions in order to create an appropriate environment.

The authors conclude that economic factors alone may not be sufficient to explain the development of human capital. Sometimes the issue of culture dominates priorities. These are questions that can be rigorously tested in future research and raise an exciting set of questions.

Knowledge Economy Indicators at State Level

Mahajan, Chandra and Sarkar, in their chapter entitled 'An Approach to Developing Knowledge Economy Indicators for Individual States', have adapted the World Bank approach for assessing the KM attainment of the states. According to the World Bank Knowledge Assessment Methodology (KAM), the knowledge economy framework consists of four pillars. These are education and training, innovation and technological advancement, information infrastructure and a proper economic and institutional regime. While the authors are still in the process of finalizing the variables to be measured for three of the four pillars, they have computed the normalized score for the information infrastructure pillar for states. Delhi and Punjab are the two highest-ranking states on the information infrastructure pillar while Jharkhand and Chhattisgarh are the bottom two states. A suggestion has been made in the chapter to interpret the state Knowledge Economy Indicator (KEI). The state KEI has been proposed to be calculated by taking the average of the normalized scores on the four pillars of the knowledge economy for each state. The state KEI in any period is a measure of the relative performance of the state compared to other states, in moving towards a knowledge economy. One can compare the state KEI in a reference year (for example, 2000) to the state KEI in the current year. Also cited is a methodology for assessing the effect of knowledge economy indicators on economic growth. This is done by fitting a regression model with the dependent variable being annual economic growth and the independent variables being knowledge economy indicators together with other variables.

Growth of Learning Organizations

Companies worldwide have used the concept of KM to harness the potential of individuals and teams, and use it as a strategy for success. The chapter on 'Knowledge Management Initiative and Practice for Moving towards Learning Organization and Business Excellence' by Joshi, Jha and Mahajan is an attempt to establish a linkage between KM and learning organization, and how it helps in moving towards business excellence. Business excellence, with respect to improved performance of people and processes, customer satisfaction and creation of a better society, is achieved through appropriate use of knowledge assets of individuals and teams. A learning organization is a group of people continuously enhancing their capacity to create what they want to create.

There are several themes, which emerge from various perspectives on learning organizations. They are as follows:

1. In order to grow, organizations need to learn continuously.
2. Both individuals and organizations learn, using different methods, producing different outcomes.
3. Information storage, processing and sharing are important.
4. Context (structure and culture) contributes to organizational learning.

Knowledge management and learning organization should be taken up as an integrated and reinforcing concept. This approach may exploit newly acquired knowledge for continuous learning. As knowledge mandates an adaptive and responsive culture, this integrative approach may facilitate knowledge creation and transfer throughout the organization. This will enable organizations to develop a shared vision among its stakeholders and ability to realize it. The end result is quality improvements across the organization, be it quality of knowledge, quality of relationships, quality of decision making and improved performance.

Widening the Conceptual Framework of Knowledge

The meaning of knowledge is understood by all but the concept is defined variously and vaguely.

It is necessary to distinguish between data, information and knowledge to understand the differences and relationships in this continuum. The terms 'information' and 'data' are often used interchangeably with the term 'knowledge'. These terms have different meanings. In general, data are raw facts. For data to be useful for making decisions or interpreting patterns, it has to be processed to obtain information. Knowledge is perceived as meaningful information. While data and information are characterized by their 'organization', information and knowledge are differentiated by 'interpretation' (Bhatt 2001). Knowledge is an understanding gained through experience, reasoning, intuition and learning. Individuals expand their knowledge when others share their knowledge, and one's knowledge is combined with the knowledge of others to create new knowledge (CIO Council 2001).

Knowledge is derived from information. It results from making comparisons, identifying consequences and making connections. Sometimes wisdom and insight are also included in the definition of knowledge. Wisdom is the utilization of accumulated knowledge. Knowledge also includes judgement and 'rules of thumb' developed over time through trial and error. Davenport and Prusak (1998) defined knowledge as a fluid mix of framed experience, values, contextual information, expert insight and grounded intuition that provides an environment of and framework for evaluating and incorporating new experience and information. Knowledge pyramid, shown in Figure 1 is a way of representing the continuum graphically (Cong and Pandya 2004).

Figure 1   Continuum from Data to Wisdom

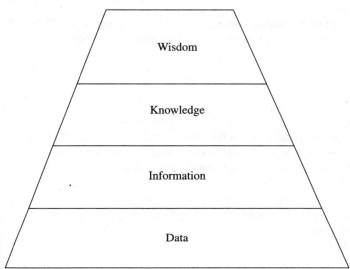

Knowledge is becoming an important resource and is considered the key source of comparative and competitive advantage (Swan and Newell 2000). For some, knowledge is 'economic ideas' (Wigg 1997) or 'intellectual capital' (Stewart 1997) and is talked about in terms of 'stockpiles', 'reservoirs', 'exchange', 'capture' and 'utilization', without understanding its epistemology—knowing it exists and understanding its context, and hence, its importance (Swan and Newell 2000).

Our understanding of knowledge is evolving. The concept of knowledge may be extended to the 'conscious' and the 'sub-conscious'. Sharma, in his chapter on 'New Approaches to Management Research and Knowledge Building: Division, D-Vision and Direct Vision Approaches and Their Convergence', has attempted to elaborate on the concept in the framework of different quantum states of mind. He states that there are mainly three quantum states of mind, namely, Division, D-Vision and Direct Vision. He also identifies a fourth state that represents convergence wherein mind operates at the convergence level as well as at the extended sensory perception level. In Division state, the mind operates at the divided vision level. In this state, a problem is divided into sub-problems and solutions are sought through this process of division. In D-Vision state, the mind looks at all the aspects of the problem simultaneously. In Direct Vision state, the mind operates at the direct-perception level, wherein it is at the intuitive and revelation level leading to tacit knowledge. Division approach is at the core of the 'Western Enlightenment', D-Vision at the core of 'Eastern Awakening' and Direct Vision approach at the core of 'Many Routes to *Nirvana*' representing three historical processes and three major thought currents that have influenced the world in many ways.

Management researchers have largely been influenced by the 'Western Enlightenment' tradition. There is a need to expand the horizons of management and social science research, and knowledge creation by following other paths, namely, the 'Eastern Awakening' and 'Many Routes to *Nirvana*'. In addition to the three quantum states of mind, there is also the fourth quantum state that represents the convergence state and could be referred to as the DEAN (Direct Enlightenment Awakening and *Nirvana*) state of mind. In this state of mind, 'Western Enlightenment', 'Eastern Awakening' and 'Many Routes to *Nirvana*' find a new convergence.

A summing up of an informal discussion on these issues, prepared by Divya Kirti Gupta, entitled 'Towards Knowledge Society—A Discussion', is presented as Appendix to this book.

Change Management Processes

Koreth describes, in his brief chapter 'A Note on Change Management Processes', an operational strategy to bring in change. According to him, for a long time, global research in change processes has been focusing on small group dynamics. In recent years, that is, since 1985, attention is being paid to large-group dynamics in order to facilitate multi-stakeholder collaboration and change in:

1. Organizations (of various kinds, both private and public);
2. communities (urban and rural);
3. professional groups; and
4. cities and states.

Research, experimental work and practice in small-group and large-group dynamics have resulted in the demonstration of two successful change processes, namely,

1. Future Search Process (FSP) and
2. Large-Group Interactive Process (LGIP).

These two methodologies are based on the following principles:

1. All the multiple stakeholders need to be identified, represented and involved full-time in the process.
2. The process is experiential, combining rational/cognitive and emotive/relationship factors, in tandem. The change process cannot be only rational or informational.
3. The process is participative, consultative and works through small group dynamics (within the large-group dynamics process).
4. Multiple stakeholders will usually have some common interests, some differing interests and some opposing or conflicting interests. These two (FSP and LGIP) processes help the participants to discover common ground, develop common solutions and generate/sustain their own energy to implement change or new projects successfully.
5. The 'Future Search Process' (as the term implies) focuses on 'The Future of X', in a certain time-span typically of five years although it could range from 3 to 10 years, depending on the nature of the project. The FSP creates and sustains strong ownership in all the participants and they take on personal responsibility and accountability for detailed planning, resource generation and execution. The FSP works typically with 80–100 stakeholders in a large open hall. In FSP everyone is a resource as also a participant in an experiential, action-learning process. If FSP feels it needs more expertise than it possesses, it can find it outside the group.

6. While the FSP focuses on creating a preferred future, the LGIP (250 to 500 stakeholder-participants) focuses on resolving current issues or finding and implementing agreed solutions to current problems. This process also helps distil common ground, common interests, common goals and common solutions, with a strong sense of ownership and commitment to implementation. The combined pool of knowledge, experience and competence is tapped through the processes of large-group dynamics and small-group dynamics.

These two proven processes are relevant to developing strategies of change management for transformation to the knowledge economy.

Human Resource Development for the Knowledge Economy

The emergence of knowledge economy will require a wide variety of expertise. All sectors of the economy and all levels of occupations are affected by the transformation of the economy. Skills need to be relevant not only for the operational needs of economic activities but also for their upgradation and improvement. A host of new activities, processes and technologies are likely to come up throwing up the need for some new occupations. Thus, the occupational profile and the content of occupations will witness large changes. For developing the appropriate occupational profile, education and training systems will have to cater to skill development needs of the emerging economy. Development of human resource will, therefore, be a critical component for the success of the initiative to evolve a knowledge economy.

One chapter is discussed under this theme: 'Identifying New Knowledge Streams in the Evolving Knowledge Economy' by Prema Rajagopalan and M.S. Mathews

Emerging Knowledge Streams/Disciplines

The chapter by Rajagopalan and Mathews is based on internal consultations within IIT-Madras and it outlines the teaching and research areas in engineering and technology considered important in the context of a knowledge economy. Their findings are summarized as follows:

1. Power and communications

    (*i*) Power quality
    (*ii*) Industry-oriented communications

2. Computer science

    (*i*) Cryptography and Security network
    (*ii*) Very Large Scale Integrated (VLSI) networks
    (*iii*) Bio-informatics
    (iv) Data mining

3. Biotechnology

   (*i*)   Biotechnology applications in industry, agriculture and healthcare
   (*ii*)   Bio-informatics

4. Infrastructure

   (*i*)   Transport
   (*ii*)   Power
   (*iii*)   Housing
   (*iv*)   Telecommunications
   (*v*)   Water supply and sanitation

5. Nanotechnology

   (*i*)   Solar energy
   (*ii*)   Carbon nanotubes

6. Energy

   (*i*)   Generation, conversion, conservation, storage and distribution
   (*ii*)   Mainstreaming energy from renewable sources
   (*iii*)   Decentralization of power generation from fossil fuels

7. Manufacturing

   (*i*)   Machine tools engineering
   (*ii*)   Manufacturing processes

8. Mechatronics

   (*i*)   Automation
   (*ii*)   Robotics

For making the programmes relevant and useful, various strategies have been suggested in the chapter. They include

1   interaction with industry;
2. sponsorship of students by industry for Master's programmes;
3. reverse engineering for producing innovations;
4. inter-disciplinary cooperation; and
5. networking of institutions.

Suggestions made in the chapter will undergo further processing through discussions with the industry. Expansion of such efforts has other dimensions as well. Some of them are referred to as follows:

1. Range of disciplines: New disciplines need to be identified in other areas as well, for example, physical sciences, life sciences, social sciences.
2. Levels of education: In addition to degree and postgraduate levels, programmes have to be introduced at diploma (polytechnics) and certificate (ITI) levels.
3. Quality of education: Existing institutions and programmes should be improved. Attention has to be paid to contents and their relevance, pedagogy, evaluation, infrastructure, teachers' quality and training.
4. In-service training: Because of fast changes in technology, and consequently skill requirements, workers of all levels should be provided training interventions periodically. As such, an exhaustive plan of training a variety of occupations at various stages of their career has to be evolved.
5. Informal economy: Training, induction as well as mid-career, has to be imparted to workers in the informal economy. This has been a hitherto neglected area.

Scope and Significance of Knowledge, Technology, R&D and Innovation Management for the Emerging Knowledge Economy

The transformation to a knowledge economy will entail changes in the thinking and working of organizations and people who have the potential for contributing to or benefiting from it. Stakeholders will need to develop a deeper understanding of the role of knowledge, technology, R&D, innovation, and so on in the growth of the knowledge economy. Efforts will, therefore, be required for advocacy, sensitization, adoption, education and dissemination of knowledge economy and its imperatives amongst the stakeholders.

The key stakeholders could be classified broadly as follows:

1. Policy makers and implementers, that is, relevant government departments
2. Academic institutions, for example, educational, training and research institutes
3. Corporate sector, industry associations and small-scale industries
4. Workers organizations
5. Non-governmental organizations (NGOs), especially those engaged in the promotion of and skill development for the informal economy
6. School/college/university students and unemployed persons
7. International agencies

The following eight chapters are discussed under this topic:

1. 'Key Stakeholders for the Knowledge Economy' by Prema Rajagopalan and M.S. Mathews
2. 'Knowledge, Science and Technology' by Abid Hussain

3. 'Innovation in Knowledge Economy' by Rajeeva Ratna Shah
4. 'Intellectual Property Rights (IPR) in Knowledge Management(KM)' by A.K. Sengupta
5. 'Research Planning and Management in a Knowledge-Intensive R&D Organization: The Case of CSIR-India' by Naresh Kumar
6. 'Strategy and Structure in the Knowledge Enterprise' by Arun P. Sinha
7. 'Expectations of SME Sector from Knowledge Economy' by K.K. Sarkar
8. 'New Public Management in the Emerging Knowledge Economy' by T.S. Krishna Murthy

Stakeholders

In their chapter on 'Key Stakeholders for the Knowledge Economy', Rajagopalan and Mathews report the findings of a survey conducted amongst selected industrial and R&D establishments located in Chennai. They looked at eight organizations engaged in areas critical to the nation's economy. The responses of the organizations define the existing linkages between the academia and industry in the following terms:

1. Visits of the industry team to engineering colleges all over the country, where students are addressed and apprised of opportunities of working with their organization.
2. Faculty of elite institutions taking up collaborative research including funding for such endeavours by the industry.
3. Sponsoring the industry staff for higher degrees in reputed educational institutions with whom Memoranda of Understanding have been signed.
4. Recruitment missions and sporadic contacts with the academia.

Some initiatives were suggested by the respondents to enlarge the scope of linkages. They include

1. taking part in regular teaching of some units of existing courses in academic institutions;
2. participation in and providing inputs for designing new courses that would be important;
3. offering internships to engineering undergraduates, but laid a minimum period of six months for the programme to be effective;
4. facilitating collaboration with interested faculty so that research can help solve shop-floor problems; and
5. sponsoring their staff for higher education in academic institutions.

Regarding training fresh graduates, IT industries expect generic skills and they have a regular scheme of providing specific skills to them. Others unanimously felt a large gap between what the students learn and what is actually required. Some industries spend almost a year training their new recruits and consider this time as some kind of a loss. 'A passing comment on graduates from elite institutions is that they are theoretically good but do not have sufficient knowledge to handle problems' (see Chapter 11).

Sunrise industries seem to have a healthy relationship with the government. Their contribution to employment growth as well as economic growth is recognized. At the same time, the government, as a funding agency for R&D, spends a large share of research funds on work of interest to such industries. The legacy industries are not too happy. They feel that their contribution to the country's development should not be under-rated, and the support in terms of policies and programmes is inadequate and non-facilitating. Preferential treatment for small and medium enterprises (SMEs) further weakens support of the government to large industries of the old economy.

It may be stated here that discussions of linkages between industry and academic institutions have been going on for a long time. The All India Council for Technical Education (AICTE) has a Board for Industry–Institute Interaction. The Council for Scientific and Industrial Research (CSIR) has been aiming to, among others, improve and enlarge the communication channels with customers and stakeholders; involve and associate professionally equipped personnel/group in each laboratory and/or external (foreign/Indian) organizations/consultants in business development and marketing activities; and permit select CSIR laboratories to set up separate companies/legal entities for business development and marketing (see website of CSIR at www.csir.res.in for more details). There has been some progress by way of campus recruitment, funding of consultancy projects, and so on but the association is limited to top-level institutions and companies. Much more needs to be done by each constituency to take the linkages to visible levels. For instance:

1. Academic institutions should regard industry-related work as a mainstream activity and give due credit to their researchers/faculty for successful assignments. Also, they should develop a professional approach in terms of quality of output, budgets, time schedules, and so on.
2. Industry should consider supporting long-term initiatives such as instituting chairs, funding acquisition of expensive equipment/software, starting specialized programmes, and so on.

Science and Technology

Abid Hussain, in his chapter on 'Knowledge, Science and Technology', looks at knowledge as an all-pervasive entity which will expand and become our most valuable resource. Science and technology (S&T) helps us to take advantage of old and new knowledge, inventions and discoveries, innovations, R&D, and so on.

Man has always had an urge to study the nature and its principles. The curiosity led to inventions and discoveries as a conquest of the mind. At the ground level, technology and science or rather knowledge was converted into various products and services. The success of nations today is not due to their having land, labour and capital, but those nations that have access to knowledge have been able to bring about many great changes utilizing the remaining factors of production. Knowledge has broken the barriers which were preventing outside ideas and thoughts from coming into the market. Today, knowledge flows easily and new ideas are accessible to everybody without let or hindrance. We can neither stop competition, nor can we prevent people from coming into our country, making things and selling them. Consumers will decide what they wish to buy and their choice will depend on their getting the best value for money.

People of India have the talent, drive and enterprise to succeed in a competitive environment, as proved by them in other countries. Their efforts will be fruitful if backed by suitable policy measures. One of the measures required for the purpose is spread of education of all levels. Another measure is to promote a culture of innovation. A connected issue is the regime of patents. We have to train people in the industry and outside in reading and understanding the patents and getting along with the related work. In this context, we should also look at the traditional knowledge available in India.

Nehru had underscored the need for developing a scientific temper. Knowledge of S&T is extremely important and it has to be intertwined with cultural values. We should be willing to do things that are correct and things that are new and worth doing, and we should be prepared to break the barriers for going ahead.

Innovation and Knowledge

A knowledge economy is somewhat different from a conventional market economy, explains Rajeeva Ratna Shah in his chapter on 'Innovation in Knowledge Economy'. The current market economy is based on capital, and capital shrinks with sharing. Knowledge, on the other hand, increases with sharing. While a market economy functions purely on the basis of competition, in a knowledge economy, competition is going to be there eventually but there is an increasing role of collaboration in innovation activities even amongst competitors. India stands way behind the developed countries and even behind developing countries such as Brazil and China in terms of innovative capacity. This shows that India has a long way to go to overcome competition for superiority, which is intense, to realize its potential as a knowledge power.

Innovation goes beyond technology innovation. It includes technology information, product information, process information, product innovation, process innovation, market innovation, and so on. Innovation leads to the creation of intellectual property and intellectual property will be, in a knowledge economy, the hallmark of competitiveness. It is the modern technology sector that is contributing mainly to knowledge and innovation. This sector comprises activities such as nanotechnology, computers, networks and biotechnology. It is important to consider the legacy economy also for competitiveness, for in the legacy sector major interventions are required. That is why it would be necessary to identify the building blocks and promote innovations therein for creating India as a new manufacturing power. To this end, we need to take care of innovation, technology, design, micro-cost monitoring, ICT applications to management processes, ICT application to technology processes and global benchmarking of quality.

Innovation assumes strong individual intellectual power. For developing the human resource with this purpose, creativity should be nurtured. This also implies that bright young persons should be taking up careers in R&D and innovation. This has not been happening in recent years. The government is now considering proposals to attract talented young persons to higher education in science through the award of scholarships and fellowships on a large scale.

For making investment in R&D efficient in terms of wealth generation, private sector should play a larger role. However, government initiative will be necessary to make it possible for the private sector to create expensive facilities, possibly through incentives and with the involvement of industry associations. As has been noticed in other countries, a great deal of pre-competitive collaborative research may have to be taken up by competitors.

While dwelling on technology support to design, supply chain management, customer relations management, manufacturing, nano-manufacturing, and so on and technology benchmarking, the chapter also looks at instances of ICT applications in society. In this context, two examples of creation of unique IDs have been described, one for villages and the other for individuals and firms.

Intellectual Property Rights

In his chapter on 'Intellectual Property Rights (IPR) in Knowledge Management (KM)', Sengupta has discussed some of the pertinent topics related to IPR together with their relevance to KM. The status of the IPR and R&D in India has also been briefly brought up, as well as the state of the knowledge society in this country. For an effective KM system to be in place, the issue of ownership of the intellectual property of knowledge can be of paramount importance. Safeguarding the IPR in a transparent, efficient and effective manner facilitates identification, creation, acquisition and sharing of knowledge. This is particularly relevant for bringing out the tacit knowledge residing with experts and people with experience, grass-root innovators and traditional knowledge holders.

Intellectual property rights formalize people to own their creativity and innovation in the same way that they can own physical property. The owner of intellectual property (IP) can control and be rewarded for its use, and this encourages further innovation and creativity to the benefit of the society. It will often not be possible to protect IP and gain IPR without their having been applied for and granted. Although there are many types of IP, the chapter is confined mainly to patents. An IPR database becomes a fairly detailed archive of globally accessible knowledge whose exploitation is subject to national IPR laws. A proper use of the IPR databases, therefore, forms an essential part of a global KM process.

Innovations, almost in all cases, require efforts and resources, sometimes substantial in financial terms. Therefore, protection of IPR for all such innovations needs to be a priority so that eventual commercialization can take place.

Two of the major issues relating to IPR have been highlighted. They are as follows:

1. Sharing of credit/rewards by the scientist and the employing organization, and
2. Intellectual Property Rights in case of collaborative and sponsored research.

The first India Patent Act was introduced in 1856. It was modified and amended in 1911. After independence, a more comprehensive bill on patent rights was enacted in 1970. In the Patent Act, 1970, emphasis was on acquisition of technology from the developed world in order to build infrastructure in all sectors of the economy. Provision for registering product patents in the 1970 Act was not included. Instead, process patents were the primary instruments in protecting IP. The awareness about IPR was low among the scientific community in the country and licensing regulations and laws discouraged patent registrations from abroad. Patenting activity increased at a fairly rapid rate since 1950s until 1970, when the new and weak patent law was implemented. There was a significant fall thereafter in patenting, especially in the areas of chemicals, food, rubber and plastic products.

The level of patenting activity in India remained low until early 1990s, when India became a member of the World Trade Organization (WTO). The agreement on Trade Related Intellectual Property Rights (TRIPS) in the WTO necessitated harmonization of the relevant Indian patent-related laws with the international standards, and accordingly several new legislations and amendments in existing laws were enacted by the Parliament. The number of applications for patenting in India, which was around 3,000 per year until 1994 (compared with the US figure of 300,000), rose to 17,500 in 2004–05. This number is expected to increase further in the future, especially after the 2005 amendment. In the expanding knowledge economy in India, there is a clear demand for accelerating the processes of identification, development, dissemination and uptake of innovations. Besides the modern scientific knowledge, the Indian civilization has traditional knowledge and grass-roots-level innovative practices, largely in the rural and tribal areas. Safeguarding the IPR of these grass-roots innovators and traditional knowledge holders would be a first step in the process of bringing them out into the open. With the new IPR regime in place, an interactive KM system can be envisioned with the involvement of all the stakeholders in the economy.

Planning and Management of R&D

Planning and management of research in an organization whose major activity is research is a complex task. Various systems and procedures have to be installed for effective management of resources—material and intellectual. In public-funded research institutions, accountability becomes even greater. Naresh Kumar has presented, in his chapter entitled, 'Research Planning and Management in a Knowledge-Intensive R&D Organization: The Case of CSIR-India', a case study of the Council of Scientific and Industrial Research (CSIR) which is a public-funded body having 38 laboratories located all over the country. Tracing the changes that took place over the years in the management systems of research in CSIR, the author shows how CSIR evolved as a knowledge-intensive, multi-location, multi-sectoral industrial R&D organization. Lessons drawn from this transformation are summarized here.

The organization has to develop a vision for its long-term role. The vision should characterize the organization in terms of areas of work, expertise level and its development, facilities, type of research, funding and revenue model, service to users and society, national and international benchmarking, interface with stakeholders, consultative mechanisms, assessment and evaluation systems, and so on. An important feature of knowledge-intensive institutions is networking.

This experience of networking presented in the two examples cited in the chapter shows that in R&D/technology management, ultimately it is the network partners' stake which determines the success of networking. Networking has now been made an integral part of R&D and technology management in the whole of CSIR.

Knowledge Enterprises

Knowledge enterprises are characterized by a high rate of utilization of knowledge and its rapid obsolescence. In such enterprises, knowledge is a main driver of competitiveness.

Sinha has described in his chapter on 'Strategy and Structure in the Knowledge Enterprise' the features of such organizations and the key features of the strategies that such organizations can employ to ensure success. He has also outlined the salient features of the structures that can aid their achievement of goals.

Amongst the stakeholders, the buyers and users are two critical and distinct players. In some cases, it is the end-user customer, rather than the buyer, who is more relevant. Knowledge process outsourcing (KPO) companies for instance have assignments from a wide range of consultants. In the investment domain, the end-user may be an individual or a mutual fund that needs the advice of the consultant, which in turn seeks a specific set of data or analytics that the KPO company can provide.

A key business stakeholder, other than the founders, is a venture capital entity, especially in the early stages of a knowledge enterprise. Search for business stakeholders is an ongoing concern. In many cases, the founders establish and develop the enterprises so as to make them saleable at the right opportunity.

Knowledge enterprises face unique challenges of (*a*) risk and uncertainty regarding the potential of market for a technology; (*b*) proprietary technology especially when the technology may be co-operatively developed by competitors who work on independent parts; (*c*) low-entry barriers since many of the real challengers to an existing successful enterprise come from the 'garage', such as 'Apple' and 'Google'; (*d*) learning curve effect resulting in a rapid decline in the price of knowledge products and (*e*) first-time users, as is the case with buyers for many knowledge enterprises, making difficult the marketing task of inducing customers to overcome product concerns and buy. Among the strategic moves the author has highlighted are fast to the market, differentiation on features or technology, consumer trial, upgradation of technology and alliance with key suppliers.

Typical features of the structure of a knowledge enterprise include (*a*) less of barriers across the structure; (*b*) more of collaborations; and (*c*) higher capacity for change and rapid learning.

While knowledge enterprises could be spread over a large variety of activities, relatively more knowledge-intensive enterprises could be technology development players, technology acquirers, technology utilizers or vendors and implementers.

Small and Medium Enterprises

Sarkar, in his chapter on 'Expectations of SME Sector from Knowledge Economy', presents the point of view of SMEs, especially with regard to their sustainability in a knowledge economy. He suggests how SMEs can become more competitive in a knowledge economy.

Small and Medium Enterprises are important in view of the significant role they can play in promoting inclusive growth through expansion of opportunities of productive, sustainable and widely dispersed employment at competitively lower per capita costs. For SMEs to be effective in this role, they need diffusion of new knowledge for technology upgradation. A vast number of SMEs are 'unregistered' and are thus in the unorganized sector. Such units as are in the unorganized sector should also have access to knowledge, invention and innovation, enabling them to update their technology, products and services.

One of the measures for the benefit of the unorganized sector and for updating the knowledge of its workers could be the expansion and renovation of the Industrial Training Institutes (ITIs) located in various states and improvement of their curriculum to make it more compatible with the products and skill needs of the unorganized sector. The author suggests, for improving the ITIs, the following:

1. Accreditation of ITIs,
2. Re-training and certification of instructors; and
3. Connectivity with R&D organizations.

While the Government of India has come out with a set of strategies, for example, cluster development for the SME sector, technology upgradation of the small-scale industries under capital-linked subsidy scheme, and many other facilities. Encouraged by such support, SMEs are going in for product innovation in their own way.

The Small Industries Development Organization, Ministry of Small Scale Industries, Government of India, has a number of field units such as the regional testing centres, field testing stations, production centres, tool room/tool designing institutes, product-cum-process development centres, central footwear training institutes and entrepreneurship development training institutes. Again there are small industries service institutes in all the states. However, regarding the working of such field units and institutes, measures have become necessary for their development and modernization so as to make them more relevant and research oriented to cater to the growing needs of the unorganized sector.

The author suggests certain measures for facilitating the integration of SME in a knowledge economy. They include the following:

1. The creative element in the output of the SME sector can also be regarded as intellectual property and is, therefore, subject matter of intellectual copyright, as a specific expression of an idea and not the idea itself.
2. Small and medium enterprisess are not aware of the mechanisms and methodology of protecting their rights. Therefore, there is an emergent need to sensitize the SMEs on this issue.
3. Small and medium enterprises are not aware about the new developments in technology, invention, design, and so on. As such, there is a need for the penetration of Internet in the SME sector and introduction of e-business so that the SMEs can get the benefits of the same.
4. When the defence establishments develop indigenous designs to meet the requirements of components as export substitution, it would be befitting if the defence establishments utilize the ingenuity of the small component manufacturing units by giving them support by way of designs with appropriate raw materials. Since SMEs are deficient in resources and outreach, defence establishments need to be relatively more proactive.
5. Small and tiny units cannot by themselves have access to knowledge, innovations and research, so there should be a nodal agency to store information on innovations, design and products for dissemination to interested units.

As the author concludes, 'Knowledge should be utilized for creation of new and better products and services and more and more of employment. It should have its application in labour-intensive organizations which are employment-oriented and need to improve productivity and incomes of its workers.'

Public Management

A knowledge society would be characterized by the application of knowledge not only in business, industry, education and healthcare but also in governance and public administration. Today, the two important challenges facing many developing countries, including India, are appalling poverty and protection of democracy from terrorism and violence. In emerging democracies such as India, standards of governance are disturbingly low despite economic growth. Further, standards of governance in dealing with these twin challenges are deteriorating because of negligence and indifference of public administration. This daunting challenge can be met successfully through reforms in public administration to improve the quality of governance.

Krishna Murthy, in his chapter on 'New Public Management in the Emerging Knowledge Economy', brings out the existing problems in public administration and the reforms necessary to resolve them in order to suit the needs of a knowledge economy. He supports the argument that the present pressing problems demand a significant change in the style of governance. Public administration should have a human face and efficacy rather than the traditional and historical concepts of the bygone era. Increased emphasis on quality performance, social justice and humane approach would be the important ingredients of the new public management.

Citizens of today demand accountability in governance putting pressure on public servants, both civil servants and politicians. Right to information has strengthened the momentum towards public control and scrutiny over public administration. Further, such NGOs have come into existence so as to make increasing demands for transparency and accountability in public administration.

International market forces and free flow of capital between nations warrant a larger regulatory role for the governments, with knowledge and economic growth getting interlinked. It is widely recognized that the knowledge economy is an emerging star in the global political horizon.

Aspirations of people increase in a knowledge-oriented society resulting in a rising feeling of dissatisfaction especially among the youth. The interacting conflict of changes—both outside the individual and society as well as within the individual and society—are causing frictions that pose challenges to the governments. People are demanding greater liberty, equality and freedom, and their aspirations, in the context of the present knowledge explosion, cannot be ignored by the governments.

An important concern of the public is corruption in public life. Corruption takes a heavy economic toll, affects the operation of markets, constrains economic development and delivery of services and distorts institutions including bureaucracy. Lack of transparency coupled with secrecy that shrouds government decisions and operations facilitate corruption. Another important feature hurting interests of people is inefficiency and delay in providing public services. For the first time, the entire population is seriously expecting the government to provide better quality of services more efficiently, in the backdrop of human rights awareness and judicial activism. The demands on public administration will increase as knowledge power acquires more importance and fuels increased expectations especially because of the increasing role of media.

Public administrators have to blend knowledge power with political power in the interest of social peace and progress. In the new order, imperfections and inefficiencies can be neither ignored nor tolerated. Innovations and initiatives for social improvement will have to be given top priority. Indian brains are occupying important positions in the knowledge economies; we are capable of succeeding in meeting the new challenge posed in our own country by the emerging knowledge economy.

Creating a Network of Knowledge Institutions

Networks are becoming increasingly important in the modern economy and present a powerful combination for the future of KM. Interdependence between networks and KM leads to the development of framework for knowledge networking.

Since knowledge demands the processes of generation, preservation and sharing, networks offer a mechanism for undertaking these tasks. Institutions and organizations have different objectives, activities and foci. For them to be networked, there has to be commonality as well as complementarity in their tasks. For different constituencies, there can be different networks just as there can be networks of micro-perspective and macro-perspective. A network of knowledge institutions will, thus, have knowledge as its focus and could comprise sub-networks of constituents, if so desired. Key functionaries in the member institutions should be committed to work for a mutually agreed set of objectives to make the network successful.

The following four chapters are included for discussion on this topic:

1. 'Networking of Knowledge Institutions' by M.S. Mathews and Prema Rajagopalan
2. 'International Networking for Knowledge Management' by Arundhati Chattopadhyay, G.S. Krishnan and U.S. Singh
3. 'International Partnering for Capacity Building in IMTT: An IIFT Initiative' by Niraj Kumar
4. 'Sensitivity to Self-Organization and Effectiveness of IT Networks in the Social Sector' by K. Sankaran

Perspective of an Educational Institution

Mathews and Rajagopalan define, in their chapter on 'Networking of Knowledge Institutions', the characteristics of knowledge networks. Important functions of such networks include creation and dissemination of new knowledge and increasing the rate of creation of knowledge. Also, networks should provide clear, recognizable benefits to all participants.

The authors also describe the concept of knowledge groups and communities. Knowledge communities are groups of people who share common challenges, opportunities or a passion for a given topic, and who collaborate to deepen their understanding of that topic through ongoing learning and knowledge sharing. The example of knowledge network of Honeywell is cited. Honeywell is an organization which has an effective KM system in place. Networking has helped the company to perform better with respect to innovation and development of new technologies.

The authors also present the experience of a networking project in the academia in which IIT-Madras is a partner and is supported by European Union (EU). The chapter concludes by proposing conceptual models for networking of knowledge institutions in India. The following three models have been presented:

1. Earthquake design of a concrete building: A technology model of networking of seven IITs for solving the earthquake engineering problem.
2. Disaster management systems technology model: A technology management model of networking of IITs, IIMs, IMI for disaster management.
3. Sustainable development: A knowledge model of networking IITs, IIMs, national law schools, medical colleges, colleges of arts and sciences, and so on.

Perspective of a Consultancy Organization

The chapter by Chattopadhyay, Krishnan and Singh on 'International Networking for Knowledge Management' discusses the correlation between knowledge and development and characteristics of knowledge networks. They make the point that 'Knowledge needs to be a part of a dynamic system where not only those institutions and networks that create scientific, technical, and social knowledge are integrated but also ensures linkage among the people who understand and utilize this knowledge for socio-economic benefits of the nation'.

Networks can be formal or informal; the latter add members informally and evolve a community of practices. Formal networks, on the other hand, have a formal membership procedure, whether qualification or rule based, with an approval mechanism (which can be automated). Essentially, formal networks will be based on common interests of members and have a specified methodology of interaction. Members could be either individuals or organizations.

The broader ownership issues of the knowledge networks are also touched upon. In a knowledge network usually all are equal partners sharing the same objectives and values and are open to each other. However, it is critical to understand the 'ownership' of knowledge that is created and is passing through the networks, as it may have implications of property rights.

The chapter subsequently illustrates India's concerns and requirements as to the uses of national and international networks. The factors, methodology and application of knowledge networks are also discussed. Finally, a case example of an international knowledge network in the form of Asian Productivity Organization has been illustrated.

Networking for a Specific Project

Kumar has presented, in his chapter on 'International Partnering for Capacity Building in IMTT: An IIFT Initiative', a specific case of networking of four institutions in Europe (UK and Poland) and Asia (China and India) for developing a new international Master's programme on innovation management and technology transfer while developing human resources in each partner institution. The proposal is under implementation and, hence, the chapter outlines the features of the proposed collaboration. The project indicates, first, the realization that formal educational programmes in KM (specialization in innovation management and technology transfer, in this case) have become necessary, and, second, that international networking models are being developed in the area of educational planning for KM as well.

The creation of a knowledge network for India will require the association of a large number of diverse institutions and organizations. It is important to link all the stakeholders, namely, policy makers and implementers, educational institutions, research institutions, industry and industry associations, workers organizations and NGOs. Since a network, for being effective, must have well-defined objectives and significantly serve the interests of its members, the knowledge network may have to comprise a number of networks or sub-networks serving individual constituencies. Thus, the knowledge network could be a network of networks. It should provide an opportunity to individuals to interact, on the one hand, and it may have linkages at the international level, on the other.

Role of Social Capital

In his chapter on Sensitivity to Self-Organization and Effectiveness of IT Networks in the Social Sector, Sankaran brings in the concept of self-organization and its role in networks involving the social sector. He finds that there are innumerable examples of successful networking of business organizations, facilitated by advances in IT. However, there is more to these networks than technology alone. There has been a re-definition of what should and should not be shared, what is meant by loyalty, identity of organizations and that of individuals, willingness to trade efficiency for flexibility, greater tolerance for trial and error, and so on. These issues go deeper than mere availability and use of hardware, software and associated technical knowledge. Such factors, which are beyond the technical realm, could be roughly termed as self-organization-promoting factors. Because of such factors, much evolution of networks has not taken place where social infrastructure is involved. Sankaran argues that an understanding and appreciation of cultural and social factors that promote self-organization among those who are trying to bring about effective social IT networks will create more effective networks.

The objectives of the organizations and the society may be furthered when individuals, as members of their respective organizations, interact in a purposeful and mutually interdependent manner. However, in normal situations, an understanding of the mutuality and cultivation of give-and-take may be missing. Policy makers and the intended beneficiaries require a new mindset that recognizes the value of inter-dependencies, multiple viewpoints, plurality, and so on. In such a situation, the role of the expert will not be to provide knowledge but to gather streaks of wisdom to generate collective good.

Citing the findings of a survey, the author argues for a more inclusive and open approach to IT network creation that is sensitive not only to the need for technical abilities but also to social, cultural and behavioural factors. Sensitivity to latter factors should be with a view to create more of self-organization. Sensitivity to such factors in network designers and policy makers may bring about significant enhancement in the effectiveness of knowledge networks.

Application of Knowledge Management for Achieving Societal Objectives

Knowledge management can benefit society in various ways. Some of the benefits may be indirect, for example, growth of a specific industry whether IT or ITeS, raising the productivity of a production process. Any measure that expands consumers' choices, reduces costs, increases business and production activities, raises employment and income levels, and so on would constitute a benefit to society. Broadly, such issues have been discussed above. Here, interest lies in those initiatives that would benefit society directly. For instance, any improvement in the social sector activities such as governance, education, healthcare or any impact on masses, especially those who are poor, disempowered, disadvantaged or deprived, could be considered as direct benefits to society. Such benefits would largely imply social development. They merit a separate discussion.

Five chapters are grouped under this topic. They are as follows:

1. 'Promoting the Use of Knowledge Management as a Tool for Securing Larger Good of the Society' by Surinder Batra
2. 'Knowledge Management and Human Development' by Mainak Sarkar and Siddharth Mahajan
3. 'Knowledge Management as a Change Driver' by Sanjay Dhar

4. 'A Digital Ecosystem Model for Competitive Agriculture in the Knowledge Economy' by Runa Sarkar and Jayanta Chatterjee
5. 'Development Leadership in a Knowledge Economy' by Nagendra P. Singh

Conceptual Issues

In his chapter on 'Promoting the Use of Knowledge Management as a Tool for Securing Larger Good of the Society', Batra looks at the relationship between KM and larger good of the society. He postulates that development can be taken as a good proxy for the larger good of the society and there can be no development without knowledge. Although KM as a discipline primarily began with the corporate sector, it is increasingly being considered relevant in the development sector and is being used by several international development agencies.

Stakeholders in the development arena include national governments, local target groups for various thrust areas of development, development agencies, external experts and knowledge workers. Each of these stakeholders has its own formal or informal repositories of explicit knowledge as well as a huge amount of unarticulated tacit knowledge of considerable value. Knowledge in the development sector continually spreads on its own and does not, as a result, remain in private ownership for long. Sooner or later it moves into the public domain. However, just as in the corporate sector, there are barriers and cultural impediments in knowledge sharing in the development sector. Knowledge management, in the development domain, has essentially led to shifting the border between explicit and tacit knowledge of various stakeholders towards more of explicit knowledge and facilitated global knowledge sharing.

The author then gives examples of KM applications at the World Bank, starting with its vision to be known as the 'Knowledge Bank' in the late 1990s. Knowledge management applications at some other development agencies are also discussed, and the lessons drawn through these applications have been highlighted.

The Indian knowledge society will have three key drivers, namely, (*a*) societal transformation for a just and equitable society, (*b*) wealth generation; and (*c*) protection of the traditional form of knowledge. Core areas that will spearhead India's march towards a knowledge society would be both technology and service driven. The difference between an IT-driven society and a knowledge-driven society lies in the role of multiple technology growth engines. Multiple technologies and management structures will have to be woven together to provide a strong foundation to the Indian knowledge society. With the use of IT, multiple technologies can be combined to realize a knowledge-propelled society. Further, IT can facilitate conversion of even traditional sectors to knowledge-intensive sectors by embedding new knowledge through multiple technologies.

In a knowledge society, people who are able to convert knowledge into skilled action become its real capital. Therefore, generation of trained and skilled human resources is a key challenge. A knowledge economy requires India to develop workers who are flexible and analytical, and who can be the driving force for innovation and growth. Further, a vibrant and dynamic knowledge society has to benefit every member of the society. As such, all segments of the society should become consumers of knowledge products. Thus, the knowledge society would have knowledge workers who create quality knowledge products and enlightened citizens who consume such products. A knowledge superpower can only be built if the civil society is nearly 100 per cent literate and has a capacity to absorb new and relevant knowledge. Therefore, development of human capital with thrust on skill upgradation, generation, assimilation, dissemination and use of knowledge would be a fundamental feature of a knowledge society. An external view is then provided from the example of Mexico where pursuit of the concept of 'knowledge cities', 'knowledge citizens' and 'evolutionary learning communities' is currently under full swing.

The chapter concludes that though significant internal efficiency gains through KM have been reported, it has not taken the shape of a concrete tool which can be simply applied to the known and unknown development challenges of any country. The policy makers have re-discovered that knowledge and skill development are crucial for promoting larger good of society. Further, not only do we require knowledge workers, we also require knowledge consumers and knowledge citizens, if we want a sustainable knowledge society. The creation of such a society begins by enabling and empowering individuals in the community so that they may develop the competencies and sensibilities to meet their personal, economic, social and environmental needs.

Sarkar and Mahajan, in their chapter on 'Knowledge Management and Human Development', look at the state as a provider of government services and, in that sense, similar to a large company, though of a not-for-profit or altruistic kind. It is, therefore, fair to ask whether KM practices that have succeeded in companies can be suitably adapted and implemented at the societal level. And what would be the problems in doing so?

As far as human development is concerned, the authors recognize that there are two types of knowledge: one, that directly affects human development, such as knowledge regarding a new vaccine, public health, and the other, technical knowledge that affects development primarily through enhancing growth in income and employment, or in other words, knowledge that has an indirect impact. They contend that the latter type of knowledge is as important as the former since growth, although not a precondition for human development, definitely helps in a large measure in achieving it.

It is widely believed that large disparities in the availability of knowledge, known as 'knowledge gaps', exist in the world. The role of the government, therefore, is to design and implement a system that helps in closing this knowledge gap. One of the key drivers of growth is technological progress. Therefore, the closing of the knowledge gap between the rich and poor countries can considerably increase their growth rates which in turn can significantly improve their levels of human development. Recent improvements in telecommunications technology and a steep fall in prices of such technologies have also meant that today a villager in a remote part of India can have access to knowledge. This phenomenon was unimaginable as recently as a couple of decades ago. It must also be noted that the gains from globalization will accrue primarily to those countries that are successful in managing knowledge, and the gap between the winners and losers is only likely to widen over time.

Knowledge in the context of a company is 'intellectual capital'. In other words, it is what distinguishes itself from its competitors and contributes towards its core competency. Therefore, knowledge in the business context has to be proprietary since it is what adds value to the company. Knowledge in this case is intellectual property and needs to be protected by the company. Now consider knowledge that is relevant to human development such as the availability of a vaccine for a particular disease. Knowledge in this context is called a 'public good', which has two characteristics, non-excludability and non-rivalry. The public good nature of knowledge in this context means that private profit motive is unlikely to generate and disseminate this knowledge. Therefore, governments and other non-profit agencies have to take the lead. Whereas standard KM is related to managing knowledge that is either already available or can be created within the company, in the context of human development the approach needs to be modified in particular because of the public good nature of such knowledge.

Generating knowledge through R&D is an expensive process and, therefore, it is done primarily by developed countries. Also such solutions may not be readily applicable in the context of developing countries such as India. Therefore, the government needs to develop its own approach to this problem. First, to the extent possible, encourage the inflow of new technologies. Second, encourage the creation of indigenous technologies that are more appropriate for India. Third, universities and other educational institutions should be encouraged to contribute to R&D. Last, private sector should be incentivized to participate in R&D. For absorbing knowledge, factors that facilitate the process include education particularly of girls and other disadvantaged groups, technical education and lifelong education, and awareness development. Dissemination can be improved through social networks and means of communication. In this context, while the private sector may be providing communication facilities, government needs to put in place regulations, standards and incentives for the private sector to establish networks in rural low-income areas as well.

A company needs to consider leadership, culture and measurement issues for implementing KM. Without the active participation of employees, a KM programme would be difficult to initiate and maintain. Therefore, it is important to set up adequate incentives for employees to share knowledge-based assets while implementing KM. Second, technology is an enabler but technology alone is not enough. Ways in which technology can be helpful in implementing KM include knowledge repositories, CoP, expert locator systems, chat forums and bulletin boards. For implementing KM, the company has to isolate knowledge-based assets from the enormous amount of data available with them. Knowledge-based assets take many forms. These include information about the external business environment, internal business processes and customers. Information about internal business processes includes their standard operating procedures (SOPs), that is, the set of actions necessary to maintain processes at the current desired quality level. Knowledge about customers is a key input for maintaining profitability of companies. Customer preferences and buying patterns need to be monitored. Analysing customer data and acting upon it will help in creating customer loyalty and generating repeat purchases from customers. Customer relationship management (CRM) initiatives in companies are already doing this, but there could be a need to have tighter integration between CRM initiatives and KM.

Knowledge management may be implemented in phases. A typical schedule would comprise infrastructure evaluation, KM system analysis, design and development, deployment and metrics for evaluation.

Knowledge management implementation may face a number of problems. Based on case studies, the following problems have been pointed out in the chapter:

1. There is lack of ICT infrastructure including low penetration levels of computers and internet.
2. In the face of the existence of the large digital divide, in the short run a more feasible option would be to use a more direct approach, whereby villagers are approached directly at village fairs. Such an approach, being labour intensive, can only be undertaken with the help and cooperation of other stakeholders such as local government bodies and NGOs operating in the area.
3. Conflicting goals, interests and biases among the stakeholders: In a country as large and diverse as India there cannot be a single solution; one has to look at a multitude of solutions. A useful approach is to demonstrate effectiveness very clearly and also not offend local conventions.
4. Although the content may be developed in English, it needs to be translated into local languages and be easily comprehensible to people with fairly low levels of education, and preferably use of audio–video should be made to illustrate the point. Local content, that is, information on local events, and so on, can make such a system popular and easily accessible to the users.

5. Another problem faced by companies is the need to set up an incentive system that adequately rewards contributors who share their knowledge.
6. The impact of KM is difficult to measure in companies; it is likely to be even more difficult at the societal level.
7. A problem that is likely to become larger and increasingly complex in the coming years is the issue of intellectual property.

Finally, the chapter gives concrete examples of KM for human development and also highlights some of the issues raised earlier. In the light of their analysis, the authors suggest that an incremental approach should be adopted coupled with a steady monitoring of progress so that changes are made in the approach accordingly.

Knowledge Management as a Change Driver

Sanjay Dhar's chapter on 'Knowledge Management as a Change Driver' focuses on the processes of application of KM. While knowledge can be used to effect the re-alignment of social forces in a manner as to make the world a more just and humane place, and ensuring that effective sharing and use of knowledge can be used as a means of approaching the ideal of a society of equal opportunities, the goal of equal opportunities and sharing of resources is not achieved, for knowledge gaps become the foundations of developmental gaps by inhibiting developmental processes. Some of the knowledge asymmetries that exist in society are pointed out here.

The potential beneficiaries of developmental support are unable to access, and are even unaware of, their rights and processes to get support that would enable them to come out of inequitable commercial relationships and transactions. The problem is compounded by corruption. The producers of economic goods, especially in agriculture and cottage industries, are unable to receive due share of the price at which the goods are sold to the ultimate consumers. The target groups of development initiatives do not get the intended benefits for a number of reasons that include inability of the developmental agencies to understand the specific support that would help their targets to achieve a better quality of life and the most effective process to provide that support, lack of awareness of targets of the development programmes as to how successful change management occurs in their own context, inability of the agencies to identify specific practices that will make their projects successful and the lack of consonance between the efforts of the agencies and those of beneficiaries. There is also the inability of the underclass to get the rightful returns on their knowledge, since they are not familiar with their IPR.

Knowledge management can be used as a means of reducing knowledge asymmetry by ensuring effective flow of relevant knowledge in support of the change processes for social development. Some of the objectives that KM can support include greater transparency in the working of institutions, providing market information and opportunities to the underclass, effective change management by ensuring effective knowledge transfers between developmental agencies, using knowledge creation processes to transform local knowledge from tacit knowledge held within a few successful people to explicit knowledge shared within the target community and using KM processes to enable the underclass to benefit from its own collective knowledge through better documentation and management of intellectual property.

The five elements of a knowledge-based strategy of development are described as follows:

1. Developmental portal: a gateway to all the development practitioners for accessing and sharing knowledge about work being done for social development.
2. Institutional forum: to facilitate sharing of knowledge about the success and failures of different social developmental initiatives.
3. Social infrastructure: to be facilitated by grassroots knowledge brokers who would provide facilitation for KM processes within the communities who are the intended beneficiaries of the developmental processes.
4. Technological infrastructure: to enable village-level access to the knowledge portal and means of benefiting from knowledge about markets for their products.
5. Institutional mechanism: for the protection of intellectual property of local innovators.

Managing social development is essentially a process of managing change. One way of managing change is to shift the momentum in favour of the desired change. Knowledge management practices and processes being used extensively in the industry can be utilized to bring in the desired change in developmental activities.

Agriculture and Knowledge Economy

Sarkar and Chatterjee discuss the application of KM in agriculture in their chapter on 'A Digital Ecosystem Model for Competitive Agriculture in the Knowledge Economy'. They underscore the importance of agriculture by stating that agriculture continues to be the occupation and way of life for more than half of India's population and, therefore, ensuring a thriving agricultural economy is critical for India's global competitiveness to be inclusive. A globally competitive Indian economy must have knowledge-driven agriculture, for agriculture has already reached the limits of land and water. Also, cropping patterns in hinterlands of India should respond to global commodity markets in real time. For this purpose, farmers will need sophisticated decision support inputs to anticipate future market scenarios. This would involve quick dissemination of information from the research system to the farmers. Indian agriculture would need to establish a real-time and adaptive knowledge-exchange network. The network would need to build real time feedback routes from the fields to the laboratory and derive necessary traction from other industrial and business KM technologies and processes, for example, user-to-user exchange, expert-to-expert exchange and KM-oriented standards for information storage, retrieval and aggregation with analytics. The chapter reports initial empirical findings from one such collaborative project.

The digital ecosystem entails a series of interconnected and intra-dependent digital platforms, created at key institutional levels (international, national and local/community) augmented by technical (ICT) and social networking processes that facilitate horizontal and vertical knowledge sharing. The empirical findings show that the 'ecosystem' approach speeds up the process of identification, development and uptake of innovation.

Once the model is validated, it can lead to the development of a digital business ecosystem that can be effective for large multi-plant enterprises or SME clusters facing similar challenges of competitiveness in a rapidly globalizing knowledge-driven economy.

Development Leadership

In his chapter on 'Development Leadership in a Knowledge Economy', Nagendra Singh points out that knowledge is a critical resource for the growth of a knowledge economy. As a result, knowledge workers, who constitute an emerging category of human resource, require attention. Their characteristics add to the complexities of managing the process wherever they are in key positions. In any setting where the degree of technology-centric process and predominance of knowledge workers are high, the degree of management complexities will also be high. Innovation and competition are important pillars of a knowledge economy. This being so, education has to be paid due attention so that the economy can remain at the cutting edge. In this context, the author brings to the fore the issues of leadership's policies and approach. The thrust of his presentation is on education policy and the development of values among the youth, appropriate for a knowledge economy. In support of his argument, the author has selected the example of BPO (business process outsourcing) industry.

Two points have been made relating to the BPO industry. First, despite the large demand for workers in the BPO sector, which will continue to grow for some time, the education system has not come up with programmes to prepare students for this activity. A major requirement for working in the BPO sector is command over English language and proper accent—normally American. A large number of teaching shops have come up to provide such training. Such establishments are out to make a quick buck with little concern for quality. Second, employment in the BPO sector is promoting consumerism. Young people are living their dreams like never before. They are soaring higher and far away from anything that is run-of-the-mill. Life is no longer about high education, status, career growth and job security. For them, it is about excitement, adventure, passion, money and a lot of fun. The youth now want to grab jobs at an early age, get large incomes and become consumers of the market economy. There is little aspiration or motivation to pursue higher education and to learn job-related skills. The kind of workplace environment and lifestyle they are chasing are creating socio-psychological problems. Quoting a study, the author contends that 40 per cent employees of 10 BPO organizations had got into serious health problems, and 21 per cent had got into illicit relationships. Thus, serious questions arise with regard to the education policy as also to the preparation of the nation's next generation. The chapter concludes by emphasizing that it is time the leadership aimed at integrated development rather than showing fast economic growth without social development.

References

Bhatt, G.D. 2001. 'KM in Organisations: Examining the Interaction between Technologies, Techniques, and People', *Journal of Knowledge Management*, 5(1): 68–75.

CIO Council. 2001. *Managing Knowledge @ Work, An Overview of Knowledge Management*. Knowledge Management Working Group of the Federal Chief Information Officers Council, August.

Cong, Xiaoming and V. Pandya Kaushik. 2004. 'Issues of Knowledge Management in the Public Sector', *Electronic Journal of Knowledge Management*, 1(2): 25–33.

Davenport, T.H. and L. Prusak. 1998. *Working Knowledge: How Organisations Manage What They Know*. Boston, MA: Harvard Business School Press.

Hughes, Alan, S. Michael and Scott Morton. 2005. 'ICT and Productivity Growth—The Paradox Resolved?', MIT Sloan School of Management, Working Paper 4579–05, Cambridge, MA, November 2005.

Nonaka, I. and H. Takeuchi. 1995. *The Knowledge-Creating Company: How Japanese Companies Create the Dynamics of Innovation*. Oxford University Press.

Office of the Minister for Communications & Information Technology. 2006. 'Ten Point Agenda: Declared by Hon'ble Minister of Communications & Information Technology, Thiru. Dayanidhi Maran on 24.05.2006'. Available at http://dmaran.nic.in/initiatives2006.htm, accessed on 11 April 2007.

Polanyi, Michael. 1958/1998. *Personal Knowledge. Towards a Post Critical Philosophy*. London: Routledge.

———. 1966. *The Tacit Dimension*. New York: Doubleday.

Stewart, T.A. 1997. *Intellectual Capital: The New Wealth of Nations*. New York: Doubleday.

Swan, J. and S. Newell. 2000. 'Linking Knowledge Management and Innovation', in H.R. Hansen, M. Bichler and H. Mahrer (eds), *Proceedings of the 8th European Conference on Information Systems*, pp. 591–98. Vienna University of Economics and Business Administration.

Wigg, K.M. 1997. 'Knowledge Management: An Introduction and Perspective', *Journal of Knowledge Management*, 1(1): 6–14.

Part 1

Directions of Change towards a Knowledge Economy

1   Mapping the Directions of Transition from Industrial Economy to Knowledge Economy*

VINOD KUMAR, HARSHA SINVHAL AND VINAY K. NANGIA

Introduction

Knowledge is increasingly becoming a more valuable asset than traditionally focused labour and capital used by economists for developing models of economic growth. Yet knowledge being abstract and subjective is difficult to evaluate. Managing knowledge is a process which involves a multi-period decision framework starting from investments in research and development (R&D), to diffusion of knowledge, to creation of innovations and finally to capturing value through commercialization of inventions and innovations. The whole process is ridden with uncertainties and difficulties in managing the complexities. The public policy challenge confronting governments is, therefore, to design programmes and systems that would reduce uncertainties and at the same time promote cooperative development.

Information technology (IT) is a knowledge-intensive industry, critical to India's growth and development. The Department of Information Technology (DIT) of the Ministry of Communications and Information Technology (MCIT), as a key knowledge ministry, has an important role to play in building the country's preparedness to usher in the knowledge economy.

The DIT sanctioned a project on 'National Competitiveness in the Knowledge Economy' in 2006 for developing a framework for collaborative linkages to meet the emerging challenges. This is a multi-institutional, multi-disciplinary 3-year project.

The proposal submitted by Indian Institute of Technology-Roorkee (IIT-R) to DIT for its consideration was, therefore, intended to create a wider and deeper understanding of the issues and actions involved in making an effective transition to a knowledge economy. After initial discussions in December 2005, the proposal was submitted in January 2006.

*The authors thank Prof. Ravinder K. Zutshi of the Department of Management, Long Island University, New York, USA and Vice-President, ISPIM (International Society for Professional Innovation Management) for his thoughts and views expressed during a number of interactions on this subject.

Following are the broad objectives of the proposal:

1. Mapping the directions of transition from industrial economy to knowledge economy.
2. Developing strategies of change management for transformation from industrial age to information age.
3. Identifying new knowledge streams/disciplines likely to emerge in the evolving knowledge economy and suggesting specialized courses to help meet manpower requirements of the knowledge economy.
4. Generating deeper understanding, among key stakeholders, of the scope and significance of knowledge, technology, R&D and innovation management for the emerging knowledge economy, and developing model course-curricula for adoption by other knowledge institutions.
5. Anticipating trends and identifying issues for formulating policy initiatives.
6. Preparing policy recommendations for efficient, smooth and speedy transformation.
7. Creating a network of knowledge institutions.
8. Promoting the use of knowledge management (KM) as a tool for securing larger good of the society.

These objectives were to be pursued by the following approaches:

1. Bringing together national and international expertise to address issues of knowledge management.
2. Initiating discussions and dialogue with the stakeholders.
3. Sensitizing the stakeholders to the possibilities and opportunities thrown up by new technologies for enhancing efficiency and productivity.
4. Surfacing the concerns of communities most affected by disruptive technologies.
5. Disseminating results of consultations/deliberations with a view to getting inputs for policy initiatives and development of alternative models.
6. Extending the knowledge pool to people in public and private domains with a view to encouraging innovative capabilities for sustainable economic development.
7. Suggesting new educational programmes/courses for development of skilled human resources for the knowledge economy.
8. Integrating the outcome of studies, reports, seminars, conferences, and so on and coming up with policy recommendations.

A key feature of the proposal is that it is a multi-institutional project drawing upon complementary capabilities of four leading national institutions. These are IIT-R, Indian Institute of Technology-Madras (IIT-M); International Management Institute (IMI), New Delhi and National Productivity Council (NPC), New Delhi. These institutions with existing activities and experience relevant to the project area will also be able to draw upon international experience and trends.

The principal investigator and another investigator from IIT-R made a presentation at the Working Group Meeting at MCIT on 27 February 2006. Administrative approval was granted for the project on 29 March 2006 and funds were released in May 2006.

In order to achieve the overall purpose of the project, one of the stated objectives is 'Mapping the directions of transition from Industrial Economy to Knowledge Economy'. This chapter deals with this specific objective.

Many experts refer to a 'new economy', with characteristics of a post-industrial society, as first elaborated by Daniel Bell (1973) and later by Peter Drucker (1989). David J. Skyrme (1999) stated that John Naisbitt (1982) coined the term 'megatrend' to describe a fundamental underlying trend that shapes the future. His book identified 10 trends, including the shifts from an industrial society to an information society, a national economy to a global economy and hierarchies to networking. These trends are evident even today, but there are more important ones besides these. Three of these that Skyrme considered especially important are

1. the power of technology and especially the acceptance of the internet as a key tool of business and commerce;
2. virtualization—the ability to work and trade over large geographic distances; and
3. the emergence of knowledge as a key focus of policy and strategy.

These megatrends as noticed and stated by experts help in visualizing the future, which in turn helps in formulating strategies to face the challenges likely to emerge in the years ahead. It is, therefore, pertinent to study first the megatrends and then map the transition in a somewhat narrower sense.

In order to prepare for meeting future challenges, it is necessary to identify certain key areas which shall play a dominant role in the lives of the people, society and nations. The following 13 areas have been identified where action is likely to be of great importance:

1. Demography
2. Socio-economic scenario
3. Technology (IT-based and non-IT-based)
4. Environment
5. Natural resources (renewable and non-renewable)
6. Energy (renewable and non-renewable)
7. Water management
8. Inequalities
9. Health
10. Military
11. Geo-political realities
12. Agriculture
13. Global systems

One of the methodologies for studying in detail the role of the 13 areas in shaping a knowledge economy could be to get commissioned research conducted by experts in these areas. Experts could be requested to work on the following common guidelines:

1. The study is being conducted for a limited purpose as a subset of the overall project, 'National Competitiveness in the Knowledge Economy'. It is, therefore, expected that the purpose of the study remains in line with the objective of the project. Project details shall be provided to the experts.
2. The study shall largely confine to the main area of the work awarded but is not limited to that. The impact of developments in respective areas on society, business, government and education must be brought out in detail.

3. Each expert shall be requested to discuss the outline of the work proposed to be done by him and freeze the framework of the study before the commencement of work.
4. Experts shall be requested to make projections at least for the years 2020 and 2030 or 2040. They may put in additional milestones.
5. There may be more than one commissioned research in certain areas like health, technology and global systems, where the scope of work is large.
6. Total time for completing the study shall vary from four to six months from the date of award of the work depending on the total quantum of work estimated in each case.
7. The studies can be awarded to individuals or institutions of repute.

Reports of the studies could be used for making a consolidated report by an expert who will do the overall study, editing and compilation of the final report. The contents of these reports shall be presented by respective experts in a conference. A brainstorming session of the experts shall precede finalization of the report.

Areas Chosen for Megatrend Studies

Demography

Demography will play a major role in a knowledge society. Population and age profile, rather than gender profile, will affect the human and intellectual capital. Inter- and intra-regional migration will be a rule rather than an exception. Human capital movement will decide the way industry and economy flourish. In the foreseeable future, India is going to be a nation of young people while the so-called developed nations may have a major portion of the population as old. How will this affect the knowledge economy? The demographic trends may become a major factor in deciding the state of global and national economy. The studies may be split further into sub-topics like national and global demography, or India vs. China or comparative demography of various continents, namely, Asia, America and Europe.

Socio-economic Scenario

The fast pace of globalization is going to bring about unprecedented changes in the socio-economic status of nations and lifestyles of people. The values and culture in an era are highly influenced by socio-economic status and related factors. These factors also affect, to a certain extent, the political thought processes. The divide between the 'haves' and the 'have-nots' has given rise to political and social upheavals in the past. Will there be a knowledge divide in times to come? How the knowledge economy will change the socio-economic scenario or be governed by it needs to be studied in order to prepare the nation for the challenges it shall face in the times to come. The study shall be divided into social, cultural and political scenarios, and so on. It will cover regional aspects globally and at the country level. It may also include study of various castes and communities, their role in nation building and the Indian diaspora the world over.

IT-based and Non-IT-based Technology

Globalization has been the cause as well as the effect of rapid advances in technology, particularly in transportation, health, information and communication technologies. Technology development has played a major role in deciding the economic status of nations today. Information technology has, to a large extent, removed time and space constraints. In the current scenario, information is a major force to reckon with. Information is power. Information technology spurs growth. Will this position continue in the knowledge economy, or will IT be used in future merely as a tool while advances in non-IT fields overtake IT and once again govern the economy? The study is expected to examine the status of the sunset industries and use of technology in such industries. Which are the sunrise industries today and how long are these going to last? Which are the technologies and industries of the future? What is the likely direction and future of technologies in areas like nanotechnology, material science, biosciences, biotechnology, and so on? Which new inter-disciplinary subjects and topics will emerge?

Environment

It is now well understood that environment and its conservation is of vital importance for the survival of human race. How will we protect the environment? How much are we ready to pay for conservation? How do we strike a balance and set priorities to face the challenges of growing population and their needs, meet their aspirations and, at the same time, conserve the environment? In a knowledge economy, will the nations which are ahead force nations lagging behind to do the 'dirty' work and produce and take over the 'elite' businesses themselves? We have to predict the scenario to be able to decide strategies for meeting the challenges. What is likely to be the policy framework globally and at the national level? What kind of interventions will be required and what will be the regulatory framework?

Natural Resources—Renewable and Non-renewable

With the given resource base, per capita availability of natural resources will get reduced as population continues to grow. To deal with the situation, we may find new reserves or change the way we live. In the alternative, we may develop altogether new ways of exploring and/or producing new resources economically. This could become a significant factor in the emergence of the major economic power. In times to come the possibility of a decline in the importance of natural resources in determining the economic strength of nations cannot be ruled out. Studying trends will help in looking at future scenarios and options for deciding strategies.

Energy Resources—Renewable and Non-renewable

Per capita energy consumption is an important indicator which reflects the economic status of a nation, region or society. A study to project the energy scenarios will help decide the relative positions of various nations in the years to come. Will the tropical nations which have climatic advantages have an edge in the new world order?

Water Management

Water is a renewable resource. However, fresh water which is fit for human consumption is becoming scarce due to pollution. Per capita water consumption is directly related to economic status. How will the world meet fresh water requirements for the growing population? How will we combat pollution? Will we drink only that water which has been condensed from the atmosphere? What will be its effect on climate? Will there be wars over water? Water covers nearly three-quarters of the earth's surface but only half of 1 per cent is available for human consumption. Saltwater makes up about 97 per cent of the earth's water while most of the remaining water lies frozen at the poles. Will desalination of seawater be a practical solution to water scarcity problems?

The study will try to answer some of these questions as to how the knowledge society will deal with the water situation.

National, Regional and Global Inequalities

As John F. Kennedy said in his inaugural address as President of the USA on 20 January 1961, 'A free society which cannot help the many who are poor cannot save the few who are rich.' What factors will decide the national, regional and global inequalities, and evolve strategies to bridge the gaps? Will knowledge economy widen the divide or bridge it? How can the knowledge economy help in creating the world a better place with more equitable distribution of resources? How will knowledge economy deal with the issues related to equal rights and opportunities, irrespective of colour, race and gender? The study in addition to inequalities of wealth and gender will address the issues of digital divide, knowledge divide, and so on.

Health

In any society, health is a major factor which contributes to its economic strength. With advancements in science and technology the average life expectancy worldwide has increased. Will the nature's law of 'survival of the fittest' be challenged? Will advancement in knowledge lead to a less healthy and aged society in which a majority of the old live on the produce of the few? Where will major health facilities and services of the world reside in the emerging globalized world? What will be the new health systems and practices in the future? What kinds of new diseases and their cures will come up? Will there be drastic changes in medicinal systems and practices?

Military

Large-scale migration of people in the knowledge economy may dilute national identities. The global village concept may make the present-day 'military' requirements and strategies unimportant. Today, every nation spends a sizeable portion of its budget on defence. Military sales are a sizeable portion of international trade. A change in this scenario in the knowledge economy may have a major effect on the role of military and military-related economic activities. What challenges will it pose in relation to the national, regional and world power equations, and what will be its effect on the economy? What kinds of warfare in future are expected to take place? What shall be the type, kind, style and composition of defence forces of the future? What kind of military institutions and organizations evolve in future?

Geo-political Realities

New geo-political realities and equations may emerge in the knowledge economy based on the availability of knowledge and its transfer mechanism. This may help decide the worth of a nation. What will be the parameters of measuring military power? Will the military power or 'currency' or 'monetary' values be replaced by 'knowledge' values? Parameters to evaluate worth of a particular knowledge, which means or is equal to power, may have to be worked out. This may then affect the way politics works in the overall world scenario. It may also influence how people, societies, nations, regions and world will be ruled. Hence studying various geo-political realities of the future is essential to plan and maintain competitiveness in the knowledge economy.

Agriculture

In the present-day civilization, agriculture or farming is the oldest occupation. It is also called the primary sector. Developed countries have moved away from agriculture to industry and services as major contributors to their national income whereas developing countries still depend largely on agriculture as a source of national income. Many of the developing countries use agriculture as a source of subsistence. Nearly two-thirds of our nation's population has agriculture as their main occupation. Advances in technology have been constantly reducing this percentage. In 'developed' nations, 3–4 per cent of the population can produce food for all. With better technology and knowledge of modern techniques, in developing countries also there may be a major shift of population from agriculture to other sectors.

In the agricultural sector, the main issues are

1. food security;
2. efficiency and effectiveness of production that covers yield and cropping pattern;
3. marketing of the agricultural produce at reasonable prices;
4. storage and distribution; and
5. contribution of agriculture to the national economy vis-à-vis the number of persons engaged in or dependent on agriculture.

What can be the effect of knowledge economy on the agricultural sector and how will it ensure a better life for the majority of our population? This is a key area as far as India is concerned and hence it needs a detailed study.

Global Systems

What will be the shape, size and dimensions of future global systems? Following are some of the areas where this kind of study can be made:

1. Financial: Will there be international bodies like the Bank of International Settlements, or will new systems for global financial order evolve?
2. Trade: Will new bodies and systems evolve in addition to those that exist today such as the World Trade Organization (WTO), International Chamber of Commerce (ICC), and so on?
3. Legal: What is going to be the system for global law making and system for dispensing justice? Will the International Court of Justice undergo changes? Will new bodies and systems come into existence?
4. Global systems of cooperation: Will organizations like the International Monetary Fund (IMF), United Nations (UN) and the World Bank remain relevant? Will they change or disappear and be replaced by new ones?

References

Bell, D. 1973. *The Coming of the Post-industrial Society*. New York: Basic Books.
Drucker, P.F. 1989. *The New Realities*. New York: Harper & Row.
Naisbitt, J. 1982. *Megatrends: Ten New Directions Transforming Our Lives*. New York: Warner Books.
Skyrme, D.J. 1999. 'Knowledge Commerce: Succeeding in a Global Knowledge Marketplace', paper presented at the Knowledge Economy Conference, Beijing, 1–3 November.

2   Conceptual and Assessment Dimensions of Knowledge Management: An Overview

Vidhu Shekhar Jha, Siddharth Mahajan and Himanshu Joshi

Introduction

Knowledge management (KM) as a business practice is being widely adopted by companies. It is the process through which organizations generate value from their knowledge-based assets. Generating value from these assets involves sharing them among employees. Information technology (IT) acts as an enabler in implementing KM in companies. Information technology tools enhance the transfer of knowledge-based assets across departmental boundaries within a company. In addition, in order to implement KM a company needs to consider leadership, culture and measurement issues.

Companies are overloaded with data and information. Only a small part of this data and information is useful knowledge that helps managers make good decisions. Knowledge is broadly classified into two types: explicit and tacit. Explicit knowledge includes all information that can be documented. Examples of explicit knowledge include business plans, white papers, technical reports, patents, demand forecasts, market analysis and customer and competitor information. Tacit knowledge is that which cannot be documented. Often managers act on information they have to make decisions based on their past experience of similar situations. Thus for making good decisions, managers rely on, among others, tacit knowledge, which includes components of gut feel and experience. It is difficult to map out and articulate the precise process of arriving at the decision. So, this is how tacit knowledge has a bearing on decision taking. Sometimes when demand for a new product is to be forecast, multiple experts are called in to express their perceptions of likely demand for the product. This is an established method of forecasting called judgemental forecasting and uses the Delphi method. This method is used to reconcile differences between the demand estimates of the experts and arrive at a consensus. How the experts use their experience of earlier products, together with their knowledge of the market, to arrive at demand estimates for the new product, is difficult to document. Again this process relies on tacit knowledge. As a part of a KM initiative, it is important to generate and share tacit knowledge in the organization.

Literature Survey

Rao (2005) identifies the following actions through which KM can occur in companies: (*a*) identify intangible assets; (*b*) prioritize critical knowledge issues; (*c*) accelerate learning patterns within the organization; (*d*) identify and diffuse best practices; (*e*) increase innovation; and (*f*) increase collaborative activities and a knowledge-sharing culture as a result of the increased awareness of the benefits of KM. Santosus and Surmacz (2006) define KM as the process through which organizations generate value from their knowledge-based assets. Generating value would involve sharing these assets among employees and departments so as to formulate best practices.

In order to understand the status of implementation of KM within the company it is important to have metrics for KM assessment. A tool that incorporates a number of metrics and is used widely for strategy implementation is the Skandia Navigator.

In the Skandia Navigator (Edvinsson and Malone 1997) measures are organized into five categories. These are (*a*) financial: this includes standard financial measures of performance; (*b*) customer: this looks at measures of customer satisfaction and retention; (*c*) process: this focuses on the company's processes and how they are organized to deliver value; (*d*) renewal and development: how the organization is preparing for the future considering such areas as customers, markets and products; and (*e*) employee related: this considers such issues as productivity and values.

Rao (2005) considers five types of KM metrics which would help assess the level of KM implementation within a company. These are (*a*) technology metrics: number of e-mails, number of online forums, website traffic, number of search queries; (*b*) process metrics: response time to queries, meeting international certification standards; (*c*) knowledge metrics: number of employee ideas submitted, best practices created, active communities of practice (CoP); (*d*) employee metrics: peer validation, feeling of empowerment; and (*e*) business metrics: reduced cost, increased market share, improved productivity.

There are two knowledge management assessment tools (KMATs) for assessing the level of KM implementation in a company. One of them was developed by the American Productivity & Quality Center (APQC) and Arthur Anderson (AA), and the other by Maier and Moseley (2003).

The KMAT developed by APQC and AA is divided into five sections: KM process, leadership, culture, technology and measurement. Within each section four to six questions are used to assess the KM capability within that area. In the KMAT developed by Maier and Moseley, the implementation of KM is assessed in five dimensions: identification and creation, collection and capture, storage and organization, sharing and distribution, and application and use. This tool consists of 30 statements on which respondents have to give their response.

Key Issues and Concerns for Knowledge Management Implementation and Assessment

Two main types of issues need to be considered while implementing KM. These are cultural and employee issues, and issues related to technology.

Cultural and Employee Issues

Without the active participation of employees, a KM programme would be difficult to start. In many organizations, employees are valued for their expertise and their knowledge of markets, customers, suppliers and processes. This knowledge helps to generate value for the company. If employees are asked to share these very knowledge-based assets, which make them valuable to the company, they may resent. They may not feel like participating in a KM programme. Therefore, it is very important to set up adequate incentives for employees to share knowledge-based assets while implementing KM. These incentives should be tied to the performance appraisal of the employees. Also employees need to be sensitized to the fact that sharing knowledge-based assets with other employees generates more value for the company. This can be done through games, simulation exercises, workshops and by relating anecdotal evidence of how value was created by sharing knowledge-based assets. For employees to share information it is important for them to know who the experts are in any particular area and how they can be located.

Technology is an Enabler but Technology Alone is Not Enough

Knowledge management is implemented by having CoP, wherein experts in a particular specialized area gather to share their experiences of what worked and what did not and also on how to improve processes. This is a way of sharing tacit knowledge. In addition there are expert locator systems and directories wherein experts in each area are identified and their contact information stored. There are knowledge repositories with search capabilities, wherein many white papers, business plans and technical documents are stored for easy access by all employees. There are chat forums and bulletin boards, wherein employees can raise queries and experts can reply. The technology to implement KM includes intranets, off-the-shelf e-mail packages and collaboration tools to implement community building. There are data mining and data warehousing tools and search engines for implementing expert locator systems and knowledge repositories. Finally, there are discussion and chat technologies to implement chat forums and bulletin boards. While this technology is essential to implement KM, having technology solutions alone will not start the KM programme. Employees need to have incentives to share information. At the same time, there should not be an information overload. The quality of data and information should be monitored so that only those knowledge-based assets are stored and maintained which would help managers make good decisions and add value.

Companies today are generating a lot of data as part of their daily operations. A lot of this information may not be timely or accurate. The problem is how to isolate knowledge-based assets from this enormous amount of data. Knowledge-based assets are those which would help managers make good decisions. Good decisions result when insights into business operations and internal processes are formed by analysing these knowledge-based assets.

For converting information into knowledge-based assets, it is important that information be presented to employees in such a form that it can be easily acted upon and analysed. For this purpose, information may need to be consolidated and prioritized. In many companies there is now a concept of digital dashboard wherein key metrics of interest are posted for easy access. These metrics are updated on a regular basis so that all employees are aware of them and necessary action can be taken if performance on any metric is causing concern. For example, companies could be using the balanced scorecard to organize their digital dashboard. This consists of metrics in the following four areas:

1. Financial
2. Customer
3. Internal business processes
4. Learning and growth

These four types of areas are linked in a sequence. The learning organization will develop people competencies. This will in turn result in improved business processes. Improved processes will result in higher levels of customer satisfaction and customer retention. This will finally improve the financial indicators.

Knowledge-based assets take many forms. These include information about the external business environment, internal business processes and customers. A lot of information about the external environment is important to make decisions at the strategic, tactical and operational levels. This would include information about the market, suppliers, competitors, substitute products and emerging technologies that would impact either the production or the delivery of the good or service. Information about internal business processes includes their standard operating procedures (SOPs), that is, the set of actions necessary to maintain processes at the current desired quality level. It includes information about those input parameters of the process that most impact the quality level of the output. These critical parameters are called critical to quality (CTQ). It includes information contained in control charts which set upper and lower limits on key process parameters. If parameters are outside these limits then it implies that with a very high chance the process is out of control and will produce more than the allowed margin of defective products.

Knowledge about customers is a key factor for profitability of companies. Customer preferences and buying patterns need to be monitored. This knowledge will help in designing pricing and promotion schemes that will generate sales. It will help in choosing distribution channel configurations that provide better service while lowering costs at the same time. Analysing customer data and acting upon it will help in creating customer loyalty and generating repeat purchases from customers. It will help in identifying the most profitable customer segments and then designing special products for their needs. It will help in finding those customers who are about to leave and then providing incentives to retain them. Customer relationship management (CRM) initiatives in companies are already doing these but there could be a need to have tighter integration between CRM initiatives and KM.

Examples of KM Initiatives in Indian Companies

Examples of two companies, namely, Tata Steel and Wipro, are outlined here for looking at their KM initiatives. These are based on case studies prepared by Kumar (2004) and Rajakannu (n.d.).

Tata Steel

The KM programme at Tata Steel was started in the late 1990s. A knowledge repository was placed on the corporate intranet. The repository contained technical documents and anecdotal information regarding the successes and failures of employees in their workplace. Contributions of employees to the knowledge repository were screened by experts before being placed on the site. Two issues that needed to be considered while establishing the knowledge repository were the volume of contributions as well as their quality. A culture of knowledge sharing had to be created. Employees were hesitant to part with their expertise or their experiences, as in their view this information made them valuable to the company. The quality of contributions also needed to be maintained. The contributions had to be such that those who used them added value and made better decisions.

A year after the knowledge repository was established, knowledge communities were formed. These were groups of employees and experts in a particular area who gathered together to share their experiences and learn from one another. They also conducted brainstorming sessions on how to improve processes within their area. Thus, tacit knowledge was shared. Knowledge communities were formed in 21 areas including iron making, steel making, mining, cost engineering and energy management.

The next step was to establish a reward and recognition system to firmly establish KM within the company. Essentially, rewards were meant for two distinct activities, that is, contributing to development of knowledge-based assets and using knowledge-based assets to add value for the company. Developing knowledge-based assets could involve contributing to the knowledge repository or answering queries of other employees that were placed on the intranet. This initiative at Tata Steel was integrated in their journey for business excellence based on the JRD (Jehangir Ratanji Dadabhoy) Quality Value (JRDQV) award for business excellence modelled on the American award for business excellence, namely, Malcolm Baldridge National Quality Award (MBNQA) for American companies.

The implementation of KM in Tata Steel provided many benefits to the company. Knowledge-based assets became widely available in the organization resulting in increased productivity. The duplication of efforts was reduced as best practices were adopted and repetition of mistakes was avoided. An environment of learning, knowledge sharing and innovation was created.

Wipro

Knowledge management initiatives were started at Wipro by appointing a full-time KM head together with a KM team. The KM team consisted of about 15 members brought together from various domains such as finance, manufacturing, e-business and data warehousing. Core competencies that members of the KM team should possess were also identified. Besides the core team, extended teams consisting of line managers and experts within each domain were formed.

The following goals of the KM initiative were identified:

1. To develop the ability of employees to access relevant information in time and link employees who needed information with experts who had the same.
2. To share best practices, reduce duplication of efforts and avoid repetition of mistakes.
3. To capture explicit knowledge and tacit knowledge of employees in order to avoid loss of expertise to the company if an employee left.

KNET is a knowledge repository in Wipro with currently over 2,900 documents in 132 categories. KNET contains case studies, white papers, presentations and technical documents. The extended teams in each domain act as editorial boards and review the documents before they are hosted on KNET. In addition, Wipro has a KM system specially designed for sales support and technical support. The sales support system helps the sales personnel have quick access to relevant documents to answer customer queries. It also provides relevant information and statistics about Wipro on a real-time basis. The technical support to KM system helps the developer community at Wipro in having ready access to technical documents necessary to create software products. It also stores details about previous projects so that learning from them can be effectively utilized in implementing current projects. Efforts are also underway to link the CRM system in Wipro with the KM initiative. Communities of practice have been established to bring together experts within a domain to share best practices and improve processes. Thus, tacit knowledge is shared.

Wipro is currently in the process of establishing a measurement system. The aim is to link efforts in the KM initiative with key business metrics related to profitability, customer satisfaction and time to market. Another effort is to establish a rewards and recognition system for employees. This will encourage employees to actively participate in the KM initiative and develop a culture of knowledge sharing in the organization.

Benchmarking KM Initiative Using KMAT

Two KMATs are discussed here. These are benchmarking tools for KM.

Just as in the case of quality, benchmarking initiatives can also be taken up in KM. Benchmarking refers to identifying best practices outside the company and then incorporating them with possible modifications within the company. A popular benchmarking tool in KM is the one developed by the APQC and AA. This tool allows companies to evaluate their strengths and weaknesses in managing knowledge-based assets. Another benchmarking tool, also known as KMAT, was developed by Maier and Moseley (2003). The two assessment tools are discussed here.

KMAT Developed by APQC and Arthur Anderson

The tool developed by APQC and AA is divided into five sections: KM process, leadership, culture, technology and measurement. Within each section, four to six questions assess the KM capability within that area. The answer to each question follows a scale from 1 to 5, that is, going from poor to excellent. The scores on each question within a section are added up to get a total score for that section (see Appendix I).

In the first section, namely the KM process, the questions attempt to find out the following:

1. Does the organization have processes in place to identify knowledge gaps and then close them?
2. Has the organization formalized the process of transferring best practices and also documenting them? This would require establishment of a knowledge repository where, in addition to technical documents and white papers, anecdotal information of successes and failures of employees should be stored.

3. Is tacit knowledge, that is, knowledge that is difficult to document, transferred across the organization? This requires CoP to be established in the organization.

In the second section, namely leadership, questions address the following issues:

1. Is managing organizational knowledge an essential part of strategy?
2. Does the organization use learning to support its core competencies?
3. Are employees compensated for their contribution to organizational knowledge?

To make the managing of organizational knowledge an essential part of strategy, support to the KM initiative has to come from the top leadership. In an organization such as Wipro, the head of KM could also be the Chief Quality Officer. Quality is important in making business processes achieve their targeted performance and thus achieve financial goals and improve customer satisfaction measures for the company. If the Chief Quality Officer is made head of KM, the KM initiative automatically receives a boost. To compensate employees for their contribution to organizational knowledge, it is necessary to have a rewards and recognition system in place. Contribution to organizational knowledge could be achieved by contributing to the knowledge repository, by answering queries of other employees on the intranet or by being on the editorial board and screening other employees' contributions to the knowledge repository.

In the third section, that is, culture, some of the following issues are looked at:

1. Does the organization encourage knowledge sharing and is there an environment of openness and trust within the organization?
2. Do employees take responsibility for their learning and do initiatives for carrying out innovation drive the learning process?

It takes time for an organization to develop a culture of knowledge sharing. Immediate reaction of employees to a proposal for knowledge sharing is that they feel reluctant to share their expertise and experiences. It is these very aspects that make employees valuable to the company. Through workshops, simulation exercises and management games, employees have to be sensitized to the fact that an environment of knowledge sharing is beneficial to the company. This cultural change in the company could even be more important to the KM initiative than the IT tools used to implement KM.

The fourth section, on technology, addresses the following issues:

1. Does technology effectively link all members of the organization to one another and also to customers?
2. Are information systems real time and integrated, and whether technology that supports collaboration is available to employees?

The final section considers KM measurement. This includes some of the following considerations:

1. Has the organization developed ways to link KM initiatives to financial results?
2. Has the organization developed a specific set of indicators to manage knowledge?

3. Do the sets of measures used balance hard and soft as well as financial and non-financial indicators?
4. Does the organization allocate resources towards efforts that measurably increase its knowledge base?

KMAT Developed by Maier and Moseley

The KMAT developed by Maier and Moseley is also used to assess how well developed the KM practice within the company is. Implementation of KM is assessed in five dimensions: identification and creation; collection and capture; storage and organization; sharing and distribution; and application and use. The tool consists of 30 statements on which respondents have to give their response. The response is on a scale of 1–6, going from 'strongly agree' to 'strongly disagree'. For each of the five KM dimensions, six statements are used (see Appendix II).

The first dimension, knowledge identification and creation, deals with how effective the company is in transforming data and information into knowledge-based assets. These knowledge-based assets will then help employees in making good decisions. It is assessed by answers to such questions as:

1. Does the company have a culture in which experience is valued?
2. Have experts in each domain been identified?
3. Are brainstorming sessions used to generate new ideas?
4. Are multiple viewpoints encouraged in arriving at decisions?

The second dimension, knowledge collection and capture, deals with how well knowledge is captured once it has been identified. It is assessed by response statements to such questions as:

1. Are jobs documented?
2. Can employees easily post documents on the intranet or save them to a network server?
3. Is gathering information and knowledge from others an integral part of the job description of employees?

The third dimension deals with knowledge storage and organization. Once knowledge has been captured it has to be stored and organized properly for easy retrieval by employees who need to use it. Also, employees in an organization are based in different departments and have different managerial responsibilities going all the way from operational decision making to long-term strategic decision making. Knowledge has to be stored and organized in such a way that employees in different departments and with different responsibilities can have easy access to it. This dimension is assessed through such questions as:

1. Is a knowledge repository present?
2. Is information from different sources stored in an integrated manner and cross-referenced?
3. Is stored information organized in a way that makes it easy to locate?

The fourth dimension deals with knowledge sharing and dissemination. If effective knowledge sharing occurs it results in improvement of business processes and creates a culture of learning and innovation in the organization. All of this increases efficiency and makes an organization more competitive in the market. It is measured by looking into such issues as:

1. Is there an intranet for the organization from where employees can retrieve relevant documents?
2. Are documents proactively shared by employees?
3. Is a rewards and recognition system in place to create a culture of knowledge sharing in the organization?

The final dimension deals with knowledge application and use. To successfully incept this dimension in the organization, the previous four dimensions have to be incorporated first. This dimension is assessed by examining such aspects as:

1. Is the collective experience of employees an integral part of decision making?
2. Are stored knowledge and best practices used for training and staff development?
3. Are advanced technologies such as data mining and data warehousing used for strategic and operational decision making?

The questionnaire can be administered to all employees in the organization. Average score of the organization or division on each of the five dimensions can be determined. Based on the actual value of the score, a grading scheme on the effectiveness of the organization on that dimension has been developed. Based on the same questionnaire, it is also possible to grade the organization on its explicit and tacit KM practices.

Conclusions

The first step in KM is that both explicit and tacit knowledge within the company boundaries be captured effectively. The second step is that these knowledge-based assets be made available to those who require them to make decisions. For this it is important that employees know that the information is available and that too in a form that is easy to use. Therefore, the key is to link the decision makers with the knowledge-based assets that will help them arrive at good decisions. So, the end result of a good KM is better decision making by all employees, resulting in competitive advantage to the company.

The two KMAT tools together provide a good way to assess the level of KM implementation in companies. The first tool assesses KM implementation based on the issues of leadership, culture, technology and measurement. The second tool looks at how knowledge in a company is identified, captured, stored, shared and applied. These tools have already been used in companies abroad to assess KM implementation. It has been proposed to use these tools to assess KM implementation in Indian companies in the near future.

Appendix I: The Knowledge Management Assessment Tool (KMAT)

The Knowledge Management Assessment Tool (KMAT) was developed by the American Productivity & Quality Center (APQC) and Arthur Andersen (AA) in 1995 to help organizations self-assess where their strengths and opportunities lie in managing knowledge.

The tool is divided into five sections: the KM process; leadership; culture; technology and measurement. The following is a subset of the items and information in the KMAT, with a simplified scoring system.

Directions: Read the following statements and evaluate your organization's performance. The scale is as follows:

1 = no, 2 = poor, 3 = fair, 4 = good and 5 = excellent

I. The Knowledge Management Process

P1.   Knowledge gaps are systematically identified and well-defined processes are used to close them.

_____1   _____2   _____3   _____4   _____5

P2.   A sophisticated and ethical intelligence gathering mechanism has been developed.

_____1   _____2   _____3   _____4   _____5

P3.   All members of the organization are involved in looking for ideas in traditional and non-traditional places.

_____1   _____2   _____3   _____4   _____5

P4.   The organization has formalized the process of transferring best practices, including documentation and lessons learnt.

_____1   _____2   _____3   _____4   _____5

P5.   'Tacit' knowledge (what employees know how to do, but cannot express) is valued and transferred across the organization.

_____1   _____2   _____3   _____4   _____5

Total of items P1 through P5. _____

II. Leadership in Knowledge Management

L1.   Managing organizational knowledge is central to the organization's strategy.

_____1   _____2   _____3   _____4   _____5

L2. The organization understands the revenue-generating potential of its knowledge assets and develops strategies for marketing and selling them.

_____1   _____2   _____3   _____4   _____5

L3. The organization uses learning to support existing core competencies and create new ones.

_____1   _____2   _____3   _____4   _____5

L4. Individuals are hired, evaluated and compensated for their contributions to the development of organizational knowledge.

_____1   _____2   _____3   _____4   _____5

Total of items L1 through L4. _____

III.   Knowledge Management Culture

C1. The organization encourages and facilitates knowledge sharing.

_____1   _____2   _____3   _____4   _____5

C2. A climate of openness and trust permeates the organization.

_____1   _____2   _____3   _____4   _____5

C3. Customer value creation is acknowledged as major objective of knowledge management.

_____1   _____2   _____3   _____4   _____5

C4. Flexibility and a desire to innovate drive the learning process.

_____1   _____2   _____3   _____4   _____5

C5. Employees take responsibility for their own learning.

_____1   _____2   _____3   _____4   _____5

Total of items C1 through C5. _____

IV. Knowledge Management Technology

T1. Technology links all members of the enterprise to one another and to all relevant external publics.

_____1   _____2   _____3   _____4   _____5

T2.   Technology creates an institutional memory that is accessible to the entire enterprise.

_____1   _____2   _____3   _____4   _____5

T3.   Technology brings the organization closer to its customers.

_____1   _____2   _____3   _____4   _____5

T4.   The organization fosters development of 'human centred' information technology.

_____1   _____2   _____3   _____4   _____5

T5.   Technology that supports collaboration is rapidly placed in the hands of employees.

_____1   _____2   _____3   _____4   _____5

T6.   Information systems are real-time, integrated, and 'smart'.

_____1   _____2   _____3   _____4   _____5

Total of items T1 through T6. _____

V.   Knowledge Management Measurement

M1.   The organization has invented ways to link knowledge to financial results.

_____1   _____2   _____3   _____4   _____5

M2.   The organization has developed a specific set of indicators to manage knowledge.

_____1   _____2   _____3   _____4   _____5

M3.   The organization's set of measures balances hard and soft as well as financial and non-financial indicators.

_____1   _____2   _____3   _____4   _____5

M4.   The organization allocates resources toward efforts that measurably increase its knowledge base.

_____1   _____2   _____3   _____4   _____5

Total of items M1 through M4. _____

Source: APQC, USA and AA, Consulting, USA (1995).

Appendix II: The Knowledge Management Assessment Tool

Instructions: This survey is designed to allow you to register your opinions regarding your organization and its external relationships. Please review each of the following statements and circle the response that best represents your opinion about your organization, using the following scale.

6 = Strongly Agree   5 = Agree   4 = Mildly Agree
3 = Mildly Disagree   2 = Disagree   1 = Strongly Disagree

1. The generation of new ideas and knowledge is highly valued.

    1   2   3   4   5   6

2. Job analyses are frequently performed to determine job duties and requirements.

    1   2   3   4   5   6

3. An electronic knowledge base exists to store new ideas, knowledge, solutions and best practices.

    1   2   3   4   5   6

4. Documents are proactively shared with employees.

    1   2   3   4   5   6

5. The collective experience of employees is an integral part of decision making.

    1   2   3   4   5   6

6. Suggestions and multiple viewpoints are often sought for decision making and organization development.

    1   2   3   4   5   6

7. The development of job documentation is encouraged.

    1   2   3   4   5   6

8. Information from many sources is stored in an integrated manner and cross-referenced, facilitating better communication and decision making.

    1   2   3   4   5   6

9. No policies or technical security issues prevent the sharing of information and knowledge.

    1   2   3   4   5   6

10. Job responsibilities are carried out and decisions are made based on all the necessary information and knowledge.

    1   2   3   4   5   6

11. Experience is highly valued.

    1   2   3   4   5   6

12. Documents can be posted on an organizational internet portal or saved on a network server.

    1   2   3   4   5   6

13. The information and knowledge you receive is accurate and up-to-date.

    1   2   3   4   5   6

14. An organizational intranet portal exists where information and knowledge relevant to job requirements may be retrieved.

    1   2   3   4   5   6

15. New ideas and knowledge are frequently applied.

    1   2   3   4   5   6

16. Brainstorming and other similar techniques are often used to generate and record new ideas and knowledge.

    1   2   3   4   5   6

17. New ideas and knowledge are recorded for future use.

    1   2   3   4   5   6

18. It is common practice to store work documents on an organizational server, rather than on personal computers.

    1   2   3   4   5   6

19. Electronic and/or non-electronic collaboration, teamwork and cooperation are a part of doing business.

    1   2   3   4   5   6

20. Recorded knowledge and best practices are used for training, staff development and organizational development.

    1   2   3   4   5   6

21.   Tips and tools, job aids and case studies of best practices are available for performance objectives.

1   2   3   4   5   6

22.   On-the-job time is available to gather information and knowledge from others.

1   2   3   4   5   6

23.   Information is stored and organized in a way that makes it intuitively easy and quick to locate.

1   2   3   4   5   6

24.   Collaborative meetings to gather information and share knowledge are productive.

1   2   3   4   5   6

25.   Advanced technologies such as data warehousing, mining and modelling are used to leverage data and infor-mation for strategic decision making.

1   2   3   4   5   6

26.   There is a directory of experts for each major knowledge domain.

1   2   3   4   5   6

27.   Concept mapping is a common technique used to gather new information and knowledge.

1   2   3   4   5   6

28.   Documents stored on an organizational server or intranet contain timely and useful knowledge for our job responsibilities.

1   2   3   4   5   6

29.   Incentives are in place that motivate staff to share knowledge.

1   2   3   4   5   6

30.   Expert systems and knowledge bases are used to aid in decision making.

1   2   3   4   5   6

Source: Maier and Moseley (2003).

Bibliography

Dalkir, K. 2005. *Knowledge Management in Theory and Practice*. Oxford, UK: Elsevier Butterworth-Heinemann.

Economist Intelligence Unit. 2005. 'Managing Knowledge for Competitive Advantage.' Sponsored by Tata Consultancy Services. Available at http://www.eiu.com, accessed in September 2006.

Edvinsson, L. and M.S. Malone. 1997. *Intellectual Capital: Realizing Your Company's True Value by Finding Its Hidden Roots*. New York: Harper Business.

Grossman, M. 2006. 'An Overview of Knowledge Management Assessment Approaches', *The Journal of American Academy of Business*, 8(2): 242–47.

Kaplan, R.S. and D.P. Norton. 1996. *The Balanced Scorecard: Translating Strategy into Action*. Boston: HBS.

Klimko, G. 2001. 'Knowledge Management and Maturity Models: Building Common Understanding', Proceedings of the 2nd European Conference on Knowledge Management, Bled, Slovenia, 8–9 November 2001.

Kumar, A. 2004. *Knowledge Management at Tata Steel*. ICFAI Center for Management Research.

Maier, D.J. and J.L. Moseley. 2003. 'The Knowledge Management Assessment Tool (KMAT)', *The 2003 Annual: Volume 1, Training*. USA: John Wiley and Sons.

Rajakannu, M. n.d. *Wipro's Collaboration and KM Journey*, White Paper, Wipro Technologies. Available at http://www.wipro.com/webpages/insights/kmjourney.htm, accessed in September 2006.

Rao, M. 2005. 'Overview of KM Tools', in M. Rao (ed.), *Knowledge Management Tools and Techniques: Practitioners and Experts Evaluate KM Solutions*. Oxford, UK: Elsevier Butterworth-Heinemann.

Santosus, M. and J. Surmacz. 2006. 'The ABCs of Knowledge Management.' Knowledge Management Research Center. Available at http://www.cio.com/article/40343/ABC, accessed in September 2006.

3 Knowledge Management in a Manufacturing Organization

RAVI PRAKASH

Introduction

In the present scenario, a transition is taking place from industrial to knowledge economy, especially in countries like India. We have nothing to lose and everything to gain from such a transition because we have a huge number of scientific and technological manpower, which forms a very large scientific knowledge pool. We hear of call centres, job outsourcing by the West, and so on, and these are all related to our knowledge pool. Hence, it is high time we understand and utilize knowledge management (KM) concepts more systematically. There is a strong need to fully understand the significance of KM, technology management, research and development (R&D) management, innovation management and intellectual property rights (IPR) management in the knowledge economy. Also, there is a need to network the knowledge institutions. It should be appreciated that KM would lead to benefits which will be reaped by the society.

Knowledge acquisition involves identification and capturing of knowledge, know-how, expertise and other intellectual capital (IPR issues). Knowledge management usually refers to the ways organizations gather, manage and use the knowledge that has been acquired over a time span. Knowledge management is like a business model, which embraces knowledge as an organizational asset to derive sustainable business advantage. As an area belonging to management discipline, it promotes an integrated approach to create and accumulate knowledge of people in an organization and disseminate it where and when it is needed. It enables people to use the knowledge of others in an environment of collaboration. It improves performance and organizational learning through application in a range of specific processes and practices.

Knowledge transfer (an aspect of KM) has always existed in one form or the other, for example, through on-job discussions with colleagues, formal apprenticeship, professional training and mentoring programmes. Knowledge management programmes seek to evaluate and manage the process of compilation and application of intellectual capital.

The importance of KM has become more apparent due to accelerating pace of change of industrial, political and service environments, staff attrition (especially that resulting from years of downsizing and re-engineering), growth in organizational scope, geographic dispersion associated with globalization of markets, global integration, increase in networked organizations, growing knowledge intensity of goods and services, revolution in information technology, and so on. Some of the specific business factors that highlight the importance of KM are listed as follows:

1. Markets are becoming increasingly competitive and the rate of innovation is rising.
2. Competitive pressures reduce the size of the workforce that holds valuable business knowledge.
3. The reduction in staffing creates a need to replace informal knowledge with formal methods.
4. The time available to acquire experience and knowledge has diminished.
5. Early retirements and increasing mobility of the work force lead to loss of knowledge.
6. There is a need to manage increasing complexity as many small operating companies undertake transnational sourcing operations.
7. Changes in strategic direction may result in the loss of knowledge in a specific area.
8. Most of the work is information based.
9. Organizations compete on the basis of knowledge.
10. Products and services are becoming increasingly complex, endowing them with a significant information component.

The following are some of the integral components of KM:

1. To generate new knowledge.
2. To access valuable knowledge from outside sources.
3. To use accessible knowledge in decision making.
4. To embed knowledge in processes, products, and/or services.
5. To represent knowledge in documents, databases, and software.
6. To facilitate knowledge growth through culture and incentives.
7. To transfer existing knowledge to other parts of the organization.
8. To measure the value of knowledge assets and/or impact of KM.

Application of Knowledge Management

Knowledge management plays a major role in manufacturing, financial services and energy sectors. At the same time, it is becoming increasingly important in business services, communications, government processes, education, healthcare, insurance, retail/wholesale trade, transportation, chemical industries, technology, and many more. Knowledge management draws inputs from a wide range of disciplines and technologies like cognitive science, expert systems, artificial intelligence and knowledge-based management systems, computer-supported collaborative work, library and information science, technical writing, document management, decision support systems, semantic networks, relational and object databases, simulation, and so on.

It is worth mentioning that Hewlett-Packard, by sharing expertise already available in the company but not known to their development teams, brought out new products to the market at a much faster rate.

Similarly, Skandia Assurance developed new measures of intellectual capital and, focusing their managers on increasing its value, have grown revenues much faster. Texas Instruments too, by sharing best practice between its semiconductor fabrication plants, saved the equivalent of investment in a new plant. Last but not the least, Dow Chemicals, by focusing on active management of its patent portfolio, have generated over $125 million in revenue from licensing and other ways of exploiting their intellectual properties of intangible assets.

These organizations are amongst the world's best-known organizations and they cover a wide range of applications of KM. Lessons learnt from these organizations show that even simple technologies can generate great performance when empowered by smart minds of motivated and committed people. Also, it may be pointed out here that unless data and information are translated into meaningful decisions and actions are taken for sustained performance, the purpose will not be served. Knowledge management provides the way, as has been proved by these world-class companies, and it has now become indispensable in the policy, strategy and implementation processes of corporations all over the world. The global KM market reached a level of US $8.8 billion during the year 2005.

In Indian manufacturing, financial services, telecom and professional service organizations, a great upsurge in KM applications has been observed. In 1999–2000, KM investment was around Rs 27.7 crore. Within two years it has almost doubled and is expected to touch a figure of Rs 180 crore in the year 2007.

Knowledge Management in Manufacturing Organizations

As mentioned earlier, the manufacturing industry in India accounts for a significant chunk of KM applications. The major factors that accelerated the growth of KM in the manufacturing industry are as follows:

1. Manufacturing is becoming more collaborative than ever before with information from suppliers, sub-contractors and customers required to be compiled in a common knowledge base.
2. Requirement of history of previous product runs/projects regarding configuration, yield, machines, ISO documentation, and so on.
3. Desperate need for improvement in productivity with shrinking profit margins, shorter life cycles, outsourcing and cost control.
4. Need for every entity involved in manufacturing to get consistent, complete and timely knowledge/ information.
5. Need for re-organization of professional skills due to ever changing technology.
6. Migration of experts in search of better job opportunities.
7. New recruits take long time to acquire the required professionalism.
8. Weak collective learning/capacity for innovation.

However, these accelerators are also met by some inhibitors at the same time. These inhibitors are as follows:

1. Lack of complete understanding of KM
2. Delay in decision making for implementing KM
3. Change management issues
4. Lack of incentives for sharing information
5. Security of the intellectual capital
6. High cost of software and services

Adopting Knowledge Management in Manufacturing Organizations

Adopting any change in an organization is normally a challenging task. The task becomes even more difficult when it needs to be done at all levels of management. Various strategies that should be followed while adopting KM in manufacturing industry are as follows:

1. All the information, including work-related files and orders dispatched, must be transferred to a central pool using information technology (IT) systems.
2. Best practices must be available centrally.
3. Data should be captured about customers at the point of sales.
4. Research and development (R&D) should be used to leverage application of the concepts of KM.
5. Methods should be devised to create greater value from existing intellectual assets.
6. Efforts should be made to create strategies for focusing on individuals' innovation and knowledge creation.
7. There should be a firm commitment at all the levels of management to a knowledge-focused strategy.

Hypothetical Example of a Typical Indian Manufacturing Organization

Let us consider a hypothetical Indian manufacturing company called XYZ which has an IT culture with a certain level of maturity. Let us further assume that it has an average of 500 employees with a separate IT department. However, benefits of IT are not yet fully derived by the company as is reflected by the low level of automation, conversion of data to knowledge, and so on. XYZ Co. will not be able to compete in the market and would face sourcing restrictions due to lack of timely information, planning constraints and knowledge drain. Most of the Indian companies face similar scenarios.

Hence, XYZ Co. needs to develop a KM system. For this purpose, the company should do the following:

1. Need not depend on the knowledge of currently available experts/specialists.
2. Should look for new avenues of procurement.

3. Should be able to manage procurement of raw materials from different resources.
4. Should ensure sufficient knowledge of production planning.
5. Should not face downtime due to non-availability of inventory attributable to lack of proficiency in inventory management.
6. Must get equipped with sufficient information to handle variations in climatic conditions.

The architecture for KM in a manufacturing industry should be based on an integrated system comprising knowledge manager, enterprise resource planning (ERP) system and process tracker. Enterprise resource planning module consists of production management, production planning, trade promotion, quality control, inventory management, packing and forwarding, purchase, maintenance, personnel and payroll, finance, receipts and payments, and management information system. Process tracker involves capture, transfer and renewal of information as major processes; it is a feedback system in which feedback is sent by the user of process/products to the knowledge manager. Knowledge manager captures this information to modify it and to convert it as an input to the knowledge base. Transfer of this knowledge base should be available to the user for future reference. Knowledge capturing involves codification, indexing, classification, aggregation and discussion. Transferring is a series of processes by which the organization distributes information and knowledge. By transferring information, the organization permits the user to incorporate, transform and apply the accessible knowledge for turning information into a value-creating process. The renewal of data implies that knowledge has to be adapted, transformed, destroyed and renewed all the time in the process. When all the three entities, namely, ERP system, knowledge manager and process tracker, work in tandem, then previously mentioned strategies for KM are accomplished.

Tools that are needed by a knowledge manager include

1. configurable interface,
2. data integrator,
3. business intelligence,
4. content and document manager, and
5. knowledge enabler.

A manufacturing organization like XYZ can reap the following benefits after achieving successful implementation of KM:

1. It would create a knowledge base of various batch runs (product category-wise), percentage yield achieved, reasons for improved/reduced yield, process parameters/quality control measures affected, and so on.
2. It would be able to track production personnel efficiencies, their training/skill needs.
3. It will provide downtime analysis, categorization and breakdown forecast, maintenance scheduling and planning.
4. There will be a production process simulation for a new product or product mix.
5. The system would be able to capture information electronically.
6. There will be reduced load on personnel.
7. Workers' skill profile will improve.

8. It will be possible to capture all interactions with quality assurance department, production, production planning and control for future use.
9. It will conserve energy and materials, and lead to consistency in operations.
10. Final yield will improve.

These points illustrate the importance of KM.

Conclusion

To summarize, it may be said that in the manufacturing sector, KM is all about coming together, keeping together and working together.

Bibliography

Lee, G. and R.E. Cole. 2003. 'From a Firm-Based to a Community-Based Model of Knowledge Creation: The Case of the Linux Kernel Development', *Organization Science*, 14(6): 633–49.

Macintosh, A., J. Fraser and D. Lochhead. 2002. 'Smart-Gov: A Knowledge-Based Platform for Electronic Transactional Services', Proceedings of DEXA 2002, the 1st International Conference on Electronic Government, E-GOV 2002, Aix-en-Provence, France, 2–5 September 2002.

Malhotra, Y. 2004. 'Integrating Knowledge Management Technologies in Organizational Business Processes: Getting Real Time Enterprises to Deliver Real Business Performance', *Journal of Knowledge Management*, 9(1): 7–28.

Ruggles, R. 1997. *Knowledge Management Tool.* Newton, MA: Butterworth-Heinemann.

Tiwana, A. 2001. *The Essential Guide to Knowledge Management, E-Business and CRM Applications.* Singapore: Pearson Education Asia, Addison Wesley Longman (Singapore).

4 Structure and Behaviour of IT Firms in India

K. NARAYANAN AND SAVITA BHAT

Introduction

With increasing liberalization and necessity to face competition it is imperative that India concentrates, revives and supports the industries that have the capability to do well. The information technology (IT) sector is one such sector in India that has the potential to grow, provide employment and internationalize. It is now recognized that information and communication technologies (ICT) can help in having social equity and sustainable development in India (Kaushik and Singh 2004; Mehta and Kalra 2006). Further, the drive to use ICT to transform India into a knowledge economy (Tripathi 2006) has increased the importance of computer hardware, software and services industry in India.

Over the last decade the IT industry in India has grown at a very high pace, becoming one of the important industries contributing to Indian exports. As of today, in India, the software and IT services industry employs 1 million people approximately and by 2008 these industries are expected to employ 2.2 million Indians. Mainly driven by the IT industry (also oil and construction) the Bombay Stock Exchange (BSE) benchmark sensex had touched 12,000 from 7,500 over a period of one year in the new millennium.

This chapter attempts to analyse the structure and behaviour of the IT firms in India. In particular, an attempt has been made to understand the pattern of growth (in fixed assets as well as sales turnover) for the three segments of IT industry, namely, computer hardware, software and IT-enabled services (ITeS). The importance of age of the firm in determining differences in the growth and technological behaviour of the firms is also highlighted. This is especially important in the context of designing policy measures like tax holiday and other concessions for firms in this industry in a developing country like India. For this study a balanced panel data sample of 155 firms covering hardware, software and services sub-sectors of the IT industry for a period of six years from 2000 to 2005 has been used.

The following section gives an overview of the IT industry in India. Later, the chapter analyses the growth, profits and technological behaviour of the sample derived from the IT industry in India. The final section gives the summary and conclusions of the present study.

Overview of IT Industry in India

Historical Perspective

The initiation of IT industry in India dates back to early 1960s. During the 1960s and 1970s, the Government of India kept self-sufficiency as the aim in computers and electronics to be achieved in three steps:

1. There should be Indian participation in ownership and control of foreign computer subsidiaries in the country.
2. Indian producers should become capable of meeting the computer requirements with foreign units meeting only the most complex and large technical needs.
3. India should be able to obtain and manufacture the most advanced systems available in the international market.

In this period International Business Machines (IBM) and International Computers Limited (ICL) were the two main players in India of which IBM alone accounted for 70 per cent of the sales. The government proposed that Indian nationals should share the ownership to which the companies responded negatively. In fact IBM, claiming that its international presence required centralized coordination and control, threatened to leave India. International Computers Limited split its operations into two, a manufacturing unit with 40 per cent Indian ownership and a sales unit with no Indian involvement. The government formed a Department of Electronics (DoE) and a new Electronics Commission to formulate and oversee implementation of policies. Electronics Corporation of India Ltd (ECIL) was formed for microcomputer production.

In 1975, Burroughs (US) entered into a joint venture agreement with Tata Consultancy Services (TCS) to export software and printers. Computer Maintenance Corporation (CMC) was also established with a monopoly to maintain all foreign computer systems. Under renewed pressure from the government to share ownership, IBM quit India in 1978. This exposed the government's resolve to pursue its policy of advancement at any cost and the market opened up to many Indian competitors like the Hindustan Computers Limited (HCL), DCM Data Products and Operations Research Group (ORG) to design and assemble systems. International Data Machines (IDM) marketed and serviced microsystems. All these together probably employed about 4,000 employees.

During the 1980s, the government encouraged the export of software and computer peripherals while permitting import of mainframes and supercomputers. This was basically due to the aim of modernizing the Indian IT industry, which was far behind the contemporary research and product frontiers in other countries. In 1984, DoE announced a new computer policy to promote manufacture of latest technology computers at internationally comparable prices. Imports (parts and know-how) were liberalized at low duties to support domestic hardware manufacturers (Parthasarathy 2005). In the year 1986, DoE announced a Software Export Development and Training Policy. Duty was cut to 60 per cent, which was subsequently cut to 25 per cent in 1992, and 100 per cent income tax exemption was announced on profits from software export. Most of the regulations were made lenient in this period. As a result, production shot up by 100 per cent while prices fell to 50 per cent and slowly computers became affordable.

Promotion and Liberalization

In this period, DoE also invested in knowledge-based computer systems (KBCS) programme with five Indian Institutes of technology (IITs), Indian Institute of Science (IISc) and National Center for Software Technology (NCST). National Informatics Center set up NICNET, a satellite-based communication network covering over 439 cities and towns, to computerize government business at all levels. Further, during the 1990s, the DoE was reprioritized by the government to promote IT rather than regulate it. Liberalization became more effective. Import duty for software, which was 112 per cent in 1991 due to devaluation of rupee, fell to 10 per cent by 1995. By 1993, duplication of software was permitted and piracy was made punishable. In 1996, Videsh Sanchar Nigam Limited (VSNL) started internet services. Encouragement in the form of tax incentives, infrastructure, free licensing to Internet Service Providers (ISPs), permission to lay cables or setting up gateways, and so on was given to the industry as value of internet was recognized. Software technology parks were set up in the 1990s to provide duty-free imports of capital goods, high-speed data communication links and tax holidays for 10 years. In the year 2000, the IT Act was enacted. This Act underscores the legal infrastructure for e-commerce and e-governance in India (see Basu and Jones 2005 for details). A summary of policies and their effects over the years is shown in Table 4.1.

Table 4.1   Summary of Indian Policies for IT Sector and Their Effects

Time period	Important policies	Effects
1960s and 1970s	Indian participation in ownership and control of foreign subsidiaries mandatory.	Foreign firms like IBM quit India and domestic firms flourished with approximately 4,000 employees working in the industry.
	In 1984, imports of parts and know-how liberalized at low duties to support domestic hardware manufacturers with duty cut to 60 per cent in 1986.	Foreign equity participation involving technology transfer. Increase in foreign trade on IT products and services (both imports and exports).
1990s	1. Income tax exemption up to 100 per cent for software export profits.	
	2. Duty cut to 25 per cent in 1992 for import of parts and know-how.	
	3. By 1993, duplication of software was permitted and piracy was made punishable.	
	4. Import duty on software fell to 10 per cent in 1995 due to devaluation of rupee.	Production shot up by 100 per cent and prices fell to 50 per cent.
	5. Encouragement given in the form of tax incentives, infrastructure, free licensing to ISPs, permission to lay cables or setting up gateways, and so on.	Exports of software.
	6. Software technology parks set up to provide duty-free imports of capital goods, high-speed data communication links and tax holidays for 10 years	

(*Table 4.1 continued*)

(*Table 4.1 continued*)

Time period	Important policies	Effects
2000 to 2006	Emphasis on the legal infrastructure for e-commerce in India via the IT Act.	1. Indian IT output value rose from $1.73 billion in 1994–1995 to $17.5 billion, a jump of 900 per cent. 2. IT software and services accounted for 3–4 per cent of GDP and around 35 per cent of exports. 3. Software exports rose from Rs 14 crore in 1995–1996 to Rs 103, 200 crore in 2005–2006. 4. As of today, the software and IT services sectors employ 1 million people approximately. 5. BSE benchmark sensex has touched 12,000 from 7,500 over a period of one year.

Source: Compiled by authors, based on literature review.

Indian IT output value has risen from $1.73 billion in 1994–1995 to $17.5 billion, a jump of 900 per cent. Information technology software and services accounted for 3–4 per cent of gross domestic product (GDP) and around 35 per cent of exports. Software exports have risen from Rs 14 crore in 1995–1996 to Rs. 103, 200 crore in 2005–2006. The annual growth rate of India's software exports has been consistently over 50 per cent. Within 3 to 4 years, India is expected to achieve $50 billion worth of exports as the industry continues to grow. As mentioned earlier, currently the software and IT services sectors employ nearly one million people and by 2008 they are expected to employ about 2.2 million Indians. Mainly driven by the IT industry (along with oil and construction) the BSE benchmark sensex has touched 12,000 over a period of one year from 7,500.

Segments of IT Industry

The IT industry in India can be broadly divided into IT services, software products, and ITeS and e-businesses. They have a large export market with a small domestic component as well. The ITeS industries like call centres, back offices, and so on have also shot up from the small beginning in early 1990s with American Express, British Airways and General Electric (GE). The only thing which may stand in the way may be the infrastructure which has not kept pace with the requirements of the industry as seen in many cities like Bangalore, Mumbai, Hyderabad, and so on. Also, trained manpower that has not kept up with the advances in the industry has to be retrained by the companies most of the time. Then there is something called the last mile problem. The communication networks have reached the towns but from there to the villages is a jump yet to be made. That requires intense investment and engineering due to the terrain involved. Also, the IT industry depends on the high-cost telecom structure imported from abroad. Efforts should be made to develop them in-house.

Table 4.2 gives the statistics on electronic production during the period 2000–2001 to 2005–2006. Data for this analysis has been taken from the website of the Department of Information Technology

(DIT), Government of India. As is evident from Table 4.2, during each financial year from 2000–2001 to 2005–2006, software production (sum of rows 5 and 6 in table) has contributed to more than 50 per cent of the total electronic production. Again, one can clearly infer by comparing rows 5 and 6 of the table that most of the software produced is exported. Further, the percentage share of software for exports in total electronic production has steadily increased from approximately 41 per cent in 2000–2001 to nearly 56 per cent in 2005–2006. It should be noted that in 1990 the Indian government had announced 100 per cent income tax exemption on software export profits after which India has been witnessing phenomenal increase in software production and exports.

Table 4.2   Value of Electronics Production during 2000–2001 to 2005–2006

(Rupees Crore)

S. no.	Item	2000–2001	2001–2002	2002–2003	2003–2004	2004–2005	2005–2006
1.	Consumer Electronics	11,950 (17.36)	12,700 (15.85)	13,800 (14.23)	15,200 (12.85)	16,800 (11.02)	18,500 (9.96)
2.	Industrial Electronics	4,000 (5.81)	4,500 (5.62)	5,550 (5.72)	6,100 (5.16)	8,300 (5.45)	9,300 (5.01)
3.	Computers	3,400 (4.94)	3,550 (4.43)	4,250 (4.38)	6,800 (5.73)	8,800 (5.77)	10,500 (5.66)
4.	Equipments and Components	11,750 (17.07)	12,000 (14.98)	13,900 (14.33)	15,700 (13.27)	16,600 (10.89)	17,700 (9.53)
5.	Software for Exports	28,350 (41.18)	36,500 (45.55)	46,100 (47.53)	58,240 (49.23)	80,180 (52.60)	103,200 (55.59)
6.	Domestic Software	9,400 (13.65)	10,874 (13.57)	13,400 (13.81)	16,250 (13.74)	21,740 (14.26)	26,460 (14.25)
7.	Total	68,850	80,124	97,000	118,290	152,420	185,660

Source: Adapted from Department of Information Technology, Government of India website: *http://www.mit.gov.in/dbid/eproduction.asp*

Note: Figures in parentheses denote percentage share of total.

Some of the recent studies (Bhaduri and Ray 2004; Narayanan 2007; Patibandla and Peterson 2002; Siddharthan and Nollen 2004) have looked into the factors determining competitiveness of firms in the IT industry in India. In general, these studies have re-established the idea that continuous technological upgradation is an important factor for keeping the industry competitive.

Patibandla and Peterson (2002) in their study find the role of transnational corporations (TNCs), especially of tacit knowledge transfer, to be important in the competitive evolution of software segment in India. Narayanan (2007) too finds foreign equity participation to positively determine export competitiveness of firms in the IT industry. At the same time Bhaduri and Ray (2004) find that, because of the small product life of computer hardware, know-how technology is especially important for export competitiveness of electrical/electronics (software and services excluded) firms.

Siddharthan and Nollen (2004) divided the sample for Indian IT sector into three groups—multinational enterprise (MNE) affiliates, technology importers that do not have foreign equity participation but make lump sum royalties or license payments to import technology and domestic firms that neither import technology nor have foreign equity participation. They find that MNE affiliates in this industry are using only one of the arms-length technology purchases and tacit technological skills from their foreign equity holder firms, to compete in the foreign markets.

Empirical Analysis

This section would deal with the analysis of the sample data drawn from the Indian IT industry. The next subsection would give the source and structure of the data used in the present analysis. Subsequent subsection would analyse the growth, profits and technological behaviour of the firms in this industry.

Sample, data and time period

The IT industry data for the present chapter has been obtained from the Prowess database provided by the Center for Monitoring Indian Economy that has data on listed companies in India. The sample period considered is from 2000 to 2005. Since the panel used for the analysis is a balanced panel, the data on 155 companies that were incorporated before year 2000 of IT industry have been extracted.

Data on the year of incorporation, economic activity, gross fixed assets (GFA), sales turnover, profit before tax (PBT), research and development (R&D) and foreign equity have been collected for each of the 155 firms. Analysis has been carried out with the help of STATA software.

On the basis of the economic activity information on these 155 firms, the authors could divide the sample into 19 hardware, 127 software and 9 IT service providers. Age of these firms ranged from one year to more than 50 years (as in the year 2000). Further, of the 155 companies, nearly one-fourth invested on R&D and 20 per cent had ownership (or were subsidiaries) of foreign companies.

Growth, profits and technological behaviour

This subsection would try to understand, with the help of tables, the structure and behaviour of firms in the sample from IT industry. Table 4.3 gives the summary of compound growth rates of GFA, sales turnover and average PBT for the full sample as well as for the three segments of the IT industry.

As can be observed from Table 4.3, when compared to the hardware segment the compound growth rate of services is the highest, followed by software. This clearly reinstates that presently Indian IT industry is growing due to its software and services segments. However, when it comes to profits, the average PBT is the highest for the software segment with both hardware and services lagging far behind.

Table 4.4 shows a summary of growth rates and profits of the firms according to age groups (as in year 2000) for the three segments of the industry. The variable age acts as proxy for experience and specialization developed by the firms in production, management and marketing. Compared to start-ups, experienced firms have the advantage of knowing the market and the players giving them an edge in exports and performance. In developing countries such as India, after liberalization, newer firms may find the domestic markets to be already crammed with older firms' products and therefore may try to

Table 4.3   Summary of Compound Growth Rate of Gross Fixed Assets (GFA), Compound Growth Rate of Sales Turnover and Average Profit before Tax

S. no. segment	No. of firms	Compound growth rate (in percentage) of gross fixed assets (mean with standard deviation in parenthesis)	Compound growth rate (in percentage) of sales turnover (mean with standard deviation in parenthesis)	Average profit before tax (in rupees crore) during the period 2000–2005 (with standard deviation in parenthesis)
1. Hardware	19	7.84 (23.51)	−0.86 (25.97)	5.14 (17.35)
2. Software	127	19.55 (28.75)	20.40 (47.83)	33.72 (143.10)
3. Service	9	58.48 (69.73)	53.89 (55.13)	−16.50 (70.28)
4. All	155	20.38 (33.14)	19.74 (47.21)	27.30 (131.35)

Source: Compiled by authors, based on sample data extracted from Prowess database.

seek the foreign markets right from the outset. As Bhaduri and Ray (2004) too note, the younger firms with latest equipment and technology might be more competitive than older firms in the Indian high-tech industries.

As is clear from Table 4.4, in general for all the three segments of IT industry, the youngest firms (firms in the age group of 1–5 years) have the highest growth rates followed by the age group of 10–15 years. Medium-aged firms that were established after 1991 have low growth rates. Firms established during the early 1990s were mainly export oriented. Therefore, these firms are likely to have been affected by the slowdown in the US market post 2000.

When it comes to profits, the youngest firms in the software and services are not doing well as compared to the oldest firms. As Indian economy opened up, IT clusters were set up in various parts in India (Okada 2006). However, most of the companies in these clusters belonged to novice entrepreneurs and only a few were set up by old established firms like Infosys Technologies Ltd, Wipro Ltd and Tata

Table 4.4   Age-group-wise Summary of Compound Growth Rate of Gross Fixed Assets (GFA), Compound Growth Rate of Sales Turnover and Profit before Tax

	S. no.	Age group as in year 2000 → Sectors ↓	1–5 years	6–10 years	10–15 years	Above 15 years	Total no. of observations
Compound Growth Rate (in %) of Gross Fixed Assets (Mean with Standard Deviation in Parenthesis)	1.	All	28.10 (32.48) [43]	14.37 (27.43) [63]	25.96 (47.07) [30]	14.02 (20.26) [19]	155
	2.	Hardware	23.55 (23.49) [6]	−4.73 (22.77) [8]	15.84 (21.98) [2]	4.60 (9.39) [3]	19
	3.	Software	26.31 (30.49) [35]	17.11 (27.73) [52]	20.13 (32.52) [26]	10.64 (17.23) [14]	127
	4.	Service	72.99 (75.49) [2]	17.69 (14.80) [3]	111.86 (146.57) [2]	51.79 (8.69) [2]	9

(Table 4.4 continued)

(Table 4.4 continued)

	S. no.	Age group as in year →2000 Sectors	1–5 years	6–10 years	10–15 years	Above 15 years	Total no. of observations
Compound Growth Rate (in %) of Sales Turnover (Mean with Standard Deviation in Parenthesis)	5.	All	38.80 (59.91) [43]	11.89 (42.48) [63]	14.87 (36.50) [30]	10.30 (33.44) [19]	155
	6.	Hardware	14.37 (18.14) [6]	−18.42 (29.39) [8]	10.60 (6.10) [2]	7.84 (5.49) [3]	19
	7.	Software	39.00 (60.83) [35]	15.86 (43.19) [52]	12.44 (36.87) [26]	5.54 (34.37) [14]	127
	8.	Service	108.49 (100.09) [2]	24.05 (32.06) [3]	50.72 (42.99) [2]	47.24 (40.60) [2]	9
Average Profit before Tax (in Rupees Crore) (with Standard Deviation in Parenthesis)	9.	All	0.14 (33.37) [43]	13.39 (43.21) [63]	32.22 (104.27) [30]	127.12 (328.73) [19]	155
	10.	Hardware	5.54 (9.49) [6]	8.05 (26.05) [8]	−1.95 (1.45) [2]	1.32 (1.70) [3]	19
	11.	Software	5.05 (12.04) [35]	14.95 (46.48) [52]	36.67 (111.56) [26]	169.64 (377.03) [14]	127
	12.	Service	−101.93 (139.75) [2]	0.62 (0.88) [3]	8.57 (13.16) [2]	18.20 (25.92) [2]	9

Source: Compiled by authors, based on sample data extracted from Prowess database.
Note: Number of observations for each of the cases is in square brackets.

Infotech Ltd (Okada 2006). The older, well-established large firms have *niche* markets for themselves and so can have high profits with moderate growth rates. The younger firms, on the other hand, are not yet established and have to be content with lower profits. Further, operating costs incurred by the software and service firms are mainly in the form of wages and salaries for skilled employees, which eat away a major chunk of profits made by the younger, generally small, growing firms.

Table 4.4 also shows that the service sector records the highest average compound growth rates for all the age groups among the three segments of IT industry. Increase in business process outsourcing (BPO) and call centre services from foreign clients is the likely reason for the high growth of the service segment as compared to other segments. At the same time, the average profits of the youngest service firms (1–5 years) are negative. This could be mainly because of the high level of initial capital investments required in establishing service firms, especially BPO firms (Okada 2006).

The hardware firms in general have lower growth rates as compared to software and services. This is not surprising since India's policies have been partial towards the growth of software and services as compared to the hardware segment. Again, large multinational companies (MNCs) in the hardware segment in India, such as Hewlett-Packard India and IBM, have shifted their R&D centres to cities like Bangalore to produce embedded software for their hardware products (Okada 2006). Thus, the hardware giants are more into production of high-end specialized software rather than hardware. The smaller hardware players are mostly selling assembled imported computers and peripherals.

As was mentioned earlier, studies dealing with Indian IT sector have, by and large, stated that technological investments play an important role in determining the competitiveness of firms in this industry. Table 4.5 tries to look at the number of firms investing in two important modes of technology investment, namely, in-house R&D and foreign equity participation, in the present sample.

As is clear from Table 4.5, 40 per cent [(38 + 31 −7)/155] of the firms in this sample are investing in technological activities of in-house R&D and/or foreign equity participation. In-house R&D is more popular with more than 25 per cent of the hardware and software firms using in-house R&D technique as compared to around 20 per cent using foreign equity for technological upgradation. Kumar (2005) too notes that established Indian companies are now trying to export more sophisticated, higher value-added software and services that would give them higher margins. However, the relative amount of in-house R&D investment in product R&D in Indian IT software firms is much less as compared to similar-sized firms in other nations.

Foreign equity participation is evident even in the youngest group of software firms, which is not the case in hardware and service firms. Again, only software firms are using a combination of R&D with foreign equity. For the hardware and oldest software firms, R&D and intra-firm transfer of technology through foreign equity participation seem to be substitutes.

Table 4.5   **Age-group-wise Summary of Number of Firms Doing R&D, Having Foreign Equity (FE) and Having FE with R&D during the Period 2000–2005**

	S. no.	Age group as in year 2000 → Segments	Firms using technological mode	1–5 years	6–10 years	10–15 Years	Above 15 years	Total no. of observations
Research and Development (R&D)	1.	All	38 (24.5%)	7	13	12	6	155
	2.	Hardware	6 (31.6%)	1	3	2	–	19
	3.	Software	32 (25.2%)	6	10	10	6	127
	4.	Service	–	–	–	–	–	9
Foreign Equity Participation (FE)	5.	All	31 (20%)	6	16	3	6	155
	6.	Hardware	4 (21%)	–	2	–	2	19
	7.	Software	25 (19.7%)	6	14	2	3	127
	8.	Service	2 (22%)	–	–	1	1	9
Both R&D and FE	9.	All	7 (4.5%)	2	4	1	–	155
	10.	Hardware	–	–	–	–	–	19
	11.	Software	7 (5.5%)	2	4	1	–	127
	12.	Service	–	–	–	–	–	9

Source: Compiled by authors, based on sample data extracted from Prowess database.

It is interesting to note that none of the nine service firms in the sample does in-house R&D though two of the older service firms have foreign equity participation. IT- enabled services such as call centres and BPO being provided by the Indian firms seem to have remained low-end routine jobs, which can be easily carried out on a large scale by the abundant labour force available in India. As Okada (2006) too notes, ITeS providers in Bangalore are mainly engaged in activities requiring low skill levels with some of the ITeS/BPO working as low cost centres only for their affiliates abroad.

Tables 4.6 and 4.7 give the frequency distribution of firms as per the compound growth rate of GFA and sales turnover, respectively. Mean of average PBT for each of the growth rate ranges has also been

Table 4.6   Frequency Distribution of Firms as per the Compound Growth Rate of Gross Fixed Assets (GFA)

S. no.	Ranges of compound growth rate of GFA (in %)	Number of firms				No. of R&D doing firms	No. of firms with FE	Mean of average PBT for the frequency range (in rupees crore)
		Total	Hardware	Software	Service			
1.	Less than and equal to 0	28	4	24	–	6 (1H, 5S)	2 (1H, 1S)	3.25
2.	Greater than 0 up to 10	35	9	24	2	10 (3H, 7S)	10 (3H, 7S)	5.52
3.	Greater than 10 up to 25	36	2	32	2	9 (9S)	5 (5S)	54.61
4.	Greater than 25 up to 50	42	3	37	2	12 (2H, 10S)	10 (9S, 1SE)	44.96
5.	Greater than 50	14	1	10	3	1 (1S)	4 (3S, 1SE)	6.66

Source: Compiled by authors, based on sample data extracted from Prowess database.
Note: Here H = hardware firms, S = software firms and SE = services firms.

Table 4.7   Frequency Distribution of Firms as per Compound Growth Rate of Sales

S. no.	Ranges of compound growth rate of turnover (in %)	Number of firms				No. of R&D doing firms	No. of firms with FE	Mean of average PBT for the frequency range (in rupees crore)
		Total	Hardware	Software	Service			
1.	Less than and equal to 0	53	7	45	1	10 (1H, 9S)	11 (2H, 9S)	4.53
2.	Greater than 0 up to 10	19	5	14	–	4 (1H, 3S)	3 (1H, 2S)	4.07
3.	Greater than 10 up to 25	33	6	24	3	14 (4H, 10S)	5 (1H, 4S)	40.46
4.	Greater than 25 up to 50	25	1	23	1	6 (6S)	7 (7S)	92.38
5.	Greater Than 50	25	–	21	4	4 (4S)	5 (3S, 2SE)	10.78

Source: Compiled by authors, based on sample data extracted from Prowess database.
Note: H = hardware firms; S = software firms; SE = services firms.

supplied in the last column of both tables. Further, the number of firms doing R&D and having foreign equity has also been indicated for each range.

As is clear from Tables 4.6 and 4.7, a majority of hardware firms have growth rates in lower ranges as compared to the software and services firms. In other words, India is still having software and services-led growth in the IT sector. Incidentally, the highest profits are earned in the growth ranges (greater than 10 up to 25 in Table 4.6 and greater than 25 up to 50 in Table 4.7) where only software firms are investing on technological activities. From the last columns in both the tables, one can clearly see the trade-off between profits and growth where average profits initially increase with the increase in growth rates up to a peak level after which they decrease with further increase in growth rates.

Summary and Conclusions

The present study attempted to examine the structure and behaviour of firms in the IT industry in India in the new millennium. A balanced panel consisting of 155 firms taken over a period of six years (2000–2005) was analysed in the study. The main findings of the present study can be summarized as follows:

1. There are differences in the growth rates of firms belonging to different segments of the Indian IT industry. In the beginning of the new millennium too, software and services segments drive the growth of Indian IT sector with hardware remaining a low-growing segment.
2. The growth rates of firms in this industry differ with their age. The youngest firms (1–5 years) have the highest growth rates. Medium-age firms that were established during early 1990s have low growth rates. It seems that the slowdown in the US market has affected these firms, which generally follow an export-oriented policy though the products that they offer are standard ones.
3. Technological activity such as in-house R&D and foreign equity participation is quite low in the industry. Among the technologically active ones, in-house R&D investment is more popular than foreign equity participation in case of both the software and hardware firms. However, the IT service sector does not seem to be using much of in-house R&D for achieving further technological sophistication that is so essential for their sustainability in the long run.
4. Of the three IT segments, software has the highest average age. Again, the older software and services firms are making more profits as compared to the younger ones. This could be mainly because many of the established software firms in India are trying to venture into high-end jobs that would give them higher margins. Thus, the government needs to help the start-up firms in getting into production of sophisticated software and services from the beginning itself.

In the past few years many new firms have joined the IT industry; mergers and acquisitions have also taken place (Okada 2006). The present study has not looked into this aspect. Nevertheless, the findings of this study, which are based on an analysis of sample firms that have survived throughout the six years in the new millennium, does give insights regarding the prevailing structure and conduct of IT firms in India. The study reinstates that Indian IT sector is enjoying software and service segments led growth. Further, there is a need to encourage the IT industry, especially service firms, to use more sophisticated technologies, and to invest in in-house R&D to discover new areas of operation, so that the focus is shifted from low-end routine jobs to high value-added jobs. Also, around the time when the policy makers are trying to reduce concessions offered to the IT industry, the study has important policy implications whereby specific concessions like tax holiday could be extended to the new, rather than to old firms, and the nature of subsidy could shift to promote technological capabilities in general and R&D investments in particular.

References

Basu, S. and R. Jones. 2005. 'Indian Information and Technology Act 2000: Review of the Regulatory Powers under the Act', *International Review of Law Computers & Technology*, 19(2): 209–30.

Bhaduri, S. and A.S. Ray. 2004. 'Exporting through Technological Capability: Econometric Evidence from India's Pharmaceutical and Electrical/Electronics Firms', *Oxford Development Studies*, 32(1): 87–100.

Kaushik, P.D. and N. Singh. 2004. 'Information Technology and Broad-Based Development: Preliminary Lessons from North India', *World Development*, 32(4): 591–607.

Kumar, N. 2005. 'Indian Software Industry Development: National and International Perspectives', in A. Saith and M. Vijayabaskar (eds), *ICTs and Indian Economic Development*, pp. 93–130. New Delhi: Sage.

Mehta, S. and M. Kalra. 2006. 'Information and Communication Technologies: A Bridge for Social Equity and Sustainable Development in India', *The International Information & Library Review*, 38: 147–60.

Narayanan, K. 2007. 'Technology Acquisition and Competitiveness: Evidence from Indian IT industry', in S.R. Hashim and N.S. Siddharthan (eds), *High-Tech Industries, Employment and Global Competitiveness*, pp. 70–96. New Delhi: Routledge.

Okada, A. 2006. 'Small firms in the Indian Software Clusters: Building Global Competitiveness', paper presented at International Seminar on Knowledge-Based Industries, Employment and Global Competitiveness, organized by the Forum for Global Knowledge Sharing, Delhi, India, 6–7 October 2006.

Parthasarathy, B. 2005. 'The Political Economy of the Computer Software Industry in Bangalore, India', in A. Saith and M. Vijayabaskar (eds), *ICTs and Indian Economic Development*, pp. 198–230. New Delhi: Sage.

Patibandla, M. and B. Petersen. 2002. 'Role of Transnational Corporations in the Evolution of a High-Tech Industry: The Case of India's Software Industry', *World Development*, 30(9): 1561–77.

Siddharthan, N.S. and S. Nollen. 2004. 'MNE Affiliation, Firm Size and Exports Revisited: A Study of Information Technology Firms in India', *The Journal of Development Studies*, 40(6): 146–68.

Tripathi, M. 2006. 'Transforming India into A Knowledge Economy through information Communication Technologies—Current Developments', *The International Information & Library Review*, 38: 139–46.

Part 2

Trends and Issues in Formulating Policy
Initiatives and Developing Strategies of
Change Management

5 India's Transition to Knowledge Economy: Variation across States*

ARINDAM BANIK AND PRADIP K. BHAUMIK

Introduction

The concept of human capital may be quite old but its relevance and use has increased with greater adoption of skill-augmenting technologies. The Organisation for Economic Co-operation and Development (OECD) (1998) has defined human capital as the knowledge, skills, competence and other attributes embodied in individuals that are relevant to economic activity. Accordingly, human capital may also be viewed as a factor of production just like—but distinct from—economic capital and labour. Economic capital may provide a necessary, but not sufficient, condition for the production of goods and services. In fact, for production of services, as distinct from the production of goods, this may be the most important factor of production; and with services emerging as the largest sector in most economies, human capital is gradually emerging both as a scarce resource and as an important contributor to international competitiveness. Developing economies suffer not only from a shortage of economic capital but also from a severe shortage of human capital although they might simultaneously have an abundance of labour. This is also borne out by studies reporting higher rates of return on investments in human capital in developing economies than in developed ones (Hartog 1999).

Development of human capital may be considered as a primary requirement for achieving economic development. Every year, economic aid is disbursed, investments are undertaken, policies are framed and elaborate plans are announced to develop human capital in many developing economies. The actual outcomes are not always as planned. It has been argued that quite often economic activities either fail in achieving their stated goals or get delayed due to non-availability of competent persons in a country. This is also true in India where there has been significant growth in the number of schools in many states due to the government's successful intervention. But in terms of quality they are often poor at both the primary and secondary levels. It is now established that primary education generates the highest rates of return; secondary level has lower returns while tertiary level has higher returns than the secondary

*The authors are grateful to Professors Ashoka Chandra, Ishwar Dayal and M.K. Khanijo for their useful suggestions.

level (Banik and Bhaumik 2002). In recent times, researchers (for example, Banik and Bhaumik 2005, 2006a) have argued that aid- or grant-driven development activities are not successful in many developing economies due to non-availability of appropriate human capital having the requisite skills.

The concept of human capital development is useful in understanding economic development. Some theories stress the importance of human development for societies to prosper economically and also for sustainable development (Knack and Keefer 1997). Granovetter (1995) underscores that virtually all economic behaviour is embedded in networks of human development. It is often argued that human capital can make economic transactions more efficient by providing economic participants with access to more information, thus enabling them to coordinate activities for mutual benefit. Rodrik (1998) finds that human capital plays a significant part in shaping the outcomes of economic action at both macro- and micro-levels. Based on community-level field work in Tanzania, Narayan (1997) illustrated that effective social and human capital helped the community studied in a variety of ways—such as, more effective government services were made available, spread of information on agriculture was facilitated, pooling together of the group's resources could be made possible and people were able to participate in the formal credit market.

On a related issue, it is often argued that the rationale for poverty alleviation programmes in developing countries lies in the imperfections in the factor markets. Accordingly, sophisticated intervention programmes have been designed and implemented without rural roots. Krishna (2001) finds that the human capital view poses a fundamental challenge to this type of development enterprise. Indeed, the author emphasized that the development agencies should consider 'investment' in human capital.

Theory also points to a number of possible benefits of human skill development for developing countries. North (1990) finds that incentives that are built into the institutional framework for skill development—and accordingly play a decisive role in shaping the kinds of skills and knowledge—are more effective. In the East Asian context, for example, it is the egalitarian education policies which have played a pivotal role in their economic growth (Birdsall et al. 1998). It is further argued that the increased equality has led to enhanced political and social stability, thereby creating a better investment environment (Stiglitz 2000). The cognitive skills, in addition to increasing the literacy rate, may be considered as a pre-condition for economic development. Lucas (1988) and Stiglitz (1988) illustrate that this pre-condition may explain the seeming failure of capital to flow to the capital-poor countries in spite of the higher marginal return to capital. The lack of complementary factors such as non-availability of skilled labour further added to the problem of capital flow to the capital-poor countries. Pritchett (2001) examined two aspects of quality of education and skills. In some countries, schooling has been enormously effective in transmitting knowledge and skills while in others it has been essentially worthless and has created no skills.

There has been a dearth of empirical literature in the Indian context analysing the diverse pictures that relate the transformation from manufacturing to knowledge economy across Indian states. This is important in the Indian context because of the fact that the country is benefiting due to positive contribution made by a select group of states and their education system.

Studies (for example, Guiso et al. 2006) often argued that it may not be appropriate to establish a link between economic incentives and economic outcomes. In other words, economic explanations are only partial analysis. Indeed the impact of culture on expectations and preferences sometimes plays an important role. Sometimes long-standing cultural traditions are the result of a society-wide (for example, religious group, ethnicity) optimization process. This culture is not continually altered in step with the changes that individuals experience during their lifetimes. This aspect may have some bearings in explaining the issues of convergence and divergence in respect of human capital across different Indian states.

This chapter develops comparisons between human and economic capital in developing economies and then discusses the structure of human capital development in the Indian context. It then examines the convergence and divergence aspects across Indian states with the help of various state characteristics. Finally, conclusions are derived.

Economic and Human Capital in Developing Economies

Economic capital, physical capital or simply capital is one of the factors of production and consists of goods that have been produced for the purpose of producing other goods. Examples of capital include buildings, equipment and inventories. Capital does not consist of final goods and services, but rather involves items that are used to further the production of final goods and services. Human capital on the other hand, is embodied in human beings and consists of knowledge, skills and other attributes relevant to economic activity. Human capital may be needed to use economic capital efficiently, especially as more sophisticated technologies are used in the production processes.

Table 5.1 summarizes the differences between human capital and other factors of production usually considered in classical and neo-classical economics from a developing economy perspective. Among other things, it shows the interdependence of economic and human capital—the productivity of economic capital depends on the intensity of human capital and vice versa.

Convergence and Divergence Issues

Economists find a causal link in the prediction of unconditional convergence across countries/states and it is only possible if the level of technical knowledge (and its change), rate of savings, rate of population growth and the rate of depreciation are all the same. In reality, countries/states differ in many aspects.

Table 5.1   A Comparison of Economic Capital, Human Capital and Labour from a Developing Economy Perspective

Attribute	Economic Capital	Human Capital	Labour
Availability	Scarce	Scarce	Plentiful
Price	International	Low	Very low
Productivity	Depends on human capital intensity	Depends on economic capital intensity	Depends on the intensity of the other two capitals
Accretion	Investment in equipment, technology, material	Investment in education, training	Increase in population
Attrition	Depreciation	Non-use of skill, retirement, death	Natural losses
Source	Savings, aid, foreign investment	Labour	Previous generation
Time to Acquire	Low	High	Very low

Source: www.Indiastat.com

A weaker version, called conditional convergence, states that for controlling possible differences in cross-country/states parameters, such as the rates of savings, initially poor countries/states grow faster.

Several studies in the Indian context have documented the persistence and growth of inequality across states with the help of structural parameters. Ghosh and De (2000) brought out the link between variable infrastructure development and growth in income and showed that areas with better infrastructure experienced faster income growth. Datt and Ravallion (1998) pointed out the extremely variable initial conditions in rural development and human capital development that was obtained in rural development as causes for persistent and often increases in spatial inequality. Ahluwalia (2002) found that variation in flows of private investment led to spatial variation in income. Cashin and Sahay (1996) explained spatial inequality and convergence as an artefact of internal migration.

In recent times, neo-classical growth paradigm has been used extensively due to its theoretical underpinning to understand the inter-regional and inter-country growth differences in the standard of living (Cass 1965; Ramsey 1928; Solow 1956). One of the basic predictions of the neo-classical growth theory is that economies with lower capital-labour ratio tend to grow faster than those with higher capital-labour ratio. It predicts that if the economies are similar with respect to their tastes and preferences and technology, then there is an inverse relationship between the initial level of per capita income and its growth rate due to implications of diminishing returns to reproducible capital. The lower the initial level of per capita income, the higher the growth rate of per capita income. Within this neo-classical growth framework a number of studies have attempted to examine the differences in growth rates and convergence across regions and countries (Barro and Sala-i-Martin 1995; Baumol 1986; DeLong 1988; Lucas 1988; Mankiw et al. 1992).

The steady-state path may not be the only answer to the prosperity of the states. This is particularly relevant in the Indian context where certain states are in the process of transformation from manufacturing to services (knowledge economy) based exclusively on human capital. More interestingly, a few states have remained in manufacturing despite a tremendous labour shortage and dependence on supply of labour from backward states. For example, Gujarat, Maharashtra and Delhi appear to be major destinations of foreign investors. In fact during the past 10 years these three states have been growing at the rate of Asian 'tiger' economies in their better days. Southern states such as Tamil Nadu, Karnataka and Andhra Pradesh are equally competitive now in this context. On most measures investors have shown a preference for states that possess a well-developed infrastructure and governance. Other factors determining the attractiveness of a state in courting FDI are availability of manpower, power supply, raw material availability, transportation facility, appropriate incentives for industry, water supply, availability of finance, and tax holidays and subsidies. In addition, the most important considerations on the part of investors are transparency in dealings, quick approvals, sound infrastructure and consistency in policy.

In this context it may be mentioned here that Gujarat and Maharashtra, two large western states, notched up the fastest growth between 1991 and 1998 whereas growth rates in half of the 14 biggest states of India actually declined (Banik and Bhaumik 2006b). On a per head basis the difference is even starker. Some states where growth is slow including the two biggest states, Uttar Pradesh and Bihar, also have fastest growing population.

Analysis

Our analysis is based on data published by the Centre for Monitoring Indian Economy (CMIE). We have also used data from two other sources such as Indiastat.com and Economic Survey 2005–2006 published by the Government of India. We have considered a single year, that is, 2003–2004, for the purpose. This way we are not in a position to interpret the time dimension of the transition. However despite this limitation, we are able to capture the current trends. Incidentally, our effort may be useful in getting interesting insights that are as yet not available in the theoretical analysis.

Figures 5.1 and 5.2 show the current structure of selected state economies with the help of broad primary and secondary sectors' contribution to state domestic product (SDP) in 2003–2004.

Three clear pictures are discernible from Figures 5.1 and 5.3. One, contribution of the tertiary sector to the respective state domestic product appears to be dominating for the southern states. Two, as regards the northern states, the role of the primary sector is distinct. Gujarat on the other hand, has taken a commanding position with the help of its secondary sector (Figure 5.3). This postulates the possibility of convergence and divergence across states.

Figures 5.4–5.6 reveal the beneficial effects of investment in human capital and institutions across states. Quite significantly, the new economy services contributed to national state domestic product (NSDP) in southern states and hence the rise in their per capita income. Interestingly, West Bengal and Maharashtra have recently entered these areas. Basic literacy on the other hand had little role to play in raising the per capita income (Figure 5.7). This implies the need for further investment in human capital. Currently this unskilled population is in the wrong line of work. The cities are now hungry for skilled population. Poor children in backward states are less likely to be at school despite the government regulation of education till age 16. Figure 5.8 depicts these facts.

Interestingly, the rise of 'knowledge industries' is a new aspect of India's future development. This is the Indian edition of 'leapfrog' where human capital in the high-technology sector has acted as a powerful engine of growth. We find that states (such as Gujarat, Maharashtra) which are relatively well

Figure 5.1   Structure of the Economy (Tertiary Contribution-wise)

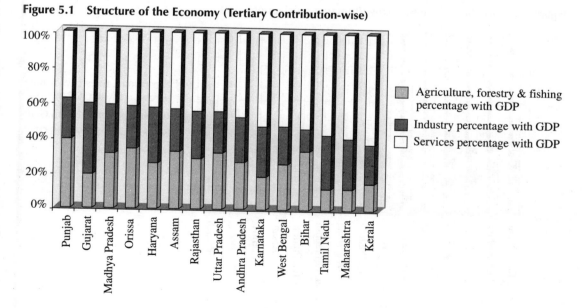

Source: www.Indiastat.com.

Figure 5.2 Structure of the Economy (Secondary Contribution-wise)

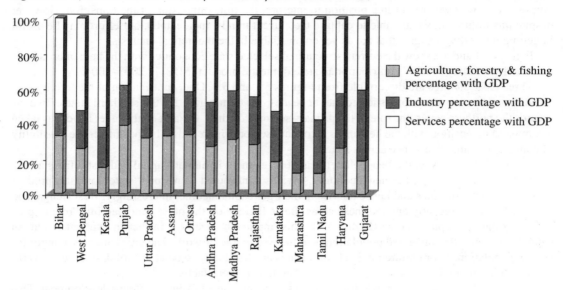

Source: www.Indiastat.com.

Figure 5.3 Structure of the Economy (Primary Contribution-wise)

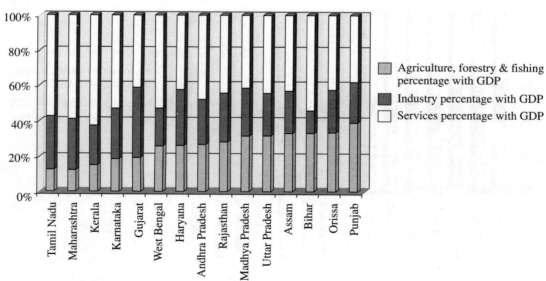

Source: www.Indiastat.com.

Figure 5.4   New Services versus Gross Domestic Product (GDP)

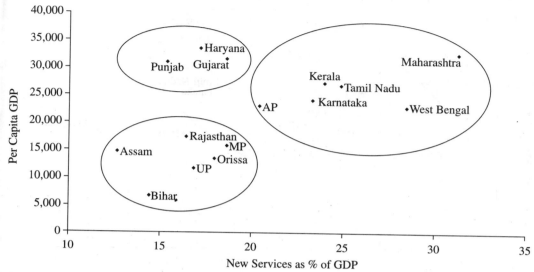

Source: www.Indiastat.com.

Figure 5.5   New Services versus All Services

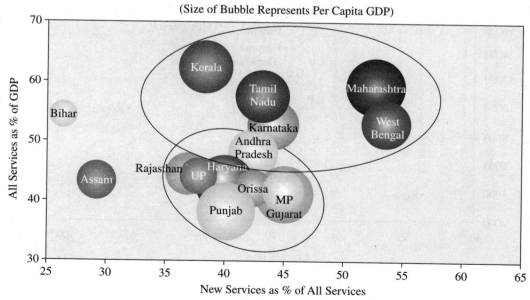

Source: www.Indiastat.com.

Figure 5.6   Manufacturing and New Services

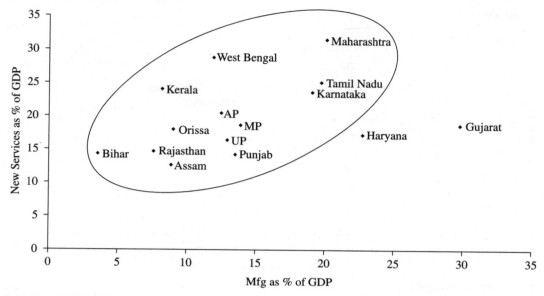

Source: www.Indiastat.com.

Figure 5.7   Per Capita Net State Domestic Product (NSDP) versus Literacy Rate

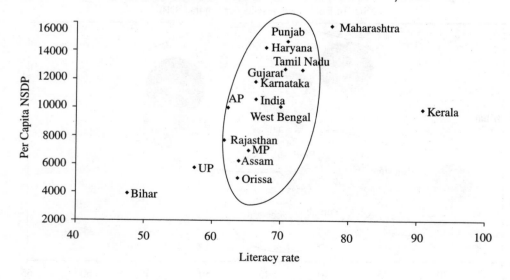

Source: www.Indiastat.com.

Figure 5.8   Per Capita Net State Domestic Product (NSDP) versus Percentage Below Poverty Line (BPL)

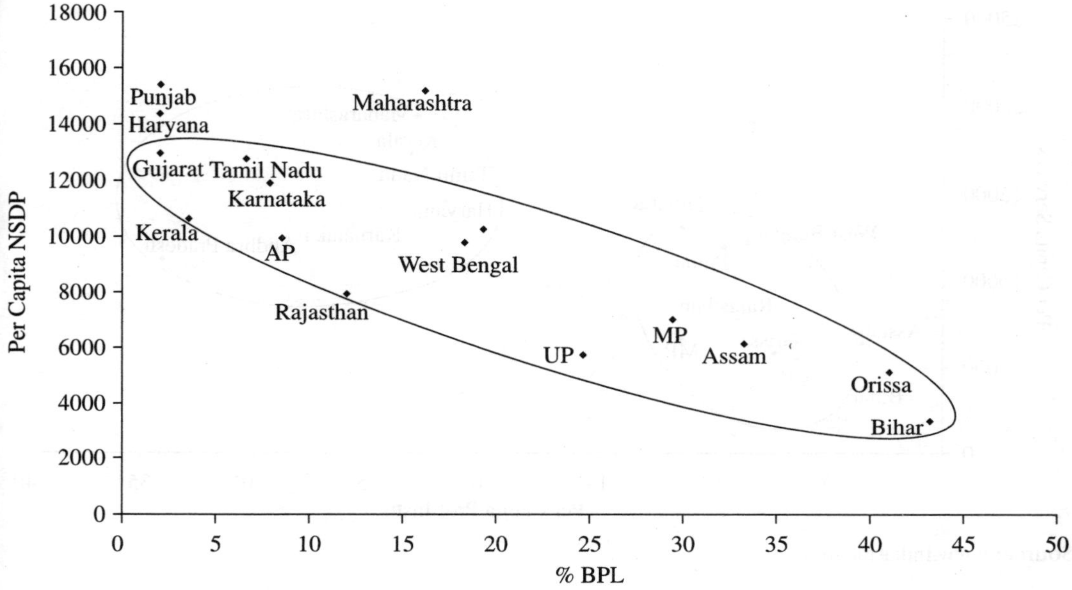

Source: www.Indiastat.com.

developed due to manufacturing, have human capital in the low-technology sector, less intervention by the state sector and geographical closeness to prosperous cities.

Is the infrastructure enough across states to support the transformation from manufacturing to knowledge economy? Figures 5.9 and 5.10 portray interesting pictures. States which are relatively well developed due to high technology (computers, software), have created human capital from endogenous factors such as pro-active policies and other interventions in order to create an appropriate environment (Figure 5.11).

Does Culture Affect Economic Outcomes?

At the household level, economic decisions are often made in accordance with prior beliefs. For example, the choice of schools/colleges, professions to be taken up or particular area for setting up residence are not determined by economic reasons alone. In certain situations, ethnicity may play an important role. Take the case of Gujarat. Logically the state should transform through growth in new economy services. Instead, the state has remained strong in manufacturing because ethnic backgrounds affect people's choices. Here entrepreneurship plays a contributory role. To quote Becker (1996, p.16),

> Individuals have less control over the culture than other social capital. They cannot alter their ethnicity, race or family history, and only with difficulty can they change their country or religion. Because of the difficulty of changing culture and its low depreciation rate, culture is largely a 'given' to individuals throughout their lifetimes.

Figure 5.9   Services and Educational Institutes (Per Capita)

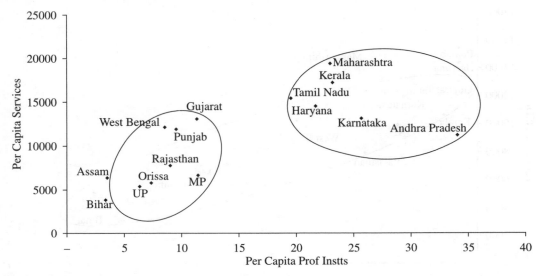

Source: www.Indiastat.com.

Figure 5.10   Electrification versus Literacy

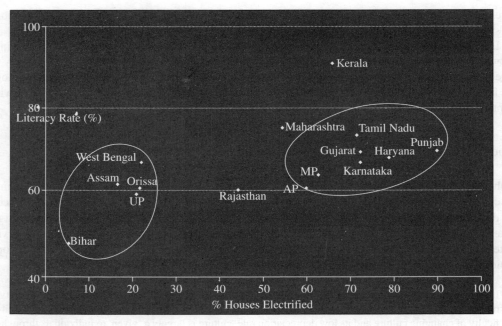

Source: www.Indiastat.com.

Figure 5.11   Expenditure on Education versus Literacy

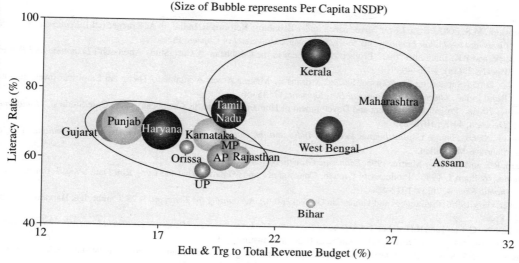

Source: www.Indiastat.com.

Sometimes culture affects beliefs and values. It can also affect broader political outcomes. The prosperity of Gujarat is again an example. Social capital, at least as intended by Putnam (1993) can be seen as a combination of values (people feel a moral duty to go and vote) and beliefs (people expect to be ostracized by their community if they behave in an un-civic way or if an individual has a problem, solve it in a co-operative way).

Conclusions

This chapter argues that human capital is embodied in human beings and consists of knowledge, skills and other attributes relevant to economic activity. Human capital may be needed to use economic capital efficiently, especially as more sophisticated technologies are used in the production processes. The study shows the interdependence of economic and human capital—the productivity of economic capital depends on the intensity of human capital and vice versa.

Our findings reveal that the rise of 'knowledge industries' is a new aspect of India's future development. This is the Indian edition of 'leapfrog' where human capital in the high-technology sector has acted as a powerful engine of growth. We find that states such as Gujarat and Maharashtra, which are relatively well developed due to manufacturing, have human capital in the low-technology sector, less intervention by the state sector and their geographical closeness to prosperous cities. The research shows that economic factors alone may not be sufficient to explain the development of human capital. Sometimes the issue of culture dominates priorities. These are questions that can be rigorously tested in future research and raise an exciting set of possibilities.

References

Ahluwalia, M.S. 2002. 'State Level Performance under Economic Reforms in India', in A. Krueger (ed.), *Economic Policy Reforms and the Indian Economy*, pp. 99–125. Chicago: University of Chicago Press.

Banik, A. and P.K. Bhaumik. 2002. 'Project Management in the Caribbean: A Case Study Approach', *Economic and Political Weekly*, 37(39): 4036–40.

———. 2005. 'Supporting the Poor but Skilled Artisans by Making Assets Available to Them: An Empirical Investigation in Rural India', *Journal of International Development*, 17: 45–66.

———. 2006a. 'Project Management and Development of Human Capital in the Caribbean: Three Case Studies', *Management Decision*, 44(8): 1076–89.

———. 2006b. *Foreign Capital Inflows to China, India and the Caribbean: Trends, Assessments and Determinants*. London: Palgrave-Macmillan.

Barro, R.J. and X. Sala-i-Martin. 1995. *Economic Growth*. New York: McGraw-Hill.

Baumol, William J. 1986. 'Productivity Growth, Convergence and Welfare: What the Long Run Data Show?' *American Economic Review*, 76(3): 1072–85.

Becker, Gary 1996. 'Preferences and Values', in G. Becker (ed.), *Accounting for Taste*, pp. 3–23. Cambridge: Harvard University Press.

Birdsall, N., G. Carol and R.H. Sabot. 1998. *Beyond Tradeoffs: Market Reforms and Equitable Growth in Latin America*. Washington, DC: Inter-American Development Bank and Brookings Institution Press.

Cashin, P. and R. Sahay. 1996. 'International Migration, Center-State grants, and Economic Growth in the States of India', Working Paper, *International Monetary Fund Staff Papers*, 43(1), IMF, Washington D.C.

Cass, David 1965. 'Optimum Growth in an Aggregate Model of Capital Accumulation', *Review of Economic Studies*, 37(3): 233–40.

Datt, Gaurav and Martin Ravallion. 1998. 'Why Have Some Indian States Done Better than Others at Reducing Rural Poverty?' *Economica*, 65(257): 17–38.

DeLong, J.B. 1988. 'Productivity Growth, Convergence and Welfare: A Comment', *American Economic Review*, 78(5): 1138–55.

Ghosh, B. and P. De. 2000. 'Linkage between Infrastructure and Income among Indian States: A Tale of Rising Disparity since Independence', *Indian Journal of Applied Economics*, 20(2): 391–431.

Granovetter, M. 1995. *Getting a Job: A Study of Contacts and Careers*. Chicago: University of Chicago Press.

Guiso, L., P. Sapienza and L. Zingales. 2006. 'Does Culture Affect Economic Outcomes', *Journal of Economic Perspectives*, 20(2): 23–48.

Hartog, J. 1999. 'Behind the Veil of Human Capital', *The OECD Observer*, 215 (January): 37–39.

Knack, S. and P. Keefer. 1997. 'Does Social Capital Have an Economic Payoff? A Cross Country Investigation', *Quarterly Journal of Economics*, 112(4): 1251–1288.

Krishna, A. 2001. 'Moving from the Stock of Social Capital to the Flow of Benefits: The Role of Agency', *World Development*, 29(6 June): 925–43.

Lucas, R.E. 1988. 'On the Mechanics of Economic Development', *Journal of Monetary Economics*, 22(1): 3–42.

Mankiw, N. Gregory, David Romer and David N. Weil. 1992. 'A Contribution to the Empirics of Economic Growth', *Quarterly Journal of Economics*, 107(2): 407–37.

Narayan, D. 1997. *Complementarity and Substitution: Social Capital, Poverty Reduction and the State*. Washington, DC: World Bank, Poverty Group.

North, D. 1990. *Institutions, Institutional Change and Economic Performance*. Cambridge: Cambridge University Press.

OECD. 1998. *Human Capital Investment: An International Comparison*, Center for Educational Research and Innovation, Paris, mimeo.

Pritchett, L. 2001. 'Where Has All the Education Gone?' The *World Bank Economic Review*, 15(3): 367–91.

Putnam, Robert D. 1993. *Making Democracy Work*. Princeton, NJ: Princeton University Press.

Ramsey, F. P. 1928. 'A Mathematical Theory of Saving', *Economic Journal*, 38 (December): 543–59.

Rodrik, D. 1998. 'Why Do More Open Economies Have Bigger Governments?' *Journal of Political Economy*, 106(5): 997–1032.

Solow, Robert M. 1956. 'A Contribution to the Theory of Economic Growth', *Quarterly Journal of Economics*, 70(1): 65–94.

Stiglitz, J.E. 1988. 'Economic Organization, Information and Development', in C. Hollis and T. N. Srinivasan (eds), *Handbook of Development Economics*, pp. 543–630. New York: Elsevier Science Publishers.

———. 2000. 'Development Thinking at the Millennium-Key Note Address', Annual World Conference on Development Economics. Washington, DC: World Bank.

6 An Approach to Developing Knowledge Economy Indicators for Individual States

SIDDHARTH MAHAJAN, ASHOKA CHANDRA AND MAINAK SARKAR

Introduction

In a knowledge economy, knowledge would be created, harnessed and applied in various sectors of the economy. There would be a constant search for new knowledge (or identification of useful knowledge which already exists), and then it would be applied to value-adding activities in any sector. Every sector would have an increasing component of knowledge. It would involve creating new products and finding new ways of making existing products. Knowledge would become the primary resource for creating value. Just as information technology (IT) and IT-enabled services (ITeS) drive the present information economy, research and development (R&D) and innovation would drive the knowledge economy.

According to the World Bank Knowledge Assessment Methodology (KAM) (see Chen and Dahlman 2005; Dahlman and Utz 2005), the knowledge economy framework consists of four pillars. These are: education and training, innovation and technological advancement, information infrastructure, and a proper economic and institutional regime. Continuous development along these four pillars would lead an economy to becoming a knowledge economy, wherein knowledge would be the main resource for economic growth.

Four Pillars of the Knowledge Economy

We describe here the four pillars of the knowledge economy.

Education and Training

An educated and skilled workforce is necessary for a knowledge economy so that it can improve skills continuously and participate in the creation, dissemination and utilization of knowledge. A technically skilled workforce with technical secondary education and tertiary education is needed to create new economically viable technologies. These technologies can be put to use to create new products and services or produce existing products and services in a more efficient manner. A technologically skilled workforce will also be able to tap into the global network of new technologies being developed and see which ones could be more easily adapted to their economic and social setting. Primary-level education for all is necessary so that the population can be informed consumers of new technologies. Also primary education would be necessary to utilize available information on a variety of topics in a better way.

Innovation and Technological Advancement

Technological advancement in a knowledge economy would result in improved design, production and delivery of goods and services. This would push productivity improvements and ultimately contribute to improved measures of the economy based on such variables as gross domestic product (GDP) per capita or GDP per worker. The innovation system refers to the entire set of institutions and of laws and procedures that define the environment for R&D and innovation in the country. The institutions comprise universities and educational institutions, firms and their R&D departments, R&D organizations of the government and consulting firms. Laws and procedures pertain to such issues as award of patents and intellectual property rights (IPR). In a knowledge economy such laws would become important because adequate measures may need to be taken to ensure that the developers of new knowledge are adequately compensated for their efforts. The network of institutions in a country together with its regulatory environment should work in such a way as to ensure the incentives for R&D work developing new products, processes and technologies.

Information Infrastructure

The information infrastructure refers broadly to information and communication technologies (ICT). This includes all hardware and software for storage, processing and transmission of information. It includes the accessibility and large-scale use of computers, phones and TVs to access information. Information and communication technologies because of their relatively low cost and widespread use, have made dissemination of information and knowledge very easy. Increased use of ICT in an economy can contribute to economic growth. When ICT are increasingly employed in the manufacturing and service sectors of an economy, they can result in productivity improvements in those sectors.

Economic and Institutional Regime

This refers to efficient functioning of the government and sound macro-economic and regulatory policies. All of these should be so aligned as to provide incentives for creation, dissemination and utilization of knowledge. In macro-economic policies, the exchange rate should reflect the true state of the currency, inflation should be low and unemployment levels also should not be high. The regulatory regime refers to those policies that encourage competition and promote efficient functioning of markets for products and services. The legal system should provide fast and easy redressal. The financial system should be able to allocate scarce capital to investment proposals yielding good returns with relatively low risks.

The KAM (Knowledge Assessment Methodology) Framework

In the basic KAM framework developed by the World Bank for a country analysis, 14 variables are used to monitor the four pillars of the knowledge economy. There are three variables for each of the four pillars and two additional variables (see the following box).

The KAM Framework of the World Bank	
Pillar	**Variables**
Education and training	Adult literacy rate; secondary enrolment; tertiary enrolment
Innovation and technological advancement	Researchers in R&D (per million population); patent applications granted by the USPTO (per million population); scientific and technical journal articles (per million population)
Information infrastructure	Telephones per 1,000 persons; computers per 1,000 persons; internet users per 1,000 persons
Economic and institutional regime	Tariff and non-tariff barriers; regulatory quality; rule of law

In addition two other variables are used. These are average annual GDP growth and Human Development Index. This evaluation methodology has been applied by the World Bank to 128 countries.

In this methodology, first a basic score on each of the 14 variables is computed for each country. Then a normalized score from 0 to 10 is assigned to each variable. A normalized score between 9 and 10 on a particular variable indicates that the country is in the top 10 percentile on the basis of its performance on that variable. Similarly, a normalized score between 8 and 9 on a particular variable indicates that a country is in the top 20 percentile but not in the top 10 percentile on the basis of its performance on that variable. The normalized score for a particular variable for a country is found by dividing the number of countries with a lower performance on that variable by the total number of countries.

Once the normalized scores for the variables have been computed, they can be averaged to get the normalized score on any one of the pillars. All the normalized scores of the 14 variables can be averaged to get the overall score of a particular country. This score is also known as the Knowledge Economy Indicator (KEI), and indicates a country's preparedness in moving towards the knowledge economy relative to other countries.

Proposed Methodology for Indian States

We plan to adapt the World Bank methodology for countries to develop knowledge economy indicators for individual states within the country. Some indicators such as gross state domestic product (GSDP) and literacy rates are available for states. However, some of the other indicators out of the 14 listed above may have to be modified to accurately reflect the preparedness of individual states in moving towards a knowledge economy. We would use databases such as Indiastat together with information available on state government websites to arrive at a final list of indicators. The aim is that these indicators should be robust, easily measurable and together cover the four pillars of the knowledge economy.

Based on our preliminary work in this direction, we can suggest some of the following variables for each of the four pillars. Data for all these variables for individual states is available on Indiastat. While we describe here the variables suggested by us for the four pillars, we shall finalize the variables after wider consultations.

1. *Education and training*: Literacy rate; enrolment per capita in basic education (classes I–V); enrolment per capita in middle education (classes VI–VIII); enrolment per capita in secondary education (classes IX–XII); enrolment per capita in higher education in each state; gross enrolment ratio; dropout rate
2. *Innovation and technological advancement*: Number of R&D projects and approved cost sponsored by Ministry of Science and Technology in each state; support to extramural R&D projects by each state
3. *Information infrastructure*: Teledensity (telephones per 100 persons) in urban areas in each state; teledensity in rural areas; internet subscribers per 10,000 persons in each state
4. *Economic regime*: Measures for venture capital accessed by states; level of entrepreneurship; institutes which help in laying of standards

Computation of Normalized Score for the Information Infrastructure Pillar for States

The information infrastructure pillar is based on three variables. These are internet subscribers per 10,000 population, teledensity in urban areas and teledensity in rural areas. For each of these variables, first we determine the actual values of the variables for the states. We then determine a normalized score on each variable for each state. The normalized score for internet subscribers per 10,000 population for a particular state, for example, is given by

$$\text{Normalized Score} = \frac{\text{No. of states below that particular state in rank based on internet subscribers}}{\text{Total number of states}}$$

Once we have normalized scores for the three variables for each state, we take the average of these three normalized scores to get an overall normalized score for the information infrastructure pillar. The data is shown in Tables 6.1–6.5.

Table 6.1 contains data on the number of Internet subscribers per 10,000 population for each state in 2003.

In Table 6.2, the states are ranked according to the number of Internet subscribers per 10,000 population in decreasing order and the normalized score for this variable for each state is calculated. Delhi and Chandigarh have the best performance on this variable while Tripura and Bihar are the bottom two states.

Table 6.1   Internet Subscribers per 10,000 Population in Each State in 2003

State/UT	Internet subscribers	Population (2001 census)	Subscribers per 10,000 population
Arunachal Pradesh	1,010	1,091,117	9.257
Andhra Pradesh	219,218	75,727,541	28.948
Assam	14,440	26,638,407	5.421
Bihar	18,895	82,878,796	2.280
Chandigarh	38,458	900,914	426.878
Chhattisgarh	9,275	20,795,956	4.460
Goa	19,449	1,343,998	144.710
Gujarat	195,072	50,596,992	38.554
Haryana	17,015	21,082,989	8.070
Himachal Pradesh	6,410	6,077,248	10.548
Jammu & Kashmir	10,235	10,069,917	10.164
Jharkhand	14,199	26,909,428	5.277
Karnataka	259,121	52,733,958	49.137
Kerala	136,458	31,838,619	42.859
Mizoram	959	891,058	10.762
Manipur	1,026	2,388,634	4.295
Meghalaya	5,285	2,306,069	22.918
Madhya Pradesh	89,501	60,385,118	14.822
Maharashtra	948,264	96,752,247	98.010
Nagaland	2,536	1,988,636	12.752
Orissa	22,343	36,706,920	6.087
Pondicherry	14,275	973,829	146.586
Punjab	69,938	6,077,248	115.082
Rajasthan	121,322	56,473,122	21.483
Tripura	1,194	3,191,168	3.742
Tamil Nadu	329,624	62,110,839	53.070
Uttaranchal	19,801	8,479,562	23.351
Uttar Pradesh	120,006	166,052,859	7.227
Sikkim	965	540,493	17.854
West Bengal	142,663	80,221,171	17.784
Delhi	650,209	13,782,976	471.748
India	**3,500,278**	**1,027,016,607**	**34.082**

Source: www.indiastat.com.

Table 6.2   Ranking of the States Based on the Number of Internet Subscribers

State/UT	No. of internet subscribers per 10,000 population	Rank	Normalized score
Delhi	471.75	1	0.968
Chandigarh	426.88	2	0.935
Pondicherry	146.59	3	0.903
Goa	144.71	4	0.871
Punjab	115.08	5	0.839

(Table 6.2 continued)

(*Table 6.2 continued*)

State/UT	No. of internet subscribers per 10,000 population	Rank	Normalized score
Maharashtra	98.01	6	0.806
Tamil Nadu	53.07	7	0.774
Karnataka	49.14	8	0.742
Kerala	42.86	9	0.710
Gujarat	38.55	10	0.677
Andhra Pradesh	28.95	11	0.645
Uttaranchal	23.35	12	0.613
Meghalaya	22.92	13	0.581
Rajasthan	21.48	14	0.548
Sikkim	17.85	15	0.516
West Bengal	17.78	16	0.484
Madhya Pradesh	14.82	17	0.452
Nagaland	12.75	18	0.419
Mizoram	10.76	19	0.387
Himachal Pradesh	10.55	20	0.355
Jammu & Kashmir	10.16	21	0.323
Arunachal Pradesh	9.26	22	0.290
Haryana	8.07	23	0.258
Uttar Pradesh	7.23	24	0.226
Orissa	6.09	25	0.194
Assam	5.42	26	0.161
Jharkhand	5.28	27	0.129
Chhattisgarh	4.46	28	0.097
Manipur	4.30	29	0.065
Tripura	3.74	30	0.032
Bihar	2.28	31	0.000

Source: www.indiastat.com.

In Table 6.3, states are ranked according to the urban teledensity (telephones per 100 persons) in 2005, and a normalized score for this variable for each state is calculated. Surprisingly, Himachal Pradesh comes up the best on this count though if the state's overall teledensity is considered taking into account both rural and urban areas, it is ranked somewhere in the middle. As expected the metros of Delhi, Chennai and Mumbai score well.

In Table 6.4, states are ranked according to rural teledensity (telephones per 100 persons) in 2005, and a normalized score for this variable for each state is calculated. Kerala and Andaman & Nicobar Islands come up the best while Jharkhand and Chhattisgarh are the bottom two states. The best teledensity figures in rural areas are about six times less than the best teledensity figures in urban areas.

In Table 6.5, the overall normalized score for the information infrastructure pillar is presented. This score has been calculated by taking the average of the normalized scores for the three variables. Only states which have data on both internet subscribers and teledensity are considered. In the final analysis, Delhi and Punjab are the two highest ranking states on the information infrastructure pillar while Jharkhand and Chhattisgarh are the bottom two states.

Table 6.3   Ranking of States Based on Urban Teledensity in 2005

State/UT	Teledensity urban	Rank	Normalized score
Himachal Pradesh	78.11	1	0.963
Delhi	52.09	2	0.926
Punjab	51.57	3	0.889
Chennai	48.03	4	0.852
Kerala	47.61	5	0.815
Mumbai	45.81	6	0.778
Karnataka	31.26	7	0.741
Andhra Pradesh	30.19	8	0.704
Gujarat	30.12	9	0.667
Haryana	29.21	10	0.630
Maharashtra (-) Mumbai	27.71	11	0.593
Kolkata	25.09	12	0.556
Tamil Nadu (-) Chennai	23.1	13	0.519
Rajasthan	22.94	14	0.481
Andaman & Nicobar Islands	22.49	15	0.444
Orissa	21.35	16	0.407
Jammu & Kashmir	19.87	17	0.370
Bihar	19.71	18	0.333
Uttar Pradesh	18.89	19	0.296
Assam	18.22	20	0.259
Madhya Pradesh	17.15	21	0.222
West Bengal (-) Kolkata	17.14	22	0.185
Uttaranchal	17.05	23	0.148
North East-I	15.93	24	0.111
North East-II	14.21	25	0.074
Jharkhand	8.56	26	0.037
Chhattisgarh	7.18	27	0.000

Source: www.indiastat.com.

Table 6.4   Ranking of States Based on Rural Teledensity in 2005

State/UT	Teledensity rural	Rank	Normalized score
Kerala	9.74	1	0.957
Andaman & Nicobar Islands	9.15	2	0.913
Himachal Pradesh	6.82	3	0.870
Punjab	5.34	4	0.826
Haryana	2.9	5	0.783
Tamil Nadu (-) Chennai	2.86	6	0.739
Gujarat	2.63	7	0.696
Maharashtra (-) Mumbai	2.59	8	0.652
Karnataka	2.49	9	0.609

(Table 6.4 continued)

(Table 6.4 continued)

State/UT	Teledensity rural	Rank	Normalized score
Andhra Pradesh	2.37	10	0.565
Uttaranchal	1.68	11	0.522
Rajasthan	1.45	12	0.478
North East-I	1.24	13	0.435
North East-II	1.21	14	0.391
Orissa	1.05	15	0.348
West Bengal (-) Kolkata	1.05	16	0.304
Jammu & Kashmir	0.78	17	0.261
Assam	0.67	18	0.217
Madhya Pradesh	0.67	19	0.174
Bihar	0.57	20	0.130
Uttar Pradesh	0.52	21	0.087
Jharkhand	0.51	22	0.043
Chhattisgarh	0.46	23	0.000

Source: www.indiastat.com.

Table 6.5   Overall Normalized Score for the Information Infrastructure Pillar

State/UT	Overall normalized score for information infrastructure
Delhi	0.947
Punjab	0.851
Kerala	0.827
Himachal Pradesh	0.729
Karnataka	0.697
Maharashtra	0.684
Gujarat	0.680
Tamil Nadu	0.677
Andhra Pradesh	0.638
Haryana	0.557
Rajasthan	0.503
Uttaranchal	0.428
West Bengal	0.324
Jammu & Kashmir	0.318
Orissa	0.316
Madhya Pradesh	0.283
Assam	0.213
Uttar Pradesh	0.203
Bihar	0.155
Jharkhand	0.070
Chhattisgarh	0.032

Source: www.indiastat.com.

Tracking Performance of a Particular State over Time

We next discuss how we can graphically compare a state's performance at different points of time. We first interpret the state KEI. The state KEI is calculated by taking the average of the normalized scores on the four pillars of the knowledge economy for each state. In the previous section, we had discussed how the normalized score for the information infrastructure pillar is calculated. We calculate similarly the normalized scores over the remaining three pillars and average these four scores to get the state KEI.

A state KEI between 0.9 and 1.0 implies that the state is in the top 10 percentile amongst the states in moving towards a knowledge economy. Similarly a state KEI between 0.2 and 0.3 implies that a state is in the bottom 30 percentile but above the bottom 20 percentile in moving towards a knowledge economy. This indicates that the state KEI in any period is a measure of the relative performance of the state compared to other states, in moving towards a knowledge economy.

We can compare the state KEI in a reference year (for example, 2000) with the state KEI in the current year. A higher value of state KEI in the current year compared to its value in the reference year indicates that the state has improved its performance relative to other states. This can be seen in Figure 6.1. On the x axis, we plot state KEI in the base year and on the y axis, state KEI in the current year. The solid line bisecting the figure is the line $y = x$, that is, the state KEI in the current period is the same as the KEI in the base period. A point in the upper left part of the figure above the line indicates that the state has improved its relative performance (state KEI in the current period is higher than state KEI in

Figure 6.1   Comparing Performance of a State over Time

State KEI in the most
recent period

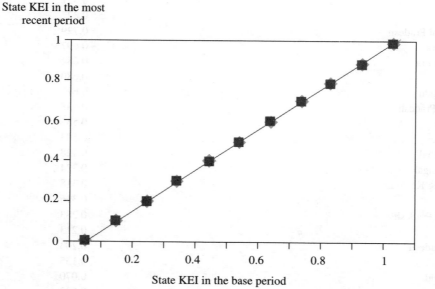

State KEI in the base period

Source: www.indiastat.com.

the base period). Similarly, a point in the bottom right part of the figure below the line indicates that the state has worsened its relative performance (state KEI in the current period is lower than state KEI in the base period).

Relation between Annual Economic Growth and Knowledge Economy Indicators at the Country Level

Chen and Dahlman (2004) assessed the effect of knowledge economy indicators on economic growth. This has been done by fitting a regression model with the dependent variable being annual economic growth and the independent variables being knowledge economy indicators together with other variables. Their model and results are discussed below.

Consider an economy aggregate production function

$$Y = AF(K,L)$$

where Y is the level of aggregate output, K is the level of capital stock, L is the size of the labour force and A is the total factor productivity which measures level of technology.

One example of a production function is the Cobb–Douglas production function

$$Y = AK^{\alpha}L^{\beta}$$

where α is the elasticity of output to capital and β is the elasticity of output to labour.

From this equation, we can write the following:

$$\Delta Y/Y = \alpha\Delta K/K + \beta\Delta L/L + \Delta A/A$$

That is, growth in aggregate output or economic growth depends on growth in capital stock, growth in the labour force and growth in total factor productivity.

The knowledge economy indicators affect the growth in total factor productivity and therefore impact economic growth. The specification of the production function which allows for this is given by:

$$Y = A(g,e,r,i)\ F(K,L)$$

where g represents the economic and institutional regime, e represents education and training, r represents the level of technological innovation and i represents information and communication infrastructure.

To estimate the effect of knowledge economy indicators on economic growth, the above production function is converted to the following specification:

$$\Delta Y/Y = \alpha\Delta K/K + \beta\Delta L/L + a_1 G + a_2 E + a_3 R + a_4 I$$

We describe here how these variables are determined.

Variable G relates to the economic and institutional regime. This is a zero-one variable and has been related to the openness in trade of the particular country. Openness in trade depends on what percentage of the total product lines are covered by non-tariff barriers, what is the average tariff rate on imports and whether private firms contribute to the bulk of the exports. Openness in trade is a proxy for some other considerations such as macro-economic stability and a well-developed private sector.

Variable E represents education and training of the workforce or the average human capital stock per worker. Variable E is defined as:

$$E = e^{rs}$$

where s is the average number of years of schooling of the workforce and r is the Mincerian rate of return to an additional year of schooling. Variable r has been determined in a different paper for 62 countries for different periods.

Variable R representing the level of technological innovation is measured in two ways: first, by the logarithm of the annual number of patents granted by the USTPO, and second, by the logarithm of the annual number of published scientific and technical journal articles.

Variable I represents the information and communication infrastructure and it has again been measured in two ways—these are the number of internet users per 1,000 persons and the number of phones per 1,000 persons.

Some of the main results of the chapter from empirical analysis are as follows. If we consider the education and training pillar, an increase of 20 per cent in the average years of schooling of a population tends to increase the average annual economic growth by 0.15 percentage points. If we consider technological innovation, a 20 per cent increase in the annual number of USTPO patents granted is associated with an increase of 3.8 percentage points in annual economic growth. Finally, if we consider information and communication infrastructure, an increase in the number of phones per 1,000 persons by 20 per cent increases the annual economic growth by 0.11 percentage points.

A similar analysis to the one given in the above paper could be done at the state level. We could consider the effect of knowledge economy indicators for each state on the annual growth in state GDP. This would be the second stage. As a first step we need to have the values of the knowledge economy indicators at the state level.

Future Work and Benefits

We would describe three or four variables for each of the four pillars of the knowledge economy. These variables would be measured for each of the states. Normalized scores for each state on each variable will be calculated. There would be an average normalized score for each state on each of the four pillars. This has already been done for the information infrastructure pillar. Finally there would be a calculation of a state KEI for each state. There would be a ranking of states based on this index.

This exercise would develop a set of indicators that would indicate the preparedness of any particular state in moving towards a knowledge economy. The most important benefit of this work is that it would focus the attention of key decision makers in state governments on indicators that reflect how well the state is progressing towards a knowledge economy. Once attention has been focused on these indicators, resources could be allocated to improve performance on those specific indicators, which need greater attention.

The set of indicators developed could also be used as a benchmarking tool. A state could benchmark itself with other states in the same geographical region or with other states with the same economic performance. A state could also compare its performance over time as described. A certain year could be chosen as a base year and performance in the present year compared with the base year.

References

Chen, D.H.C. and C.J. Dahlman. 2004. 'Knowledge and Development: A Cross-Section Approach', *Knowledge for Development Programme*. Washington D.C.: World Bank Institute.
——. 2005. 'The Knowledge Economy, the KAM Methodology and World Bank Operations', *Knowledge for Development Programme*. Washington D.C.: World Bank Institute.
Dahlman, C. and A. Utz. 2005. *India and the Knowledge Economy: Leveraging Strengths and Opportunities*. Washington D.C.: World Bank Institute.

7 Knowledge Management Initiative and Practice for Moving towards Learning Organization and Business Excellence

Himanshu Joshi, Vidhu Shekhar Jha and Siddharth Mahajan

Introduction

Building a creative and a learning organization is recognized as a pre-requisite for business excellence (Evans and Lindsay 1999). As an approach towards creating a learning organization, knowledge management (KM) has gained wide acceptance for harnessing the intellectual assets with an organization to gain competitive advantage.

Although organizations practice KM in some form or other, it is important to understand the role of knowledge and capability assets in evolving a learning organization.

Just managing knowledge is not the goal. The goal is to leverage the potential of KM to increase organizational performance through learning. Achieving and sustaining competitive advantage requires organizations to learn better and faster from their experiences. Knowledge management programmes, processes and tools support organizational learning for achieving business excellence.

Relationship between Knowledge Management and Learning Organization

Knowledge Management

Although the study of knowledge has its roots in antiquity, the field of 'knowledge management' as a self-conscious discipline is a recent phenomenon. According to Peter Drucker, the collective knowledge residing in the minds of its employees, customers, suppliers, and so on is the most vital resource for an organization's growth, even more than the traditional factors of production, namely, land, labour and capital (Grossman 2006).

Organizations articulate the concept of KM in terms of intellectual capital, intellectual property, knowledge assets and business intelligence. Corporate knowledge is being viewed as one of important sustainable untapped sources of competitive advantage in business. There is always a new idea waiting to be discovered, new ways of doing things, new products, new strategies and new markets (McElroy 2000).

One of the greatest challenges organizations face today is how to manage their intellectual capital. Business environment has now entered a knowledge era, where knowledge has become power, and learning rapidly has become a pre-eminent strategy for success. Thus, knowledge is rapidly becoming more important to organizations than financial resources, market positions, technology and other tangible assets. In today's knowledge economy there is a paradigm shift in focus towards intangible assets, which has contributed to improvement of business processes. Learning organizations competently manage knowledge as one of their major strategies for success in the knowledge economy.

But KM does not happen by chance. A culture which promotes knowledge creation and provides for appropriate support processes is essential for KM. Therefore, if organizations are to fully benefit from the principles of KM, they must focus on how the cognitive capacity of their employees and support processes for KM can be enhanced and measured to provide timely information for improvement. The cognitive capacity (in the form of heuristics and intuitions) and the support processes (such as culture, products and services) are the two most important constructs with KM.

Literature on learning organizations does not mention knowledge explicitly. Some authors only briefly mention knowledge in passing but do not expand on the relationship between the two (Loermans 2002).

Figure 7.1 shows the importance of cognitive and support processes in KM. The level of KM in an organization whose employees perform organizational tasks routinely can be assessed by ascertaining whether they are able or unable to contribute to any improvements in the organizational business processes. Equally, support from the organization in providing the facilities that support and optimize KM is an important issue. Based on the level of cognitive capacities of employees and support services existing in the organization, the condition can be classified as Integrated Knowledge Management, Partial Knowledge Management and Absence of Knowledge Management in an organization.

Effective KM requires not only addressing the mindset of the employees but also putting in place the necessary support services that facilitate an environment for knowledge creation and learning. An organization should always seek employees who demonstrate stimulating behaviour, acquire knowledge and know how to adapt to change. Similarly, cultural and technological support must be interwoven with the organizational processes.

Knowledge acquisition process is of two types: inward/internal and outward/external. Internal knowledge acquisition owes much to total quality management (TQM) idea of internal benchmarking and learning from experience. External knowledge is acquired to bring in innovative ideas and develop effective operating systems. The ability to learn from internal and external business environments has become one of the principal value-adding resources for learning organizations.

Learning Organization

Peter Senge (1992) defines learning organization as 'A group of people continuously enhancing their capacity to create what they want to create'. For organizations to anticipate and respond to complexities

Figure 7.1   Knowledge Management with Respect to Cognitive and Support Processes

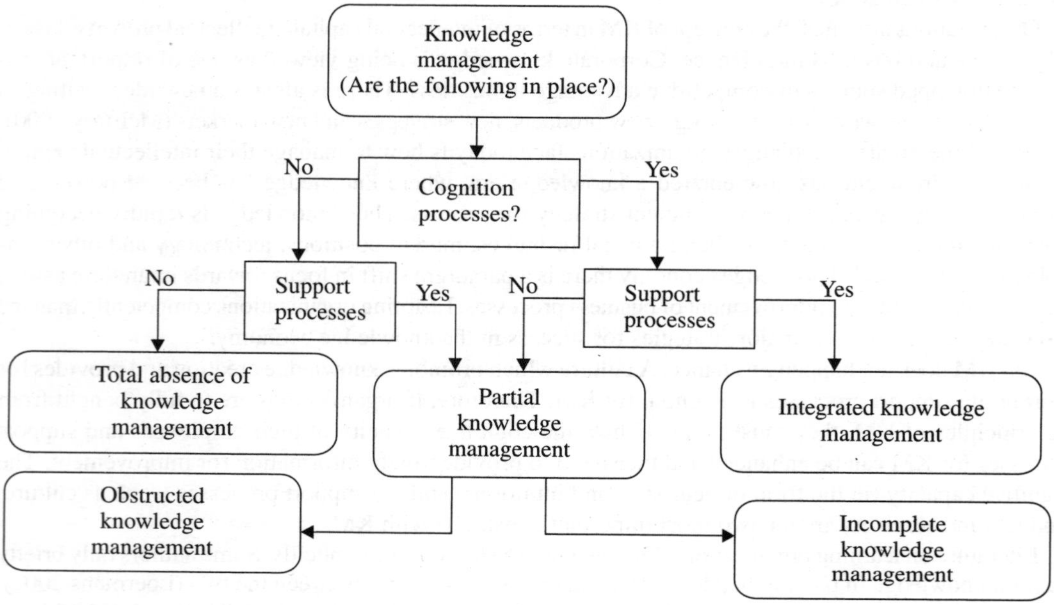

Source: Adapted from Kululanga and McCaffer (2001).

and uncertainties, they have to consciously and comprehensively gather, organize, share and analyse its knowledge in terms of resources, documents and people skills. The rate at which organizations learn and adapt to the changing environment may become the sustainable source of competitive advantage.

A learning organization is one that, according to Senge (1992), has acquired 'systems thinking' by mastering the four disciplines of 'shared values', 'personal mastery', 'mental models' and 'team learning'. System thinking has become known as the fifth discipline. It is closely related to Deming's concept of 'knowledge system'. This system talks about profound knowledge, which is knowledge universal to all businesses, large or small. Once the individual understands the system of profound knowledge, he will apply its principles in every kind of relationship with other people. This will enable him to make better decisions for organizational transformation.

A learning organization and its people make use of their experience and others' to improve their performance. Continuous learning is built into the system and the value of continuous learning is espoused, driven and role-modelled by the top management leadership within the organization. Further, communication within all the levels of management is open and widespread. People at all levels are included in the decision-making process and are recognized for their contribution towards learning and disseminating the knowledge acquired to other employees. Some of the success stories that have shown the characteristics of a learning organizations are GE, Johnson & Johnson, Toyota Motors, Southwest Airlines, Intel, Cisco Systems, Tata Steel and Infosys Technologies; there are many other organizations as well. What is common to these companies is their founding values, and their desire to create new products and markets, new approaches and greater customer value.

Since organizations learn only through individuals who learn (Senge 1992), it is necessary to look closely at how individuals learn. In this respect, it is worth noting that individual learning is a necessary but not sufficient condition for organizational learning. Hence, there is a need for having 'shared rules'.

Argyris and Schön (1978) distinguish among three different types of learning: single-loop and double-loop as well as deutro-loop learning—also called triple-loop learning. This is shown in Figure 7.2.

Figure 7.2   Single-loop, Double-loop and Triple-loop Learning

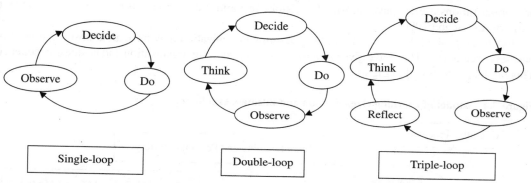

Source: Adapted from Argyris and Schön (1978).

The model of Figure 7.2 has the processes shown in Figure 7.3.
The three variables of Figure 7.3 are explained as follows:

1. *Governing variables:* Those dimensions that people are trying to keep within acceptable limits.
2. *Action strategies*: The moves and plans used by people to keep their governing values within.
3. *Consequences*: What happens as a result of an action. These can be both intended (intention and outcome are same) and unintended (intention and outcome different).

When something goes wrong and an error is detected, a convenient way is to look for another strategy that will give the desired outcome. This error detection and correction process constitutes

Figure 7.3   Single-loop and Double-loop Learning

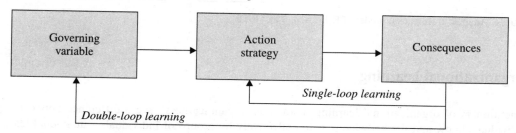

Source: Adapted from Argyris (2001).

single-loop learning. Single-loop learning is like a thermostat that learns when it is too hot or too cold and turns the heat on or off. Single-loop learning seems to be present when goals, values, frameworks and, to a significant extent, strategies are taken for granted. The emphasis is on 'techniques and making techniques more efficient'.

Double-loop learning occurs when an error is detected and corrected in ways that involve the modification of the organization's underlying norms, policies and objectives. Double-loop learning, thus, 'involves questioning the role of the framing and learning systems which underlie actual goals and strategies'. Chris Argyris' intervention research argues that double-loop learning is necessary if practitioners and organizations are to make informed decisions in rapidly changing and often uncertain contexts (Argyris and Schön 1996).

Eskildsen et al. (1999) suggest that the 'Learning Organization may have an almost 1:1 impact on business excellence'. They have given a causal model for learning organization and business excellence. This model is illustrated in Figure 7.4.

Figure 7.4   Model of Learning Organization and Business Excellence

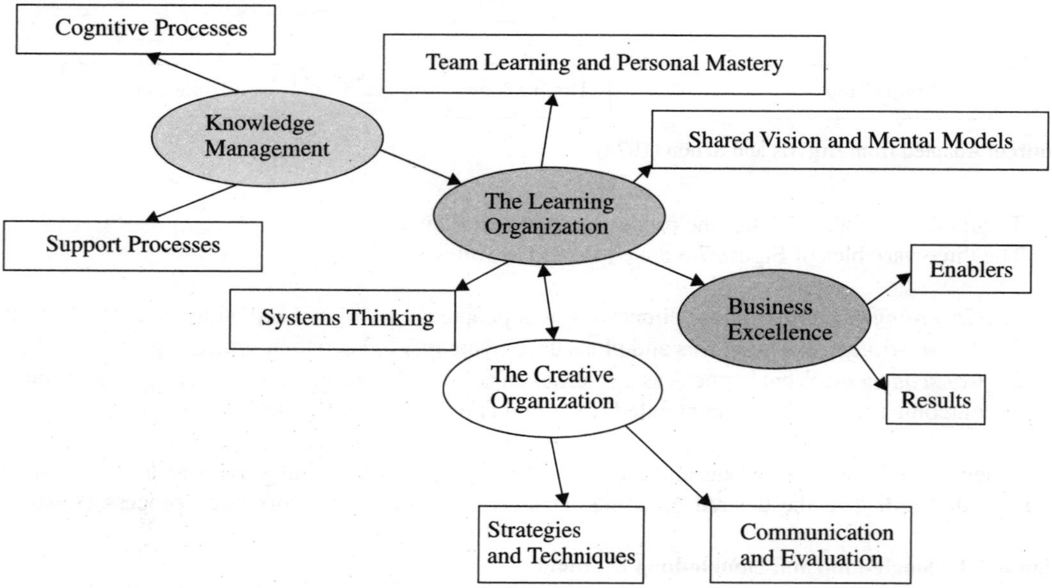

Source: Adapted from causal model of Eskildsen et al. (1999).

Organizational Learning

Practitioners of organizational learning, known as 'organolearners', see a difference between what individuals know and the knowledge held collectively by groups of individuals—individual learning leads to individual knowledge, organizational learning leads to collective knowledge. Conflict between them occurs at times and can be seen as a stimulant for innovation and creativity. Older ideas give way to newer, more effective ones as people in business, for instance, attempt to resolve their individual and group differences (McElroy 2000).

Kim's organizational learning model is composed of two separate, but related, learning cycles: individual learning and organizational learning. Individual learning is a four-phase iterative learning cycle, as mentioned earlier in this chapter: observe, assess, design and implement. Learning begins with observation, with seeing events and patterns. One makes an assessment or diagnosis about what one has observed and then designs a theory based on the observations and data collected. This theory influences the development of a response which leads to the implementation of certain actions. These actions and their results are observed, initiating a second iteration of the learning cycle. Feedback for improvements is shown as environmental response in Figure 7.5. This model combines individual learning and organizational learning and shows the importance of interplay between them if learning at either level is to occur, that is, individual learning is informed by organizational knowledge (mental models) and, conversely, organizational knowledge is produced collectively by individuals.

Figure 7.5   Organizational Learning Model of Daniel Kim

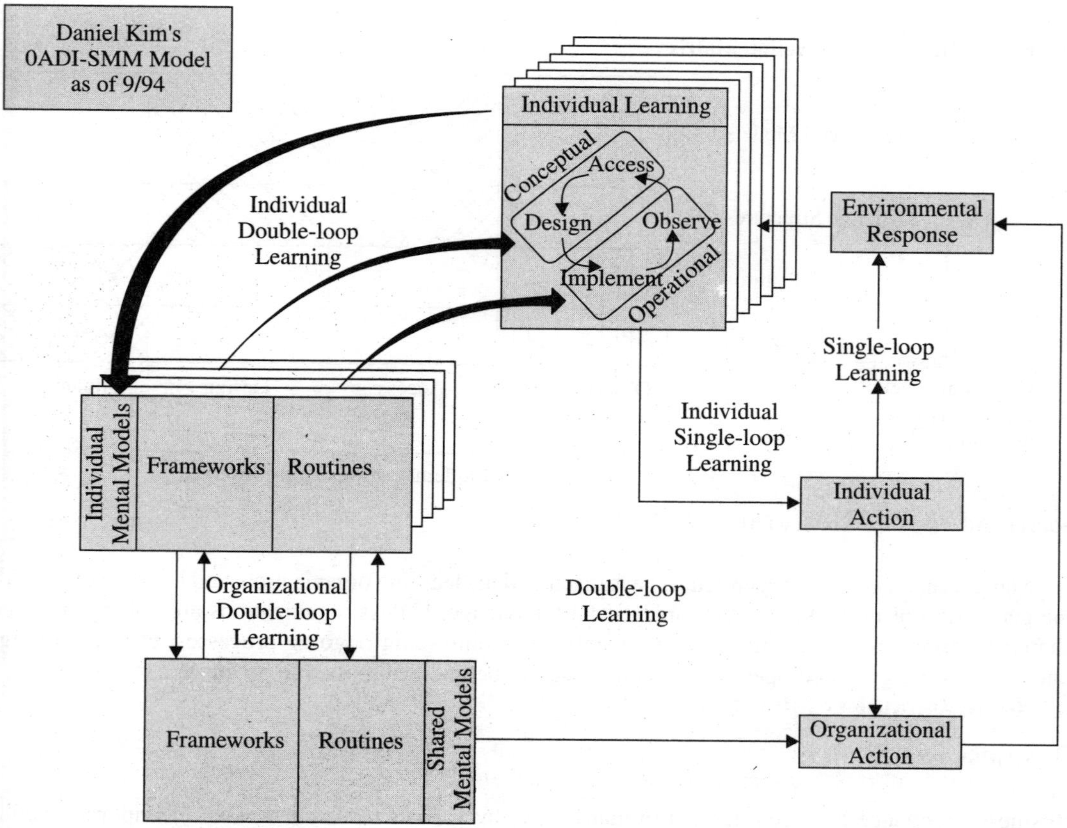

Source: Adapted from McElroy (2000).

There are several inferences that emerge from various perspectives on learning organizations:

1. In order to grow, organizations need to continuously learn.
2. Both individuals and organizations learn, using different methods, producing different outcomes.
3. Information storage, processing and sharing are important.
4. Context (structure and culture) contributes to organizational learning.

These inferences integrating knowledge and learning form a starting point for linking KM and organizational learning practices (Gorelick et al. 2004).

It has been established that a learning organization generates new knowledge which helps to sustain its competitive advantage. However, just creating knowledge does not mean that knowledge is being efficiently and effectively used or managed. A learning organization manages its knowledge and ensures that a proper environment exists in the organization to facilitate knowledge transfer and sharing. This helps in creation of knowledge, both at individual and organizational levels. Individual and teams use this improved value-added knowledge to make more-informed decisions. This cycle of events is an ongoing process where individuals and organizations continuously upgrade their skills and knowledge towards achieving business excellence (Figure 7.6).

Figure 7.6   The Learning Action Matrix

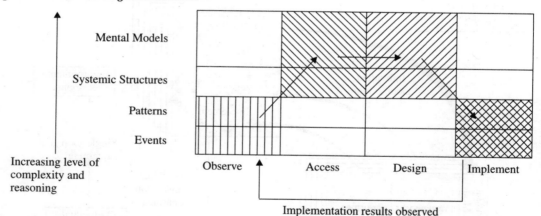

Source: Adapted from Shibley (2001).

Many researchers and academicians have discussed the learning organization, and its connection with the generation of individual and organizational knowledge. Unless organizations are able to embrace shared learning and knowledge creation as mutually reinforcing ongoing processes, use of learning/knowledge synergy for competitive advantage cannot be realized to its true potential.

Business Excellence

Business excellence has been defined in many ways by various researchers. One of important definitions given is 'The overall way of working that results in balanced stakeholder (customer, employees, society, shareholders) satisfaction so increasing the probability of long-term success as a business' (Raisbeck, FFQM).

Joseph Juran, Kaoru Ishikawa and Edward Deming were the pioneers of the TQM movement (Evans and Dean 1999). Their basic assumptions of TQM focused on customer, people, processes in organizations, role of top management, and continuous improvement for all processes and systems. According to them, the cost of poor quality is far greater than the cost of designing and developing new products and services. Organizations are systems of interrelated units and for TQM to succeed, all the components within the organizations must be collectively involved. Therefore, individuals and teams in the organization have to continuously learn and innovate to improve their quality of work.

According to the TQM founders, TQM interventions or activities must be guided by four change principles, namely, work processes, variability, analysis and continuous improvement. Product design and production processes must be improved; variance must be controlled to ensure high quality; data must be systematically collected and analysed in a problem-solving cycle; and commitment must be made to continuous learning by the employees about their work (Selladurai 2000).

Themes linking KM and learning organizations are a starting point to link them to enhanced organizational capacity towards making better business decisions and actions. This transformation is dependent on implementing the right knowledge and learning strategy.

Organizational Transformation and Proposed Benefits

Knowledge is seen in different ways in different organizations and the use of knowledge may also vary amongst them. Depending on the knowledge gap and the manner in which it exists, the focus of improvement and building a learning organization is different. An important aspect of attempting business excellence lies in understanding the guiding principles of a learning organization such as the creation of foundations for learning like adaptive culture (team work, information sharing), knowledge workers (training and reward system), commitment of management (leadership and behaviour modelling provided by key executives and managers), and involvement and participation of stakeholders (employee involvement processes, customer-focused processes).

The framework linking knowledge management, learning organization and business excellence can be explained better by a simple example. An individual, who joins a new organization, has certain assumptions, values, norms and rules, which influence his decision making. Because individual employees hold a wealth of experience and knowledge about their company, profession and practices, they are able to apply skills and knowledge in current organizational context. Knowledge creation and sharing is bound to happen between individuals and teams through socializing at work. Knowledge should be actionable; unless used in practice, the benefits cannot be realized. The quality of knowledge creation and sharing depends on specific situations within their culture. These situations could be the kind of leadership and top management support, teamwork, structures, communication techniques, and so on. Hence, organizational culture has an important role in the creation of individual and organizational capabilities.

Learning is an activity performed by individuals who facilitate organizational learning. Also, learning is a result of cognitive refinement and behavioural adjustment, and of the mutual reinforcement between the two. This requires an environment where experimenting with new approaches is encouraged and errors are not perceived as failures (Love et al. 2004).

To create a learning organization, it is critical that employees are motivated to learn, and they have the necessary system support to use and disseminate their newly acquired knowledge. In this process of capacity creation and development, learning takes place at individual and collective levels. The result is improved performance through creation of a learning culture. This culture facilitates synergizing the interplay between these two interdependents resulting in knowledge flow and learning from individual and team interactions. This helps in creating a foundation for achieving business excellence. This is illustrated in Figure 7.7. It presents a blueprint for achieving business excellence which recognizes KM and organizational learning to cultivate continuous improvement, learning and knowledge.

Figure 7.7   Reinforcing Model of Knowledge Management Practice towards a Learning Organization for Achieving Business Excellence

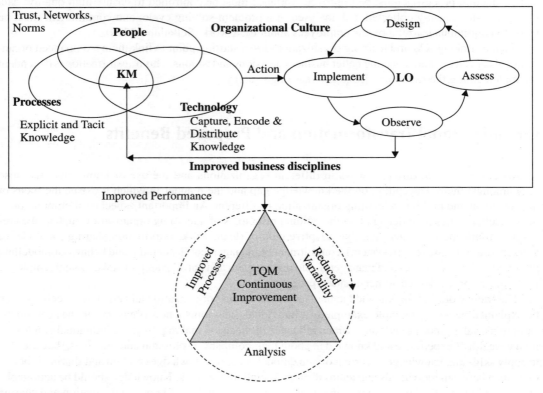

Source: Authors.

The proposed model may help in achieving business excellence and the following benefits, if KM and learning organization are taken up as an integrated and reinforcing concept. This approach may exploit newly acquired knowledge for continuous learning. As knowledge mandates an adaptive and responsive culture, this integrative approach may facilitate knowledge creation and transfer throughout the organization. This will enable organizations to develop a shared vision among its stakeholders and the ability to realize it. The end result is quality improvements across the organization, be it quality of knowledge, quality of relationships, quality of decision making or improved performance.

Conclusions

Knowledge and learning are fundamental factors that need to be addressed if business excellence is to be achieved. There are many approaches to the development of KM as a strategy to achieve business excellence. Organizations need to assess themselves and get answers to questions like where are we, where do we want to be and how do we get there! People, processes and technology can help in effective KM, which can lead to the development and implementation of a learning organization.

Establishing a learning organization through knowledge creation and sharing is not easy. Yet organizations have been doing it for achieving business excellence. This approach to transformation has given a new dimension to organizational learning to enable organizations and its employees to understand what they actually need, when they need it and what needs to be done to improve overall organizational performance.

The key to becoming a learning organization is to evaluate existing situation and identify areas where learning is needed. Also important is an emphasis on allocation of resources to ensure that proper learning can be delivered to those who need it, at the appropriate time and in the right format. This exercise mandates a long-term strategic focus with systems built in to monitor the new developments to respond accordingly. This requires effective leadership, an implementation strategy, strong internal and external partnerships, effective technology enablers and measures to track business impact.

Furthermore, neither the learning organization concept which is people-oriented and focuses on learning as a process, nor the KM concept which focuses on knowledge as a resource, can stand alone and contribute towards achieving business excellence. Knowledge management and learning organizations are complementary concepts which should be seen as one integrated programme, process, philosophy and approach to achieve business excellence through stakeholders' satisfaction for sustainable competitive advantage.

References

Argyris, C. 2001. 'Theories of Action, Double-Loop Learning and Organizational Learning'. Available online at http://www.infed.org/thinkers/argyris.htm, accessed on 26 October 2006.

Argyris, C. and D.A. Schön. 1978. *Organizational Learning: A Theory of Action Perspective*. Reading, MA: Addison-Wesley Publishing Company.

———. 1996. *Organizational Learning II: Theory, Method and Practice*. Reading, MA: Addison-Wesley Publishing Company.

Eskildsen, Jackob K., Jens Dahlgaard and Anders Norgaard. 1999. 'The Impact of Creativity and Learning on Business Excellence', *Total Quality Management*, 10(425): S523–30.

Evans, James R. and W.J. Dean, Jr. 1999. *Total Quality: Management, Organization and Strategy.* South-Western Educational Publishing.

Evans, James R. and W.M. Lindsay. 1999. *The Management and Control of Quality,* 4th Edn. St Paul, MN: West Publishing Company.

Gorelick, Carol, Nick Milton and Kurt April. 2004. *Performance through Learning—Knowledge Management in Practice.* Boston, MA: Butterworth-Heinemann.

Grossman, Martin. 2006. 'An Overview of Knowledge Management Assessment Approaches', *The Journal of American Academy of Business,* 8(2): 242–47.

Kululanga, K.G. and R. McCaffer. 2001. 'Measuring Knowledge Management for Construction Organizations', *Engineering Construction and Architectural Management,* 8(5/6): 346–54.

Loermans, Jozef. 2002. 'Synergizing the Learning Organization and Knowledge Management', *Journal of Knowledge Management,* 6(3): 285–94.

Love, Peter E.D., Jimmy C. Huang, David J. Edwards and Irani Zahir. 2004. 'Nurturing a Learning Organization in Construction: A Focus on Strategic Shift, Organizational Transformation, Customer Orientation and Quality Centered Learning', *Construction Innovation Information, Process, Management,* 4(2): 113–26.

McElroy, Mark W. 2000. 'Integrating Complexity Theory, Knowledge Management and Organizational Learning', *Journal of Knowledge Management,* 4(3): 195–303.

Selladurai, Raj. 2000. 'A Look at Total Quality Management's (TQM) Effectiveness', Proceedings of the Eleventh Annual Conference of the Production and Operations Management Society, POMS-2000, San Antonio, TX, 1–4 April.

Senge, Peter M. 1992. *The Fifth Discipline.* London: Century Business.

8 New Approaches to Management Research and Knowledge Building: Division, D-Vision and Direct Vision Approaches and Their Convergence*

SUBHASH SHARMA

Introduction

This chapter presents different approaches to viewing reality around us depending upon different quantum states of mind. These approaches are referred to as Division, D-Vision and Direct Vision approaches to problem solving, decision making and creating new knowledge. We will also explore the usefulness of these approaches in the field of management research as well as in improving the knowledge competence of the society and its institutions.

Before we define the Division, D-Vision and Direct Vision quantum states of mind, we present a framework of linkage between knowledge and wisdom. This framework, presented in Figure 8.1, suggests that knowledge and wisdom are linked through action–reflection process.

Figure 8.1 Knowledge–Wisdom Cycle

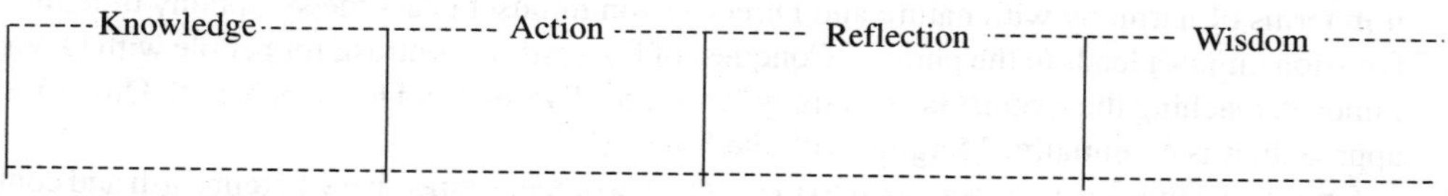

Source: Sharma 2006: 9.

---

*This chapter extends author's ideas available in his various publications. Ideas presented in this chapter were also presented at the COSMAR 2006, Department of Management Studies, Indian Institute of Science, Bangalore, 21 September 2006 and at the Research Seminar on Management Perspectives, Indian Business Academy (IBA), Greater Noida, 5 October 2006.

It may be indicated that this framework extends Paulo Freire's idea of action and reflection as a learning process. The gap between knowledge and wisdom is bridged through action and reflection. Managerial or social action is usually based on prior knowledge/theory/concept about a phenomenon and results of action are reflected upon to develop insights. This process leads us towards wisdom. Thus, wisdom results from existing knowledge and it has the potentiality of expanding the horizons of existing knowledge. Knowledge–action–reflection process leads to better insights and helps in developing and sharpening the intuitive faculty. It also helps in development of tacit knowledge.

We can also represent the above framework in the form of wisdom equation:

$$\textbf{Wisdom = Reason + Intuition (W = R + I)}$$

According to this definition, a knowledge society should further evolve as 'wisdom society' and ultimately reach the state of sacro-civic society wherein all routes to reality find due importance in human existence.

To understand the different routes to reality, we should focus on different quantum states of mind. Broadly there are three quantum states of mind, namely, Division, D-Vision and Direct Vision. Later we will identify a fourth state that represents the convergence state wherein mind operates at the convergence level as well as at the extended sensory perception (ESP) level. There are many examples of creative individuals with ESP. For example, Beethoven was deaf, yet he composed outstanding music; Milton was blind, even then he produced excellent poetry; Surdas was blind, yet he sang many memorable *bhajan*s, and Ramanujan is known as a man who knew infinity. Thus, there is a close linkage between creativity and ESP. It may be indicated that an individual's ESP competence could improve through experience as well as encounters with reality and events in one's life. It can improve through the action–reflection process. Even shocks and surprises could possibly alter neuron structures leading to ESP. Further, various meditation techniques may also help in improving ESP competence and ESP power. Tacit knowledge could also result from ESP as a result of professional experience of the practitioner.

In Division state, mind operates at the divided vision level. A problem is divided into sub-problems and solutions are sought through this process of division. In D-Vision state, the mind takes a rainbow view wherein all colours are seen simultaneously. In Direct Vision state, the mind operates at the direct-perception (*darshan*) level wherein it is at the intuitive and revelation level leading to tacit knowledge.

These three quantum states of mind lead to three different ways of knowing and solving problems. In the following discussion, we cite a number of examples from our day-to-day experiences to show the application of these three approaches. Illustrative examples are as follows:

1. Division mindset views human existence in terms of conflict with nature. D-Vision mindset views it in terms of harmony with nature and Direct-vision mindset hears the symphony of nature.
2. Division mindset leads to the phrase, 'Conquest of Everest'. In contrast, for people with D-Vision mindset, reaching the Everest is essentially 'Quest for Everest' and for people with Direct Vision approach, it is essentially 'Merging with the Everest'.
3. In feminism, Division approach leads to man versus woman perspective wherein clash and conflict are highlighted. D-Vision approach views the issues in terms of man–woman complementarity and Direct Vision approach leads to yin–yang (originated in ancient Chinese philosophy and metaphysics, which describes two primal opposing but complementary principles or cosmic forces) integration.

4. Division mindset leads us to 'clash of civilizations'. This worldview of Huntington is essentially rooted in his Division mindset. In contrast, D-Vision mindset suggests the 'dialogue of civilizations' and Direct-vision approach leads us to 'confluence of civilizations'. Thus, the worldview changes from clash to co-existence to confluence in consonance with three quantum states of mind.

5. In Division approach, human being is merely a 'factor of production'. In D-Vision approach he/she is a co-creator and co-venturist and in Direct Vision approach he/she is a 'being', who is also considered by some as 'divine being'.

6. In Division approach, labour and capital are in perpetual conflict. In D-Vision approach there is search for complementarity and in Direct Vision approach there is harmonization. Trusteeship model of organizations emerges from the second and third approaches and it aims at transforming 'lines of conflict' (loc) into 'lines of confidence' (loc) and 'lines of connectivity' (loc).

7. It may be indicated that in Division state, mind operates at the reason/analytical level, in D-Vision state, it operates at an intuitive level and in Direct Vision state, it operates at an integrative level.

8. Three quantum states also represent the scientist, artist and *rishi* mindsets.

9. In Division approach there is dichotomy and distance between subject and object. In D-Vision approach, this distance reduces. In Direct Vision, there is subject–object fusion, for example, 'dancer becomes the dance'. Thus, Division approach is essentially Newtonian in nature, D-Vision approach is closer to 'Quantum physics' and Direct Vision approach is 'Vedantic' in nature.

Many other examples from organizational, social, political and managerial contexts can be cited to illustrate the three quantum states of mind. For example, most of the public policy is rooted in Division approach. Further, most of the 'isms' are also rooted in Division worldview. For liberation of the mind from various isms, it is important to create a mind-shift from Division approach to D-Vision and Direct Vision approaches. Table 8.1 summarizes the three approaches to viewing realities around us based on the three quantum states of mind.

Table 8.1   Quantum States of Mind and Views of Reality: Some Illustrations

S. no.	Division	D-Vision	Direct-Vision
1.	Conflict with nature	Harmony with nature	Symphony of nature
2.	Conquest of Everest	Quest for Everest	Merging with the Everest
3.	Feminism: man versus woman	Man–woman complementarity	Yin–Yang integration
4.	Clash of civilizations	Dialogue of civilizations	Confluence of civilizations
5.	Human being as a 'factor of production'	Human being as a co-creator and co-venturist	Human being as a divine being
6.	Labour and capital are in perpetual conflict	Labour and capital are complementary	Labour and capital are in harmony
7.	Analytical mind	Intuitive mind	Integrative mind
8.	Scientist mindset	Artist mindset	*Rishi* mindset
9.	Subject–object dichotomy and distancing	Subject–object nearness	Subject–object fusion

Source: Sharma 2007: 250–51.

Quantum States of Mind: Reconciling Theories of Evolution

The foregoing discussion on the quantum states of mind leads us to reconciliation of the following three theories of evolution:

1. Darwin's theory
2. Aurobindo's theory
3. *Avatara* theory

Darwin's theory was essentially a 'body-centric' theory of evolution wherein man evolved as the 'body' responding to random mutations in the manner of stimulus–response/shock–response (S-R) behaviour, thereby fitting with respect to the environment. Darwin's quantum state of mind was essentially 'body-centric'/'matter-centric' and this is reflected in his world view.

Aurobindo's theory of evolution refers to evolution of mind. Human beings are endowed with intelligence and this represents the unique characteristic of human beings as distinct from animals. Hence, evolution should be seen as evolution of mind. Thus, this theory is mind-centric and can be referred to as S-I-R (stimulus–intelligence–response) approach to evolution. In formulating his theory of evolution, Aurobindo's quantum state of mind was 'mind-centric' and this is reflected in his evolutionary theory.

The *Avatara* theory essentially refers to the evolution of consciousness and is spirit/consciousness centric. S-V-R (stimulus–*vivek* [discriminating ability]–response) is implicit in this model. Thus, the idea of 'ethical' response is represented in this approach. Ancient *rishi*s were operating from 'consciousness-centric' quantum state of mind and this is reflected in their formulation of the *Avatara* world view.

While Darwin's theory leads us to 'survival of the fittest', Aurobindo's theory suggests 'survival of the most unique' and *Avatara* theory suggests 'arrival of the best to lead the rest'.

The reconciliation suggests that there is co-evolution of body, mind and spirit (BMS) and there is no conflict among the various theories, as these theories are looking at the evolution phenomenon from different levels, namely, from matter, mind and consciousness (MMC) levels. This approach to viewing reality from different levels has interesting implications for human and social development. While Darwin's theory provides only a limited hope for the human beings, the reconciliation of various evolution theories provides us a new vision of human being in terms of his/her potentiality of evolving as a 'cosmic being' through evolution of mind and consciousness.

Three Researchers Walking on a `Thought Road´: Convergence of Division, D-Vision and Direct Vision Approaches

The discussion on the three quantum states of mind leads us to the metaphor of three researchers walking on a 'thought road'. For the researcher walking on the left side of the road, Division approach is the best way to do research by keeping a distance between the observer and the observed; that is the best way to capture the reality out there. For the researcher walking on the right side of the road, reality out there can be captured through the D-Vision or the 'rainbow' approach. The third researcher believes in the Direct Vision approach and suggests that the way to create paradigm shifts is through Direct-perception ('*darshan*') approach. There are many ways of '*darshan*'; there are many routes to *nirvana*.

The Division approach was at the core of the 'Western Enlightenment', D-Vision at the core of 'Eastern Awakening' and Direct Vision approach at the core of 'Many Routes to *Nirvana*' representing three historical processes and three major thought currents that have influenced the world in many ways.

Management researchers have largely been influenced by the 'Western Enlightenment' tradition. There is a need to expand the horizons of management and social science research and knowledge creation by following other paths, namely, the 'Eastern Awakening' and 'Many Routes to *Nirvana*'.

It may be indicated that in addition to the aforementioned three quantum states of mind, we also have the fourth quantum state that represents the convergence state and could be referred to as the DEAN (Direct Enlightenment Awakening and *Nirvana*) state of mind. In this state, 'Western Enlightenment', 'Eastern Awakening' and 'Many Routes to *Nirvana*' find a new convergence. Figure 8.2 presents the metaphor of three researchers finding a convergence in the 'DEAN' approach.

Figure 8.2   Three Researchers Metaphor—Convergence among Western Enlightenment, Eastern Awakening and Many Routes to *Nirvana*

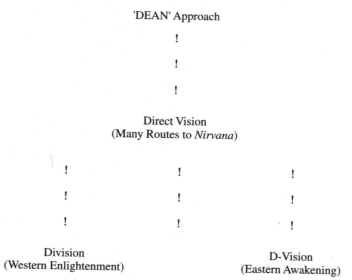

Source: Author.

A knowledge society should recognize all the three thought currents of knowledge creation. During recent years, 'Eastern Awakening' and the idea of 'Many Routes to *Nirvana*' have been getting some attention leading to new age knowledge movements. For example, 'Many Routes to *Nirvana*' has brought in the question of values to the forefront of social discourse.

Towards Four Quadrants of Knowledge Creation:
A Typology of Thinkers and Knowledge Creators

The discussion so far leads us to another typology of thinkers and knowledge creators. Knowledge creation could be based on 'mono' versus 'poly' perspectives of reality. For example, for a theist, there are two views to theism, namely, monotheistic and polytheistic approaches. This idea is also applicable to other domains of knowledge, for example, holistic perspective versus segmented perspective. Further, as discussed earlier, mind could operate from Division (a close equivalent could be '*Dwaitic*' world view) or Direct Vision (a close equivalent could be '*Adwaitic*' world view). When these ideas are presented in a graphical format, we arrive at four quadrants view of knowledge and knowledge creation. This is presented in Figure 8.3.

Figure 8.3 Quadrant View of Knowledge and Knowledge Creation

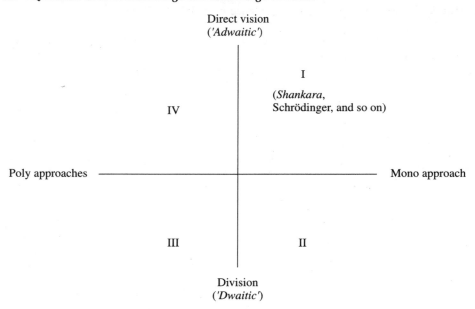

Source: Sharma 2006: 141.

Quadrant-I Thinkers

Illustrations of quadrant-I include *Shankara* and Schrödinger. Thinkers in this quadrant provide us deep insights on micro–macro links. In the field of religion, they are monotheistic-*adwaitic* in their approach. Quadrant-I social thinkers take a holistic view of social issues and problems. Gandhi also belongs to this quadrant.

Quadrant-II Thinkers

Quadrant-II thinkers are 'unity in diversity' type. Although they may look at the reality from diversity perspective, they are able to see its ultimate linkage with an overarching framework. Subject matter specialists with a sense of holistic links belong to this category of thinkers.

Quadrant-III Thinkers

They represent 'philosophical parochialism' and are essentially ethno-centric and segmented-view oriented. 'Narrow empiricism' belongs to this quadrant.

Quadrant-IV Thinkers

They represent divided vision though the claim is universalistic. For example, Marxist thinkers belong to this quadrant.

The above framework helps us in understanding the viewpoints of different thinkers in science, social contexts, religion, philosophy and spirituality.

Towards a Complementary Perspective to Knowledge Creation

It may be indicated that different ways of viewing reality can play a complementary role, thereby avoiding a conflict among science (Division approach), art (D-Vision approach), philosophy (Direct Vision/*Darshan* approach) and spirituality (DEAN vision/Divine-Vision approach). These different approaches to viewing reality could be represented in many different ways. For example, science, art, philosophy and spirituality could be considered as four steps to knowledge creation. In this four-step model, science is the first step of knowledge creation and development. Further, if we represent science and art on the horizontal axis in consonance with left and right side of the brain, and philosophy and spirituality on the vertical axis in consonance with the back and frontal side of the brain, we arrive at a framework of four-dimensional as well as four-directional view of knowledge wherein an event or a phenomenon is viewed from four perspectives/directions in the manner of the '*syadvad*' or multiple perspectives approach. This four-directional view could also be referred to as 'knowledge *swastika*' wherein there is complementarity of four approaches to knowledge creation, namely, science, art, philosophy and spirituality. It could also be represented by 'doctor's symbol' of plus or cross wherein horizontal side of 'doctor's cross' represents science, and art and vertical side represents philosophy and spirituality. No doubt, an ideal doctor uses all the four approaches, that is, Division, D-Vision, Direct Vision and 'DEAN' Vision, in appropriate combinations and according to the requirement. In fact, all fields of knowledge draw upon the four approaches. It may be further indicated that in this metaphor of four-directional view, science, art, philosophy and spirituality can be represented by West, East, South and North directions of viewing the same reality. In Indian map it also has a metaphorical meaning. Himalayas are in the north, representing spirituality, *Shankara*'s birth place is in the south representing philosophy, Shantiniketan is in the east representing art and Bhabha Atomic Research Centre (BARC) is in the west representing science. It may be reiterated once again that these four roads to reality play a complementary role. They also represent a new convergence of three historical thought currents, namely, 'Western Enlightenment', 'Eastern Awakening' and 'Many Routes to *Nirvana*'.

In a knowledge society all the routes to reality, namely, science, art, philosophy and spirituality, are equally respected. Viewed from this perspective, India is already a knowledge society awaiting an official recognition!

Bibliography

Bebek, Borana. 1982. *The Third City: Philosophy at War with Positivism*. London: Routledge and Kegan Paul.

Capra, Fritjof. 1976. *The Tao of Physics*. Toronto: Bantam Books.

Goswami, Amit and Maggie Goswami. 1997. *Science and Spirituality: A Quantum Integration*. New Delhi: Munshiram Manoharlal Publisher.

Gupta, Chandra Bhan. 2000. *Adwaita Rahasya: Secrets of Creation Revealed*. New Delhi: Macmillan India.

Jitatmananda, Swami. 1991. *Holistic Science and Vedanta*. Bombay: Bhartiya Vidya Bhavan.

Karikal, Shivram. 1994. *Vedic Thought and Western Psychology*. Mangalore: Arthi Publications.

Mehar, Baba. 1963. *The Everything and the Nothing*. Bombay: Mehar House Publications.

Menon, Sangeetha, B.V. Sreekantan, Anindya Sinha, Philip Clayton and R. Narasimhan (eds). 2004. *Science and Beyond: Cosmology, Consciousness and Technology in the Indic Traditions*. Bangalore: National Institute of Advanced Studies.

Rao, Ramakrishna. 2005. 'Psychology in the Indian Tradition: A Classical Model with Contemporary Relevance', *Psychological Studies*, 50(1): 1–8.

Sharma, Subhash. 1996 and 2006. *Management in New Age: Western Windows Eastern Doors*. New Delhi: New Age International Publishers.

———. 1999. *Quantum Rope: Science, Mysticism & Management*. New Delhi: New Age International Publishers.

———. 2001a. *Arrows of Time: From the Black Holes to the Nirvana Point*. New Delhi: New Age International Publishers.

———. 2001b. 'Routes to Reality: Scientific and Rishi Approaches', *Journal of Human Values*, 7(1): 75–83.

———. 2005. 'Space Time Consciousness: Towards a Speculative Convergence of Science & Spirituality Through Unfolding of Universal Spiritual Consciousness (USC)', in Sharath Ananthamurthy, Meera Chakravorty and M.C. Radhakrishna (eds), *Landscape of Matter: Conference Proceedings on the Concept of Matter*, pp. 207–16. Bangalore: Prasaranga, Bangalore University.

———. 2005. 'Quantum States of Mind: Ordinary Perception to Extra-ordinary Perception', *Psychological Studies*, 50(1): 9–15.

———. 2006a. 'Vedanta as Ved-Ananta: A New Unfolding of Universal Spiritual Consciousness (USC)', *Chinmaya Management Review*, 5(1): 26–32.

———. 2006b. 'DEAN Approach to Leadership and Management', *Southern Economist*, 15 June, p. 12.

———. 2007. *New Mantras in Corporate Corridors: From Ancient Roots to Global Routes*. New Delhi: New Age International Publishers.

Talbot, Michael 1981. *Mysticism and the New Physics*. New York: Bantam Books.

Wilber, Ken. 2000. *Integral Psychology: Consciousness, Spirit, Psychology, Therapy*. London: Shambala.

9 A Note on Change Management Processes

M.D.G. KORETH

1. The focus clearly is on the imperatives of change with regard to competitiveness in the knowledge economy.
2. Therefore, we need reliable, proven models and processes of real-time strategic change.
3. Over the last 60 years, global research in change-processes have focused on 'small group dynamics' (SGD), and since 1985 on 'large group dynamics' (LGD), to facilitate multi-stakeholder collaboration and change in

   (*i*)   organizations (of various kinds, both private and public);
   (*ii*) communities (urban and rural);
   (*iii*) professional groups; and
   (*iv*) cities and states.

4. Research, experimental work, and practice in SGD and LGD have produced two successful change-processes:

   (*i*) the Future Search Process (FSP) and
   (*ii*) the Large-Group Interactive Process (LGIP).

5. Although these two methodologies have some variances, they are both based on the following essential principles:

   (*i*)   All the multiple stakeholders need to be identified, represented and involved full time in the process.
   (*ii*) The process is experiential, combining rational/cognitive and emotive relationship factors in tandem. The change-process cannot be only rational or informational.
   (*iii*) The process is participative, consultative and works through SGD (within the LGD process).
   (*iv*) Multiple stakeholders will usually have some common interests, some differing interests and some opposing or conflicting interests. These two (FSP and LGIP) processes help the

participants to 'discover common ground', develop common solutions and generate/sustain their own energy to implement change or new projects successfully.

(v) The FSP (as the term implies) focuses on 'the Future of X', in a 5-year time span typically (the time horizon could range from 3 to 10 years, depending on the nature of the project). The FSP creates and sustains strong 'ownership' in all the stakeholders—the 'future project' becomes their own project, rather than someone else's project, and they take on personal responsibility and accountability for detailed planning, resource generation and execution. In fact, Russell Ackoff (one of the gurus of operations research) now is convinced that to implement projects flawlessly, we should 'first future; then plan', as he puts it. The FSP works with 80–100 stakeholders in a large open hall (since everyone needs to have eye contact with everyone else). The process needs to be designed and facilitated by two or three trained and experienced LGD/FSP practitioners. But there are no lectures or 'inputs/ advice from experts'. The 80–100 stakeholder-participants who are relevant to the project of the future will themselves be bringing an average of 20 years experience, expertise and knowledge each to the table—hence a total of 1,500–2,000 years of knowledge, data, experience, expertise will be available during the three days of the FSP, to be pooled and drawn from. But the FSP is not a conference or a seminar where papers are read or presentations made—everyone is a resource, and everyone is a participant in an experiential, action-learning process. Even the two nights of sleep in between the three days of the FSP are extremely vital to the process—research has established that during sleep, each day's experiences continue to be subconsciously processed, assimilated and transformed, in each participant's mind, thus leading to a 'paradigm shift' in the mindset on the third day only. If the FSP feels it needs more expertise than it possesses, it will find ways and means of locating, accessing and tapping into such expertise or domain competencies, which lie outside the group.

(vi) While the FSP focuses on creating a preferred future, the LGIP (250–500 stakeholder-participants) focuses on resolving current issues or finding and implementing agreed solutions to current problems. This process also helps distil common ground, common interests, common goals and common solutions, with a strong sense of 'ownership' and commitment to implementation. Again, there are no lectures, papers presented or training inputs—the combined pool of 5,000–10,000 years of knowledge, experience and competence are tapped through the processes of 'LGD' and 'SGD'.

(vii) Prior to both the change-models being implemented, specific preparatory steps are needed—the key ones are

- consulting the Apex Group or Top Team, discussing the nature of the project, helpful factors, hindering factors and getting their commitment;
- interviewing a cross-section of all stakeholder groups to understand their perceptions of, and their willingness to, get involved in the proposed project;
- a Design Team Workshop with a cross-section of 30–35 representatives of all stakeholders; and
- a Support Team Workshop who needs to understand the nature of the project, in order to process the outputs emerging out of each session of the workshop, and create a continuous feedback cycle.

In terms of the imperatives of change with reference to the knowledge economy, these two proven, research-based, practice-based 'change management' processes are relevant. They are also vital to developing strategies of change management for transformation from the industrial age to the information age.

Part 3

Human Resource Development for the Knowledge Economy

10 Identifying New Knowledge Streams in the Evolving Knowledge Economy

PREMA RAJAGOPALAN AND M.S. MATHEWS

Introduction

According to the new growth theory, the advancement of knowledge is a key determinant of long-term economic growth. Spillovers of knowledge (external effect on human capital) across firms can help prevent the phenomenon of diminishing returns to the accumulation of capital formation. In addition, one commodity that increases by giving/sharing is knowledge. Besides, knowledge is critical not only to economic growth, but also to any society's long-term development.

In this context, Indian Institute of Technology-Madras (IIT-M) has been working on identifying such streams of knowledge that need concentrated attention in the decades to come. Eight branches/specializations were identified and faculty from IIT-M was invited along with their colleagues and students to make brief presentations on the emerging frontier areas of research and those areas that would be of direct relevance to the Indian context. This chapter is based on the two workshops held at IIT-M. The eight areas/branches so identified include

1. Power and Communication
2. Computer Science
3. Biotechnology
4. Infrastructure
5. Nanotechnology
6. Energy
7. Manufacturing
8. Mechatronics

Power and Communication

Major thrust areas were presented by the participants at the brainstorming exercise. In the field of electrical engineering, the most important stream to be addressed was 'power'. Trained manpower in the area of 'power quality' was essential. Course curricula and research problems needed to be charted out based on interaction with industry (power supplying and consuming agents), electricity boards and other stakeholders.

In addition, suggestions were made to emulate models that have proved successful in the 'communication' stream development. Close interaction with industry was emphasized. Training students for a Master's degree sponsored by the industry (majority of them from small companies) can result in immediate returns. Students learn to solve actual problems under academic guidance complemented by mentoring and nurturing by their sponsors. A need was felt to alter pedagogy—to integrate laboratory with theory—and even alter the method of teaching for better skill training and sustainable learning.

Computer Science

In the area of computer science and engineering, four major areas were identified for training manpower in large numbers. These were:

1. Cryptography and security network
2. VLSI or very large scale integrated networks
3. Bioinformatics
4. Data mining

With various kinds of terrorist activities expanding in the country and worldwide, development of Crypto Tool Industries is a field that needs immediate attention. Computational biotechnology is an interdisciplinary area to be developed by biotechnology departments and computer science specialists.

Biotechnology

Two major areas were identified in the field of biotechnology. One of them related to the traditional biotech applications in industry/agriculture and healthcare. While there seemed to be impressive course syllabi in many colleges offering the programme, the interface between teaching and industry needs to be strengthened. The availability of trained scientists to handle the courses is lacking in most situations. The revolution in the other area, namely bioinformatics, has led to the reconstruction of genetic circuits. Knowledge obtained in this area should be put across to the public (which can help prioritize areas) and other stakeholders to facilitate crystallization of courses and relevant research areas for funding.

Infrastructure

With respect to infrastructure, major areas that need critical attention are transport, power, housing, telecommunication, water supply and sanitation. An overlap of priority areas emerges across branches. It was pointed out that the lack of comprehensive planning and management of infrastructure facilities will hinder India's economic growth. Courses and skill development should focus on design process, material availability, climate compatibility, life cycle costs, and so on in any investment in infrastructure development. In the current scenario, it was recorded that most educational institutions give little importance to these concepts and their relevance in the Indian context.

Nanotechnology

Nanotechnology could be addressed from several dimensions. Those of immediate relevance in contributing to the country's economy relate to tapping solar energy to replace fossil fuels. New challenges to identify new nanotechnology structures are emerging for designing new polymers for providing 100 per cent efficiency in storage and distribution. Detailed description of the carbon nanotubes (CNT) and their importance in interventions in healthcare, environmental pollution and energy were discussed. Courses on the technology, design and building of CNT and its applications would greatly facilitate the country not only in solving some of the energy, healthcare and other country-specific problems, but also contribute to frontier area of research in the international map of science. The stream being frontier and recent, it was suggested that a network of institutions working on this area would help in making rapid strides in the country as a whole.

Energy

The role of energy technology and its contribution to the country's sustainable economy is another major stream to be addressed. It was stressed that food and energy, instead of being separated, must on the contrary be coupled. Major manifestations of energy—such as energy generation, energy conversion, energy conservation, energy storage and energy distribution—must be dealt with in some detail in the courses to be designed. While touching upon mainstreaming renewable energy, the grid system and power distribution were referred to. A strong plea was made for decentralized power generation from fossil fuels and consumption to be made locally, and this may radically alter the Indian energy scenario. No coherent or concise courses as of now are available in this area. A warning bell was sounded that if the country does not attend to this area seriously, it would run out of power in the next 20 years. A shift from conventional engineering courses (branches) to evolving new inter-disciplinary streams in the context of the nation's needs was recommended. Illustration on the disadvantages of promoting Jatropha (a bio-diesel, produced from the seeds of *Jatropha Curcas*, a plant that can grow in wastelands) was explained.

Manufacturing

Manufacturing, it was pointed out, is being treated as a low-priority area where the number of available experts is also declining. Paradoxically, the dependence on developed countries for machinery is only increasing. This is not a good situation if India has to effectively compete in the new knowledge economy, for dependence has a high cost. The machine tool industry needs to be revived and the manufacturing process should be made a people-friendly activity. This, however, can be facilitated only by national policies, industrial acts and the will of the government. The process of reverse engineering may be encouraged to produce new innovations—thereby suggesting even new pedagogies. The quality of training should include both know-how and know-why of manufacturing. One should think of innovative courses to create a knowledge base and skilled personnel in manufacturing.

Mechatronics

The new emerging field of mechatronics is a fusion of mechanical, electrical, electronics and computing. Examples of research in this field are in automation of any human activity, robotics. A major need for training in mechatronics, apart from the applied products, is to facilitate effective communication among various engineering branches and remove the uncertainties associated with electronics or computing. While mechatronics is being taught in some institutions, the courses are offered as specialized modules without any focus on demands from industry. This gap should be bridged in the new attempt. Inputs from the industry even in syllabus preparation should be encouraged. Reverse engineering again was suggested as a possible strategy to engineer interest in new design and innovation.

Conclusions and Issues for Discussion

How does one facilitate a sustainable knowledge economy? The first step is to recognize the existence of multiple knowledge economies in the global context. The scope and dimensions of each economy can range from a small community of a country (like localized energy generation/consumption practices) to a regional integration of even many countries (like communication/roads). Each individual knowledge economy then is best developed based upon its distinct characteristics (for example, Jatropha cultivation or material availability and climatic variations in building infrastructure). Knowledge systems then should facilitate a set of related economic institutions—financial institutions or production units—and continue to reciprocally interact in the larger context of goals of the country.

The following are some of the issues that can be discussed further:

1. What other subject areas are important for improving India's competitiveness in the knowledge economy?
2. What mechanisms can be evolved to quickly develop detailed syllabi and curricula in these frontier areas?
3. What mechanisms can be evolved to train critical 'teaching manpower' in these frontier areas?
4. How can these frontier subjects be taught in higher education institutes in the country?

Part 4

Scope and Significance of Knowledge,
Technology, R&D and Innovation
Management for the Emerging
Knowledge Economy

11 Key Stakeholders for the Knowledge Economy

Prema Rajagopalan and M.S. Mathews

Introduction

The systematic organization of knowledge production and control provides a co-ordination mechanism to the social system in addition to the traditional mechanisms of economic exchange and political decision making. In other words, university–industry–government relations develop in terms of institutional arrangements for three major functions of the socio-economic system. These are

1. wealth generation and retention;
2. novelty production; and
3. control at the interfaces of these dynamics.

There exist two layers of networks—one where they constrain each other's behaviour and the other where they shape each other's expectations.

In this context, one of the major thrusts in the development of the knowledge economy is to explore the existing linkages among the triple helix (university, industry and government) and generate deeper understanding of their role in the knowledge economy. Indian Institute of Technology-Madras (IIT-M) attempted, as a first step, to approach and obtain response from some of the industries and research and develop-ment (R&D) laboratories within the city of Chennai to gain insights on the strong and weak links with the academia and the government.

Survey Findings

Organizations Covered

Eight sectors identified as significant thrust areas for development were covered. A list of firms/labs and areas are as follows:

1. Computer Science—Infosys
2. Communication—Midas
3. Biotechnology—Orchid Pharma
4. Infrastructure—Pricewaterhouse Coopers
5. Nanotechnology—High Energy Battery
6. Energy—Center for Fuel Cell Technology
7. Manufacturing—Caterpillar
8. Mechatronics—Ashok Leyland

Areas of Research and Products

The first question addressed to each of these stakeholders was on their specialty products and current areas of R&D. From the list of companies it would be clear that their products were diverse; they ranged from high-efficiency automobiles and high-energy batteries based on nanotechnology to communication software and antibiotics, and research in hydrogen technology to building high-quality roads. All these products, amongst others, have been identified as critical to India's development goals. The companies and their personnel took great pride in their research endeavours. For instance, the scientist from the fuel cell technology lab (supported by the Department of Science & Technology) felt that the importance of hydrogen technology cannot be neglected, as the country will soon face an energy crisis. In the case of manufacturing, one of the respondents said, 'We take great care in the safety and health of the work environment and the outside. We have replaced all our asbestos material—whether as roof or in the equipments used.' They consider this accountability and responsibility essential in any industry. While the communication group has many success stories of outreach in the rural areas, the nanotech batteries using carbon nanotubes is yet to gain similar visibility. In sum, across industries and R&D laboratories, the products were of significant relevance to the country and so were their research activities.

Linkages with Academia

This question elicited a variety of responses. The curiosity was to understand the linkages at various levels. Infosys was proud of its 'Campus Connect' programmes. In this programme regular visits are made by Infosys team to many engineering colleges all over the country, where students are addressed and apprised of opportunities of working with Infosys. The second level of linkage has been with the faculty of elite institutions taking up collaborative research including funding for such endeavours. A third type of linkage has been in the form of regularly sponsoring the industry staff for higher degrees in the Indian Institutes of Techology (IITs), Anna University, and so on where company memorandums of understanding (MoUs) are signed as well. A fourth type of linkage exists only in recruitment and irregular/sporadic contacts with the academia. However, in unison, all concurred on the need for strengthening the linkages with the academia.

Existing Problems and Possible Strategies

Referring to the triple helix model and the nature of possible relations, it may be relevant to state here that linkages can be both vertical and horizontal. Vertical communications refer to the constraints through institutional arrangements, whereas horizontal ones relate to factors outside of institutional arrangements. Responses from stakeholders, while outlining existing problems, clearly bring out the dynamics of relations among the three main agents. Their experiences are summed up as follows.

Areas like manufacturing are no more attractive as students do not prefer core engineering jobs anymore. They find it undesirable to travel long distances and be in the thick of manufacturing (on-site) jobs. In other areas, due to the very specialized nature of their research areas, for example, mechatronics or hydrogen technology, which are multidisciplinary, the scope of any effective interaction with academia is restricted. In this category, we may also include biotechnology firms that are worried about patenting issues and excessive competition.

This did not prevent our respondents from coming up with viable options for altering the scenario. Several initiatives were suggested as follows. The industry can

1. take part in regular teaching of some units of existing courses in academic institutions;
2. participate in giving inputs for designing new courses that would be important;
3. offer internships for engineering undergraduates, but lay a minimum period of six months for the programme to be effective;
4. facilitate collaboration with interested faculty so that research can help solve on-floor problems; and
5. sponsor their staff for theoretical training and higher education to academic institutions.

Skill Expectations from Potential Recruits

Apart from the information technology (IT) industry, which looks only for basic analytical skills and takes it upon itself to impart necessary job-related skills through training for anything between one and three months, all others unanimously felt that, in terms of skills, there is a large gap between what the students learn and what is actually required. Some industries spend almost a year training their new recruits to upgrade them to meet the skill requirements. Such a long training period is a loss of time if the industry has to advance rapidly in research and product commissioning (for example, exposure to real-time operating system in automobile manufacturing). So much so that non-engineering people are heading divisions, but they are unable to think out of the box and more creatively (for instance, a lawyer heading the Asia-Pacific operations of a manufacturing industry). A large resource of technical manpower exists in India and strategies need to be devised to train them and retain them in the context of the country's future requirements. A passing comment on graduates from elite institutions is that they are theoretically good but do not have sufficient knowledge to handle problems in the field.

Contribution to the Country and Support from the Government

On the first part related to contribution, while the contribution of communication and IT can be measured, amongst others, in terms of the number of jobs they have created, importance of research in frontier areas is recognized by the government and funded well. The fruits of such research will turn into benefits in the future. One section of the respondents is very optimistic on this issue. On the other hand, respondents from areas like manufacturing and infrastructure feel that while their contribution to the country's development cannot be doubted, support in terms of policies (to enable revival and retention of the foundations of an industrial economy) and programmes is inadequate and non-facilitating. Infrastructure has an indirect impact but the same is not given due priority. An earnest plea was made to highlight this dimension. In the words of a respondent, 'It is the survival of the fastest and not the fittest!' Sometimes priority to small and medium enterprises eliminates the eligibility of large-scale industries for support. This imbalance needs to be rectified.

Conclusions

This chapter, based on a survey conducted by IIT-M, has attempted to present the views of the stakeholders from the industry and R&D with respect to their linkages with academia and government, and their role in the future knowledge economy. Building on the information, one can attempt to formulate strategies to model a network of knowledge institutions. In sum, it can be said that a triple helix model can help us identify mismatches between institutional arrangements and their functions. Insights drawn—as enunciated in some responses—can provide a rich arena for problem solving. Conflicts of interest can first be deconstructed and then reconstructed both analytically and practically by enabling new institutional arrangements. The dynamics of this relationship must be made viable both at the micro and macro levels of the economy.

Specific points emerging from the chapter could be summarized as follows:

1. A number of industries and R&D organizations in the private sector are doing commendable work in frontier areas important for the knowledge economy. However, they highlighted genuine problems in terms of regulations, restrictions on research funding, and so on. They need to be discussed and conveyed to the policy makers.
2. There is a need to identify the shortcomings in the present curriculum and devise mechanisms to overcome the same.
3. An effective platform for face-to-face interaction among the academia, industry and state (triple helix) needs to be created.

12 Knowledge, Science and Technology*

ABID HUSSAIN

Introduction

Of all the contemporary issues, the most important is the role of technology in development and in the growth of the societies. This is such an important subject that it is being considered and discussed widely. It may not be easy to find solutions to most of the issues of the present era but it would be useful to think as to what is it that makes the process of finding solutions faster and enables the society to take advantage of old and new knowledge, inventions and discoveries, innovations, research and development (R&D), science and technology (S&T), and so on. Knowledge men, knowledge products, knowledge markets, think of anything, knowledge is the all-pervasive *mantra* which will expand and become the most valuable resource.

In this era of knowledge, lifestyles have changed. Jobs might be the same but the way in which tasks are executed has changed. Facilities for work have changed and the environment in which economic activities are undertaken has changed. The contribution being made by science and technology (S&T) to society is unprecedented. Those days are gone when it took about seven months for the Queen of Spain to know that Columbus had discovered America. It took more than seven weeks for the best of minds, the best of people in Paris and London, to know that Lincoln had been assassinated. But in today's world, anything that happens anywhere in the world at any point of time is known instantly and is often seen in real time. A few decades ago, it could hardly be visualized that a time would come when a camera will be placed in the outer space and it would take pictures of the earth. There are stations that have been built in the outer space and men and women have been sent into the space and to the moon. People on earth have seen Neil Armstrong walking on the surface of the moon; it was seen as if it was taking place in the backyard of human habitation.

---

*This chapter is based on an oral presentation made by the author.

Science and Technology

Science and Technology as a Change Agent

Considering the activity of production, the way in which agricultural production has increased is unbelievable. It is true that the green revolution here, which owes a lot to S&T, has not been able to cover the entire agricultural scene of this country. But, to get about two-thirds of the population out of poverty is no mean achievement. Admittedly, there are millions of people in India who do not get enough to eat, sleep on the pavements or do not have safe drinking water. But notwithstanding these shortcomings, the tremendous amount of change which has come about in the last one or two generations is remarkably huge.

It is interesting to analyse how S&T became a motivating force, a driving force to reshape the lives of generations. There has always been an urge to find out what nature is and the rules and principles which guide the nature and become the lessons of science. There have been numerous inventions and discoveries, but most of these were the conquest of curiosity, the conquest of the mind, and those were the subject matter of consideration at the intellectual and philosophic levels. At the ground level, S&T or rather knowledge was being converted into products and services.

Science and Technology as a Factor of Production

Classical and neo-classical economics have always considered four important factors of production—man, land, capital and technology. In their combination, technology was there but of an elementary nature. Emphasis was laid on human muscle, believing that muscles can provide the necessary power. While use was made of mineral and other natural resources, which lay hidden under the earth or were there above the earth, their value was not realized adequately for a long time with the result that much more was wasted than was used for quite a long period. It was thought that capital, that is, liquid money, was the most important factor of production. Also, it was believed that production could go up if, in addition to availability of capital, there were more men to do the work or when there were natural resources available to make things. Capital comes out of savings; savings come out of crushing to some extent, as was done in India, the consumer urges and needs. Technology was always there. At all points of time, S&T was being harnessed. But S&T was given fourth ranking amongst the factors of production. Later it was discovered that of the four factors of production, the paramount factor was S&T.

In today's world, a nation may have plenty of wealth—minerals, jewels, gold, platinum or anything—it may not be a great power; it may have long stretches of land under its occupation, yet it may not be a great nation; it may have access to oil but then again it does not count for much. But those nations that have access to knowledge have been able to bring about many great changes utilizing the remaining factors of production. That is the key to success today. Some countries may be having oil somewhere under their part of the earth and they may be making money out of it, but to become a great nation, they have to add value to that oil; they have to convert that oil into chemicals; they have to convert that oil into materials. This transformation is achieved by those who have access to S&T. With such imperatives, S&T has become the primary and the most significant factor of production. It is this recognition which entails a great change and great difference to the entire world and its development.

Changing International Environment

For facilitating development, nations have to cultivate, disseminate and build S&T in a society. Science and technology is like light that brightens the whole place. One cannot possess and hold it. One cannot have a monopoly over it. Tomorrow it would be obsolete; tomorrow something better would be available from somewhere else. Therefore, it is not easy to be holding on to S&T. Also, technology has to be within its useful life; one cannot use technology which has been beaten out of its life by users.

Production and growth are based mostly on S&T. One should be ahead of others if one's products are to be sold in the market. Competition has become a necessary element which makes it clear that one cannot make a new product, sell it and find the willingness of the consumer to accept it, unless the product is value based, less expensive and is available in good time. This can happen only when those factors are under control so as to make S&T available for use. Therefore, S&T has to be identified and managed in a manner which will make it possible to use it. In the early days of independence, it was believed that by raising the walls through protection, this country could make products, may be inferior and less attractive than others, and yet in the market within in the country such products would sell. So, advances in S&T had little significance for the production system. Unfortunately that era is over. Science and technology itself has shattered the walls which were preventing outside ideas or outside thoughts from coming into the market. Today, the international environment has become different with the result that new ideas, new designs and new products and services come galloping into the national economy. Competition cannot be checked with such barriers as we built earlier; people cannot be stopped from coming into this country for making products and selling them.

Market, Competition and Innovation

Consumers Choice

There was a time when the notion of nationalism was synonymous with the idea of protection but not so any more. The consumer will rebel against it. Some time back in America, a campaign was started against Japanese goods and the slogan was 'Be American, Buy American'. That was similar to what was being said in India, that is, 'Be Indian, Buy Indian'. But, within a week the American people rebelled against that message. They rejected those slogans which implored Americans to buy only American goods. They argued that they were not prepared to pay for the inefficiency of General Motors or Ford Motor or a US television company. If the Japanese television is better than theirs, if it is less costly, if it is more efficient, they will go for it. Their logic was that they were working, and so were their spouses, sometimes day and night or double shifts, they were doing so not to pay for the inefficiency of American businessman but to lead a better life themselves. That is the thinking in almost all the countries today including India. One may be looking for the lights and bulbs for Diwali which are Indian but when one finds the Chinese bulbs better, brighter and cheaper, one will buy the Chinese products. Thus, in this era of competition, new walls cannot be raised against products produced abroad.

Competition

This country is endowed with talent. Indians may not have been good with muscle power, they may not have been good in handling machines, but they always had certain instincts called abstraction and knowledge. Brahmin in this sense is not a caste, it is the brain power, it is the people who devote themselves to the service called knowledge. In a book Aristotle said, 'From India, I would like not elephants, not jewels, it's not gold, it's not Kohinoor, but the Brahminical mind and the philosophy.' The Director General of UNESCO, Federico Mayer, had said that knowledge flows from West to East and wisdom flows from East to West. While Indians are the inheritors of the tradition of knowledge, they have to get out of the mindset that they can produce, they can earn, they can live a great and prosperous life by cocooning themselves within India and not letting competition come from outside or within the country.

Potential of Indian Scientists

When it comes to knowledge, Indians are able to compete with the best in the world. It is wonderful to see in America that there is not a single Indian who is begging in the streets, or cleaning or sweeping floors, as Indians were largely doing at one time in England and other countries. These men and women from this country, with 7 dollars in their pockets, went to America, a strange country, with a strange language and strange habits and culture, and made a mark for themselves. Today, there is not a single hospital in America where they do not have an Indian doctor; there is not a single good laboratory where they do not have Indian scientists. A number of noble laureates from the universities have been working with young Indian boys and girls. Today, even in the Wall Street, Indians are working at senior levels in financial firms. Silicon Valley has the flavour of Indian *masalas* (spices) and curry everywhere. Indian scientists have the potential to be amongst the best. The issue is that the system must be able to respond to realize that potential.

If the scientists are not able to contribute, if they have become rigid on their views and are not looking forward to new ideas, it is because of the system in which they are caught. If the shackling effect of the system is taken out and incentives and creativity are permitted to play their role, development will be faster. This realization must pervade the industry also. Industrialists will also have to be prepared for competition and not ask for the controllers to get into the business.

Role of Education

When the process of economic liberalization was launched in 1991, some people felt that the Finance Minister was 'opening the cage and the tigers in the cage will rush out'. There were others who felt otherwise. They held the view that business and industry had got so much used to protection that they had lost the will to strive. The willingness to strive is essential for competing and succeeding. Solow, the economist who won the Noble Prize, worked very hard on finding out what makes more production come out of the productive machines. He proved that the cumulative contribution of the three factors of production, namely, land, labour and capital, was less than the residual contribution that was being made by S&T. He proved that 1 dollar of new S&T inducted in production produces 10 more dollars of output. Science and technology is the most important factor for increasing productivity of production processes.

What is it that makes S&T flourish in a country? The answer is simple; education is the basis. Unless and until education flows from top to bottom and educated persons are spread from bottom to top, S&T-oriented society cannot emerge. It is unfeasible to have inadequately educated men designing factories, developing new products, providing IT services to the world or sending satellites up above the earth—or even running buses, trains and airlines or treating sick and suffering. Today, it is gratifying to see that in spite of several aspects of education which are unsatisfactory, emphasis is on educating the people, so that they may be able to become the foot soldiers of S&T in the coming years. It is an inspiring sight to see, in a village or a small township, small children carrying books—very heavy, may be too heavy—and running in the direction of the school. The school may not have a teacher yet there is a strong desire that the school should be there. In some schools the blackboard may not have a chalk to write with but the desire to teach and learn is there. This urge has already developed among the masses and it is for the government, private organizations and civil society to take it forward.

Culture of Innovation

Besides education, there are other things also to be done to make S&T work. A country cannot go on just inventing things; that is not possible. That is where innovation has become necessary and important. Japan was not the country where the automobile was developed and its manufacturing started. It was England, Germany and America that were in the forefront. Japan took it up much later and yet Japan overtook all these leading countries. In the same car, the Japanese have installed an air conditioner, a watch and a music system, though none of these was meant originally for the car. These and some other innovative changes made the product so different from the original one that it became accepted as the best in the world. Even those who created the car had to feel humbled before what Japan was able to do. Korean example of innovative culture is even more amazing. Korea was a unaggressive country and had no particular ambitions at that point of time, and India was relatively ahead. Yet Korea has been able to emerge as an Asian tiger while India is struggling to be noticed at the international level. India started manufacturing Ambassador Cars based on a British model. Korea also took up manufacturing cars of the same model.

In 5–10 years, Korea came out with various new models altogether and India continued with the initial model of Ambassador for decades. Such instances depict a pathetic picture of non-innovative ways of doing things, of living happily with what has already been given, of being indifferent to how the competitors are moving ahead, of preventing others from competing with us and then feeling that we have been able to achieve a great deal. The upshot is that one has got to borrow technology. There is no point in re-inventing the wheel. A country must modernize a product, change it, moderate it, or do whatever else it might do, so that it is able to project its contribution to the product. Time has come when India should have a platform for launching innovations. Other countries recognize such opportunities in India. The best of industries and others are opening up their research centres in India and utilizing the talent of Indian S&T personnel.

Intellectual Property

A climate of innovations brings under sharp focus the issue of intellectual property rights (IPR). It becomes important to learn how to read patents, interpret them and develop new products from the existing patents. A whole class of people have to be trained in the industry, outside the industry, everywhere, so that they are able to read the patents, understand them, resolve the related issues, and facilitate the application of S&T and innovations. There is a lot of traditional knowledge available in India. Ways must be found to give it new shape, to make it available widely and to harness that knowledge.

There are 5,000 patent institutions for teaching people in China while India has barely two such institutes. The rest of the set-ups are like debating societies; they hardly take up work on understanding, analyzing and finding out as to what a specific patent product is and how it could be utilized. In addition, there are numerous traditional medicines, traditional herbs and other products that are largely un-documented, and they can be made use of. In this context, a massive wealth exists today at the base of the pyramid. There are poor mothers in the villages who provide effective and safe medicines to their children the likes of which are not known even in the Western, scientific, knowledge world. Extensive knowledge known to such rural folks needs to be brought out. Sometimes attempts are made in the West to patent traditional Indian products as happened in the case of Basmati rice and turmeric. It should be ensured that India is not deprived of its intellectual property in this manner. Documenting such intellectual property has started in India. A beginning has been made but there is a lot more that can and needs to be done.

Concluding Remarks

While appreciating the value of knowledge and S&T, it has to be understood that imparting of education is extremely necessary. It has also to be accepted that competition gives us the urge to improve the products. For accepting and implementing new ideas, it is important to develop the right mindset. Nehru always used to emphasize the value of the scientific mind, the scientific way of thinking and the scientific temper. Scientific temper means that we must have the courage to break the barriers in our thinking and analyze new ideas. It implies that we seek the best, understand it completely and examine its shortcomings, and see how better than the best can come out. We may have the best of technology at a point of time but we must attempt to improve upon it for the future. Such a state of mind comes up when we just do not submit ourselves to the knowledge or prescription given by our superiors, predecessors or others. In Bhagavad Gita, Krishna said to Arjuna something like this, 'Oh Arjuna! I have given you all the knowledge you need. I have solved all your problems which were bothering you. I have given you an idea as to what is right, what is wrong, what is *Dharma* and what is *Adharma*. Now it is for you to decide and do what is right.' Krishna was definitely far wiser but he left it to Arjuna to decide the course of action. He said, 'I have given you everything; nobody will see me in the form that you have seen; nobody will have access to the type of knowledge that I have given to you; but that's not enough. You have to get into action yourself.'

By questioning conventional wisdom or what the elders or superiors say, it is not that we have to be disrespectful of them or disobey them. But we must have the courage to point out what is wrong and prove it in a scientific manner. Knowledge of S&T is extremely important and it has to be intertwined with cultural values. It is not easy to find improved ways of working and invent things, yet it has to be done. As a person said to a traveller, 'Are you looking for a pathway in this forest? There is none here but when you walk the path it will be formed.' When it comes to a question of doing something correct, doing something new, doing something good, we should be prepared to acquire knowledge, break the barriers and progress ahead. This is what S&T is about.

13 Innovation in Knowledge Economy*

RAJEEVA RATNA SHAH

Introduction

Knowledge is an essentiality related to development. The three pillars of development which have already been identified by the United Nations (UN), are economic development, environment development and socio-cultural development. These three pillars should be put together for balanced development. Knowledge is critical to the strengthening of the three pillars.

For economic development, knowledge has become so important that at certain stage of development, the economy is characterized as a knowledge economy. This is a nuance that needs to be understood. Knowledge economy changes the scenario in the sense that it will have the wherewithal and the means to have access to data—mine it, warehouse it and mine it at will—which was not so earlier. India can create capacity; it has the processing power which has been growing fast; it has bandwidths which are trebling every 24 months and it has networks which are growing very fast.

One of the factors that contributed to the success of information technology (IT) in this country is the fact that the Department of Electronics (DoE), which was overseeing IT in earlier years, did not see itself as a regulator or as a controller; it saw itself as a facilitator. It tried not only to facilitate but also to foresee events as they were coming, and even go beyond the vision of the industry to set the base and the horizons for the industry. As a result, India is now perceived at the international level as an IT power. India should now strive to move further and transform its economy into a knowledge economy.

Innovation and Competitiveness

Innovation

In the National Innovative Capacity Index, standing way behind the developed coun-tries and even behind Brazil and China in terms of innovative capacity, the latest ranking of India is 33, and we have a

---

*This chapter is based on an oral presentation made by the author.

long way to go to improve it. In this spectrum of 43 nations, at one end is the USA with an index of 31 and at the other end is India having an index of 21. Within these 10 numbers, there are about 41 nations arranged in between. The competition for superiority is intense.

Innovation is not merely technology innovation. It is about technology information, product information, process information, product innovation, process innovation, market innovation, and so on. Innovation leads to creation of intellectual property. Intellectual property is going to be the hallmark of competitiveness. It is the intellectual property where the ownership is going to reside in future and all other activities in manufacturing are likely to become outsourced. That is going to be the locus of movement of the knowledge economy. In such a scenario, probably owning of physical facility is not going to be important in case of knowledge industries. It will be important to own the application, and there resides ownership. If ownership of various innovative products is available, that is, intellectual capital is available, then the rest of it, namely, manufacturing, can be outsourced; fabrication becomes an outsourced proposition. So in a knowledge economy, fabrication will become increasingly outsourced, intellectual property is what will bring in the dividends.

Key Drivers of Innovation

Technology

The modern technology sector is contributing mainly to knowledge and innovation. This sector comprises activities such as nanotechnology, computers, networks and biotechnology.

Leaving apart the knowledge sector, which moves on its own momentum, in a knowledge economy the legacy sector will behave differently and therefore the entire manufacturing processes would be impacted though in a totally different manner. It is important to consider the legacy economy here for competitiveness because within the knowledge economy itself and the various knowledge sectors of economy, India is already moving at a speed where it could propel itself into leadership positions. It is in the legacy sector where major interventions are required and that is why it would be necessary to identify the building blocks for creating India as a new manufacturing power. In order to drive competitiveness worldwide, seven points need to be taken care of: innovation, technology, design, micro-cost monitoring, information and communication technologies (ICT) applications to management processes, ICT application to technology processes and global benchmarking of quality.

Global Competitiveness

In global competitiveness also, India ranks pretty low. In 2002, India's ranking in the world in growth competitiveness was 48 while it was 37 in micro-economic competitiveness.

Preparation of Human Resource

Innovation basically assumes that there is a strong individual intellectual power behind it. For making the human resource innovation oriented, creativity has to be nurtured and grown right from the young age. This also implies that bright young persons should be taking up careers in research and development (R&D), and innovation. This has not been happening in India in recent years. However, the government is conscious of this fact and is trying to improve the human material which can innovate. Towards this, the government is creating some 10,000 scholarships of about Rs. 1 lakh each for bright students. The intention of such a scheme is to tap the talent at post-12th-class stage and bring talented students into research stream. The scholarship could be Rs 1 lakh a year during undergraduation, Rs 2 lakh during postgraduation and even higher at Ph.D. level. In this manner, it may be possible to lock in promising intellectual manpower with outstanding prospects for jobs because this manpower is going to be *crème de la crème*. They would be taken out even before the Indian Institutes of Technology (IITs) pick out their lot from it. That is the quality of manpower that should power R&D, and create innovation. The Planning Commission is working on this proposal and hopefully it will be a part of the 11th Five Year Plan. This scheme will be one of the major drivers of innovation. The second element in the key drivers for the legacy sector is R&D on technology for effecting economies.

Role of Public and Private Sectors

Innovation stems from two sources. One of them is public-funded R&D which generates knowledge that leads to innovation. The second avenue is private-funded R&D which is the driver of innovation that is wealth generating. Public-funded R&D may lead to patents. However, patents so generated may remain largely in the records and may not get capitalized and converted into wealth. While it is common practice to measure the volume of R&D in terms of public expenditure as a percentage of gross domestic product (GDP), it is more important but rare to measure it as a contribution of value to the society, value to the economy and value of the wealth that it is generating. Even in the economies that have 3 per cent and above public expenditure on R&D, it is not the public expenditure which is leading to wealth-creating patents as much as the expenditure by the corporate—the corporate budget on R&D.

The issues that are being addressed here relate largely to the firm level. But in each of them there is a role that can be played by the government. For instance, with regard to innovation, India is not innovating fast enough. At the moment, the *crème de la crème* goes to the IITs; the next lot goes to the next level of selection; and after that what remains as residue is going into research. So the best-quality manpower that should go into research is going elsewhere. Research as a function has not been given primacy in the social fabric. This situation needs to be reversed. This reversal of trend cannot be initiated by a firm; this has to be done by the government. That is one of the policy interventions that would be required. On the technology front, there is a great deal that can be done at the firm level. Firm-level R&D, regrettably, is falling. Besides, R&D that is being undertaken at the firm level is of poor quality. India is way behind others on this front. Huawei and ZTE—the two public sector companies in China—have during the course of the last 20 years traversed such a long distance in R&D that they are challenging the likes of CISCO of USA in telecom equipment. They have now mastered reverse engineering. They have reverse-engineered most of their products and now they are getting into creation of wealth through intellectual property. They have a presence all over the world in some 27 locations and they are spending something like 25 per cent of their profits on R&D. Firms have to take the lead and get into innovation though there is a whole lot of work that needs to be done above the firm level as well. There is a great deal of pre-competitive collaborative research which needs to take place, for instance, on materials. Some materials may have significance to say 250 odd firms in an industry but none of them has the wherewithal to invest in the development of those materials, particularly nano-materials. That is where the associations of industries can come in and facilitate joint initiatives. The government can incentivize them to take up such collective work.

Then there are certain common facilities which may be required by an industry with such a heavy investment that not even a major player can make. In the auto industry, for instance, the automatic cash back facility was at 2 billion dollars investment; no single player was willing to put in that much. Dependent on that investment would be the scaling of auto exports to the global economies. So a state-of-the-art auto test facility has to be set up. Now the government is setting up that facility because such a scale of investment goes beyond the capabilities of any single firm. This is on the technology level. On the design level, the government has one of the finest institutions that is now getting into high-tech areas also. The National Institute of Design (NID) has the capabilities for designing automobiles. They have now set up a centre in Bangalore which is designing chips and getting into microelectronics. Thus, design is another element where government has already taken an initiative. Probably what the government can do is to establish NID centres in three or four locations. Each of them should be unique and need not be a replica of any other. They could be specialized centres under the NID umbrella.

On micro-cost monitoring, the government need not do anything since it is something which is totally within the realm of the firm-level decision making. Firms need to do all the necessary research. The cyber space provides a whole lot of material which they can extract from. Supply chain management (SCM), customer relationship management (CRM) and enterprise resource planning (ERP) are techniques which are well known. Vendors as well as firms are aware of them. There is some kind of reluctance sometimes to get into some of these. But, with the passage of time, more and more firms are accepting these ICT-based modern management techniques.

Whatever is necessary to make India a powerhouse of innovation and intellectual property creation should be done. The fact is that, as in all other countries, the public domain investment in R&D is generating less of intellectual wealth. Today, the Council of Scientific and Industrial Research (CSIR) institutions (38 laboratories) are generating patents somewhat less than 200 a year while CISCO and the Intel research laboratories in India are generating almost equal number of patents. Thus, value that is created through private enterprise is higher because their R&D investment is aimed at getting them immediate profits. Public funding of R&D may not generate wealth through commercialization of results as much as the private-funded R&D does, but it is essential for generating knowledge and capacity building that is so critical for taking up innovative work in both public and private sectors.

The S&T ministries, each one of them, had their outlays doubled in the last three years and in some cases they have tripled in absolute terms. For investment in R&D as a percentage of GDP in an economy, where distribution takes priority over so many other things, it is not fair to apply the same proportions as in developed countries. Today the political emphasis in the country is creating a just social order. Equality, justice and fraternity, three of the props of the Constitution of India, relate to a just social order. The fourth one, that is, liberty, relates to the individual—the freedom of the individual, the individuality and ability to bring out the best, the originality of the individual, the diversity in the individual and the power of innovation that comes from that. The prevailing 9 per cent growth is intended to imply 9 per cent inclusive growth. The emphasis is on inclusion which means the public expenditure is going to be putting up very high priority on inclusion.

Public–Private Partnership

The social debate at the moment is on unshackling education so as to enable private enterprise to contribute. The Planning Commission has been putting its weight on the side of unshackling. Even in bio-informatics and human resource development (HRD) in the twilight zones of various domains, which are going to be stitched soon by the All India Council for Technical Education (AICTE)—a statutory body set up by the government for the promotion and regulation of technical education in the country—it is necessary to create manpower which is versatile in more than one domain. So, HRD programmes are needed to create, for instance, info-bio manpower and info-bio-nano manpower. Various such combinations will be required. Information technology applies to even legal domain. A certain kind of manpower is needed which is not just legal by training, not just IT by training, but which knows its law and the technology. These are some of the directions in which the government may have to take the lead. If National Association of Software and Services Companies (NASSCOM) has to succeed, it must have, amongst other things, very strong programmes relating to ICT and its applications, which can be delivered in Chinese, Arabic and Spanish, besides English. These three foreign languages will require a large number of people. Spanish is spoken in Latin America just as Chinese and Arabic are understood by a very large part of the world, the latter in the Middle East and North Africa. These are some of the strategic interventions that are needed.

For intervention in terms of intellectual property creation, the government has a role in incentivizing various industry associations to get on to some cross-cutting research which relates to the industry as a whole and involves large investments. This could be more like pre-competitive collaborative research, the kind that Media Lab Asia was supposed to do, where various corporates were supposed to pitch in. But it did not happen, because that process was brought not on its merits but for certain peripheral considerations. This does not mean that it cannot happen. That is one part of the issue.

The other part is certain strategic innovation where we should have creation of institutions of excellence in various knowledge domains like nanotechnology. This is one of the weak areas at the moment. That is where the experiment of Media Lab Asia should be looked at once again. A very major strategic intervention was attempted in trying to create the Media Lab Asia with the collaboration of Massachusetts Institute of Technology (MIT), USA. In the Media Lab Asia, a system was created whereby it would be a partnership between Indian corporates, foreign corporates and Indian government. The Indian government agreed to provide up to Rs 60 crore per year as an upfront grant and committed itself to doing so for the next 5 or 10 years. It was felt that one of the things that was blocking the Indian scientific research was that we were not setting our targets globally. We were not looking at the global research platforms and not taking maximum advantage out of them. We thought that we needed to give top scientists global mobility. Therefore, we decided that we would cross the barriers relating to salaries and remuneration, and so on, and the scientists engaged in this work could be considered for higher remuneration. We engaged a chief executive who was the chief executive of Hewlett-Packard for the Asia Pacific region. He was drawing a salary of around US $300,000 at that time and we hired him for something like US $50,000 or 60,000. Since he was an Indian, he was willing to come back to the country even though the remuneration, in nominal terms, was lower. But the entire IIT system opposed it. As a result, the plan was rejected and the CEO had to go for no fault of his. These are some of the impediments to making very large strategic interventions. As a result, sometimes they eventually fall apart.

In the Media Lab Asia case, the government was trying to establish the laboratory to market link. Bridging the digital divide was set as the core area for Media Lab Asia. It was realized that the megatrends of technology in the 21st century would be different from the megatrends in the 19th and 20th centuries. In the earlier centuries, scientists were exploring the natural phenomena. They were focusing more on the macro-world; they were not getting so much into the understanding of the micro and infinitesimal—whether it is the atoms and sub-molecular particles or nanotechnology or bits and bytes which is ICT or genes which is biotechnology or the network. In the 21st century the R&D is dealing with the infinitesimal. It is able to deal with it now and not earlier because earlier all the computing that was being done and the storage were undertaken manually in the human brain. Now it is being done in magnetic medium and through computing powers which are ever increasing. This enables us to deal with a large amount of data. When we are dealing with sub-molecular structures or bits and bytes or genes and neurons, each one of them has to have a descriptor and we have to deal with them as individual entities and we need to store a whole lot of information which was manually impossible to store. This means that now we need super-computing for each of these applications. What distinguishes IT which relates to bits and bytes is that since it carries information, it carries information about sub-molecular particles from the nano-world, information about genes, information about neurons. Therefore, IT becomes the hyphen that joins or binds various knowledge domains.

Technology and R&D

Technology Foresight

A key factor in the development of competitiveness in a knowledge economy is technology development. One has to be on the lookout for opportunities for developing new technologies and innovations. One has to follow global trends in both business and technology domains and raise questions relating to economics, society, governance, and so on for the purpose of finding solutions through technology development.

Patents

Patenting is an avenue of protecting the rights of those who have invested in the development of technology and ensuring fair economic returns to them. Patents also indicate the level of innovative activities in a country. Amongst the top 10 countries with regard to the number of US patents registered by them per million population in 2001, developing countries like Taiwan and Israel figure but countries like India and China do not. Thus, as a technology-innovating economy, India has a long way to go.

The ability to innovate and seek patents also depends on the type of industries and R&D that are dominant on the industrial scene of a country. As trends go, some industries witness large levels of innovation at a particular point of time. Patenting activity is relatively large in sectors such as drugs, semiconductors and microbiology. Therefore, countries will display large innovative capacity if their funding on R&D is large in such fertile areas.

Capturing the traditional knowledge is one of the features of the knowledge economy, and it is closely related to the intellectual property rights (IPR) issue. It is also related to WTO issues. A lot of work has already been done, and many traditional herbs and traditional medicines, and their formulation have been worked out and placed on the prior art search of about 1 million pages. This is more in the realm of herbal drugs. This is one kind of traditional knowledge which will have future productive use. Such knowledge we must in all circumstances procure. There are other kinds of traditional knowledge which relate to, for example, folklore and how folk songs have proceeded over the ages and how folk art has proceeded from one century to another. Probably some motifs taken from folk art could be used appropriately in the future but the potential for productive use of such knowledge is not as much. There are two missions operating in this area. One of them is the national mission for manuscripts for preserving manuscript resources from all over India, and another mission recently announced by the Minister of Culture is documentation of intangible cultural heritage of India. It is planned to document all the folklore or intangible heritage in various regions of India. While all forms of traditional knowledge is valuable, we have to see which part of traditional knowledge is more sensitive to being stored in because of the wealth that is contained in it. Patenting needs to look at these aspects as well.

ICT Support to Design

Designing is for cost competitiveness, functional effectiveness and higher productivity. One can design also for durability and greater reliability. Design is not merely about the aesthetics and economics of products but also for so many aspects which are part of the design objectives. Designing in a knowledge economy becomes different, for it goes a few steps further. In a knowledge economy there is a system that enables designers to link themselves with the suppliers and the customers in a holistic manner. They can get the feedback from all of them into the design stage and can go on improving upon the design or the product and the system.

First there is a product development stage, then there is product verification stage and, after demonstration, there is the feedback for refining the product further. Then there are the stages of product validation and product implementation.

Micro-cost Monitoring

Micro-cost monitoring is becoming an important element because every little bit that can be done to reduce the cost is going to contribute to the economy of mass consumption. Mass consumption economies like India, China and Brazil are going to be highly price sensitive and whatever cost reduction can be brought about would immediately enlarge the size of the market. As such, cost monitoring becomes very important. For this purpose, one needs not only to have intensive data relating to one's own industry but also to look at what others are doing, what kind of competition is going on inside India, what level of competition is operating outside India and what are the various cost-cutting options that they are using, so that we may choose our options and apply them.

ICT Applications to Management Processes

Supply Chain Management (SCM)

In the supply chain, the world over, large original equipment manufacturers (OEMs) are moving towards design outsourcing and integrated business model. So design outsourcing is becoming a part of SCM.

Design is where knowledge-based capabilities are strong; after it is outsourced and accepted, it is reintegrated. Initially when manufacturing was outsourced, a large number of parties were associated. Large OEMs are now implementing SCM strategies oriented towards their major suppliers' capabilities trickling down to small and medium enterprises (SMEs). Then they start doing ABC analysis based on the performance of various suppliers and thus they start narrowing down the number of suppliers; because the larger the number of suppliers, the weaker is the chain. This is the broad approach through which SCM enables OEMs to proceed further and have absolutely cast-iron-strong, loyal and well-performing suppliers so that they can be knit into the production framework.

Customer Relationship Management

Customer Relationship Management (CRM) (see Box 13.1) is a system that allows us to

1. manage business relationship with the customer;
2. implement the strategy that puts the customer first;
3. interact and get intimate with the customer and solidify the customer's loyalty;
4. enhance understanding of and track customer habits;
5. link together data with all parts of the business;
6. warehouse all information of the customer; and
7. maximize advantage to the company on the basis of all the above.

Box 13.1   Customer Relationship Management (CRM)

- Systems that allow you to manage relationship
- Strategy that puts the customer first, it's getting intimate with the customer—solidifying loyalty
- Understanding and tracking customer habits
- Links data together from all parts of the business
- Warehouse of all the info of your customer
- Maximizer, ACT!, Salesforce.com, Pivotal

ICT Applications to Technology Processes

Manufacturing

Enterprise-level functions—execution, tactical and strategies—are organized vertically. Horizontally, there are project development, operations, marketing and sales, finance and human resources. Computer-aided manufacture, computer-aided design and computer-aided execution are largely at the execution level where ICT is intensively involved. Various other applications are on the operation side. The most important feature is that the three major ICT applications, namely, SCM, CRM and Enterprise Resource Planning (ERP), facilitate a holistic look at all the stakeholders, and integrate them and weave them into one holistic vision of where the enterprise should be.

Nano-manufacturing

Manufacturing can be at the macro level, the micro level or the nano level. In a knowledge-based economy, one has to understand the nuances of each level of manufacturing. Nanotechnology is concerned with the design and manufacturing of molecular scale devices by manipulation and placement of individual atoms and molecules with precision on the atomic scale. The basic difference in nano-fabrication is that it is not a top-down fabrication. It is a bottom-up fabrication where one is putting up a sub-assembly and then building upon it as opposed to the 'top-down' fabrication techniques employed in microelectronics technology. The head of a pin is 1–2 millimeters, human hair is about 60–100 micrometers, a red blood cell is 2–5 micrometers and the DNA is 2.5 milli-micrometers or it is 2.5 nanometers.

Nanotechnology derives knowledge from a number of disciplines, for example, physics, chemistry, mathematics, biology, information science and has wide applications in electronics, optics, healthcare, energy, environment and the like.

There are some potential applications of nanotechnology which are mind boggling. Nanotechnology can take us to the stage when we introduce a nanoparticle inside the human body and it can tell us which of the capillaries is blocked, and it can clear the capillary in future. This is a kind of nanosurgery. Nanotechnology is not going to merely impact upon manufacturing, it is going to impact on health sciences also. Like ICT some of the knowledge-based technologies are going to have a profound impact across various domains of knowledge. Information and communication technologies is the hyphen that joins and the buckle that binds various domains of knowledge. Similarly there are some of these emerging technologies which are going to have a profound and widespread impact.

Benefits to the Society

Identification of Villages

In a knowledge society, knowledge must benefit the common man. There are various possibilities of doing so and they will expand as the society develops. As an example in the current situation, we could consider the National Rural Employment Guarantee Programme (NREGP) launched recently by the government. It is the first year of implementation of that programme. Today we can have the name of every villager and every village and its identification (ID) on the database; and we have done it. We know who is coming forward to avail of this programme and getting how many days of work, and how much payment is being made tohim. We are now working on a unique ID for every individual in the village to enable us to know what the various benefits are that are reaching him under various schemes, to what extent it is leading to amelioration of his poverty and to what extent we are able to bring about a change in his economic status. Thus, it should be possible to measure and calibrate the impact on individual poverty in future. It is a unique feature of ICT that we can go into any number of elemental records, we can go into any degree of detail, we can store information and then we can analyse the information. As the next step, we need to develop a powerful system which can convert such a management information system into a decision support system. Once the information is available and it has been properly analyzed, it should lead to decisions and interventions. This has not started happening yet but it is possible to do that.

Earlier, there were indefinite lists of villages in which villages used to come in and go out. The states would send different lists of villages on different occasions. Now the lists of villages have been firmed up at the state level. This has helped in monitoring the progress of drinking water facility village-wise. This micro-monitoring in the public domain has been introduced only to make sure that we can have targeted delivery. Thus, targeted delivery is going to be one of the major achievements of the use of ICT. What is really happening is that in NREGP, data capture is still a problem because the IT conduit is going up to the district level only; by the end of this year it will go up to the block level. Beyond that level, the IT conduit is not there. From the project site, information ought to be brought on a daily basis and fed into the computer. Since we are not able to do that, there is always a time lag. To overcome this problem, at least partly, attempt is being made to transfer information through handheld devices. The project manager will transfer that information, bring it back to the computer and charge it on the computer at least once a week. Thus, at least weekly updating will take place. This has not happened countrywide but it has already happened in Orissa and some other regions. This only goes on to show that these are the potentials through which we can improve our delivery mechanism. Once we have the data captured across the board at any point of time all over the country, then we know the correct picture. So we really need to make our updating transactions facility. Of course, this is a powerful delivery mechanism and monitoring of governmental programmes so that they are effectively implemented, but there are many dimensions of this issue which still have to receive due attention.

Identification of Citizens

India needs to create unique ID for every individual citizen. India also needs to create a unique ID for every business corporate. The unique ID system for the corporates and for the businesses is already being created. It is an electronic system. All filing of returns of companies from 15 September 2006 onwards is now on the basis of unique ID created by the Ministry of Company Affairs (MCA). The creation of the unique ID for the individuals is held up. While there are developmental pressures from, for instance, the Planning Commission, who are demanding that this should be immediately put into position so that it can converge various development programmes and see what is happening to the beneficiary, on the contrary, the Home Ministry's perspective is that the moment unique IDs are created, they will be interpreted as some kind of a certification that the individual is a citizen and citizenship gives him certain legalized status. Being apprehensive about its implications, the Home Ministry would like it to be an operation which goes through the entire quasi-judicial process of determining citizenship, particularly in those areas where there is a significant presence of foreigners. One way to resolve the issue is to take the view that the ID being proposed is not a citizen ID but a population ID. Social security would be an overlay on the population ID and not on the citizenship issue. If the ID is regarded as a citizen issue, it will have to wait till the quasi-judicial process has taken place. The Home Ministry's route will take 10 years and will require Rs 5,000–10,000 crore investment in smart cards. If the ID is regarded as a population issue, no investment in smart cards is necessary upfront. In the magnetic medium, it is possible to create the scheme for every individual resident in India. Whenever there is a government programme, the smart card can be given to the beneficiary with his unique ID. Thus, whenever he gets a benefit from any programme he will be using the same ID. Also, whenever he is expected to get a benefit, he will be willing to invest in the smart card. So the government will not be investing, the beneficiary will be investing. In this manner, the smart card can be financed by the benefit stream that is going to flow to him. If he is going to make it, then it could be a smart card with digital signature, it could be a smart card with a Radio Frequency Identification (RFID) residing on it. Depending upon his own needs, he could go in for the most sophisticated smart card and pay for it. We can thus create a scheme that becomes government enabled without government funding.

From here we proceed towards creating two courses or portals. One is governmental business portal which is now riding on MCA. It is not just for filing returns to the MCA but for all transactions relating to Income Tax Act, excise, corporate tax or wherever there is a government interface. All those transactions can be through that particular unique ID. It should be possible to have G to B portal on which all this can reside. This can be done first at the central government level. Later, it can combine the state government applications. Subsequently, municipal-level functions can be combined vertically. Conceptually, on the citizen side, there can be a citizen portal and wherever during his life cycle he needs to get into interaction with the government, all those applications can come on to it.

14 Intellectual Property Rights in Knowledge Management

A.K. SENGUPTA

Introduction

In the realm of knowledge management (KM), there are three vital processes, namely, 'knowledge identification', 'knowledge creation' and 'knowledge acquisition'. In organizational as well as societal contexts, the process of knowledge identification primarily concerns conversion of tacit knowledge that exists with people and groups into explicit and documental knowledge—on paper or on electronic contents—in order to clearly bring out what one knows and what one does not know that one knows, and make these explicit enough to be shared by people who may utilize the same for organizational or societal benefit. The knowledge creation process is one step ahead of knowledge identification in that it involves innovation and human ingenuity to bring forth new knowledge from the existing knowledge pool. Research, development, analysis, experimentation, introspection and many other activities are invariably linked with the knowledge creation process, and they often lead to basic scientific knowledge which is then used by commercial organizations for producing new or improved products and processes that benefit the society in general. Finally, there is the process of acquisition of knowledge that already exists elsewhere—with individuals, in universities, in research institutions, with the competitors. The purpose is to avoid 'reinventing the wheel' to the extent possible and to accelerate the process of enhancement of organizational capabilities through absorption and assimilation of the acquired knowledge and further creation of new knowledge.

In each of the three distinct KM processes, the issue of ownership of knowledge per se is of paramount importance. The intellectual property and ownership pertaining to a particular piece of knowledge, whether identified within, created by research and development (R&D) or acquired from outside, needs to be clearly established and protected, to ensure equitable sharing of credit and wealth generated by the eventual application of that knowledge. Protection of intellectual property rights (IPR) and generating incentives for the owners are necessary for enhancing knowledge-based approach to work, whether in the domain of industry and trade or in the grassroots-level innovations and traditional knowledge.

During the latter part of the 20th century and in early 21st century, the environmental system in which knowledge production and use took place has become complex. There are many interactions between those involved, and feedbacks from markets and industry identify important and, often, radically new areas of research. Rapid obsolescence of old products and processes, faster exploitation of discoveries and innovations in new fields and efforts of governments to use scientific expertise more effectively in the pursuit of economic and social progress have led to policies and activities aimed at producing closer links among commercial establishments, research laboratories, government institutions and professional bodies. The global nature of business, economy and science and technology (S&T) has broadened the scope of these links. Intellectual property rights have the essential function of defining relationships between those involved in these interactions for changing cultural and regulatory environments, and bringing about net social benefits by increasing the rate of innovation.

Similarly, at the grassroots level, with the level of innovations and traditional knowledge that exists in households, villages and rural economy, it is important that IPR of the knowledge holders are protected. Significant work in this area has been done by the National Innovation Foundation (NIF) (www.nifindia.org), an IIM-Ahmedabad-based organization that has in the last 20 years of efforts unearthed more than 50,000 innovations practised in rural India. Approximately 100 of these innovations have led to applications for patenting, including six for which US patents have been granted. Many of these innovations remained hidden until NIF detected them—and in some cases substantially improved upon them—before making them available for application to the world at large.

The present chapter is aimed at highlighting some of the issues concerning the interplay of IPR in the KM processes, in the industry and the grassroots and traditional knowledge sectors, particularly in the Indian context.

Intellectual Property

Concept of Intellectual Property

Intellectual property, known as IP, allows people to own their creativity and innovation in the same way that they can own physical property. The owner of IP can control and be rewarded for its use, and this encourages further innovation and creativity to the benefit of all. In some cases IP gives rise to protection for ideas but in other areas there will have to be greater elaboration of an idea before the case for protection can arise. It will often not be possible to protect IP and gain IPR unless they have been applied for and granted. Some IP protection such as copyright arises automatically, without any registration, as soon as there is a record in some form of what has been created.

As per the agreement on Trade-Related Aspects of Intellectual Property Rights (TRIPS), eight categories of IP have been defined, for which protection of ownership rights can be sought. These are (a) patents, (b) copyrights, (c) trademarks and service marks, (d) design registration, (e) layout designs for integrated circuits, (f) trade secrets and undisclosed Information, (g) geographical indications and (h) new plant varieties. In this chapter discussion shall be confined mainly to patents though other types of IP may often be as important in deliberations in KM. In the field of grassroots-level innovations and traditional knowledge, for example, geographical indications and protection of plant varieties can be of particular relevance.

IPR as an Archive of Global Innovations

Intellectual property rights system in general is a systematic process of disclosure and structured documentation of innovations that is accessible in the public domain. The system gives rise to a guarantee for ownership rights by the governments to those who created or developed the innovation in the first place, so that it can be worked on or utilized for public good by the owners or licensed to others for commercial exploitation.

Intellectual property rights database, therefore, becomes a fairly detailed archive of globally accessible knowledge whose exploitation is subject to caveats elaborated in specific national IPR laws. A proper use of the IPR databases, therefore, forms an essential part of a global knowledge management process which can not only avoid 'reinventing the wheel' but also help in cost-effective and strategic utilization of the knowledge that is already available, through appropriate licensing, transfer of rights, and so on. Patent records, for example, contain a wealth of information on each patented invention, including the identity and location of the inventors and the inventors' work domain and the technological area of the invention. In addition, patent documents also contain information on previous patents—'prior art' and 'citations'—tracing multiple links across inventions. Patent records thus can be a promising window on the knowledge economy. It is said that 80 per cent of all information relating to innovations in S&T is available in the patent databases—much more than in literature in any other form.

Accessing the IPR Archives

On a rough estimate more than 6 million patents have been granted in the world. More than 80 per cent of them is now in the public domain, that is, they are past the expiry of the protection period after the grant—a patent has a life of 20 years. These patents are published by the authorities in the respective countries where their applications were first filed and patents granted. Many of these were filed and granted in several countries individually or through the Patent Cooperation Treaty (PCT) route. These publications are generally open for access by public at large anywhere in the world, through the websites of the patent offices of the country such as www.uspto.gov (for US Patent & Trademark Office), www. ipindia.nic.in (for Indian Patent Office), www.patent.gov.uk (for UK Patent Office) and www.jpo.gov. jp (for Japan Patent Office). They are also available as printed publications.

Since novelty, originality and inventiveness are essential pre-requisites in seeking patent protection of an invention, searching of patent databases often is the starting point before applying for a patent, and also before initiating a research programme in any area of S&T. Patent search and identification of citations as well as all 'prior art' references are an art in itself, a complex procedure involving selection of 'keywords', databases, cross-referencing that need to be pursued, and so forth. While there are modern bibliometric techniques available for searching, several IT-enabled retrieval technologies also allow targeted document detection, extraction, visualization and routing of databases.

Integrating IPR in Innovation Processes

Innovation is neither about getting it right the first time nor about perfecting an idea before exposing it to other people. Successful prototypes and experiments should be allowed to be rolled out gradually in order to facilitate and integrate learning. Such structures should allow organizations and individuals to learn from best practices, inside as well as outside the public service. Finally, there needs to be 'space' for reflection, rejuvenation and forward development.

Innovation is the art of making new connections and continuously challenging the status quo—without changing things for change's sake. Hence, innovation can be defined as a frame of mind. Successful innovation is first, and most importantly, about creating value. It does so either by improving existing products, processes or services (incremental innovation) or by developing products, processes or services of value that have not existed previously (radical innovation or 'invention'). However, both kinds of innovation

1. challenge the status quo;
2. have an understanding of and insights into consumer needs; and
3. develop imaginative and novel solutions.

In addition, innovation is generally associated with the following:

1. Willingness to take risks
2. Coping with high levels of ambiguity and uncertainty
3. Original thinking
4. Passion to drive an idea through to conclusions
5. Ability to inspire passion in others

Innovation can be viewed usefully as being more about a certain frame of mind rather than a tangible product or a new technology. An innovative mindset will seek to improve and change in order to increase the value—be it a process, a product or a business model. In an innovative organization, innovation will not be the domain of a department or small group of people but the responsibility of everyone. It must, however, be recognized that innovations, whether small, incremental or radical, almost in all cases require efforts and resources, sometimes substantial in financial terms. Therefore, protection of IPR for all such innovations needs to be a priority so that eventual commercialization can take place.

IPR Issues

Individual and Organizational Research

All intellectual properties get created through skilful utilization of the 'knowledge assets', comprising human intellectual capital—knowledge, information, experience and insight—that reside in individual human beings (individuals), assisted by the 'structural' capital of organizations, namely, work environment and facilities, proprietary software systems, networks and supply chains. In deciding the ownership of IPR of inventions or innovations, the interests of the individual scientists, inventors and innovators must be taken into account along with those of the research organization and organizations that may have been associated in the research efforts. Intellectual inputs in research activities may include previously protected knowledge (background IP), pool of knowledge existing in the public domain, tacit knowledge of the people involved, commercial knowledge of markets and consumers and other 'non-scientific and non-technical' knowledge. A scientist, who worked on his own towards an invention, may apply and be recognized as the owner of an IP. However, when an IP gets created in an organizational domain, the IPR normally rests with the organization (research laboratory, academic institution or company), to which the inventors belong. It is normal practice, however, to get the names of the inventors included in the IP document (for example, the patent), along with the organization named as the applicant and eventual owner of the property. The inventors often get a share or some benefits from financial returns on the eventual commercial utilization of the IP.

Role of IPR in Research Collaboration

With the explosion and complexity of scientific and technical knowledge during the last 50 years, resources needed for production of new knowledge (financial, intellectual or organizational) are, more often than not, too large for a single organization. This is especially true for basic research, the output of which can seldom be translated directly into useful and financially profitable returns without extensive further upgradation, that is, applied R&D. Such research programmes or projects are mostly funded these days by public, government or charitable institutions, and conducted in a collaborative mode in academic, government and commercial bodies. So are many of the upgradation programmes, in which expertise needed is more readily available in universities and research institutions, rather than in the industry or the final utilizing organizations. Intellectual property rights have the essential function of defining relationships between those involved in these interactions, and new IP ground rules that are being established in order to enable the system to work effectively and efficiently, delineating the interests, rights and responsibilities of all the participant organizations and individual scientists.

Output of research work can entail IPR of various kinds—patents and other formal IPRs—and also enhancement of skills and forms of tacit knowledge of the participants. Even those taking part in the research project primarily for financial gains, for example, contract research institutions, will surely look for wider benefits such as increased knowledge and expertise in technological and commercial spheres. Not all the output may be easily translated into marketable products, but it can contribute to the overall capabilities and competencies of the companies, and other collaborating institutions.

Collaboration agreements between participating organizations are generally complex legal documents that may also have to comply with the public funding conditions. The most contentious issues often are regarding the ownership of the rights on the IP that gets generated during the implementation of the programme or project, and sharing of returns due to the eventual commercial exploitation of the same. In most countries, governments tend to be the primary providers of funding for basic and applied research that is conducted mostly in universities and research organizations. Since government funding is from public money, in most countries, including the USA, until 1980, IPR of all inventions emanating out of such research programmes usually rested with the government agency that funded the programme, and transfer and utilization of these inventions were controlled by the concerned government agency.

The situation in USA changed dramatically in December 1980 with the passing of a legislation by the name of Bayh–Dole Act (Patent and Trademark Act) that created a uniform policy among the many federal agencies that fund research. The Act enabled small businesses and non-profit organizations

(NGOs), including universities, to retain the title to the inventions made by them under the federally funded research programmes.

The Bayh–Dole Act was especially instrumental in encouraging universities to participate in technology transfer activities. Prior to the enactment of the Bayh–Dole Act, it was mandatory for institutions to give up the ownership rights of all IP developed through the federally sponsored research programmes in favour of the concerned government agencies. As a result, the US government had accumulated 30,000 patents. Only approximately 5 per cent of those patents were commercially licensed. The enactment of this legislation provided an incentive to the universities to get involved in research programmes that promised creation of IP with commercial potential, take initiatives to market their innovations and persuade the industry to make high-risk investments in collaborative programmes. Subsequent to the Bayh–Dole Act, there has been manifold increase in patent-related activities in US universities and research organizations. Many new inventions, successfully transferred to industry, have contributed to advances in medical, chemical, manufacturing, communication and software industries. Products that revolutionized the world in the last 25 years, such as internet search engines, faster modems, diagnostic tests for breast cancer and osteoporosis, lithium ion batteries used in mobile phones were developed as a result of licensing of university innovations.

Scenario of IP, R&D and Emerging Knowledge Economy in India

Historical Perspective

Historically, awareness of IP in India dates back to 1856, when the first India Patent Act was introduced. The Act was modified and amended in 1911. After independence, a more comprehensive bill on patent rights was enacted in 1970. The 'Patent Act, 1970' was enacted against the background of the country's imminent thrust on transformation from a poor 'agrarian' economy to a planned 'industrial' economy. The emphasis, at that juncture, was on acquisition of technology from the developed world in order to build infrastructure in all sectors of the economy. One fallout of this over-concern was the omission in the 1970 Act of any provision for registering 'product patents'. Instead, 'process patents' were visualized as the primary instruments for protecting IP. Know-how for proven technology products from developed countries was procured and adapted by the Indian industry. In some cases, for example, pharmaceutical products originally developed abroad, process modifications associated with cost reduction and productivity increase were carried out and similar products were manufactured in India. Not only was the awareness about IPR low among the scientific community in the country, but licensing regulations and laws discouraged patent registrations from abroad. Interestingly, patenting activity appeared to have increased at a fairly rapid rate from 1950s until 1970, when the new and weak patent law was implemented and there was a significant immediate fall in patenting, especially in the areas of chemicals, food, rubber and plastic products.

Level of Patenting Activity

The level of patenting activity in India remained low until early 1990s, when India became a member of the World Trade Organization (WTO) following the advent of economic liberalization. The agreement on TRIPS in the WTO necessitated harmonization of the Indian patent and other IP laws with the international standards, and accordingly several new legislations and amendments in the existing laws were enacted by the Parliament of India. These legislations included the Trade Marks Act, 1999; Designs Act, 2000; Copyrights (Amendment) Act, 1999; Geographical Indication of Goods Act, 1999; and Patents Act Amendments in 1994, 1999, 2002 and finally in 2005. The 2005 Patents Amendments included the admissibility of product patents and a host of other provisions that were meant to motivate individual inventors, organizations and firms to seek protection of IPRs. The number of applications for patenting in India, which hovered around a yearly figure of around 3,000 until 1994 (compared with the US figure of 300,000), had since risen to 17,500 in 2004–05. This figure is expected to increase significantly, especially after the 2005 amendment.

Trends in patenting activity over the years in India reflect a low intensity of the R&D work done in the country. The extent of R&D investment at the industry level in India in terms of percentage of sales has remained less than 1.0 for the last 50 years. In contrast, many US industrial firms devoted between 2 and 4 per cent of their turnover to R&D every year. Since 1995, there has been some increase in R&D investments by the manufacturing industry in India, especially in pharmaceutical, biotechnology and chemicals sectors, but the level continues to be way behind the international trends. With the advent of product patents, one would expect further increase in R&D intensity in these and other sectors in manufacturing. A further amendment to the Indian Patent law, incorporating the features of the US Bayh–Dole Act, could enlarge further the scope of industry–academia research partnership.

Funding of R&D

Another significant point of note in the Indian R&D scenario is the extent of participation of the government in R&D activities. The share of public investment has been consistently more than 75 per cent in Indian R&D, compared to hardly 25 per cent by the industry. In developed countries the position in this regard is just the opposite, with industry spend amounting to 70 per cent or more of the total national investment on R&D. Bulk of the public-funded R&D in India is conducted in national laboratories, universities and specialized government agencies relating to space, atomic energy and defence. The commercial potential of the research output or technologies developed in such institutions is uncertain in the short term. The awareness of IPR has been low until recently among the scientists as well as administrators. Quantum of R&D investment vis-à-vis gross national product (GNP) in the country has also been minimal—between 0.7 and 0.8 per cent—in this country, compared with 2.5–4.0 per cent in most of the developed nations. In fact, total national R&D investment in India in 2004–2005 has been estimated to be around Rs 21,640 crore (0.77 per cent of GNP, and equivalent to US $4.4 billion), which is less than the R&D spending by some of the multinational companies (MNCs) on their own. There were at least 12 companies abroad whose R&D budget in 2005 was in excess of $5 billion.

Knowledge Economy

The onset of globalization, advent of WTO and signing of the TRIPS agreement, all of which occurred in the 1990s, have stimulated the Indian economy to transform itself into a knowledge economy in the 21st century. The educational system in this country is gearing up to face the challenges of transformation, pursuing international recognition of excellence in some of the areas of higher education. There are more than 300 universities and 17,000 higher educational institutions producing approximately 3 million graduates, including 350,000 engineers and 200,000 IT professionals, each year. The R&D infrastructure in India boasts of nearly 3,000 scientific and industrial research organizations (SIROs) where more than 100,000 scientists are researching in a variety of scientific and technological fields, including such advanced areas as space research, satellite communications, atomic energy, supercomputing, nano-sciences and oceanography. The intellectual capital available in India has attracted more than 150 multinational companies (MNCs) to set up R&D centres in this country. Patents filed in USA by Indian entities of the MNCs over the last few years number a few thousands. The IT sector alone is likely to employ 2 million people by 2014 and is expected to account for 8–10 per cent of GDP by 2008. There are signs of rapid acceleration in the manufacturing sector also.

In the expanding knowledge economy in India, there is a clear demand for speeding up the process of identification, development, dissemination and uptake of innovations. An effective IPR system can go a long way in this regard. For example, the number of research and industry projects carried out in the engineering colleges and universities in a year as partial fulfilment of requirements for completing undergraduate, postgraduate and doctoral degrees in India is remarkably large and could be around 200,000 or possibly more. Even if only a modest 5 per cent of these projects have innovative ideas that have potential for societal and commercial application, 10,000 patents could come out every year. Similarly, the Indian civilization, which is at least 5,000 years old, has traditional knowledge and grassroots innovative practices, unknown to outside the user circles in rural India. Safeguarding the IPR of these grassroots innovators and traditional knowledge holders would be a first step in the process of bringing them out into the open.

Concluding Remarks

Managing the IPR of innovating individuals and organizations is an integral part of KM where, apart from identification, creation and acquisition, sharing of knowledge is an essential component. Knowledge sharing can happen only in an environment of trust, transparency and equitable distribution of pecuniary benefits, if any. Not long ago, 'knowledge was power' for people to progress in life. But in a knowledge economy, where knowledge is often used as a strategic resource for gaining competitive advantage, sharing and integrating knowledge are also key organizational processes. An efficient, effective and transparent IPR system can help in establishing such an environment. This is particularly relevant for the conversion of tacit knowledge residing with the experts and experienced people in organizations, grassroots innovators and traditional knowledge holders into explicit and documentable variety. A good IPR system will also be a faithful link between the academic freedom of the scientists, researchers and innovators, and their rights and privileges in work environment.

In 2002, President Abdul Kalam unveiled the Vision of India 2020, which called for developing an India that is free from poverty, strong in trade, commerce and S&T, and a nation bustling with energy, innovation and entrepreneurship. There is little doubt that over the last decade or so, India has made significant strides in achieving that vision of becoming a vibrant knowledge society. With the new IPR regime in place, an interactive knowledge management system can be envisioned with involvement of all the participants and stakeholders in the economy.

Bibliography

Dahlman, C. and A. Utz. 2005. *India and the Knowledge Economy.* Washington: World Development Studies, The World Bank.

Department of Science and Technology. 2005. *Science and Development Statistics 2004–05*, NSTMS. New Delhi: Government of India.

Deolalikar, A.M. and Lars-Hendrik. Roller. 1989. 'Patenting by Manufacturing Firms in India', *The Journal of Industrial Economics*, 36(3).

European Commission. 2002. 'Role of IPR in International Research Collaboration', Working Paper, 5th Framework Programme, European Commission, April.

Jaffe, A.B. and M. Traitenburg. 2002. *Patents, Citation and Innovation—A Window on the Knowledge Economy.* Cambridge, MA: MIT Press.

Knowledge Society, www.indianbusiness.nic.in/knowledgesociety/infotec.htm

Leonard, A. 1999. 'A Viable System Model: Consideration of Knowledge Management', *Journal of Knowledge Management Practice*, 8(1).

Malhotra, Y. 2003. 'Measuring Knowledge Assets of a Nation: Knowledge Systems for Development', *Knowledge Management Measurement: State of Research 2003–2004*, UN Advisory Meeting, UN Headquarters, NY, September.

National Innovation Foundation, www.nifindia.org

Swaminathan, K.V. (ed.). 2006. Workshop on Intellectual Property for Technical Institutions—Background Material, Organised by Waterfall Institute of Technology Transfer, Sponsored by AICTE, Ludhiana, March 2006.

15 Research Planning and Management in a Knowledge-intensive R&D Organization: The Case of CSIR-India*

NARESH KUMAR

Introduction

Over the past 60 years or so, India's Council of Scientific and Industrial Research (CSIR) has developed a unique research and development (R&D) management culture which has passed through several critical and defining periods of time. Whether it were the expectations from it in pre-independence India, or of the socialistic India of post-independence, or an India of open economy, it has shown organizational adaptation, survival and competence in the face of increasingly discontinuous environmental change. India's Council of Scientific and Industrial Research of today embodies organizational processes that are a synergistic mix of scientific output, as reflected in its quality research publications, a significant portfolio of registered intellectual property—primarily patents, a large number of new products and processes, a number of collaborative, cutting-edge research projects with globally known companies and the creative and innovative capacity of its scientific work force.

With its 38 national laboratories, CSIR has been occupying the centre stage of most of the scientific and technical endeavours initiated by Indian scientists in various laboratories and in academia. It is also generally recognized that CSIR has been a harbinger of scientific temper in post-independence India and is one among the world's largest publicly funded R&D organizations. India's Council of Scientific and Industrial Research of today is a knowledge-intensive, multi-location, multi-sectoral industrial R&D organization.

It was in September 1942 that CSIR India was formally set up. In the early years of its establishment the emphasis in development initiatives was on industrial development of the country and for that reason CSIR was considered to be an important, rather at that time the only, organization which could help achieve such a goal. Its first governing body (GB), having eminent persons from the government,

*This paper is based substantially on a study presented in the ninth Asia Pacific S&T Management Seminar, Tokyo, Japan, March 2004.

industry and academia as its members, charted for it ambitious plans of establishing research capabilities in all areas of scientific endeavour—a science base which would meet the industrial aspirations of young India. The GB directions led to the setting up, in the first phase, of the National Chemical Laboratory, National Physical Laboratory, National Metallurgical Laboratory, Central Fuel Research Station, Central Glass and Ceramic Research Institute, and so on and several others such as the Central Drug Research Institute, Central Road Research Institute to name a few, later. Ever since their establishment, CSIR laboratories have greatly enriched India's basic research capabilities and also added to several industrially relevant processes and products. A large number of products are a testimony to CSIR's industrial research prowess.

Research Management Practices in CSIR

The R&D management culture in CSIR has passed through several cycles, yet the research programmes have always been guided by well laid-out planning, approvals, management and review procedures.

In the initial years the GB used to consider, accord approvals and thereafter review the progress of research programmes undertaken by the individual laboratories. Discipline-wise research committees assisted the GB in these tasks. In 1951, there were 24 such committees covering a wide range of areas. Later, the newly established laboratories got adequate research facilities and manpower. Advisory boards for individual laboratories were set up which not only looked critically at the research proposals but also helped the laboratory directors in certain executive functions. These advisory boards were later split into executive committees and research advisory councils (RACs), thus creating a much needed demarcation between the executive- and research-related functions in the laboratory.

These committees usually had eminent subject specialists as members who understood the nuances of research planning and management well. All the research proposals were approved by RAC and thereafter the progress was reviewed and mid-course corrections, if needed, were carried out as per the suggestions of RAC. Subsequently the executive committee and the RAC were replaced with the management council (MC) and the research council (RC), respectively, with minor changes in their powers and functions.

In fact in the 1950s and 1960s, CSIR was informally following the well-known Plan, Do, Check and Action (PDCA) cycle for the management of its research projects. The emphasis on research of fundamental nature came later in the 1970s and 1980s. This period could aptly be called the laissez-faire period as projects with long-term objectives were common. Such projects were difficult to route through the PDCA cycle.

Moving further into time, it was realized that with boundaries between various scientific disciplines getting thinner, the need of the hour was to have a closer coordination among various laboratories. This led to CSIR setting up the coordination councils in respective science areas such as Chemical Science Coordination Council, Biological Science Coordination Council and Engineering Research Council. These coordination councils, however, could not achieve much. The primary reason for the failure of these councils was the inability of the member directors to accept a common agenda. The councils were subsequently disbanded.

Concerned as it was, CSIR GB set up, in the year 2001, ad hoc task-specific 'performance appraisal boards' (PABs) to 'check' the performance of each of its 38 laboratories. Members of these PABs were drawn from systems external to CSIR and had the mandate to judge and analyse each laboratory's performance vis-à-vis its peers within/outside India in terms of research standing, industrial relevance and preparedness to face the challenges being posed by other global knowledge-based research organizations. The PAB's iterated the 'check' and 'act' cycles to truly judge all the laboratories in terms of their output and relevance. The PAB's appraisal of each laboratory was 'reviewed' by the CSIR GB, which in one way or the other influenced the flow of grants to non-performing laboratories. The PAB review mechanism has now been institutionalized and the appraisal would take place every three years.

Over the past 60 years CSIR has constantly evolved itself.

CSIR 2001—Vision and Strategy

Ambitious R&D Management

A paradigm shift in CSIR's research management was introduced when CSIR brought about in early 1996 a policy document 'CSIR 2001—Vision and Strategy'. The vision aimed at moving CSIR from an internally driven R&D organization towards a globally competitive, more entrepreneurial and externally guided knowledge-intensive one.

According to this vision, CSIR's earlier organizational structure promoted hierarchies, retarded individual initiatives, enterprise and empowerment of scientists, and lacked instruments for promoting inter- and intra-laboratory coordination. In many cases, the performance 'accountability' and 'ownership' of the laboratory mandate by individual scientists was also found wanting. As a result, market responsiveness was not up to the desired level. For CSIR to compete in the global knowledge marketplace, it needed to restructure itself along virtual corporate lines and processes. It, therefore, led to restructuring of CSIR's central level organizational structure as per Figure 15.1 and the laboratory level as per Figure 15.2.

As a result of this policy, the advisory board and technology advisory boards (TABs) were proposed as new organs in the CSIR structure on the recommendations of the Science Advisory Committee to the Prime Minister with a view that CSIR should have the best of expert advice for programme identification, prioritization and management. The TABs functioned for a few years, served a limited purpose and were disbanded afterwards.

The vision document advocated that at the laboratory level, each laboratory was to be considered as a subsidiary corporate entity. The Director would be the CEO of the laboratory and in place of the Management Council (MC), he would have an executive board to assist him in the management of the affairs of the laboratory. Performance-related accountability, incentives and rewards would be introduced and the laboratories would be accorded autonomy in operations related to and dependent on the extent of their committed output and deliverables— the higher is the growth rate committed and achieved the higher will be the level of independence from head-quarters and the laboratory rewarded suitably. However, this new system was not adopted and the extant system of MC was continued albeit with a number of additional responsibilities assigned to the MCs.

Research councils (RCs) were assigned functional responsibility but without any operational powers and accountability. In order to derive maximum advantage of the high-quality expertise of its membership, the RC was expected to help the laboratory in deriving its vision and direction, and serve as an S&T sounding board for the ideas and programmes of the laboratories. This 'management' at the laboratory level, as per Figure 15.2, ideally fits the PDCA cycle if viewed holistically.

Figure 15.1   CSIR's Present Organizational Structure

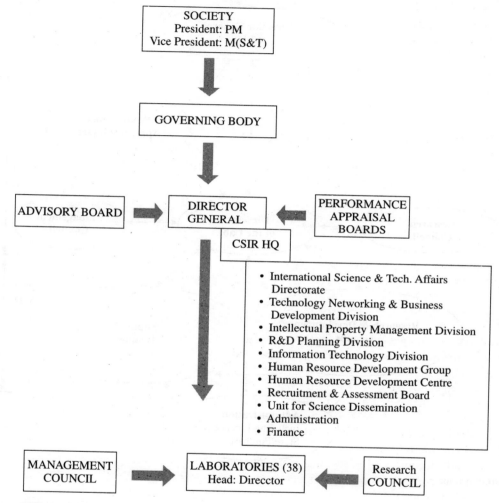

Source: CSIR Annual Reports.

Management through a Structured Planning Process

India has been following a centralized system of planning since 1952 with the formulation of Five Year Plans. Each plan had a particular thrust area of development in the 5-year period. Council of Scientific and Industrial Research too has been following this practice and it charts out its agenda for the 5-year period as also the ways and means to implement the same. For the purpose of this study only the Ninth (1997–2002) and Tenth (2002–2007) Five Year Plans of CSIR are being discussed.

Figure 15.2 Typical Organizational Structure of CSIR Lab

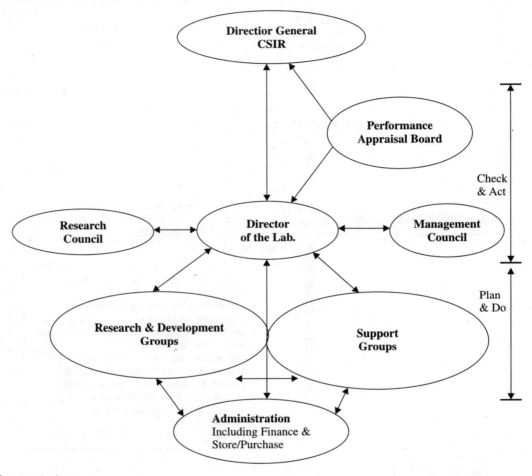

Source: Author.

Ninth Five Year Plan (1997–2002): A Sectoral Approach

For the Ninth Plan period, the Government of India placed emphasis on providing the country with seven identified basic minimum services rather than a single mandate. These services covered inter alia providing safe drinking water, primary health services, universalization of primary education, and so on. Council of Scientific and Industrial Research, on its part, adopted a sectoral approach of development and classified its programmes into 16 broad sectors, namely, aerospace; biology and biotechnology; chemicals; drugs and pharmaceuticals; earth resources and natural hazards mitigation; ecology and environment; electronics and instrumentation; energy; food and food processing; housing and construction; leather; exports of R&D and services.

Under each of the sectoral plans, CSIR's Ninth Plan Working Group broadly recommended major projects, modernization inputs and deliverables in terms of external cash flow, technology development, generation and utilization of new knowledge, and so on. The working group also recommended new schemes on (a) modernization and upgradation of R&D equipment and facilities at national laboratories and (b) intellectual property and technology management.

During this plan period, a major CSIR-coordinated programme on discovery, development and commercialization of new bioactive molecules was initiated in the year 2000. This programme involves networking 20 CSIR laboratories, 12 universities and three systems of medicine, that is, Ayurveda, Siddha and Unani. The bioactive molecules programme aimed at bio-resource collection, processing and evaluation to get leads to the development of new drugs. In 2000–2001, the government assigned CSIR the responsibility to manage and operationalize another programme of immense techno-scientific importance, namely, New Millennium Indian Technology Leadership Initiative (NMITLI). Both these programmes were, in a way, precursors of the current 'network' approach as being practiced in all the CSIR laboratories.

Performance and Review of Ninth Plan

During the period of the Ninth Plan (1997–2002), CSIR provided scientific and industrial R&D of value not only for India's sustained development but also for meeting its strategic needs as well. It spearheaded the formation of a nucleus for a civilian aircraft industry in India, global leadership position in mint oil production, national level efforts to combat malaria, and many more similar initiatives. It was in recognition of its understanding of multi-faceted technology management that CSIR was assigned the responsibility to co-ordinate and manage the activities of New Millennium Indian Technology Leadership Initiative (NMITLI) which seeks to secure for India a global leadership position based on technology. New Millennium Indian Technology Leadership Initiative has so far catalyzed and supported 25 proof-of-concept projects involving 150 R&D institutions and 50 industrial partners in niche areas where India could attain a leadership position. The network programme on bioactive molecules too yielded more than 50 leads for diverse diseases, for example, cancer, ulcer, tuberculosis and immuno-modulation.

Tenth Five Year Plan (2002–2007)

Towards the end of the Ninth Plan, CSIR carried out 'check' and 'act' cycles on its Ninth Plan Agenda ('Plan' and 'Do' cycles) through a SWOT analysis for each laboratory, and in biotechnology, chemicals, drugs and pharmaceuticals, and so on, sectors where CSIR has large interests and stakes. It was apparent from the SWOT exercises that the sectoral approach did not deliver in the Ninth Plan to the extent that was initially expected. Lack of co-ordination among stakeholders was possibly a major reason for under-performance. The CSIR strategy for the Tenth Five Year Plan period was drawn up accordingly on the basis of a careful assessment (check and act) of the needs of and opportunities in the market place in the next 5 years. Based on the opportunities so identified CSIR sought to partner strategically with the Indian industry for:

1. innovative research;
2. application and development of technology;
3. commercialization of technology; and
4. technology transfer.

It is envisaged that this partnership with the industry shall move through a well thought cycle (Figure 15.3) wherein the output of the individual components (plan, do, check and act) of the cycle would be inter- and intra-dependent.

At this point of time, India's Planning Commission sought to bring in the 'network' approach wherein only those new R&D projects would qualify for funding which had a demonstrable network among various CSIR laboratories usually from the same discipline though in a few cases the 'network' partners could be even from other disciplines. This ushered in a new era of carrying out R&D—from small laboratory-centric projects to mega multi-locational, multi-objective projects. Amongst hundreds of projects, most of them being resource thin, CSIR now has 56 networked projects (Figures 15.3 and 15.4).

Network Approach

Managing R&D

Thus, it was only towards the end of the Ninth Plan period that CSIR, on the directions of the Planning Commission, brought in a paradigm shift in the way it was carrying out its R&D programmes. The Planning Commission desired the CSIR to bring in sharp focus, in-depth accountability, greater and cohesive networking, and an overall relevance to national needs in all its research programmes.

As per the new mandate, CSIR identified 56 network projects. These projects were selected from lists of projects identified by the Planning Commission Steering Committee, CSIR's Tenth Plan Working Group and the Core Committee.

For the selection of these projects several brainstorming sessions were held within the laboratories and at the CSIR level. These sessions discussed not only the S&T sectors in which these network programmes would be taken up but also their scientific goals and the resources in terms of manpower and finance required. The planning process for these network projects was debated in a meeting of the participating institutions, the 'do' part was to be carried out in the partner laboratories, the 'check' or review was to be taken up in the regular meetings of the partners and any mid-course correction or 'action' required was to be carried out in the individual laboratories. A three-level system of monitoring has been thus built into the network project system (Figure 15.5) which has not only sharpened the focus but also brought in a great measure of accountability. This model is now in operation. Its results, which would be coming out in the final year (2006–2007) of the current Tenth Plan, would indicate the correctness of this approach.

NMITLI: Paving a Way for PPP-Driven R&D

The NMITLI was launched in the year 2000–2001 with the main objective of catalyzing innovation-centred S&T developments as a vehicle to attain for the Indian industry a global leadership position in

Figure 15.3   CSIR Tenth Five Year Plan

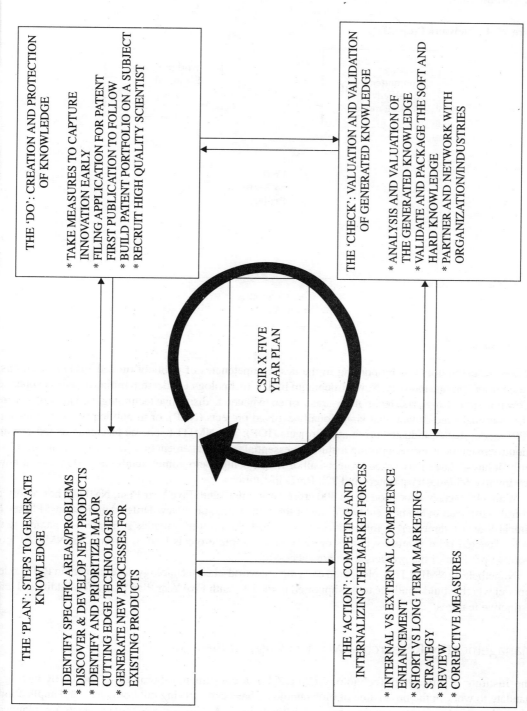

THE 'DO': CREATION AND PROTECTION OF KNOWLEDGE

* TAKE MEASURES TO CAPTURE INNOVATION EARLY
* FILING APPLICATION FOR PATENT
* FIRST PUBLICATION TO FOLLOW
* BUILD PATENT PORTFOLIO ON A SUBJECT
* RECRUIT HIGH QUALITY SCIENTIST

THE 'CHECK': VALUATION AND VALIDATION OF GENERATED KNOWLEDGE

* ANALYSIS AND VALUATION OF THE GENERATED KNOWLEDGE
* VALIDATE AND PACKAGE THE SOFT AND HARD KNOWLEDGE
* PARTNER AND NETWORK WITH ORGANIZATION/INDUSTRIES

CSIR X FIVE YEAR PLAN

THE 'PLAN': STEPS TO GENERATE KNOWLEDGE

* IDENTIFY SPECIFIC AREAS/PROBLEMS
* DISCOVER & DEVELOP NEW PRODUCTS
* IDENTIFY AND PRIORITIZE MAJOR CUTTING EDGE TECHNOLOGIES
* GENERATE NEW PROCESSES FOR EXISTING PRODUCTS

THE 'ACTION': COMPETING AND INTERNALIZING THE MARKET FORCES

* INTERNAL VS EXTERNAL COMPETENCE ENHANCEMENT
* SHORT VS LONG TERM MARKETING STRATEGY
* REVIEW
* CORRECTIVE MEASURES

Source: Author.

Figure 15.4 Network Projects

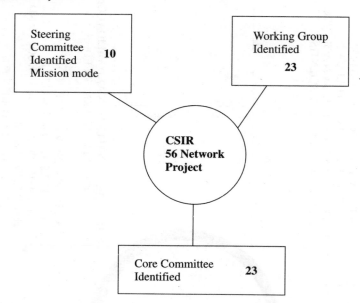

Source: Author.

selected research domains by pooling in the best competencies of publicly funded R&D institutions, academia and private industry. New Millennium Indian Technology Leadership Initiative seeks to operate in low investment-high risk technology areas, often to generate disruptive technologies. The projects are either national need driven, that is, nationally evolved projects (NEP), or in public private partnership (PPP) mode, that is, industry-originated projects (IOP). The NMITLI scheme has also created certain unique management and monitoring features so essential for management in a knowledge economy. Currently, it has 42 large networked projects, all of which being socio-commercially important. As of now they involve 65 industry partners and 222 R&D institutions.

With a budgetary allocation of Rs 300 crore during the Tenth Five Year Plan, NMITLI has reported several significant outcomes, such as filing of three Investigational New Drugs Applications; Phase III clinical trials on three herbal formulations; five world-class bio-informatics software—to name a few. As is expected from venture schemes of such nature, some projects lead to failures. In NMITLI too, about 40 per cent of the projects were not successful.

Nonetheless, NMITLI has pioneered carrying out world-class technology development in PPP mode, a model which would continue to be supported in the Eleventh Five Year Plan with a few additional and distinctive features.

Management of Research—IMTECH Case Studies

The Institute of Microbial Technology (IMTECH), a constituent laboratory of the CSIR having a mandate to work in the broad area of biotechnology, has been carrying out both basic and application-oriented research projects ever since its establishment in 1984. A majority of these projects are 'planned'

Figure 15.5   Networked R&D Project Management

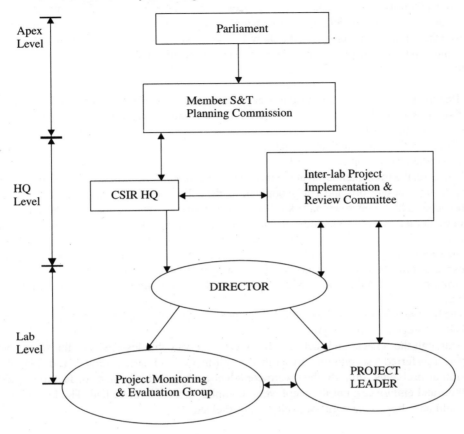

Source: Author.

in-house, carried out or 'done' in-house and 'checked' or reviewed in-house by the RC who may, if needed, introduce or suggest mid-course corrections. Some of these technologically relevant projects are a good model for case studies on R&D and technology management. The outcome of these studies provided a good feedback while planning new projects. In this chapter, two case studies are presented—one that was a failure but offered good lessons in technology management and the other, a successful one, which is now a role model for management of industrially exciting projects in a network mode.

Case Study I

An in-house project initiated to develop a cost-effective process for the production of urokinase—a thrombolytic enzyme—was identified for transfer of technology at laboratory scale. The project seemed to be imminently doable and a few industrial users approached the institute for technology licensing. The technology was licensed jointly to M/s Unichem Laboratories and Finowel Enzymes at laboratory scale

(50 litre). Apart from some commonly available consumables, the only requirement of this project was continuous availability of male urine. For the process to be economically viable, a minimum of 10,000 l/day of urine was required which, upon processing, would yield sufficient quantity of crude urokinase. Teams from these industries were given the show-how at the laboratory level for implementation on commercial scale. However, the process could never be commercialized. Reasons for failure were analyzed as follows:

1. 'Planning' of the process was right because urokinase is needed as a thrombolytic.
2. To carry out or 'do' the process was easy at the laboratory level as it needed a minimum of consumables and hardware.
3. 'Check' or the review indicated that the crude urokinase obtained had appropriate specific activity as per the pharmacopial standard.
4. However, the implementation at the industrial level failed. The reason for this failure was that in spite of the best efforts and a huge population, the collection of urine became a problem—a huge bottleneck. Major internationally known non-governmental organizations (NGOs), namely, Sulabh International, a large civic body; Brihan Mumbai Municipal Corporation; large industrial units; Unichem Ltd and Godrej Ltd, either demanded a huge amount of money to supply urinals, or the workers of the industrial units refused to use the specially fitted urinals or the units themselves expressed their inability to change their existing urine disposal systems.
5. Urine passing through the public toilets had a lot of inhibitors which affected the urokinase quality.
6. The licensee lost money, the institute lost a potential source of recurring revenue and the country had to forego a useful enzyme.
7. Although the 'check' and 'act' did throw up some valuable lessons, still the same know-how was transferred a second time to another user, M/s Cadila Pharmaceuticals Ltd, who also faced similar problems. Initially they were confident as they had a number of factories and several thousand employees, but the employees' compliance could not be had. The know-how, which could have been successful, was ultimately shelved.

This experience gave the institute an important lesson in R&D/technology management, that is, ultimately it is the network partners' stake which determines the success of networking. In this case although the know-how was simple and doable, the attitude of an NGO, a civic body and factory workers was unhelpful, for they had no stake in the product. While formulating proposals for the Tenth Five Year Plan, this lesson was kept in mind as an important element of R&D planning and management. In all the 56 network programmes and the bioactive molecules programme, every partner understood and agreed to the purpose of the programmes.

Case Study II

India is the largest producer of ethanol (ethyl alcohol) from cane molasses having an annual production of more than 3 billion litre and the requirement of the alcochem industries based on alcohol is ever increasing. One of the preferred ways to increase the production of ethanol from molasses is to have a more efficient strain of yeast. The institute's scientists have been regularly improving—genetically or through selection—such strains of yeast which increase the conversion of molasses to ethanol. In this case, immediately after the laboratory-scale work was successfully carried out it was realized that this technology can only be transferred when proven on the industrial scale, for which the institute did not have the capability. And even for industrial-scale trials the institute needed to fine-tune the laboratory-scale technology parameters at 4 kilolitre (KL) scale level. This led to the institute tying up with two institutions, one for 4 KL trials and the other for scaling up the 4 KL scale results to commercial levels. A tie-up with a sister laboratory, Regional Research Laboratory, Jammu, was sought for the 4 KL pilot-scale technology and another tie-up with India's largest producer of potable alcohol, M/s McDowell and Company, led to successful trials at factory scale with the help of McDowell's technical team at Shertally in Kerala. The end result was immediate signing of licensing agreements with five distilleries of the McDowell group itself. A critical factor for the success of this valuable experience was networking. In this case the 'planning' of the appropriate process, the 'doing' on pilot scale, the 'checking' or review of institute's lack of facilities for pilot and factory scales and the 'action' on time of tying up with a sister laboratory and an end user, formed a good example of appropriate R&D management which ultimately led to the commercial success of the R&D project. Networking established in this case was later used to sign technology licensing deals with three more distilleries.

Lessons drawn from both these case studies, reported briefly, were valuable in the management of R&D-based laboratory-generated technologies. Projects taken up in the Ninth Plan were not only in sectoral mode but also stand-alone ones with not much interface or involvement of end users or other stakeholders. While planning for the Tenth Five Year Plan, importance of networking and constant use of PDCA cycle or Deming cycle in the overall project execution were all apparent.

Networking has now been made an integral part of R&D, and technology management in the whole of CSIR. Council of Scientific and Industrial Research realizes that dynamically responsive organizations like itself have to renew themselves through strategic system modifications from time to time. Networking as a tool is perhaps the best management tool in the present times.

Conclusions

Managing R&D processes has changed over the years, moving from the earlier technology-centred model to an interaction and network-based one. And for bringing in the change, dynamically responsive, knowledge-driven research organizations like CSIR have to renew themselves periodically through strategic system modifications. With this realization, CSIR restructured its research programmes from individual or sectoral approaches to 'network' approach. This change not only ensured proper 'planning', facile 'working/doing', appropriate 'checking/review' and fast 'action' but also led to appropriate resource utilization. The programmes initiated in the beginning of the Tenth Plan have already started yielding dividend through a more focused approach, appropriate resource utilization and identification of end users early enough in the whole R&D management cycle.

Bibliography

Council of Scientific & Industrial Research. 2001. *Tenth Five Year Plan of CSIR*. New Delhi: Council of Scientific & Industrial Research.

Council of Scientific & Industrial Research. 1996. *Ninth Five Year Plan of CSIR*. New Delhi: Council of Scientific & Industrial Research.

———. 1996. *CSIR 2001: Vision & Strategy*. New Delhi: Council of Scientific & Industrial Research.

———. *Annual Reports*, 2001–2002 and 2002–2003. New Delhi: Council of Scientific & Industrial Research.

———. 2001. *Performance Appraisal Board—Constitution & Functions*.

H.R. Bhojwani (Emeritus Scientist). *Personal Communication*, (IPMD), Council of Scientific & Industrial Research.

Government of India. 2004. *India 2004: A Reference Annual*. New Delhi: Publications Division, Ministry of Information and Broadcasting, Government of India.

Rajagopal, N.R., M.A. Qureshi and B. Singh. 1991. *The CSIR Saga*. New Delhi: Publications and Information Directorate.

Rao, D.Y. 2006. 'A Review of "NMITLI"', presented at an internal meeting of CSIR, August.

16 Strategy and Structure in the Knowledge Enterprise

ARUN P. SINHA

Introduction

Knowledge enterprises have a mission primarily to create and deliver knowledge to customers. Their services can range from simple and routine to the highly complex. Call centres constitute the simplest end of the continuum. Business process outsourcing or BPO services use information technology (IT) to cater to other enterprises. They are only a little more involved than call centres, with the simplest financial accounting and share registry to more involved advertising and marketing research in the business to business (B2B) sector. Software companies that design and write software for various applications—including those for the BPOs and call centres—are the most archetypical knowledge enterprises. Whether it is the business domain, the engineering design application, software embedded in industrial controls or software for gaming consoles, there is a knowledge enterprise that builds software for it.

Most non-routine knowledge applications are those dealing in research and development (R&D) for an external client with the support of IT. The essence of such R&D assignments is that they are small modules and IT is inherent in their design. They lead to knowledge elements that can be re-used in multiple future assignments, due to synergy and economies of scale. Such business is referred to as knowledge process outsourcing (KPO).

Besides all this, knowledge-enterprise-like conditions may also involve a physical product. Due to the high rate of utilization of knowledge and its rapid obsolescence, resulting in service-like market conditions like in mobiles, digital cameras and in many industrial products with embedded software, the distinction between knowledge-related services and a pure service is blurred. In such enterprises, and in all those described above, knowledge is a major driver of competitiveness.

What are the features of such organizations? What are the key features of the strategies that such organizations can employ to ensure success, as different from product-based ones? What are the salient features of the structures that can aid their achievement of goals? These are issues the present chapter deals with. The effort here is to sketch just one link in a chain of future efforts that may be made, that will help develop a framework for understanding the knowledge enterprise.

The Knowledge Enterprise 'Ecosystem'

The overall ecosystem of the knowledge enterprise consists mainly of the buyers, business stakeholders and technology suppliers (Figure 16.1). Of course, there is the larger environment of laws and government regulation, and the broad political environment in which the international trade functions.

Buyers and users are two critical and distinct aspects. For many enterprises, it is the end user customer rather than the buyer, who is more relevant. Knowledge process outsourcing (KPO) firms, for instance, have assignments from a wide range of consultants. In the investment domain, the end user may be an individual or a mutual fund that needs the advice of the consultant, who in turn seeks a specific set of data or analytics that the KPO can provide.

A key business stakeholder, other than founders, is a venture capital entity, especially in the early stage of a knowledge enterprise. The search for business stakeholders is an ongoing concern in the life of such an enterprise. Unlike others in the economic landscape, many of the knowledge enterprises are meant for acquisition by design. The founders make conscious efforts to make them saleable.

Figure 16.1 Ecosystem of Knowledge Enterprise

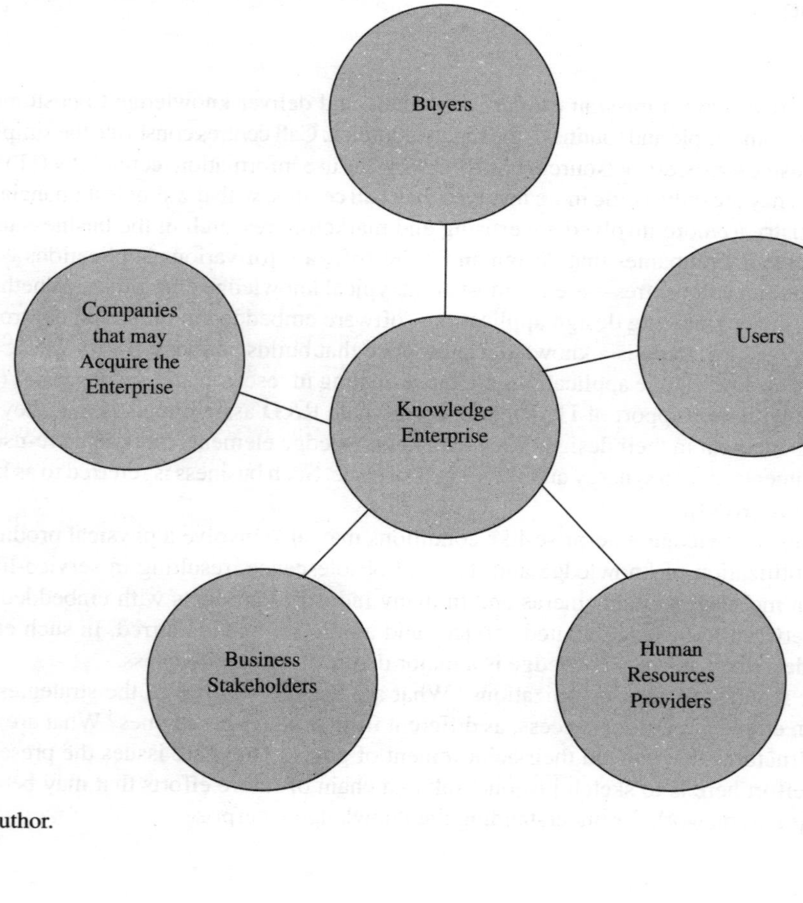

Source: Author.

Strategic Issues

Unique Strategic Challenges

Under such an ecosystem, the knowledge enterprise faces unique challenges to build a viable strategy:

1. Risk and uncertainty: Very often, the enterprise works on technology that is still to work out. Others work simultaneously on competing concepts. Which technology will work out is uncertain. It is also unclear whether buyers/users will accept it and how fast the market will grow. In many enterprises, the initial success may be fine but the overall potential of the market may be severely limited.
2. Proprietary technology: Unlike in most other sectors, the technology in a knowledge enterprise is developed within or obtained along with a merger or acquisition. Sometimes, the technology may be co-operatively developed by competitors who work on independent parts.
3. Low entry barriers: Even entrepreneurial ventures can easily enter an industry. Many of the real challengers to an existing successful enterprise come from the 'garage', 'apple' and 'google', for example.
4. Learning curve effect: There is a rapid decline in the price of knowledge products.
5. First-time users: Buyers for many knowledge enterprises are first-time users. So, the marketing task is to induce customers to overcome product concerns and buy.

Typical Strategic Moves

Some of the commonest and most well-tested moves relate to getting 'fast to the market'. When the market is already competitive, a key strategy for competition, especially in business-to-consumer (B2C), is to differentiate on features or technology, whether it is a search engine, word-processing software or CAD software.

'Consumer trial' is one natural path to build positive attitudes about a product. While being the first mover is advantageous, the customer often waits for the next generation product, so the company must always continue to 'upgrade the technology' and add features.

'Alliance' with key suppliers or with those having related or complementary skills will lead the company to new skills, capabilities and resources.

Important Features of Structure and Process

Comparing organizations in the conventional and the knowledge economies, one would find critical differences in structure and process:

1. *Less barriers across the structure*: Even a casual comparison of knowledge enterprises with conventional ones shows that there are much less barriers among

    (*i*)   different vertical ranks;
    (*ii*)   functions and disciplines;
    (*iii*)   units in different geographic locations; and
    (*iv*)   the company, its suppliers, distributors, strategic allies and customers.

2. More collaboration: Across all the above dividing lines, the knowledge enterprise is able to have a lot more of collaboration.
3. Capacity for change and rapid learning: Mainly due to the above, the knowledge enterprise is capable of fast changes. It must and does learn frequently and fast.

Discussion

In view of the largely unique strategic and competitive environment, the knowledge enterprise finds it essential to deal with rapid changes in customer needs and with fast emergence of new technologies. Being first to the market is always a good *mantra*. Yet the strategic landscape is filled with players who do the opposite as well. They acquire technologies, along with the start-ups which create them, only when it has achieved a stable and dominant position. Their margins would have declined substantially by then. So, the acquisition would be meaningful only if the company can tap a large market potential.

The larger landscape of knowledge enterprises includes those offering routine services like call centres and BPOs. Leaving these apart, the ecosystem of more complex enterprises is populated by four 'ideal-types' as displayed in Table 16.1.

Each of these four types adopts a distinct combination of strategy, structure and key tasks as follows:

1. A technology development player makes it a habit of creating new technologies and selling them off to others who can exploit them further. These players are mostly small entities and function as entrepreneurial organizations. They operate around a founder and his associates without the trappings of so-called professional management. Their key task is to find new business opportunities and new technological possibilities, and to create innovations.
2. A technology acquirer enters a field when a particular technology has reached some success and dominance. It acquires the technology and often the venture itself. It plays on volumes with somewhat less margins. Its key task is to scan for entities ripe for acquisition, negotiate acquisition and ensure a smooth integration of cultures.
3. A utilizer is an entrepreneurial venture that limits itself to growing on one or a few successful technologies that it created. The entrepreneur does not wish to create any more new technologies. It hopes to grow with its current business which appears to have a large market potential. The company uses a slowly declining pricing strategy, continues to do focused incremental R&D in the same business and develops new applications for related markets.

Table 16.1   Strategy and Structure in the Ecosystem of Knowledge Enterprises

	Technology development player	Technology acquirer	Utilizer	Vendor/implementer
Structure	Entrepreneurial	Professional-Divisionalized	Functional	Professional- Matrix
Role of Founder	Vital	May not be there	Continue	Not necessary
Size	Very Small	Large	Medium	Very Large
Key Tasks	—Find new opportunity of business through IT Create New Innovations.	—Scan for acquisition Negotiate Integrate Cultures.	Find new markets and applications.	High-quality coding Project management HR management.
Strategy	Create innovations on the strength of founder and associates. Sell to larger firm.	Locate promising technologies/start ups. Acquire through financial strength. Operate service at high efficiency.	Find new applications and markets and improvements. Use familiarity with the product as strength. Improve cost on learning curve.	Use skills of operating at low cost. Use efficient project management strengths.

Source: Author.

4. Vendors and implementers are arbitrage players. They take outsourced work from worldwide makers of products and services, and from consultants that provide IT services and install IT infrastructure in organizations. Their key task is to maintain a steady supply of IT professionals and provide efficient and high-quality programming. Their management processes have to emphasize project management skills.

Bibliography

Collins, J.D. and M. Hitt. 2006. 'Leveraging Tacit Knowledge in Alliances', *Journal of Engineering and Technology Management*, September, pp. 147–67.

Karlsson, M. 2006. *The Internationalization of Corporate R&D*. Stockholm: Swedish Institute of Policy & Research.

Kimbrough, S. and F. Murphy. 2005. 'A Study of Philadelphia Knowledge Economy', *Interfaces*, May–June.

Ravishanker, M.N. and S.L. Pan. 2006. 'The Influence of Organizational Identification on Organizational Knowledge Management', *Omega*, pp. 221–34.

17 Expectations of the SME Sector from Knowledge Economy

K.K. Sarkar

Wisdom is a weapon to ward off destruction;
It is an inner fortress which enemies cannot destroy.
—*Thirukkural 421* (200 BC)
(Abdul Kalam 2003)

Introduction

To survive and succeed in the fast-moving competitive economic and business environment, industrial enterprises and service organizations or service providers, whether large or small, need to use knowledge, skills and ideas. Creativity and innovation are *sine qua non* in the current commercial scenario of globalization, rapid technological change and intense competition.

Therefore, the issue of knowledge and innovation is important to India in all the sectors, and this issue is equally a global one. Only that country whose economy is knowledge based and innovative, bringing in, ahead of others, new products, devices, methods and systems, will lead the world.

Importance of Knowledge

The knowledge of human beings has been termed as human capital and it is their asset. The expression 'knowledge' and joint expression 'knowledge economy' are not new terms. Knowledge has always been the pivotal force in the economy, whether old or new, or whether transiting from old economy to the new economy. All individuals and organizations use knowledge for their production processes, development and expansion. The emerging era is a knowledge era where knowledge will be the most critical and important driver of growth and, as such, it has to be given due importance. For the economy to function and grow in a healthy manner, there is a need for a system for harnessing knowledge and promoting its application in various segments of the economy including service sector, educational sector, healthcare sector, and so on.

In the knowledge era, industry and service organizations, particularly in the small and medium enterprises (SMEs) sector are facing stiff competition.

Application of Knowledge in the SME Sector

New Concept and Definition of SMEs

It may be mentioned here that recently legislation has been passed by the Parliament in relation to small-scale industries, introducing the concept of 'enterprise' as against 'industry' and defining micro, small and medium enterprises (Government of India 2006). Small and medium enterprises are important in view of the significant role they can play in promoting inclusive growth through expansion of opportunities of productive, sustainable and widely dispersed employment at competitively low per capita costs. In order to make SMEs effective in this role, there is a need for the diffusion of new knowledge for technology upgradation at the enterprise level. A large number of SMEs are currently 'unregistered' and are thus in the unorganized sector. As such, units in this vast unorganized sector should have access to knowledge, invention and innovation, enabling them to update their technology, products and services.

Approach Paper for Eleventh Plan

The draft approach paper for the 11th Plan focuses on faster and inclusive growth of the economy (Planning Commission 2006). Therefore, in any plan or project for development, attempts should be made to overcome the knowledge gap and/or information gap of the unorganized sector as well. Of late, under the aegis of the Planning Commission, a Working Group for Micro and Small Scale Enterprises and Agro and Rural Industries for the 11th 5-year Plan 2007–2012 has been set up and one of its objectives is to review the existing research and development (R&D) institutions and suggest measures for their reorganization, revitalization and linkages with counterpart/corresponding R&D establishments in defence, electronics, material sciences, nanotechnology, and so on, on the one hand, and universities, colleges, Indian Institutes of Technology (IITs), Technology Information Forecasting and Assessment Council (TIFAC), and so on, on the other.

Training Institutions

For the benefit of the unorganized sector and for updating the knowledge of its workers, there is an urgent need to expand and renovate the Industrial Training Institutes (ITIs) located in various states, and to improve their curriculum to make it more compatible with the products and skill needs of the unorganized sector. Alongside, there is a need for retraining of the faculty/instructors of the ITIs. At present, ITIs are providing training in 84 trades. Training in some of these trades may have to be discontinued and some new trades may have to be taken up in order to cater to the needs of the knowledge economy.

Again there is a mushroom growth of training institutions, many of which are not up to the mark for the delivery of appropriate training. They may be deficient in terms of infrastructure, curriculum, pedagogy, instructors and evaluation procedures. As such, there is a need for accreditation of training institutions and certification of the knowledge persons, that is, instructors. All such institutions should be equipped with connectivity and R&D organizations so that being at the delivery point of knowledge they can deliver and/or disseminate information regarding new inventions, products and designs, enabling the unorganized sector to remain competitive in the domestic as well as international markets.

Support Systems

Ministry of SSI

For responding to the needs of small industries, the Ministry of Small Scale Industries (SSI), Government of India, has come out with a set of strategies for the small-scale sector, for example, cluster development, technology upgradation under capital-linked subsidy scheme, and many other facilities. Such policy support from the government is vital. Encouraged by the support of the government, SMEs, even without direct help or guidance from the government, are going in for product innovation on their own. Their initiatives on innovation provide ample evidence of the creative potential of workers in the SMEs.

Field Organizations

The Small Industries Development Organization (SIDO), Ministry of SSI, Government of India, has regional testing centres, field testing stations, production centres, tool room/tool designing institutes, product-cum-process development centres, central footwear training institutes and entrepreneurship development training institutes. Further, there are small industries service institutes in all the states. However, regarding the working of such institutes, there is an emergent need for their development and modernization to make them more contemporaneous and research-oriented to cater to the growing needs of the unorganized sector.

Areas of Development

Intellectual Property

The creative element in the output of the SME sector also can be regarded as intellectual property and is, therefore, a subject matter of intellectual copyright, as a specific expression of an idea and not the idea itself. Therefore, there is a need to protect their interests under the intellectual property right (IPR) so that there is no infringement. But unfortunately, units in the SME sector are not aware of the mechanisms and methodology of protecting their rights. As such, their creations are being copied and their market is being taken away by those who have better technology for producing the same type of products. Therefore, there is an emergent need to sensitize and educate the SME sector on this issue. The issue has become so important that IIT, Kharagpur, has introduced a specific programme on IPR. A large initiative on awareness development in the SME sector on IPR is called for.

Knowledge/Information Gap in SME Sector

Units in the SME sector are not aware or rather they are not kept informed about the new developments in technology, inventions, design, and so on. Most of them are also not conversant with the facilities and opportunities available through information technology (IT) and are, therefore, unable to derive the benefit of e-business or e-commerce. As such, there is a need for the penetration of internet in the SME sector and introduction of the revolution of e-business so that the SME sector can derive its benefits. There is a need for re-defining the road map of the development of the SME sector by either developing specific clusters existing in rural, semi-urban and urban areas or relocating them in a cluster of allied products, be they of arts and crafts, village industry products, leather and leather goods, gems and jewellery, food processing, foundry, machine tools, or any other.

Defence Production

People working in the small and informal/SME sector can be creative though they may not be equipped with formal education. They have imagination and initiative. When the defence establishments develop indigenous designs to meet the requirements of components for export substitution, it would be befitting if the defence establishments utilize the ingenuity of the small component manufacturing units by giving them support by way of designs with appropriate raw materials. Defence establishments will benefit by enlarging their supply base. Since SMEs are deficient in resources and outreach, defence establishments need to be relatively more proactive. While the small units will be helping the country by providing inputs for import substitution, they will also be adding to the growth of exports. In the process, the country will achieve a wider spread of entrepreneurship and employment.

Nodal Agency

Small and tiny units cannot by themselves have access to knowledge, innovations and research; so there must be a nodal agency to store information on innovations, designs and products for dissemination to interested units. Such an agency can best be set up by the Small and Tiny Industries Associations. All such accredited associations should have incubation centres having connectivity with IITs, IIMs and other relevant institutions.

Conclusions

There is an ancient Indian saying, '*Viddattanchya, nripatancha, noibongtulla kadachana; swadeshe pujyate raja, vidyan sarbatra pujyate; jyantirbhi bantyate noibo chore naapin niyate; daane noibo kshyang jaati vidyaratna mahadhanam*'(The scholar is never comparable with emperors. While the former is worshipped within his own territories, the latter, that is, the scholar is revered beyond bounds. The scholar's property, that is, knowledge can neither be parted with among his kin nor stolen and decayed through preaching/teaching. So the knowledge is considered as the most invaluable and priceless acquisition of scholars.). Here we observe: Knowledge is Power, knowledge is for distribution and dissemination; knowledge may be creative or destructive. Knowledge is not destroyed; it is transmuted and recreated in another form. Knowledge is, therefore, indestructible and supreme.

Knowledge does not make any distinction between the rich and the poor; all can be benefited by it. While the rich can be richer, the poor should not be poorer in a knowledge economy. The disparity between the rich and the poor should be diminished.

Knowledge should be utilized for creation of new and better products and services and employment opportunities. It should find applications in labour-intensive organizations which are employment oriented and need to improve productivity and incomes of its workers.

In the interest of small units, there is a need to protect their IPR. Also, knowledge should be made accessible to small units. In this direction, a beginning has been made by the Government of India by implementing the scheme of Gramin Tathya Prajukti Kendra (Rural Information Technology Centres), so that access to knowledge is provided in the rural areas.

References

Abdul Kalam, A.P.J. 2003. *Ignited Minds: Unleashing the Power Within India.* New Delhi: Penguin India.
Government of India. 2006. The Micro, Small and Medium Enterprises Development Act, 2006.
Planning Commission. 2006. *Towards Faster and More Inclusive Growth.* An Approach to the 11th Five Year Plan, Planning Commission, Government of India, November, 2006.

18 New Public Management in the Emerging Knowledge Economy

T.S. Krishna Murthy

Introduction

The present era can be characterized as fast changing and challenging. No doubt, human race has witnessed innumerable changes and challenges from time to time. However, the pace of change and the intensity of challenge differ vastly from one era to another because of the complexities of changing times. These challenging changes make life exciting and sometimes confusing. Today, the two important challenges facing many countries are (*a*) appalling poverty which is deepening social inequalities/tensions and (*b*) promotion and protection of democracy from terrorism and violence, which is essential for freedom, equality and social justice so as to check any arbitrary rule. In most emerging democracies, standards of governance are disturbingly low notwithstanding economic growth. What is more, the standards of governance in fighting these twin challenges are deteriorating because of negligence and indifference of public administrators on the one hand, and ever-increasing explosion in government expenditure on administration, on the other. Inevitably, this daunting challenge amidst dynamic changes can be met successfully only if reforms in public administration are urgently addressed to improve the quality of governance. Countries that fail in this mission run the risk of losing both development and freedom, and eventually people's faith in democracy. Such a consequence is a direct invitation for violence and revolution. Already, there are signs of the same in terrorism and violent revolutions at least in some regions of the world.

Concept of New Public Management

Governance

In such rather disturbingly confusing conditions, the field of public administration has of late been the subject of intense debate and discussion about a new approach styled as the 'new public management'.

The concept of new public management indeed emerged as an effective answer to improve governance. Its need was increasingly felt and sought even in developed economies especially in New Zealand and UK. In the US, it was known by a different expression, that is, 'reinventing management'. The champions of new public management argue that the present-day pressing problems demand a significant change in the style of governance. The new public management should be with a human face and efficacy challenging, and overriding traditional and historical concepts of public administration of the bygone era. The proponents of this concept are of the view that greater emphasis on quality performance with stress on social justice and humane approach would be the most important ingredient of the new public management. According to them, ideas of Max Weber of centralized bureaucratic structures in which the rules, regulations and laws are faithfully invoked and implemented in delivering public services with ruthless emphasis on procedural compliance cannot and should not work any longer (Weber 1947). Perhaps this was what Alvin Toffler had in mind when in his book entitled *Future Shock* he referred with foresight to the gradual withering of the traditional bureaucracy and its replacement by specialists, technologists and scientists (Toffler, 1970). In the present ever-changing global scenario, generated by changes in politics, economics, technology, science, social structures and leadership styles, the governments have started realizing that they cannot survive hereafter with antiquated procedures and policies without reference to human feelings and sentiments.

Accountability

Thanks to the progress in education, the citizens of today have started demanding, rightly and vociferously, accountability in governance, thereby putting tremendous pressure on public servants, both civil servants and politicians. Right to information, now being widely accepted, has indeed strengthened the momentum towards public control and scrutiny over public administration. Added to this, is the increasing competition among political parties to deliver public services or goodies to the vote banks not often necessarily for social good but with an eye on the elections. An offshoot of this is the unhealthy culture of subsidies and gifts of various kinds ranging from consumer goods to cash payments without any matching productivity or any substantial contribution to economic growth. People have increasingly started realizing the strength of their power of votes albeit rather slowly and often for wrong reasons. The might of the ballot over bullet is also being increasingly understood and felt by the citizenry. Further, a number of non-governmental organizations (NGOs) have of late come into existence with an increasing demand for transparency and accountability in public administration and public life. Today no one will argue that bad governance is tolerable or acceptable; on the other hand, people demand good governance with transparency and efficiency. Alongside democratization, a popular though silent movement for good governance has indeed begun.

In the light of these new demands, many proponents of the new public management are 'convinced that the appearance of... entrepreneurial organizations in the late twentieth century is no accident. We believe that it represents an inevitable historical shift from one paradigm to another' (Osborne and Plastrik 1997). This sense of inevitability, in turn, has led to the inference that governments around the world have converged on the principles of the new public management because they are useful in virtually any political setting, geographic region or policy area (Caiden 1991; Osborne and Plastrik 1997).

New Approach

Thus, the new public management is claimed to have emerged as a universal new paradigm warranting change in management style and strategy with emphasis on effective problem-solving techniques. The quick fix method of crisis-fighting for finding an immediate but temporary solution has become obsolete as it cannot solve problems effectively on a long-term basis. This short-term solution approach is known as 'discontinuous change'. The short-term solution is sought when a crisis prompts managers to compromise on established concepts and practices in favour of new ones to temporarily solve pressing problems. Some scholars of public administration refer to 'discontinuous change' as reform by roots while the alternative strategy is referred to as 'incremental' or 'branching' reform which occurs when managers refer to historical precedents and practices, and apply them to take appropriate decisions with reference to particular problems. The new public management, however, can be said to be neither a distinct paradigm nor an incremental change. It encompasses varied concepts and practices, often pragmatic, flexible and cost effective, so as to achieve global convergence in good governance techniques. The new public management is based on managerial discretion, customer satisfaction, cross-functional collaboration, emphasis on market mechanism, and so on. Decentralization, accountability and transparency with responsive but responsible policy-making roles for both civil servants and citizens are emphasized.

Of late, civil services tend to be too large, too expensive and often inadequately productive in the context of increasing functions assumed by governments for developmental work. Added to these is the increasing corruption in civil services in such countries exploiting ignorance and illiteracy of the people especially in developing democracies. Lewis Preston in his foreword in a recent World Bank publication *Governance and Development* rightly observed, 'Efficient and accountable management by the public sector and a predictable and transparent policy framework are critical to the efficiency of markets and governments and hence to economic development' (Lewis Preston 1992). In this background, recent efforts to reform public administration in developing countries, especially within the core civil services, have received wide attention both from the academia and governments themselves.

Increasing inability of present-day civil services to carry out critical developmental functions of the government in complex international economic environment is frequently noticed and has been increasingly criticized. This growing concern for containing the size and improving the performance of the civil service signifies a re-dimensioning and re-defining of the role of the state reflecting a fundamental shift in the direction of economic development policy. This is perhaps the reason that some leaders opined, although in a different context, that the government is best if it governs the least. Indeed the new wisdom seems to be to 'manage less—but better'. Disillusionment with centralized control of civil service management often linked with corruption is indeed the direct cause of the triggering of this new approach. The US Government Performance Results Act is an indication of the new approach (US President's Office, 1993). This emphasis on pragmatic performance is viewed by some as a complete departure from the past approaches in public administration.

Role of Knowledge

Although a debate goes on as to whether the new public management is a new paradigm different from the past principles and practices or an incremental evolution of global practices. What is important to recognize now is that the growing emphasis on democracy and development, two seemingly contradictory goals in the context of the recent developments relating to knowledge management (KM) in a global scenario, calls for giving a totally new orientation even to the new public management. Operation of international market forces and free flow of capital between nations have necessitated a larger regulatory role for the government with knowledge and economic growth getting interlinked. 'Knowledge is power' is the new *mantra*—new buzzword—in fact, a new armour in the arsenal of power, if a country is to dictate and dominate in international politics and economic relations. The growth of and interest in KM has been the most magnificent and significant development in recent times. Rightly, it has been recognized that the knowledge economy is an emerging star in the global political firmament. New public management has to fine-tune itself if public administration has to survive in this new order based on knowledge power.

Just as the aspirations of the people increase in this knowledge-oriented society, there is a rising feeling of dissatisfaction and frustration in the world today, particularly among young people. There is a burning desire amongst many of them to upset the existing order and to seek something more acceptable from the point of view of public satisfaction and public good. There is indeed an insatiable and strong urge for major change especially in the light of the Universal Declaration of Human Rights by the UN (United Nations, 1948). This urge for change to a better quality of life is in the midst of so many other changes taking place in society. It is the interacting conflict of these changes, both outside the individual and society as well as changes within the individual and the society, which is causing frequent frictions posing the biggest challenge to the governments all over. This urge of the people for greater liberty, equality and freedom, in the context of the present-day knowledge explosion, can no longer be ignored by modern governments. If the governments continue to ignore this urge, they do so at their peril.

Corruption in Public Life

One of the most important concerns affecting public peace and progress is corruption in public life. It is a phenomenon that is widespread in the society even though everybody knows that its detrimental and corrosive consequences are deadly and disastrous. Corruption exacts heavy economic costs, distorts the operation of free-market forces, slows down economic development and distorts institutions including bureaucracy in delivering services to the society. It has a vast negative influence in our fight against poverty and violence. Although surveys and studies have shown that the underdeveloped and developing countries are more corrupt than the industrialized nations, it can never be said that any country is free from corruption. That is why corruption makes every society vulnerable though the incidence of corruption has more adverse and often violent consequences in poor and developing countries.

Status of Corruption

Briefly stated, corruption is abuse of public office for private gains. Corruption occurs in many forms. It is generally understood as gifts to public servants for private gains. It would also include donation to political parties and politicians for favours to be got when they assume power. Money laundering is also considered one of the corrupt practices mainly for performing illegal acts such as drug trafficking and other anti-national and anti-social activities. Even though all the legal systems of the world include laws and institutions to fight corruption, the deficiencies in judicial systems and police administration, and bureaucratic inadequacy have strengthened the vicious spread of corruption. A recent study indicates high levels of corruption in services such as healthcare, education, power, land administration and the police (Transparency International India 2005). Another study (World Bank 2006) relating to reforming public services in India has noticed the following methods in improving public services delivery:

1. Fostering competition
2. Simplifying transactions
3. Restructuring agency processes
4. Decentralizing management
5. Building political support
6. Strengthening accountability mechanisms

The World Bank study has also pointed out individual services and states that have been able to achieve specific successes despite corrupt environment although in a limited measure.

Failure of Governance and Citizens

Normally, one would have thought and expected that, with liberalization and free-market approaches, there would be a diminishing role for the government and government servants especially with the revolutionizing changes in technology. Unfortunately, this is not so. On the contrary, with increasing population and poverty caught in a trap of vicious circle amidst increasing violence, terrorism and socialistic movements, the regulatory role of governments is expanding at a fast pace. Ironically, the increased wage bill of an expanding bureaucracy and political machinery is crowding out developmental spending on a substantial scale. Capacity gaps are found to exist in many areas. India, for example, has the highest absolute number of maternal deaths in the world, but only three full-time officers at the central level are dedicated to the task of supervising maternal health programmes. The weakness of accountability mechanisms is another barrier to improving services across the board. Bureaucratic complexity and procedures make it difficult for an ordinary citizen to navigate the system for his or her benefit. Lack of transparency and secrecy that shrouds government operations and programmes provides fertile ground for corruption and exploitation. Nor is civic pressure for change in many developing democracies robust. A national survey conducted in 2001–2002 revealed that only 8 per cent of all respondents were members of a civic association while only 2 per cent could attest to the presence of an NGO in their area working on the provision of public goods. This finding is mirrored in another national survey conducted in 1996 by the Centre for Developing Societies which found that only 4 per cent of all respondents were involved with a civic association. Although civil societies have of late been questioning and arresting discriminations, discrepancies and deviations arising out of bureaucratic lethargy, unsettling effects of market forces and political apathy, they are yet to empower people in a big way partly because of their own deficiencies and inadequacies. When the citizenry fails to organize itself to improve public services, politicians and bureaucrats lack the incentives to take the issue of poor governance seriously. Thus, the empowerment of people towards good governance suffers.

Lack of accountability in turn provides opportunities for corruption. India was ranked at the 90th place in Transparency International's Corruption Perception Index (CPI) in 2005. The country is not well organized to combat corruption. A multiplicity of overlapping anti-corruption agencies and dilatory legal processes for tackling cases, have made it difficult to bring the corrupt to book. India's election campaign finance regime also has potential for negative effects on service delivery. The unregulated cost of elections—and the lack of legitimate funding sources, including a system of public funding—has created incentives to extract rents from administrative functions, including the delivery of services to fund campaign expenses or pay back contributors. The constituency grants for the Members of Parliament in India have been found in many cases to be misused or used for unintended projects.

The second important factor in public administration in many countries causing uneasiness in the minds of people is the inefficiency and delay in providing public services. The inefficiency and delay naturally slow down development process and consequently alleviation of poverty. In fact, it is often said by economists that poverty is a vicious circle contributing to its deterioration even if some attempts are made to improve the situation by developmental inputs. Unless the net effect of developmental inputs is in a position to override the vicious circle of poverty, alleviation of poverty will be a distant dream. In the race towards development it is this poverty trap which the new public administration has to break. The colonial system of administration based on rules and regulations is not adequate. The administrators have to be not only public development-oriented but also initiative- and innovation- oriented with adequate and strong information base in a globalizing and competitive world. It is indeed this need for constant improvement in governance that led the Prime Minister Dr Manmohan Singh to observe in his recent convocation address at the Tata Institute of Social Sciences (TISS) as:

'Our democratic institutions are warps of our nationhood. After 40 years and several questions, these institutions of governance have come to stay but they are in need of constant repair, rejuvenation, revitalization, modernization and humanization.'

Rising Expectations of the People

In the initial phase of the history of human race, the struggle among various human tribes was based on religion or cult. Subsequently, the struggle among communities was based on military power. Still later, the struggle among nations came to be based on commerce, trade and industry. The present phase of struggle in human history is based on knowledge power. Starting in the middle of the 19th century, a revolution in communication began with the telegraph, expanded later to the telephone, and then the radio and TV. By using electronic signals, it became possible to transmit messages instantaneously over a distance and to do so with not only written words but also representations of voice and graphics. With the introduction of computers in the late 20th century and coupled with the development of artificial intelligence, technologies converged resulting in Anthony Oettinger's expression 'commutronics'. With revolutionary changes taking place in technology, public administration in democratic countries also needs to change itself in its style and approaches as the expectations of the people are becoming more and more demanding. For the first time the entire human race is seriously and vigorously expecting governments to provide better quality of services more efficiently, with human rights awareness increasing day by day and the judiciary taking an active role in the form of judicial activism. Demands on public administration are going to be on the increase with knowledge power acquiring more importance and fuelling increased expectations especially because of the significant strides in print and electronic media.

Governance and Social Goals

Consistent with the recent changes in public administration, the current wave of reforms in human services relating to child care and welfare, care of the aged, healthcare, education, especially of women and children, and medical and sanitation facilities, governments have been concentrating on providing emphasis in these areas through flexible funding, support to local governments and NGOs, along with suitable and effective accountability and monitoring mechanisms. New public management with its new orientation and outlook may be criticized as old wine in new bottles but the current blend of emphasis on social development with efficiency and speed will go a long way to improve the quality of governance. Taking note of these changes in the development landscape, the World Bank noted that development thinking has evolved into a broad pragmatism, going beyond mere economic growth to encompass important social goals, and stressed the need for integrated implementation of good policy initiatives with strong administrative, legal and financial institutional mechanisms. The bank's *World Development Report 1990/2000* stated:

> Globalisation, which reflects the progressive integration of the world's economics, requires national governments to reach out to international partners as the best way to manage changes affecting trade, financial flows, and the global environment. Localization, which reflects the growing desire of people for a greater say in their government, manifests itself in the assertion of regional identities. It pushes national governments to reach down to regions and cities as the best way to manage changes affecting domestic politics and patterns of growth. At both the supranational and sub-national levels, institutions of governance, negotiation, coordination, and regulation will play a critical role in promoting a new equilibrium between and within countries—and in abetting the creation of the stable environment that will make possible the implementation of development programs.

Governance and Civil Service Reforms

The pathetic state of affairs of our civil service has been beautifully summed up by Madhav Godbole, a retired civil servant himself (Godbole 2004). He writes thus:

> The years since independence have seen progressive, marked and unabashed interference in the management of civil services and excessive political interference, and arbitrary, unguided and blatant misuse of discretion in all personnel matters, even at the highest levels of bureaucracy. Introduction of self serving criterion such as 'officer enjoying the confidence of the government' for purposes of promotions, postings and transfers has led to highly personalized administration. This is against all precepts underlying the creation of permanent civil services. Rule of law, equality before law and equal protection of law are given a go by in the process. This is not the governance, which was visualized by the Constitution and is an anti-thesis of democratic and accountable government. This is nothing but authoritarian use of power by a democratically elected government. Inevitably, this has led to politicization of the services leading to the civil services becoming the instruments and handmaiden of the political party in power. Thus, the constitutional protection to civil

services has not just been eroded but has been wiped out altogether. This has led to a substantial decline in their morale and the standards of their efficiency and integrity. Public image of a civil servant is now that of a rent seeker and exploiter who has no respect for the rule of law. He has ceased to be either civil or a servant of the society. One noteworthy feature in this behalf is that the situation is equally bad and worrisome at the centre and the states, and irrespective of which political party is in power.

Stating that the need for neutral civil service is quite important for good governance, he continues as follows:

The fundamental rights play a noteworthy role in the area of administrative law due to the phenomenal increase in the functions, powers and activities of civil administration, particularly in a welfare state. A large amount of discretion has to be inevitably left in the hands of administration. This has meant close scrutiny of both the administrative laws as also the procedures to ensure that they do not bestow arbitrary and unregulated discretion in the hands of administration. This brings out the close inter-relationship between the fundamental rights and good governance. Good governance requires, among others, sound forward-looking and enlightened constitutional framework, democratic governance, independent judiciary, freedom of press, and independent, apolitical, neutral and fearless civil services owing allegiance to the Constitution and the rule of law and not to the political party in power. While a great deal has been done, debated and translated in reality in respect of the first four items, the last named item pertaining to the civil services has been totally lost sight of and has often been pushed under the carpet. And the disastrous consequences are there for all to see. It must be realized that independence of civil services is no less important or significant for the working of the Constitution than the independence of the judiciary.

Concluding Remarks

India had a rich record as an intellectual capital of the world even before some of the present-day advanced countries had any exposure to science, technology and trade. However, the emphasis on individual and scientific approach in the ancient culture resulted, on many occasions, in the neglect of social welfare and justice. While in the past, the nation had a high degree of scientific research and spiritual enquiry, its knowledge power was confined largely to the elite and to certain regions. The intellectual dominance produced distinguished individuals in science, astronomy, mathematics, astrology, literature, abstract philosophy, economics and state craft. However, such individual excellence is not adequate for social advancement especially in the competitive modern globalizing scenario. Interdependence and independence will have to coexist to survive in the global race in international geophysical and economic relations. Hence the ancient wisdom has to blend with modern strides in knowledge power. Indian public administrators—indeed public administrators all over the world—have to think afresh to blend knowledge power with political power in the interest of social peace and progress. Collectively, the Indians have progressed considerably in certain areas such as science and technology, especially information technology, management skills like organization development, financial services, and textiles and engineering sectors. In the new order, imperfections and inefficiencies can neither be ignored nor tolerated. Innovations and initiatives for social improvement will have to be given top priority. One does not have to go far to seek new strategies. India has been the centre of confluence for many religions and scriptures. Ancient texts and scriptures have enough to provide the beacon light in bringing in the new order, especially to usher in a culture of integrity and hard work. They need to be looked at with a new scientific temper. Given the facts of India's rich historical legacy in the intellectual arena and the Indian brains presently occupying important and challenging positions in the international arena, Indian society is capable of succeeding in meeting the new challenge posed by the emerging knowledge economy. What is needed, therefore, is the will of the government and of the people to move forward with emphasis on merit balanced with social justice.

References

Caiden, G.E. 1991. *Administrative Reform Comes of Age*. Berlin: Walter de Gruyter.

Godbole, M. 2004. 'Good Governance: A Distant Dream', *Economic and Political Weekly*, 39(11): 1103–06.

Osborne, D. and P. Plastric.1997. *Banishing Bureaucracy*. New York: Persius.

Preston, L.T. 1992: 'Foreword' in *Governance and Development*. Washington D.C.: World Bank.

Transparency International India. 2005. 'India Corruption Study 2005'. Available at http://www.tiindia.in/data/files/India%20C orruption%20Study-2005.pdf, accessed on 15 October 2006.

Toffler, A. 1970. *The Future Shock*. New York: Random House.

United Nations. 1948. 'Universal Declaration of Human Rights'. Available online at www.un.org/Overview/rights.html

US President's Office. 1993. 'Government Performance Results Act of 1993'. Available online at www.whitehouse.gov/omb/ mgmt-gpra/gplaw2m.html

Weber, M. 1947. *The Theory of Social and Economic Organization*, Translated by A. M. Henderson and T. Parsons. New York: Oxford University Press.

World Bank. 2000. *World Development Report 1999/2000*. New York: Oxford University Press.

World Bank. 2006. *India Reforming Public Services in India*. Washington, DC: World Bank.

Part 5

Creating a Network of Knowledge
Institutions

19 Networking of Knowledge Institutions

M.S. Mathews and Prema Rajagopalan

Introduction

One of the critical components of a successful knowledge economy is networking. Networks may be defined simply as linkage of points or nodes such that movement may occur from one of the points to any other point. Networks are nodes connected by links (Barabási 2002).

Networks are of two kinds: (*a*) physical networks and (*b*) social or organizational networks. The examples of physical networks are road and railway networks, and communication networks. Social networks could be groups of people networked for a common purpose. In this chapter, the focus is on social networks which can be defined in broader terms as knowledge networks. Seufert et al. (1999) defines knowledge networks as those that settle down among the individuals, groups and organizations. They are important not only for their mutual relationships, but also for the integrity of the activity carried out by the whole of the knowledge network.

There are two important dimensions to knowledge networks: (*a*) technological dimension and (*b*) organizational dimension. The technological dimension focuses on the computer science aspects—the software and hardware required for the network. The organizational dimension focuses on the knowledge aspect, and related management and other issues.

This chapter defines the characteristics of knowledge networks. This is followed by a discussion on knowledge groups and communities. Then it presents the experience of a networking project in the academia in which Indian Institute of Technology-Madras (IIT-M) is a partner and is supported by the European Union (EU). The chapter concludes by proposing conceptual models for networking of knowledge institutions in India.

Characteristics of Knowledge Networks

Some of the important characteristics of a knowledge network (Seufert et al. 1991) are as follows:

1. Networks exist to create and disseminate new knowledge. They are not created merely to use existing, stored knowledge but to disclose new achievements in specific areas quickly.
2. They are structured and operated to increase the rate of creation of new knowledge.
3. They provide clear, recognizable benefits to all participants.
4. Membership in networks is by invitation, based on merit or prior review of the purposes of the project.
5. Networks are usually inter-disciplinary and cross over the frontiers between sections of activity and areas of knowledge.
6. Through networking a transfer occurs between the tacit knowledge of a individual and the explicit knowledge held by organizations.

Knowledge Communities

The term 'communities of practice' was first introduced by Lave and Wenger (1991). They define it as a relationship between people and activities, and at the same time they connect with other communities or organizations.

Many major multi-national companies (MNCs) have knowledge networks. Participating members can upload new knowledge into the network and also draw knowledge from it for their own work. The members in the network can have different degrees of participation.

Honeywell is an organization which has an effective knowledge management (KM) system in place. The purpose of the KM system is to maximize the value and impact on Honeywell businesses and customers by providing technology products—business solutions meeting global standards of quality, innovation and lifetime performance.

Roles played by the system are as follows:

1. Product engineering solutions
2. Applied research and technology
3. IT/Digital enterprises solutions
4. Business process support
5. Analysis

The objective is to foster knowledge sharing and re-use culture in Honeywell in order to

1. share solutions to customer problems;
2. increase productivity and reduce cost, effort, cycle time and defect rates;
3. help cross-functional project teams to collaborate and share work through knowledge-sharing forums like communities of practice, best practice and lessons learned sessions;
4. locate people with specific skills or domain knowledge and connect them to knowledge seekers; and
5. enable easy search, access and re-use of organized information and re-usable competency-based assets available in the in-house knowledge management database.

Conclusion

Networking has helped the company to perform better with respect to innovation and development of new technologies.

Case Study: EU–Asia Network of Competence Enhancement on Public–Private Partnerships in Infrastructure Development (EAP3N)

Objective of the Network

The overall objective of the project is to improve human resource capacity within and outside of the European and Asian academic institutions to contribute to public–private partnerships (PPPs) in infrastructure development. For this purpose, an international network of competence enhancement on PPPs is initiated at Knowledge Center @ Weimar, in Germany.

Knowledge Center @ Weimar

Knowledge Center @ Weimar was founded in February 2002 by the Chair IT in Construction and Construction Economics, and serves as a competence centre in an international network with the following partner universities:

1. Stanford (USA)
2. Carnegie Mellon (USA)
3. Stellenbosch (South Africa)
4. Swiss Federal Institute of Technology (Switzerland)
5. University of Manchester (UK)

Framework for Programme

The framework of the network shown in Figure 19.1 assists in organizing, implementing, delivering and monitoring of programmes.

Devices and Methods Used in the Project

1. E-mail
2. Video conference

3. Port
4. Face-to-face meeting

Figure 19.1   Framework of Networking Programme

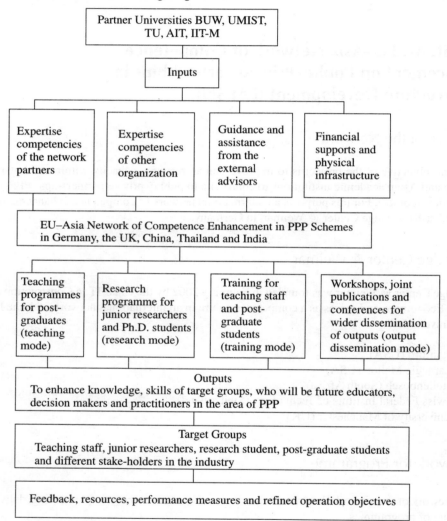

Source: 'EU–Asia Network of Competence Enhancement on Public–Private Partnership in Infrastructure Management', European Commission sponsored research projects, under the Asia-Link programme, 2004–07.

Note: BUW = Bauhaus Universität, Germany; UMIST = University of Manchester Institute of Science and Technology, UK; TU = Tsinghua University, China; AIT = Asian Institute of Technology, Thailand; IIT-M = Indian

Tasks Achieved in the Project

1. Two seminars on PPP in infrastructure development

    (*i*)   Tsinghua University, Beijing, China
    (*ii*) IIT-Madras, India

2. Built bilateral relationship among the five participating universities
3. Sharing of lectures via video conferencing amongst the partners
4. Conducted training programmes for research associates

Proposed Models for Networking of Knowledge Institutions in India

In this concluding section, three models are examined in increasing complexity. Three hypothetical problems are discussed to illustrate the models:

1. Case 1: Earthquake Design of a Concrete Building
2. Case 2: Disaster Management Systems Technology Model
3. Case 3: Sustainable Development

Case 1: Networking of Seven IITs for Solving the Earthquake Engineering Problem—Technology Model

The objective of the networking model is to put in place a knowledge network amongst seven homogeneous groups. In this case, the seven homogeneous groups are the seven civil engineering departments of the seven IITs (Figure 19.2). The problem to be solved is also well defined. If this networking problem is solved it will put in place the technologies and social dimensions of working in a network model. Once this is completed another dimension can be added by bringing in the management institutes.

Case 2: Networking of IITs, IIMs, IMI for Disaster Management

In this model, called the Technology Management model, networking of technical and management institutes is envisaged (Figure 19.3). Once this task is achieved, we can go in for the Knowledge Model.

Case 3: Networking IITs, IIMs, National Law Schools, Medical Colleges, Arts and Science Colleges, and so on

In this model, called the Knowledge Model (Figure 19.4), all the top educational institutions are networked to study inter-disciplinary problems. Although the concept looks simple and attractive, achieving integrated working is a complex task.

Figure 19.2   Networking of Seven IITs for Earthquake Engineering Technology Model

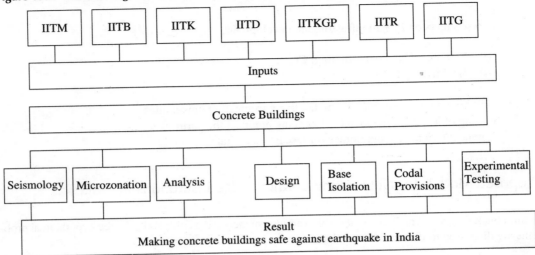

Source: Authors.

Figure 19.3   Networking of IITs, IIMs and IMI for Disaster Management Technology—Management Model

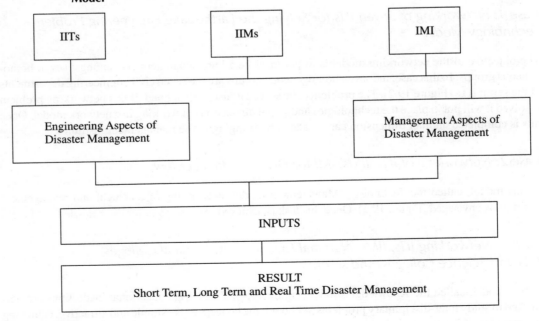

Source: Authors.

Figure 19.4   Networking of Various Institutes for the Knowledge Model

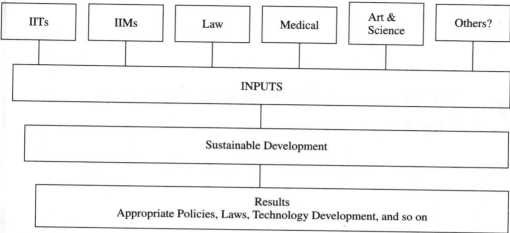

Source: Authors.

Nowadays, computer technology is necessary to achieve the above results is available. However, there are several questions in the social and organizational realm which have to be addressed before we get results. Some of these questions are as follows:

1. What is in it for me?
2. Why should I share my knowledge?
3. Why should I join a loose network, when I am at the head of our hierarchical organization?
4. Who will initiate the model and organize the work?

Bibliography

Barabási, Albert-László. 2002. *Linked: The New Science of Networks*. Cambridge, MA: Perseus Publishing.

Lave, J. and E. Wenger. 1991. *Situated Learning. Legitimate Peripheral Participation*. Cambridge, UK: Cambridge University Press.

Rao, N. Janardhana 2005. *Effective Knowledge Management, Emerging Trends*. Hyderabad: The ICFAI University Press.

Rooney, David, Greg. Hearn and Abraham Ninan. 2005. *Handbook on the Knowledge Economy*. UK: Edward Elgar.

Seufert, A., G. Krogh and A. Bach. 1999. 'Towards Knowledge Networking', *Journal of Knowledge Management*, 3(3): 180–90.

20 International Networking for Knowledge Management

ARUNDHATI CHATTOPADHYAY, G.S. KRISHNAN AND U.S. SINGH

Introduction

Globalization is a reality and the resultant liberalization within the economic system of India is irreversible. Despite its costs and turbulence that the critics of economic liberalization term as corporate-led, anti-poor, gender- and class-biased and destructive to the environment, globalization has offered India Inc. a significant opportunity to be globally competitive. The rapid growth of the Indian information technology (IT) industry is a testimony to this phenomenon. By now globalization has become synonymous with increased specialization, interdependence and integration wherein international and regional production networks (IPNs and RPNs) as well as value-added chains are integral parts.

The emergence of networks is evident in the economic field through increased movement of goods, services, knowledge, ideas, finance, people, and so on across national boundaries. In the geo-political field, international networks are set up through various forms of state-sponsored integration/mechanisms, for example, G8, Association of Southeast Asian Nations (ASEAN), South Asian Association for Regional Cooperation (SAARC) and Organisation for Economic Co-operation and Development (OECD) and in the cultural field through increased communications and opportunities to travel. The principal driving factors behind the current phase of globalization are lower barriers to trade and investment, lower transport costs, lower IT costs and the increasing role of the internet.

In general, those countries and regions within countries that have adopted liberal trade and investment policies, improved their transport and communication networks, and developed their institutional and human capital have benefited from the process through higher economic growth rates. In contrast, countries that are either late starters or have not embraced such measures voluntarily or have found difficulty in implementing such measures for reasons of geography, topography, finance or capacity have failed to reap the benefits of globalization to the same extent and are facing the possibility of being bypassed or marginalized.

Knowledge for Development

In this age of IT revolution, where new knowledge-based economies or societies are emerging, it is important to understand the basic distinction between the two commonly used metaphors, that is, 'information' and 'knowledge'. The former is a raw resource whereas the latter is a value-added resource that is generated by processing information. Conversion of information to knowledge requires skilled analysis, interpretation, refinement and adaptation. The uniqueness of a knowledge society lies in enriching the information society with innovation and value addition of products. However, if knowledge remains static, it is ineffectual. Hence, knowledge needs to be a part of a dynamic system where those institutions and networks that create scientific, technical and social knowledge are not only integrated, but also linked among the people who understand and utilize this knowledge for socio-economic benefits of the nation. The knowledge society enables value addition to preceding forms, namely, agricultural society, industrial society and information society by empowering individuals, institutions, companies, society and thereby the nation at large. Knowledge thus creates a comprehensive wealth for the nation and also improves the quality of life in the form of better health, education and infrastructure, and fulfilment of other societal needs.

Knowledge Network

Knowledge Network Concept

The *Human Development Report* (2001) published by the United Nations Development Programme (UNDP) puts forward the proposition that we have entered 'the network age' where there is synergy among various kinds of networks, namely, task networks, advocacy networks, development networks, technology networks and knowledge networks. A knowledge network refers to a network whose mandate is to generate and disseminate knowledge, usually based on research that is both problem-based and theory-based. Almost any collaborative activity involving the sharing of information among human beings can be considered a knowledge network. Such networks can arise spontaneously and almost instantaneously in response to a particular short-term need, or be created for long-term use through a process of planned development using rule-based formality and heavy-duty infrastructure. Some knowledge networks can involve millions of people while others can be very small, for example, a family can be considered a knowledge network (UNDP 2001). However, in this age of information and communication technologies (ICT), knowledge networks can exists even without direct human participation.

Knowledge networks may be either formal or informal in nature. Informal knowledge networks are usually grouped under the term 'communities of practice' that can be defined as a platform for interaction among professionals who have a real need to share each other's knowledge. People can be added to this informal network at will either by demand, or by referral or by self-selection. In this case the need to know is the driving force and the desire to achieve a specific result is the binding agent. For example, the

Community of Practice (http://www.solutionexchange-un.net.in/index.htm) that has communities dealing with issues on AIDS, decentralization, education, environment, food and nutrition security, gender, health and poverty is very useful for development practitioners in India.

In contrast, formal knowledge networks always have a formal membership procedure, whether qualification or rule based, with an approval mechanism (which can be automated). They are usually long term. Examples of formal knowledge networks are as follows:

1. Networks linked by common interest: (*i*) Professional associations, (*ii*) project teams and (*iii*) issue/advocacy networks established for public education and to exert influence on policy.
2. Networks linked by methodology: (*i*) Internet (for example, networks based on using e-mail or the web), (*ii*) meetings (for example, networks operating on the basis of a regular meeting cycle) and (*iii*) offline (for example, networks communicating by post, telephone, exchanging newsletters, CD-ROMs, videos).
3. Networks of individuals: (*i*) Association based on qualifications or profession, for example, Miners' Association, Journalists Association, (*ii*) society and (*iii*) clubs, for example, Rotary Club.
4. Networks of organizations: (*i*) Alliance, (*ii*) collaboration, (*iii*) coalition or (*iv*) confederation.

Knowledge Network System

The structure of knowledge network comprises nodes and links. Nodes are the focal points for activity or organizational processes and could be individuals, teams or even organizations, whereas links are various connecting and coordinating mechanisms, such as workflow procedures or meetings. As information flows across the links and is put to various uses, new knowledge is created. The basic elements of knowledge network are (*a*) people, (*b*) hardware, (*c*) software and (*d*) procedures like access, navigation, observation, analysis, repository and learning.

Research on knowledge-intensive business services (KIBS), such as management consultancy and software, shows that they play a central role in transferring research knowledge from centres of excellence to firms that enable them to remain innovative (Aslesen 2004). These findings on the role of consultants suggest that knowledge transfer from exploration stage (research) to exploitation stage (commercialization) is by no means straightforward and is mediated by an examination stage (value assessment or evaluation) with some possibilities discarded and only those with clear applicability retained. The transfer of tacit or implicit knowledge into explicit or codified knowledge is assisted by research of third-party intermediary (Cooke 2005). As Table 20.1 indicates, this function can be captured by the intermediary concept of 'complicit' knowledge. A third party possesses complicit knowledge probably

Table 20.1   Knowledge: From Implicit Domains to Regional Innovation Systems

	Implicit	*Complicit*	*Explicit*
Knowledge domain	Invention	Translator	Appropriation
Knowledge capability	Talent	Research	Technique
Innovation system	Institutions	Networks	Interactions

Source: Cooke (2005).

with a background in the knowledge base of the tacit knowledge holder who therefore belongs to the same 'epistemic community'. However, complicit knowledge will also extend professionally into the explicit knowledge epistemic community, probably in business of some kind. Thus, the intermediary is complicit in two epistemic communities, a scientific (or may be a symbolic, for example, creative arts) and a commercial one.

In Table 20.1, the three categories of knowledge are set against three spatial categories, the first being a 'knowledge domain' or a space where exploration knowledge originating endogenously and exogenously, and possibly capable of being recombined into a commercial innovation, is concentrated. The second refers to the 'knowledge capability'; such a domain accumulates through the recruitment and retention of talent available to work in research or commercialization of such innovations. Finally, supporting the knowledge transformation process are its institutions, which through network relationships interact in support of regional or, for clusters, localized innovation. Networks, for example, are a paradigm case of institutional complicit knowledge intermediation. Regions with such knowledge domains, capabilities and innovation systems experience increasing returns to scale and become knowledge quasi-monopolies.

National Productivity Council (NPC) is a national level organization set up to promote productivity culture in India. National Productivity Council's knowledge network comprises 207 full-time professional consultants located at 14 regional offices in India. Besides providing training and consultancy, and undertaking research in the area of productivity, NPC also implements the productivity promotion plans and programmes of the Tokyo-based Asian Productivity Organization (APO), an inter-governmental body of which the Government of India is a founder member. In NPC, a multi-disciplinary working group or interactive knowledge network is formed for carrying out major consultancy projects or assignments. Thus, members having different expertise form a part of integrated knowledge network for achieving the organizational goal.

Importance of Knowledge Network

Knowledge networks constitute the new social morphology of our societies and the diffusion of networking logic substantially modifies the operation and outcomes in processes of production, experience, power and culture. They are important not only because of the knowledge they produce and disseminate, but also because of the social organization and innovation they enable. Depending on the capacity to generate, disseminate and infuse knowledge into the economy, the domain of knowledge institutions or networks may be domestic, regional or global. Knowledge networks flourish best in environments where members are free to do research, disseminate results, and free to explore and exchange ideas without fear of reprisal. However, if coordination among members fails then 'knowledge networking' becomes 'knowledge not working'. In a multi-country knowledge network, adequate bandwidth needs to be allocated to share and cherish one another's culture—may be heritage learning, history or entertainment. Understanding and respecting one another's culture is essential for enhancing the productivity or competitiveness of an individual in a globally networked environment.

In the knowledge economy, networking among partners boosts the power of all the participating partners. Robert Metcalf's law states that the 'value' or 'power' of a network increases in proportion to the square of the number of nodes on the network. For example, let six partners, namely, the government; research/academic institutions; corporate or business houses; foreign institutional investors (FIIs); donor agencies like the World Bank, the United Nations, Asian Development Bank and Department for

International Development (DFID); and non-governmental organizations (NGOs) or civil societies join to work as networked knowledge partners with a common objective of building India into a leading economy of the new world order. The combined strength of this 'knowledge platform/network' will not be just that of six partners but it would be six squared (6^2) or 36. These institutions or partners are essential building blocks and pillars of innovation as knowledge multiplies when partners are united in a common platform. In short, the knowledge platform would be the launch pad for many innovations that are waiting to be unearthed only by the combined power of the stakeholders and produce competitive products that reach the world market. The purpose of this network platform thus would be to facilitate knowledge creation, dissemination, sharing and re-use leading to coordinated design and delivery of complex systems in the knowledge domain. These systems would be directed towards improving the quality of life of the people and creating nation's wealth.

Ownership of Knowledge within Networks

In a knowledge network, usually all are equal partners sharing the same objectives and values, and are open to each other. However, it is critical to understand the 'ownership' of knowledge that is created and passing through the networks as it may otherwise challenge the deeply embedded concepts of property rights. World Intellectual Property Organization (WIPO) provides guidelines for the ownership of copyrights and patents, and settles the battle about ownership of knowledge on well-defined terrain. Within the World Trade Organization (WTO), broad coalitions of developing countries and NGOs have challenged the legal regimes surrounding trade in intellectual property and services. These global negotiations are taking place, however, within the framework of established regimes of intellectual property.

India and Knowledge Networks

Economic Development

India with its current population of over 1 billion is facing a major challenge of uplifting its 260 million people who live below the poverty line. In order to provide these under-privileged population a decent habitat, work, income, food, access to healthcare and education, the economy needs to grow at the rate of 10 per cent per annum consistently for over a decade as against the growth rate of around 7–9 per cent per annum in recent years.

Achieving this demanding growth rate would be possible only when India's natural and human resources are fully utilized for building competence and technologies that lead to generation of additional high-income employment and value addition in all sectors of the economy, that is, agriculture, manufacturing and services. In order to achieve such economic growth and ensure a societal transformation, there is a need to build a knowledge society. One of the major initiatives in this endeavour will be the creation of relevant networks that act as platforms for the collective effort of the government, academic institutions, large and small businesses, foreign investors, and so on.

However, the efficacy of this knowledge society would be determined by the ability to create and maintain a knowledge society infrastructure, develop knowledge workers, and enhance their productivity through the creation, growth and utilization of new knowledge. The extent of development of a nation into a knowledge society is judged by the way it creates and deploys knowledge and skills in sectors like ICT, manufacturing, agriculture, education and healthcare.

Dr A.P.J. Abdul Kalam, former President of India, suggested the plan PURA (Providing Urban Amenities in Rural Areas) which facilitates the creation of employment in the rural areas itself to reduce migration from rural to urban areas in search of jobs in manufacturing and services sectors. Employment opportunities in rural areas can be created by, among others, through skill enhancement of displaced agricultural labour for undertaking value-added tasks in the rural enterprises. PURA achieves this objective by providing physical, electronic and knowledge connectivities to a cluster of villages thereby leading to their economic connectivity and prosperity. Knowledge creation and knowledge utilization are the keys to the success of a PURA programme.

President Kalam's Singapore Lecture at the Raffles Convention Center, Singapore, has also emphasized that the convergence of biotechnology, nano-science and technology, and ICT by facilitating the design, development and production of knowledge products for international markets is expected to touch every area of concern to the humanity. Concerted research and development (R&D) in these areas would require high-bandwidth connectivity such as the one proposed in the knowledge GRID. According to him, the 'world knowledge platform' with the public private partnership needs to create networks for the following objectives to make our world safe, sustainable, peaceful and prosperous:

1. Energy storage, production and conversion
2. Enhancing agricultural productivity
3. Water treatment
4. Disease diagnosis and screening
5. Drug delivery system
6. Food preservation and storage
7. Air pollution control and ventilation
8. Construction
9. Health monitoring
10. Vector/pest destruction and control
11. Hardware, software and networking products' design, development and production
12. Automobile hardware, embedded software integration
13. Gene characterization, stem cell research and invention of drugs for the diagnosis and treatment of diseases like cancer and diabetes

In addition to the above-mentioned areas, electronics, ICT and automobile sectors may also be focused especially in the areas of design and development leading to production for meeting the world's market demands.

Application of Knowledge Network for Disaster Risk Reduction in India

In India, the experiences, approaches and adopted modalities for disaster management are not comprehensively codified. As such, their knowledge remains largely with individuals as tacit knowledge. Recently it was realized that linkages among agencies, policy makers, disaster managers and specialists from allied fields of engineering, architecture, planning, seismology, hydrology, agriculture and social sciences, working on disaster management, need to be strengthened in order to derive regional best practices and coping mechanisms. National Disaster Risk Management Programme, under the Ministry of Home Affairs, GOI-UNDP is facilitating exchange of knowledge through networking for physical interaction, workshops, documentation of experiences, sharing on World Wide Web Portal (http://www.ndmindia.nic.in/), and so on.

Such a network will connect all the programme partners of Government of India comprising more than 500 institutions in the country. Subsequently, conscious effort will be put in to facilitate the evolvement of various networks such as a state network comprising all the state disaster management departments, a training institution network comprising all the administrative training institutions (ATIs) in India and other training institutions in disaster management area.

Further details of the knowledge network for disaster risk management can be ascertained by visiting the website www.ndmindia.nic.in.

Knowledge management is all about getting the right knowledge, in the right place, at the right time and knowledge networks facilitate the attainment of these objectives.

Case of an International Productivity Network

Asian Productivity Organization

The APO was established in 1961 as a regional inter-governmental organization to contribute to the socio-economic development of Asia and the Pacific through enhancing productivity. Asian Productivity Organization's vision of continuous productivity enhancement on a sustainable basis is based on three pillars, namely, (a) strengthening competitiveness, (b) harmonizing environmental protection with increasing productivity and (c) enhancing social fairness. The key roles of APO are to act as a think-tank, catalyst, adviser, institution builder and a clearing house of productivity information. Presently, APO has 20 governments as its members.

Asian Productivity Organization has created an effective international network of NPOs in its member countries who share their common zeal for productivity enhancement to improve standards of living. This network of NPOs is supported by APO through its activities, namely, seminars, training courses, observational study missions, workshops, symposia, study meetings, surveys, basic research, demonstration projects, e-learning programmes, fellowships, technical expert services and information dissemination.

These activities are effectively utilized by APO to create a larger chain effect through international networks. Some examples of such operations are as follows:

1. Publications: Asian Productivity Organization has published more than 400 volumes of reports on various research projects, surveys, symposia, study meetings and seminars. Asian Productivity Organization also brings out printed books on productivity subjects, some of which have been translated into more than 15 languages. Recently, APO introduced e-books on its website which has a library of 24 titles and is expanding.
2. Audio-visual aids: Asian Productivity Organization's audio-visual materials are for self-learning and for use in training programmes.
3. APO website: This website provides comprehensive information on APO and its activities with the long-term objective of developing it into a major internet portal on productivity. Apart

from information dissemination, the site is increasingly being used by the APO secretariat for communication with its partners, NPOs and participants, as well as for implementing web-based learning mes.

4. APO intranet and APOnet: To harness IT to renovate and improve its operating systems, APO launched its intranet system in 2001 to enable sharing of information quickly and effectively through a knowledge centre, which has three basic components: (*a*) an information hub on past APO projects and participant database, (*b*) information on member countries and their NPOs and (*c*) information on APO administrative guidelines and activities. The APOnet, set up in 2002, fosters closer communications among the APO secretariat, NPOs and participants in ongoing APO projects for better programme planning, preparation and implementation. It enables the NPOs to have access to all APO project sites through which they can view or download resource papers, participants' reports and reports of the proceedings. The APOnet is now a virtual depository of the reports, documents and papers of almost all APO projects.

5. APO e-Forum: A new internet-based platform called APO e-Forum has been launched in 2003 to achieve a multiplier effect for its programmes and to provide its participants a platform for professional networking, including real-time chat, after attending its projects.

This information gives an illustration of an international network for productivity augmentation.

Conclusions

It has been seen that international networking is an essential element of knowledge management for the future of knowledge economies. The networks have to be in the advanced technology format using ICT as well as in tacit forms through cooperation among individuals, social groups, institutions, societies, and so on in both formal and informal manner. Such international networks have to cater not only to well-established sectors of the economy, but also to the hitherto not much attended sectors and economies for the well-being of greater mass of the population. Examples of international networks like the APO are to be identified and cross-connections between them are also to be established to multiply the benefits of international networking.

References

Aslesen, H. 2004. 'Knowledge Intensive Business Services and Regional Development: Consultancy in City Regions in Norway', in P. Cooke and A. Piccaluga (eds), *Regional Economies as Knowledge Laboratories*, pp. 58–76. Cheltenham: Edward Elgar.

Cooke, Philip. 2005. 'Research, Knowledge and Open Innovation: Spatial Impacts upon Organisation of Knowledge-Intensive Industry Clusters'. Aalborg: Center for Advanced Studies, Cardiff University (Regional Studies Association: 'Regional Growth Agendas'), 31 May. Available online at http://www.regional-studies-assoc.ac.uk/events/aalborg05/cooke.pdf.

United Nations Development Programme (UNDP). 2001. *Human Development Report 2001—Making New Technologies Work for Human Development*. New York/Oxford: United Nations Development Programme/Oxford University Press.

21 International Partnering for Capacity Building in IMTT: An IIFT Initiative

Niraj Kumar

Higher Education Networking between Europe and Asia

Asia-Link Program

The Asia-Link Program was set up by the European Commission to promote regional and multilateral networking among higher education institutions in the European Union (EU) member states and developing countries in Asia. The programme aims to promote the creation of new partnerships, to reinforce existing partnerships between European and Asian universities and to create new sustainable links. The programme is funded by the EU budget, under the budget line for 'Political, economic and cultural cooperation with Asian developing countries'.

Partnership projects under Asia-Link Program can undertake activities in one or more of the following three areas:

1. Human resource development (HRD) activities aim to upgrade the skills of university teaching staff, in particular young faculty and future teachers (that is, post-graduate students) and administrators. Each project should provide for mobility of nationals from both the EU and the eligible Asian countries.
2. Curriculum development activities aim to develop curricula, by producing new/improved courses, modules or teaching/training materials. Each project, which should be innovative, covers activities relating to the preparation of curricula and course material (content definition, teaching tools, production/printing of course material), their dissemination and the training of professors/tutors to teach them.
3. Institutions and systems development grants are awarded for cooperative projects that aim to enhance the overall management of institutions of higher education through sharing of experience between Asian and European institutions (or groups/associations of institutions).

Project Abstract

This 30-month project will develop a new international Master's programme in Innovation Management and Technology Transfer (IMTT) while developing human resources in each partner institution. The four parties—in the UK, China, India and Poland—are from contrasting economic situations, providing good role models for other universities regionally in developing, transitional and developed economies. Targets will include academics and administrators at universities, would-be innovators from the public sector and from larger organizations, small and medium enterprises (SMEs), students and policy and decision makers (Table 21.1). An international expert panel commenting on structure, case study and module development will assess quality. To encourage innovation at different levels, those under-represented in innovation will be a key focus for participation, including ethnic minorities and women. Activities include workshops, module and cast study testing, e-forums and diverse publications including special edition of a referred academic journal.

Table 21.1   Target Groups and Beneficiaries

Target group	Direct	Indirect
Academics at IIFT	12	10
Academics from other universities	70	50
Public sector organizations	20	20
Large companies	20	20
Students	20	20
Policy and decision makers	10	10

Source: Contract document Asia link/UCE/10375.

Project Partners

1. University of Central England, Birmingham, UK
2. Indian Institute of Foreign Trade (IIFT), New Delhi, India
3. Dalian Maritime University, China
4. Institute of Humanity and Economics, Lodz, Poland

Project Deliverables

1. Develop new curriculum—structure and framework
2. Prepare 18 case studies and 20 new modules
3. Provide a guide for other projects
4. Develop and assess market for new programme
5. Evaluate currently available support for innovation
6. Develop a sustainability plan
7. Constitute an international expert panel of 6–12 members and a national expert committee
8. Report on potential of under-represented groups
9. Support human resource development (HRD) by conducting workshops, meetings, and so on

Qualitative Assessment

A National Expert Committee at the partner country level under the guidance of the International Expert Panel shall be supervising the quality issues and developing the programme (Box 21.1).

Box 21.1 Project Partner Views

Tentative Modules

1. The characteristics of an innovator or an innovating organization (how leadership fits into this process)
2. Creativity and innovation
3. Building a plan for commercialization; understanding the marketplace
4. Innovation and its need for entrepreneurial marketing
5. Innovation—impacts on internationalization and exporting
6. The way finance can be accessed, used and managed to support innovation
7. The role of the regional support environment and how this can encourage innovation
8. The role of universities in working with companies to support innovation
9. Knowledge capture, sharing and creation as key components of innovation
10. Clustering—how firms link together for competitive advantage and the impact of this on the innovation process
11. Clustering—how large firms impact on regions and the effects on innovation
12. Benchmarking innovation, trends and comparisons internationally
13. Benchmarking innovation support actions, internationally
14. Technology and the innovating firm
15. Women and innovation
16. Innovation and ethnicity
17. Re-inventing the organization
18. Change management and strategic planning to support large firm re-invention
19. Innovation in the public and voluntary sector
20. Ethical impact of innovation internationally
21. Technology transfer—developing expertise as in a university working with industry
22. Innovation and technology transfer, theoretical approaches
23. IPRs
24. Technology transfer management
25. Innovative motivation for technology
26. Innovative organizational culture
27. Management of competence
28. Human resource for innovation and technology management
29. Marketing of innovation
30. Management, technology and methodology
31. Knowledge management and virtual organization

Source: Project Partners' meet at Dalian, China, May 2005.

Modular Components of International Master's Programme in IMTT

Capacity Building and Institutional Framework

1. Target the human resource potential at each partner institution via current assessment.
2. Follow-up the HR assessment by action to support HRD.
3. Disseminate the project outputs by organization of events including all target groups and participation in national and international conferences, symposia, round table meetings.
4. Disseminate the project outputs to widest possible audience via diverse publication routes (see Figure 21.1).

Figure 21.1   Institutional Framework

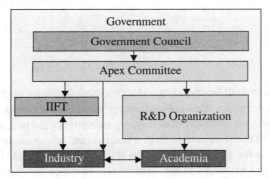

Source: IIFT Position Paper in Project Partners' Inception Meet at Delhi, January 2006.

Forward Linkages

1. Capacity building through series of seminars and follow-up workshops.
2. Knowledge dissemination through participation in seminars/conferences, both national and international.
3. Publications in international journals and international conferences.
4. Positioning IIFT as a facilitator/service provider in IMTT training and education.
5. Branding IIFT as a successful international education partner.

22 Sensitivity to Self-Organization and Effectiveness of IT Networks in the Social Sector*

K. SANKARAN

Introduction

Developments in networking among business organizations show that inter-organizational (and by logical extension, inter-institutional) entities often perform better when they are networked and work as 'open' organizations. Pursuing objectives inter-dependently, organizations (and institutions[1]) in networks have been seen to perform better in many situations than when in stand-alone mode (Adler and Kwon 2002), particularly when they are in the knowledge domain (Nahapiet and Ghoshal 1998). Several types of successful inter-organizational networks in the field of business can be identified. For instance, there are information networks through which suppliers and buyers link their activities using computers in supply-chain management programmes. Similarly, just-in-time (JIT) and business process outsourcing (BPO) may be viewed as inter-organizational arrangements that enhance overall effectiveness of network participants. The huge success of internet and firms like Google could be attributed to the power of collective minds working together based on principles of self-organization.

These networks are, no doubt, facilitated by advances in information technology (IT). Consequently it is important to examine how IT enables networking amongst organizations. However, there is more to these networks than technology alone (Brown and Duguid 2000). Open organizations with scope for self-organization force a whole lot of traditional views to stand upside down. There has been a re-definition of what should and should not be shared, what constitutes breach of loyalty, identity of organizations and of individuals, willingness to trade efficiency for flexibility, greater tolerance for trial and error, and so on. These issues go deeper than mere availability and use of hardware, software and associated

* The survey findings cited in this chapter are from the research report by a team of researchers at T.A. Pai Management Institute, Manipal, wherein the author was the principal investigator. The research was sponsored by the Department of Scientific and Industrial Research, New Delhi. It was completed in April 2006.

technical knowledge. Such factors, which are beyond the technical realm, could be roughly termed as self-organization-promoting factors.

It seems that where commercial interests are supreme, networking happens by a cooperative process—a process wherein there exists no single, hierarchically dominant, organization to drive the process. Organizational theorists surmise that what is at play is self-organization (Stacey 1996; Wheatley 1996), a form of self-interest-based organic way for the entire system to develop without central intervention by one controlling organization. For instance, the elaborate system that allows use of credit card involves a fantastic network of banks, regulators, credit rating agencies, retailers, merchandizers, debt-recovery companies, users, user advocacy groups, and so on—all working in tandem to get, say, one's travel bookings at the click of a mouse! This infrastructure (with physical and knowledge dimensions) did not come up in one day. The network is not the product of a well-designed, pre-planned, blue-print-based programme of a few experts. The network progresses over time, through trial and error, with the participant groups working entrepreneurially in their own self-interest. There was no central planning involved. All that was done at the highest level (say government) was to let these things happen with enabling legislation.

It would appear that where social infrastructure is involved, such rich evolution of networks does not take place so easily. Coordination and network flows, when social infrastructure is involved, seem primitive compared to what commercial organizations have been able to achieve. A simple example, faced in everyday life, is dug-up roads. The departments responsible for roads, water supply, electricity, sewerage, telecom, traffic, and so on are not able to coordinate their activities in an effective manner on what appears to be a simple coordination problem! Reasons for inadequate coordination may be many. Perhaps those who are supposed to bring about changes may not be having the right incentives for change. Or perhaps, control-based centralized planning may be coming in the way of organic development of coordination.

The purpose of this chapter is not to identify the reasons for lack of such coordination. Identifying reasons attributable to specific organizations may look like fault-finding. The issue still has to be addressed albeit indirectly. The thesis of this chapter is that an understanding and appreciation of cultural and social factors that promote self-organization among those who are trying to bring about effective social IT networks will create more effective (and egalitarian) networks.

Institutional sociologists and economists see society as consisting of various types of institutions and organizations. More often than not, organizational members who are otherwise rational act in ways that are collectively sub-optimal (North 1990). Self-organization may be an answer to collective under-performance that institutional arrangements are notorious for. When individuals, as members of their respective organizations, interact in a purposeful and mutually inter-dependent manner, it is likely that the objectives of the organizations and the society they are part of may be furthered (Baker 1990). An understanding of the mutuality and cultivation of give-and-take may be what is missing. Better understanding requires skill that can be learnt. Policy makers and intended beneficiaries require a new mindset, one that recognizes the value of inter-dependencies, multiple viewpoints, plurality, and so on. In such a scheme of things, the role of the expert will not be to proffer knowledge but to marshal disparate nuggets of wisdom to create collective good.

Hubris and self-importance that come with position, power and expertise, which offered a hefty premium until recently, may, in the new scheme, become liabilities. The role of 'charismatic' leadership styles—see Bradshaw (2006) who reports the views of Henry Mintzberg—may also have to be questioned. Clear demarcation between the ruler and the ruled, between brain and brawn, and so on would hopefully no more command premium. Human behaviour will be driven by purposeful action (Senge et al. 2004) even within the boundaries of organizations. If indeed this thesis is right, then there may be many benefits that can be reaped from networks, the noblest of which will be what Surowiecki (2005) calls the 'wisdom of the crowds'.

What is being suggested here would also imply that there lie certain hidden benefits 'over and above' physical and financial returns sunk in IT networks. The stock of hidden capital that provides these benefits is often called 'social capital' (Coleman 1990; Putnam et al. 1993). Several questions arise once this subtle capital that resides in human collectives is recognized. These questions may be posed as follows:

1. What prevents us from fully exploiting these advantages?
2. Can we hasten network benefits which are literally up for grabs for a perceptive society?
3. What are the lessons from the command-and-control paradigm so that mistakes should not be repeated?
4. What are the levers for encouraging self-order?

Preliminary Findings of a Survey of Social Capital

Recently, a qualitative study was undertaken on how IT facilitates social capital among institutions in the coastal areas of Karnataka. The objective was to find out the extent to which internet and IT technologies are used by institutions to

1. exchange information among them;
2. create and further 'associations' among them; and
3. receive and offer e-enabled services.

Five types of organizations were identified: businesses, professionals, service providers, non-governmental organizations (NGOs) and government. Businesses included small and medium businesses in the region which were mainly manufacturers and large traders. Professionals included doctors, accountants and lawyers. Service providers included schools, colleges and hospitals. Finally, government included some selected government departments.

The heads of organizations (or organizational units) were engaged by the research team in free-flowing interviews. A checklist was used to make sure that the interview covered all the issues that were intended to be covered. Comments of the interviewees were recorded with their consent. Findings of the survey were quite revealing.

Issues covered in the survey were divided into two types: Level 1 and Level 2. Both these levels had to do with lacunae in the existing order of things. Level 1 issues were surmountable through better resource availability and use. In other words, the lacunae could be 'corrected' by providing proper supply of technology and associated services. As opposed to this, Level 2 issues were related to how individuals view themselves and their roles in an IT-enabled society. As individuals use technology they not only process information, generate outputs, and so on but also generate a deeper connection with the world; for instance, new forms of assurances and affirmations are provided by their participation in the networked world. The Internet and communication over the Internet, become a matter of defining identity, broadcasting one's skills, offering expertise, seeking partnerships, and so on. In other words, the Internet acquires a new meaning in terms of being a social extension of oneself and one's organization. Level 2 issues are related to self-order. However, for the sake of completeness and to establish the context, Level 1 issues are also reported here.

Level 1 issues could be summarized as follows:

1. The respondents need to have better protection for their computer installations. This is indeed an opportunity for security software providers and associated services. There is also considerable need for better education regarding computer security.
2. Related to the above is the use of authentic software. Unless the users confidently demand services from software providers many of the features that they could possibly use would remain untapped. There is scope for better social capital formation between software providers and users.
3. Dial-up connections are a problem. However, this problem is slowly being taken care of by the recent foray of broadband which should become more widely available in the survey region in the months to come.
4. The absence of awareness of internet etiquette is another problem. There has to be much more training in schools, colleges and computer-training centres on how to deal with e-mail and other aspects of e-etiquette.
5. The current level of computer literacy is quite low among educated and professional persons. So there is tremendous scope for imparting education to such persons who are otherwise well educated.
6. There is inadequate trust in transacting through the Internet. Most respondents hesitate to use debit/credit cards for transactions for fear of misuse.
7. Inadequate availability of services (such as e-signature verification, e-notarization) for transacting e-documents is an issue on the supply side.

Level 2 issues could be described briefly as follows:

1. 'Blame the messenger' problem: There seems to be considerable inability and unwillingness among the respondents to differentiate between the technology per se and what it does—metaphorically, between the carrier and what is carried. Because of this, it was found that often individuals blame technology for ills such as exposure to x-rated sites by children and students. As a result, several respondents advocate 'banning and complete avoidance' rather than take technology head-on and create 'attractor fields'.
2. 'Glorified railway timetable' problem: Often the Internet is considered not more than a huge source of information. In other words, the Internet is considered as a huge database, quite akin to a railway timetable, wherein specific information is sought. But when it comes to giving information there is less of willingness and ability to share information.
3. 'Over-estimation of direct contact' problem: It is a cultural 'given' for many that matters can be expeditiously dealt with only by face-to-face interaction. In general, people are unwilling to conceive that the Internet may be used as a medium for conversation, dialogue and discussion with higher efficiencies.

4. 'Stuck on paper' problem: In matters where legality is involved, there is little awareness that technology could provide many legal safeguards that are traditionally available with 'hard copies'. Ideas of electronic signature, electronic verification, electronic notarization, and so on are 'too distant and dreamy' for many of the respondents.

5. 'Visible technology attribution' problem: There is less appreciation for the 'service' component in delivered product–service mix as compared to the 'product' component in the mix. This lop-sided view translates to inadequate provision for software, security, warranty, training, and so on. Hassle-free operation is given less importance when compared to 'whistles and bells' (advanced physical features that appear attractive but are not usable by the buyer because of lack of adequate ability vis-à-vis software) that come with the hardware at the information and communication technologies (ICT) acquisition stage. This myopia has finally resulted in many cases of individuals getting disenchanted with ICT.

6. 'Government as master' problem: There seems to be disproportionate expectation of what the government can do and must do. Whether it is making broadband connections available or providing local language scripts or reducing the price of computers, a majority of the respondents tended to view these matters as issues for the government to act upon.

7. 'Fixation of entities' problem: While discussing social capital, it was noticed that there is inadequate appreciation of the idea that relationships may be as important as entities (in relationships) themselves to achieve results. In other words, there seems to be some kind of 'fixation' on entities. What could be sensed was an inability or unwillingness to think beyond entities and visualize the possibility that existing entities could leverage on creative relationships with positive-sum-game plans. It was also possible to sense (diabolically) that primacy of entities is upheld so that there is enough scope for fixing the blame on the other (accusation) or on oneself (guilt). This attitude would certainly come in the way of development and nurturance of social capital (especially 'bridging' social capital).

Level 2 Findings and Self-organization

There appears to be a link between Level 2 limitations and self-organization. Self-organization requires clarity of objectives, willingness to learn, space for trial and error, tolerance for ambiguity, self-confidence, innovativeness, and so on. As opposed to this, what we see is a significant level of negatives: fear of taking initiative, fear of unfamiliar technologies, reluctance to share information, helplessness, dependence on authority, inadequate appreciation of the benefits of creating inter-dependent relationships, and so on.

Table 22.1 relates Level 2 issues and their attendant characteristics that essentially militate against the idea of self-organization. No doubt more work needs to be done to establish a firm link between the social, cultural and behavioural observations of the survey and the factors that facilitate (or inhibit) self-organization. This chapter is meant only to provoke thought and create dialogue and discussion on the matter.

Table 22.1   Level 2 Issues and Their Attendant Characteristics

Item	Level 2 issue	Connection to disablement of self-organization
(a)	Blame the messenger	This problem points to lack of innovativeness to conceptualize on how to use informational tools to one's own advantage. It conveys helplessness and locus of control outside oneself. This attitude is antithetical to self-organization because self-organization posits willingness and ability to experiment and create advantage for self (individual or collective) and others in mutually reinforcing ways.
(b)	Glorified railway timetable	This problem indicates fear of (or perception of futility in) sharing information. This problem may be explained as passive input taking rather than giving out (or output giving). This shows inhibition and lack of ability to share information in mutually inter-dependent and synergistic ways.
(c)	Over-estimation of direct contact	This may indicate surrender to power attributes rather than to autonomous logic and intuition. It is indicative of unhealthy attribution of power to 'the other' and helplessness for oneself, and the obverse of it; attribution of power to oneself and powerlessness to others.
(d)	Stuck on paper	Shows justificatory and risk-averse disposition which are not conducive to winning through trial and error, an important attribute of self-order.
(e)	Visible technology attribution	Shows lack of clarity on what objectives are being sought by oneself. This is antithetical to self-organization which requires greater clarity on what one's basic objectives are.
(f)	Government as master	Indicates dependence rather than autonomy and self-empowerment, essential attributes that create the context for self-organization.
(g)	Fixation on entities	Lack of holistic and process perspectives. It also indicates atomized and alienated individualism, lack of faith in collectives and inadequate understanding of one's role in creating positive-sum games, and so on attributes required to grant and accept ideas of self-organization.

Source: Author.

Conclusions

This chapter has argued for a more inclusive and open approach to IT network creation that is sensitive to not only the need for technical abilities, but also social, cultural and behavioural factors. Sensitivity to latter factors, it was argued, should be with a view to create greater self-organization. It was posited that sensitivity to such factors amongst network designers and policy makers may bring about quantum jumps in the effectiveness of networks.

Technical virtuosity, to the neglect of social, cultural and behavioural dimensions, will only create suspicion and fear of the network. This will keep the intended beneficiaries away from the network. This kind of informational exclusion will also encourage forces that perpetrate exclusion. Those who are able to use the new facilities will slowly, over time, hijack the infrastructure for their own informational advantage to create another long cycle of social disparity, this time based not on cornering tangible resources, but informational and IT asymmetry. This is something that the policy makers can help avoid. By implication, the chapter also hazards the hypothesis that sensitivity to self-organization is lacking in existing policy frameworks.

Note

1. In this chapter we will use the term 'organizations' to mean both organizations and institutions.

References

Adler, S.P. and S.W. Kwon. 2002. 'Social Capital: Prospects for a New Concept', *Academy of Management Review*, 27(1): 17–40.

Baker, W. 1990. 'Market Networks and Corporate Behavior', *American Journal of Sociology*, 96(3): 589–625.

Bradshaw, D. 2006. 'Mintzberg slams leadership', *Financial Times*, 23 October.

Brown, J.S. and P. Duguid. 2000. *The Social Life of Information*. Boston, MA: Harvard Business Press.

Coleman, J.S. 1990. *Foundations of Social Theory*. Cambridge, MA: Harvard University Press.

Nahapiet, J. and S. Ghoshal. 1998. 'Social Capital, Intellectual Capital and the Organisational Advantage', *Academy of Management Review*, 23(2): 242–66.

North, D. 1990. *Institutions, Institutional Change and Economic Performance*. Cambridge: Cambridge University Press.

Putnam, R., R. Loenardi and R.Y. Nanetti. 1993. *Making Democracy Work: Civic Traditions in Modern Italy*. Princeton, NJ: Princeton University Press.

Senge, P.M., C.O. Scharmer, J. Jaworski and B.S. Flowers. 2004. 'Awakening Faith in an Alternative Future: A Consideration of Presence—Human Purpose and the Field of the Future', *The Society for Organizational Learning Journal*, 7(5): 1–11.

Stacey, R.D. 1996. *Complexity and Creativity in Organizations*. San Francisco, CA: Berrett-Koehler.

Surowiecki, J. 2005. *The Wisdom of the Crowds*. New York: Anchor Books.

Wheatley, M. 1996. 'The Irresistible Future of Organizing'. Available online at http://www.margaretwheatley.com/articles/irresistiblefuture.html, accessed on 6 August 2008.

Part 6

Application of Knowledge Management for Achieving Social Objectives

23 Promoting the Use of Knowledge Management as a Tool for Securing Larger Good of the Society

Surinder Batra

Introduction

The title of this chapter invites several questions to which there are no ready answers. The most compelling question is, what do we mean by the larger good of the society? An internet search on the phrase 'larger good of the society' did not bring out anything significant except two brief statements in a speech by Mr Azim H. Premji, Chairman, Wipro Corporation, delivered as the 38th Convocation Address at IIT-M in July 2001. These statements were as follows:

1. 'While knowledge-based industries provided a great opportunity for creating wealth, there is need to use it for the larger good of society.'
2. 'In the millennium of the mind, knowledge-based industries like IT are in a unique position to earn wealth from outside. While earning is important, we must have mechanisms by which we use it for the larger good of our society.'

While these statements fall short of defining what is 'larger good of the society', they rightly point towards the potential of knowledge-based industries in delivering wealth for the society. Economists have always maintained that gross domestic product (GDP) and economic growth contribute to society's wealth and well-being. However, since the early 1990s, Human Development Reports from United Nations Development Programme (UNDP) have pushed the concept that human development is central to the well-being of a society. United Nations Development Programme has also come up with the Millennium Development Goals in the *Human Development Report*, 2003, which have gained international acceptance. Recently, an attempt has been made in certain quarters to define a 'Happiness Index' and rank countries according to how happy their population are. The concept of 'gross national happiness' has also been suggested, and in certain quarters, this is being described as relatively more important than GDP.

In this chapter, the view taken is that development as defined by UNDP in its human development reports is a fairly good indicator of the larger good of the society. Briefly, according to this concept, the indicator of well-being is that all people lead a full and productive life in balanced and harmonious interdependence with each other. Development is the process of enlarging people's choices, created by expanding human capabilities through knowledge, skills and health. However, providing more choices is only a partial view of development; development also means an expansion in awareness and ability to choose correctly. It also emphasizes that development, in order to be meaningful, has to be a process of mutual learning and interchange.

Development and Knowledge

Significance of Knowledge in Development

The importance of knowledge for development cannot be over-emphasized. According to the World Bank's report entitled *World Development Report—Knowledge for Development, 1998–99* (1999), knowledge is critical for development because everything we do depends upon knowledge. We need to transform our resources into useful outputs, and that requires knowledge. However, since resources are scarce, we need to use them in such a manner that ever-higher returns are achieved on our efforts and investments. That too requires knowledge. The report observes that in the current world economy, the balance between knowledge and resources has considerably shifted towards knowledge.

The OECD Report (1996) defines four types of knowledge, namely, know-what, know-why, know-how and know-who. As is evident, know-what refers to knowledge about facts, whereas know-why refers to the knowledge of scientific principles and laws of nature. Know-how refers to skills or the capability to do something, and know-who involves information about who knows what and who knows how to do what. It is axiomatic that all the four types of knowledge are crucial to any strategy for promoting development. Further, knowledge is increasingly being codified and transmitted through computer and communications networks. Also required is tacit knowledge, including the skills to use and adapt codified knowledge, which underlines the importance of continuous learning by individuals and firms. Thanks to the technology behind knowledge management (KM), it has led to moving the border between explicit and tacit knowledge towards explicating a part of the tacit knowledge. It has also resulted in a far greater potential for global knowledge sharing amongst a large diversity of stakeholders who may be considerably spread geographically.

The conscious use of KM as a discipline for promoting development has recent beginnings. According to Ferreira and Neto (2005), KM had its origin in the corporate sector but it was soon adapted by the development sector owing to its direct relevance to this sector. Knowledge management began to influence the development community, namely, the group of institutions (public and private, national and international) whose mission is promoting development of impoverished countries, in the second half of the 1990s, with the initiatives of the World Bank, the United Nations, the Global Knowledge Partnership and some other international institutions. The potential of KM in development is not sufficiently understood but the number of organizations that are giving it importance is growing every day.

Stakeholders in the Development Sector

The development sector is populated by a variety of stakeholders. National governments (and respective state governments) and various government bodies are one clear set of stakeholders, as they conceive and plan development programmes, allocate funds for their implementation and take up their implementation either directly or through other agencies. Local target groups (specific to the development programme) form another important, or rather the most important, set of stakeholders since development activities are aimed at lifting their status in the society. The third important stakeholder category is subject matter experts, for example, experts in health, education, whose knowledge and skills are retained for executing the development programmes. These experts may be from the local community or outside, or even from other countries, depending upon the requirements and whether any external development agencies are also engaged in the execution of development programmes. External development agencies themselves are another important stakeholder category. They operate in the host country in accordance with their respective country programmes, which are expected to be in conformity with the national policies. Typically, development agencies provide financial support for implementation of development programmes. However, it is not uncommon to find them operating with a policy and agenda guided by their own priorities. On many occasions, development agencies may have their own philosophy regarding what works and what does not in a given national situation. Many a time, consultants/experts nominated by the development agencies are expected to contribute to the development programmes, irrespective of whether or not they understand the realities of the local environment fully.

The point being made here is that all the stakeholders are owners of knowledge which is a mix of explicit and tacit knowledge. The extent to which knowledge has been made explicit, however, depends upon the type of stakeholder. For example, much of the knowledge of the local target group remains tacit most of the time. On the other hand, knowledge owned by development agencies and/or external experts may have a high codified content in terms of guides, manuals, documentation of learning experiences, and so on. As observed earlier, however, KM discipline facilitates transformation of tacit knowledge of many of these stakeholders into explicit knowledge. It also facilitates wider sharing of knowledge within the same category of stakeholders as well as amongst stakeholders of different categories.

Characteristics of Knowledge in the Development Context

There is a major difference in the characteristics of knowledge as seen in the context of development sector and in the corporate sector context. Ferreira and Neto (2005) have identified the following key characteristics of knowledge in a development context:

1. When an individual, an organization or a social group innovates successfully, the knowledge on which that progress is based becomes visible. As time goes on, such progress is understood and copied. Thus, one can say that knowledge 'leaks' from the innovators to a larger spectrum of society.
2. Once knowledge spreads in society, it has no private owner. Thus, most development-related knowledge becomes public good.

3. There exist several linguistic, social and cognitive barriers against knowledge diffusion across different social groups. These barriers can impede knowledge from being transferred to whoever may need this knowledge.

4. In society, the frontiers, actors and rules for KM are not well defined, and they keep on changing. Therefore, solutions required have to be flexible and robust to adapt to such fuzzy and changing conditions.

5. Culture cannot be easily changed in a society. As culture is the source of barriers in KM diffusion processes, it has implications for utilization of knowledge.

To these characteristics, one can add the following two more features identified in the World Bank Report (1999):

6. As compared to other commodities, knowledge is 'non-rivalrous'; that is, sharing of knowledge with others does not mean that it has been given away.

7. Once knowledge has been put in public domain, it is non-excludable, that is, it is difficult for its creator to prevent others from using it.

Empirical Findings on KM Applications by Development Agencies

The literature of KM applications in the development sector is replete with examples of development agencies having established KM systems in the last six to seven years. According to King and McGrath (2003), the centrality of knowledge for development cooperation agencies has led to the rapid spread of notions of KM and knowledge sharing across the agency community. The British Department for International Development (DFID) has embarked upon a knowledge-sharing project. The Japan International Cooperation Agency (JICA) is developing a new knowledge management network, as is the German Agency for Technical Cooperation. The Inter-American Development Bank, European Bank for Reconstruction and Development (EBRD), Asian Development Bank (ADB), Swedish International Development and Cooperation Agency (SIDA), and the Canadian International Development Agency are also amongt those who have embarked on knowledge projects. This trend is not confined to official development assistance. A number of existing non-governmental organizations (NGOs) have also become active in the new knowledge-based aid such as Oxfam and TearFund in Britain. Moreover, a new set of what may be termed 'knowledge NGOs' has also appeared on the development stage, including OneWorld, and the International Institute for Communications and Development.

The documentation of the experience of establishing KM systems is available on the internet for the World Bank, UNDP, United Nations Economic and Social Commission for Asia and the Pacific (UNESCAP) and ADB. Out of these, the experience of World Bank has been very well documented and an additional advantage is that it has been systematically evaluated. A snapshot evaluation of KM initiatives in SIDA, JICA, DFID and EBRD was also done by a World Bank Evaluation Team and it is a good source of information on how KM is being implemented by these agencies. In the following sections, a brief overview of the KM systems at some of these agencies is presented.

Knowledge Management Initiatives at the World Bank

The credit for initiating KM at the World Bank goes to the then World Bank President in 1996 when he, for the first time, publicly announced the vision of the bank transforming itself into a 'Knowledge Bank'. According to the Evaluation Report by the World Bank Operation Evaluation Department (Gwin 2003), the bank's stated intention was to develop a world-class KM system and to improve and expand the sharing of development knowledge with clients and partners. The objectives of this commitment were to improve the quality of the bank operations and enhance the capacity of clients to achieve development results.

The three objectives of KM envisioned by the World Bank comprise (*a*) creating knowledge; (*b*) sharing knowledge and (*c*) applying knowledge. The sources of creating knowledge are seen as economic and sector work, research evaluation, learning from the outside world and learning from their (World Bank professionals) own successes and failures. The sharing of knowledge is seen to take place with clients, partners and the outside world, as well as with its own internal professional community. The application of knowledge is seen in the form of knowledge products and services created and offered by the bank to the target groups and national governments.

Knowledge management systems at the World Bank gradually evolved from components which can be categorized as 'self-service', form of 'networks/communities of practice' (CoP) and the more thoroughly evolved form called 'facilitated knowledge transfer'. The self-service category includes corporate KM portal, knowledge repository image banks, library of learning objects, video-on-demand/webcasts, live databases and directories of expertise. The second level of evolution called networks/CoPs includes sector networks, thematic groups and advisory services. The last category of facilitated knowledge transfer includes debriefing/after-action reviews and peer learning. As one moves from the lowest level of KM (self-service) to the highest level (facilitated knowledge transfer), one observes an increasingly higher human interaction and move from explicit to tacit form of knowledge.

The bank has established nearly 80 thematic groups till date. These are essentially CoPs related to specific disciplines. These thematic groups are organized by individual sectors or across sectors, support core bank functions, are funded by sector boards and are accountable to them, and rely extensively on knowledge partnerships. Besides, there now exist 25 advisory services (help-desk facilities) for obtaining knowledge in specific fields, several sectoral knowledge collections on Web, live databases of country/sector statistics, directories (people pages), debriefings (tacit knowledge downloads), indigenous knowledge bases (such as Africa IK), global development gateway, development forum (discussion groups), B-SPAN (webcasting) and dissemination for formal/informal learning. For capturing tacit knowledge from operational experiences (what was done and how it was done), the systems developed include (*a*) video-taping of narrative ('story-telling') and (*b*) synthesis of themes in two–five minute video clips. The initiatives such as launch of Global Development Learning Network and Development Gateway are useful for connecting externally and serve as media for connecting development experts around the world. Technologies used for KM at the World Bank include (*a*) global satellite communications links connecting HQ and country offices; (*b*) video-conferencing (satellites, ISDN, IP); (*c*) interactive TV (TV broadcasting by satellite and interaction via phone, fax, e-mail); (*d*) Web—online learning applications; (*e*) Web-based video casting and (*f*) online discussions and newsletters. Other important initiatives are network and regional internal knowledge-sharing activities among the bank staff and regional- and country-level external knowledge sharing with the clients.

According to an internal evaluation report (Gwin, 2003), the World Bank has spent nearly US $220 million on the various afore-mentioned KM initiatives. These have sparked a lot of innovation with potentially significant benefits for scaling up of effective bank interventions and for empowering clients to improve development outcomes. Consequently, the bank's knowledge has become faster and easier to access. Stated advantages of the KM systems at World Bank are as follows:

1. Substantial upgrades in the bank's information management system and global connectivity
2. More systematic collection of bank's information and lessons of experience, and their active dissemination to staff, clients and partners
3. Greater interaction among all staff across the institution and with clients, around shared work areas
4. Innovations in collaborative analytical work and peer-to-peer exchange across client countries
5. Leveraging of technology for global knowledge sharing

Internal surveys at the bank reveal that a much higher percentage of World Bank staff is able to access the knowledge and information they need to do their job. They feel that they have adequate opportunities to learn new skills to do their job better. Most professionals rate very favourably the bank's delivery of global knowledge or best practices in the form of products and services as a result of KM applications. It is not surprising that the bank was recognized as the Most Admired Knowledge Enterprise (Know Network) in the years 2003, 2002, 2001 and 2000, and was named as Best Practice Partner by American Productivity & Quality Center (APQC). However, it is believed that the new KM-related activities have not been tightly linked to the bank's core tasks, which limit their effectiveness. As a result, the staff and clients do not view the new KM-related programmes as sufficiently relevant to their operational work. The report also identifies oversight and lack of incentives as major impediments. Challenges ahead in successful KM applications at the World Bank include mainstreaming KM in core operational processes, consolidating knowledge and learning objects, knowledge sharing with external agencies for capacity development and scaling up through partner institutions.

Knowledge Management Initiatives at Other Development Agencies

King and McGrath (2003) provide an interesting comparison of the KM systems at four selected international development agencies. These are

1. JICA
2. SIDA
3. EBRD
4. DFID

Some of the salient features of this comparison are as follows:

1. Knowledge management initiatives in all these four agencies focus on practical improvements of the day-to-day internal working through knowledge sharing.

2. All the agencies support the production and dissemination of developmentally useful knowledge that otherwise would be under-produced if left to either the market or national systems of knowledge generation.

3. Knowledge-sharing activities in these four agencies range from highly technological approach for formal knowledge transfer to an increasingly human-centred approach which encourages both formal and informal interactions, to an approach stressing organizational learning and partner capacity development.

4. All the agencies make use of the CoPs for knowledge sharing though the mode of operation of the CoPs varies considerably across them. For example, DFID's approach to CoPs stresses the informal nature of knowledge sharing. Typically one member of the staff has part-time responsibility for supporting their work. Also, a small number of communities already have external participation. Japan International Cooperation Agency's approach to CoPs is through formal structures and management, and opening the CoPs out to the wider Japanese development community is encouraged.

5. All agencies have developed their intranets as a way of enabling more effective internal knowledge sharing. For example, DFID's intranet site, called InSight, is aimed at better sharing of information about organizational vision and restructuring. For its staff, the new intranet is an immediately visible part of their working day.

6. Other KM systems in vogue in these development agencies are

   (*i*) electronic documentation and record management (DFID and SIDA) and

   (*ii*) electronic yellow pages which provide an electronic tool through which the tacit and codified knowledge of staff can be tapped more effectively by colleagues (EBRD and DFID).

7. All the agencies provide support to national knowledge capacities, such as global public goods' development and dissemination; research cooperation and North-South and South-South institutional partnerships and meetings.

8. At least two agencies (DFID and JICA) are supporting e-learning initiatives. In DFID's case, the Imfundo Project is narrowly focused on using information and communication technologies (ICT) to support teacher training in Africa. Japan International Cooperation Agency has embarked upon the J-Net initiative, which plans to provide distance learning through a series of 30 dedicated centres in the south.

9. Both at DFID and EBRD, all the relevant knowledge about a project is distilled into short and standardized project data sheets.

10. Agencies are increasingly moving away from the certainty of universal answers to development questions. The growing awareness of the importance of context is one of the direct consequences of the knowledge agenda.

Vision of Knowledge Society in the Indian Context

Several documents refer to a vision of knowledge society in the Indian context. For example, the report of the task force *India as Knowledge Superpower: Startegy for Transformation* (Government of India 2001) recounts that India was a leading knowledge society in the millennia gone by, thanks to the awe-inspiring contributions by our saints, poets, philosophers, scientists, astronomers and mathematicians towards new thoughts, principles and practices. India, according to the report, has the potential to capture its past glory, learn the key role of knowledge in development and become a leading knowledge society. The report observes that the Indian knowledge society will have three key drivers, namely, (*a*) societal transformation for a just and equitable society, (*b*) wealth generation and (*c*) protection of the traditional form of knowledge. The societal transformation will be centred primarily in education, healthcare, agriculture and governance, and will encompass higher employment generation, higher industrial growth, higher national efficiency and productivity, higher empowerment of women, creation of a truly transparent society and generation of significant rural prosperity. As regards the second key driver, that is, wealth generation, India's economic development will depend upon its ability to generate wealth and share it equitably. This wealth generation has to be powered by generation, dissemination and creative use of knowledge, woven around national competencies. As regards the third dimension, that is, protection of traditional knowledge, the report observes that there is a responsibility to design and implement an intellectual property right (IPR) system to protect India's indigenous innovations and traditional knowledge.

The core areas that will spearhead India's march towards a knowledge society would be both technology and service driven. Technologies will include ICT, biotechnology, oceanography, space technology, environmental technology, and so on. The service-driven areas would include, among others, disaster mitigation, weather modification, telemedicine, tele-education, native knowledge products, teleservices for national and overseas requirements, and infotainment. The report makes a point that the difference between an information technology (IT)-driven society and a knowledge-driven society resides crucially in the role of multiple technology growth engines; and that multiple technologies and management structures will have to be woven together to provide a strong foundation to the Indian knowledge society. In other words, using IT, multiple technologies can be interwoven to realize a knowledge-propelled society. Further, the use of IT even in traditional sectors can facilitate conversion of these sectors to knowledge-intensive sectors through embedding new knowledge in multiple technologies.

The Task Force Report observes that in a knowledge society, only those people who are able to convert knowledge into skilled action become its real capital. Therefore, generation of trained and skilled human resources is a key challenge. It has identified a requirement of more than three million knowledge workers in multiple technologies. Finally, the report observes that a vibrant and dynamic knowledge society has to touch every member of the society; therefore, every strata of society should become consumer of knowledge products. Thus, the basic constituents of the knowledge society would be knowledge workers who create quality knowledge products and enlightened citizens who consume such products. A knowledge superpower can only be built upon a foundation of a civil society that is nearly 100 per cent literate and has a capacity to absorb new and relevant knowledge. Therefore, a constant development of human capital with thrust on skill upgradation, generation, assimilation, dissemination and use of knowledge needs emphasis.

More recently, the importance of knowledge and skill development as a means of promoting knowledge society and making knowledge and skills as drivers of economic growth of India has become an important theme with authors concerned with India's development challenges. For example, a World Bank paper (Dar 2006) observes that India's transition to a knowledge-based economy requires a new generation of educated and skilled people. Its competitive edge will be determined by its people's ability to create, share and use knowledge effectively. A knowledge economy requires India to develop workers—knowledge workers and knowledge technologists—who are flexible and analytical and who can be the driving force for innovation and growth. To achieve this, India needs a flexible education system: basic education to provide the foundations for learning; secondary and tertiary education to develop core capabilities and core technical skills and further means of achieving lifelong learning. The education system must be attuned to the new global environment by promoting creativity, and improving the quality of education and training at all levels.

Knowledge Cities, Knowledge Citizens and Evolutionary Learning Communities

Laszlo and Laszlo (2006) refer to two main purposes of knowledge-based development (KBD), namely, economic prosperity and human development. These two purposes, according to them, are complementary but can continue to operate within a framework of 'business as usual'. They emphasize the need for a third purpose of KBD, which is to contribute to a socially and environmentally sustainable society as the enabler of an evolutionary future. To include this third purpose, there is a need to recast those who live in a knowledge economy as more than knowledge workers, namely, as knowledge citizens.

The afore-mentioned authors define knowledge citizens as better educated (formally or informally), critical and informed sections of population who are

1. ready to participate in civic life;
2. politically active;
3. interested in a better quality of life for themselves and for the next generation, including concern for healthy lifestyles and less dependence on consumption;
4. appreciative of artistic expression and cultural activities; and
5. more competent in human relations.

The knowledge citizens make possible a learning society. These authors also define a knowledge city, which may be thought of as the hardware, the infrastructure for learning and knowledge creation. The learning society is the software—the culture of learning, creativity and innovation—that distributes the benefits of access to knowledge across the society by offering a higher quality of life and greater opportunities for meaningful living.

The authors make a distinction among growth, development and evolution. Growth implies an increase in size or quantity, whereas development implies an amelioration of conditions or quality. Evolution, on the other hand, is a tendency towards greater structural complexity and organizational simplicity, more efficient modes of operation and greater dynamic harmony. The evolutionary development, therefore, seeks to promote future-oriented human activities; it involves designing new ways of learning, working and living that embody social and environmental integrity. 'It is about creating a simpler and more meaningful way of producing what we need in order to re-establish the balance between our human systems, the biosphere, and the geosphere in which they rest.'

The creation of a sustainable learning society requires bringing people together to define the paths that make sense to them through dialogue so that they may determine ways that are meaningful and feasible, given their culture, situation, talents, values and aspirations. The creation of a sustainable learning society begins by enabling and empowering individuals in community, so that they may develop the competencies and sensibilities to meet their personal, economic, social and environmental needs.

The authors quote the example of the north Mexican city of Monterrey which has developed the strategic vision of becoming a knowledge city by the year 2020. The state government's website defines a knowledge city as a geographic territory where government, business and society devise a strategic plan for the common purpose of building a knowledge-based economy. One strategy suggested to implement the large-scale involvement of citizens is through the creation of evolutionary learning communities (ELCs), which serve as spaces where citizens from diverse backgrounds and perspectives representing all sectors of society get together to learn, develop their capacities and identify opportunities for collaborative action. These activities are expected to have a direct impact in terms of the improvement of quality of life, creation of a positive future and an increase in life-affirming opportunities. The vision of the type of dialogues to be fostered within the Monterrey ELCs is of multi-sectoral gatherings (including marginalized residents, union workers, academics, professionals, women and youth, to mention but a few) that are open to participation by anyone interested in the opportunity. The Monterrey ELCs will be explicitly oriented to evolutionary learning. In other words, their learning strategy will seek to generate personal, social and environmental transformation for sustainability. The assumption behind the methodology is that there is a collective wisdom that needs to be activated and accessed, so that people can step forward to solve their own problems as well as to create new possibilities for their future.

Conclusions

This chapter traversed the journey through basic concepts of knowledge and KM as relevant to the organizational and development contexts, and has overviewed the contemporary practices and philosophies/visions of knowledge management for development, as interpreted by selected development agencies, development experts and task forces established by national governments. It emerges from this journey that KM has not taken the shape of a concrete tool which can be simply applied to the known and unknown development challenges of any country to place it on the desired growth and development trajectory. In terms of practical use, there have been significant advancements by well-known development agencies, for example, use of intranet-based KM portals for knowledge sharing, establishment of knowledge gateways and knowledge development networks, and adoption of communities of practice. However, it cannot be established as yet that these innovations have made a major paradigm shift in the development processes though significant internal efficiency gains have been reported. Interestingly, the literature appears to have come to a full circle by re-discovering and re-iterating that knowledge and skill development are crucial for promoting larger good of the society. Another highlight of the current thinking is that not only do we require knowledge workers, but we also require knowledge consumers and knowledge citizens, if we want a sustainable knowledge society. There is strong evidence to suggest that the current international thinking appreciates the concern for enabling and empowering individuals in the society to develop their competencies and sensibilities for meeting their personal, economic, social and environmental needs. To this end, the concept of ELCs serving as spaces for citizens with diverse backgrounds to learn, develop their capacities and identify opportunities for collaborative action appears a welcome new idea worth exploring.

References

Dar, A. 2006. '"The World Bank"—The Vocational Education and Training System in India"', Conference Paper at *India: Meeting the Employment Challenge: Conference on Labour & Employment Issues in India*, Institute for Human Development, New Delhi, 27–29 July.

Ferreira, S.D.M. and M. Neto. 2005. 'Knowledge Management and Social Learning: Exploring the Cognitive Dimension of Development', 1(3): 4–17. Available online at www.km4dev.org/journal

Government of India. 2001. 'India as Knowledge Superpower: Strategy for Transformation', Report of the Task Force. New Delhi: Educational Consultants India Ltd. On behalf of Planning Commission, Government of India.

Gwin, C. 2003. *Sharing Knowledge: Innovations and Remaining Challenges*, An OED Evaluation. Washington, DC: The World Bank.

King, Kenneth and Simon McGrath. 2003. *Knowledge Sharing in Development Agencies: Lessons from Four Cases*. Washington, DC: The World Bank Operations Evaluation Department (OED), The World Bank.

Laszlo, K.C. and Alexander Laszlo. 2006. 'Fostering a Sustainable Learning Society through Knowledge Based Development', ISSS-2006, Proceedings of 50th Annual Meeting of the International Society for the Systems Sciences, California, 9–14 July 2006.

Organisation for Economic Cooperation and Development (OECD). 1996. *The Knowledge-Based Economy*. Paris: OECD.

Premji, Azim H. 2001. '38th Convocation Address of IIT-Madras, July, 2001'. Available online at http://www.hinduonnet.com/2001/07/28/stories/0428401y.htm, accessed on 3 September 2006.

Prusak, Larry 1999. 'Action Review of Knowledge Management: Report & Recommendations'. Available at http://siteresources.worldbank.org/WBI/Resources/2137981099435725267/ActionReviewKM.doc, accessed on 3 September 2006.

UNDP. 1990. *Human Development Report 1990: Concept and Measurement of Human Development*. New York: Oxford University Press.

UNDP. 2001. *Human Development Report 2001: Making New Technologies Work for Human Development*. New York: Oxford University Press.

UNDP. 2003. *Human Development Report 2003: Millennium Development Goals: A Compact among Nations to End Human Poverty*. New York: Oxford University Press.

World Bank. 1999. *World Development Report—Knowledge for Development, 1998–99*. Washington D.C.: World Bank.

Website: http://en.wikipedia.org/wiki/gross_national_happiness, accessed on 3 September 2006.

24 Knowledge Management and Human Development

MAINAK SARKAR AND SIDDHARTH MAHAJAN

...economies are built not merely through the accumulation of physical capital and human skill, but on a foundation of information, learning, and adaptation. Because knowledge matters, understanding how people and societies acquire and use knowledge—and why they sometimes fail to do so—is essential to improving people's lives, especially the lives of the poorest (World Bank 1998).

Introduction

It is useful to interpret knowledge in the context of human development. Although no consensus exists, the knowledge management (KM) literature typically defines knowledge as 'actionable information', that is, information that can be used for taking a better decision (Tiwana 2002). Unlike information, which simply gives facts, knowledge allows the recipient to improve his decisions. Although information is easy to document and share and is therefore 'explicit', a large part of knowledge is embedded in the person concerned; in other words it is 'tacit'. Therefore, the sharing of information is relatively easy, but knowledge is by its nature hard to share and manage in a meaningful way. Although difficult, this is not an impossible task. Knowledge management as a business practice has been successfully implemented in a multitude of companies across the world, where success is defined as adding value and increasing the profitability of concerned companies. Knowledge management is, therefore, a set of practices that encourages the creation of new knowledge, harnessing of existing knowledge, and dissemination and utilization of such knowledge for adding value.

The state has a multitude of roles to play, but in the context of this chapter we view it as a provider of government services and, in that sense, no different from a large company albeit of a not-for-profit or altruistic kind. This chapter, therefore, asks the question whether KM practices that have succeeded in companies can be suitably adapted and implemented at the societal level, that is, whether the government can improve its ability to provide such services as health, education, governance, to its citizens through better management of knowledge. Also, what are the probable hurdles that it is likely to face in this process?

Potential benefits from successfully managing knowledge can be considerable, as international experience has shown. Here a distinction needs to be made between knowledge that directly affects human development, such as knowledge regarding a new vaccine or public health, and technical knowledge that affects development primarily through enhancing growth in income and employment, or in other words knowledge that has an indirect impact. The position taken in this chapter is that both are equally important and, therefore, government policies need to encourage the generation and dissemination of both. This view has emerged from a consensus among experts, based on a recent empirical finding across the world that growth, although not a precondition for human development, definitely helps in a large measure in achieving it. India and other developing countries are in an envious position today, since considerable technical knowledge, as well as knowledge pertaining directly to human development, has already been developed by the industrialized countries over the last century. In other words, there is no need for re-inventing the wheel. Some experts believe that countries such as India and China are in a better position today compared to the West,[1] since they do not have legacy technologies from the past (in most developed countries there are sectors which use the latest technologies and others that are more backward). Therefore, their latecomer status helps them in getting the best technologies without legacy costs of changeover, which means that they have the potential to leapfrog over developed countries. For instance, recent experience in telecommunications shows that whereas the US, one of the earliest adopters of cellular technologies, is stuck with a network that is not the most advanced, high costs of switching mean that they continue using it although better alternatives exist. However, a country such as China, which was a late adopter, was able to install a superior or more advanced system. This perception may be excessively optimistic, for most experts believe that large disparities in the availability of knowledge exist in the world, which the World Bank terms as 'knowledge gaps'. The role of the government, therefore, is to design and implement a system that helps in closing this knowledge gap. Recent improvements in telecommunications technology and a steep fall in prices of such technologies have also meant that today a villager in a remote part of India can have access to knowledge that was unimaginable even a couple of decades back.

There is a consensus among most experts that one of the best ways to combat under-development is through economic growth and one of the key drivers of growth is technological progress. Therefore, the closing of the knowledge gap between the rich and poor countries can considerably increase their growth rates which in turn can significantly improve their levels of human development. A notable example in this regard is of the so-called East Asian Miracle, that is, the tiger economies (Hong Kong, Singapore, Taiwan and Korea) that successfully transformed themselves within a generation from primarily rural, poor and agrarian societies to industrial powerhouses with enviable records of human development, so much so that the latest figures show that there is hardly any poverty in any of these countries. For instance, whereas both South Korea and Ghana started out with roughly the same per capita incomes in the 1950s, by the late 1990s Korea's per capita income was roughly six times that of Ghana. Such impressive growth rates have been observed rarely in the history of the world. Although there were a multitude of factors that contributed to this phenomenon, most experts currently hold the view that a large portion of this growth is attributable towards the successful adoption and implementation of the latest technologies from the leaders (the Western countries). This shows the potential for countries such as India in managing knowledge successfully. Also, it is to be noted that knowledge gaps exist not just between countries but within the countries as well. So, the government policy has to adequately address such gaps within the country as well, for equitable growth and the largest impact on human development.

There is also a threat from not being able to manage knowledge properly. With the world economy moving towards increasing knowledge orientation where technology plays a significant role in every aspect of value creation (production, transportation, and so on), countries that fail to adapt themselves will be left behind. Globalization has made certain countries very rich given their ability to adapt and utilize the latest technologies (Japan, Korea and more recently China), but other countries have been left way behind. Therefore, the gains from globalization will accrue primarily to those countries that are successful in managing knowledge, and the gap between the winners and losers is only likely to widen over time.

This chapter is structured as follows. The next section discusses how KM at the societal level is different from that at the company level. A later section discusses policies required for KM for human development in terms of the objectives and policies needed to achieve them. The subsequent section discusses how typically KM is implemented in a company and lessons for governments. Thereafter, a section reports some interesting case studies in this context and brings out some common hurdles that governments are likely to face in implementing a KM system. Finally there are conclusions.

Knowledge for Companies vis-à-vis Human Development

Salient features of knowledge in the context of a private business are considerably different from the type of knowledge that is relevant to society as a whole. Knowledge in the context of a company is 'intellectual capital'. In other words, it is what distinguishes a company from its competitors and contributes towards its core competency. For instance, Google is a successful company since it can create web search algorithms which are considerably superior to its competitor's offerings. It can do so because of the intellectual capital of its employees. Therefore, knowledge in the business context has to be proprietary since this is what adds value to the company. In other words, knowledge in this case is intellectual property and needs to be protected by the company. In contrast, knowledge that is relevant to human development, such as the availability of a vaccine for a particular disease, should not have restrictions on access. Knowledge in this context is what economists call a 'public good', which has two characteristics, non-excludability and non-rivalry. Non-excludability means in this context that it is information that is not desirable to be held secret; on the contrary, it should be disseminated as widely as possible. As compared to intellectual property in the context of a company, Google stays in business by protecting its copyright on its technology. Its survival depends on its ability to exclude rivals from acquiring this knowledge. Non-rivalry means that if a person X knows about the vaccine, his knowledge does not reduce the benefit of knowing about it to person Y; if anything, it might increase the benefit since there would be less incidence of the disease in the community. On the other hand, if Google loses its intellectual property it also loses its value as a company, and so its knowledge is highly rivalrous. Other examples of public good that are non-excludable and non-rivalrous are roads and infrastructure, education and public health.

The public good nature of knowledge in this context means that private profit motive is unlikely to generate and disseminate this knowledge. Therefore, governments and other non-profit agencies have to take the lead. Although society as a whole gains considerably from the generation, dissemination and utilization of such knowledge, the gains are not proprietary in nature and, therefore, cannot be captured by a private company. In other words, social returns are much higher than private returns. Need for the right policy of the state is, therefore, paramount. An excellent example in this regard is the set of innovations that are collectively known as the Green Revolution which significantly increased land yields across the world. Private companies did not undertake research in developing high-yielding variety (HYV) seeds since it is hard to make a profit through selling seeds. First, the purchasing power of farmers across much of the developing world is low; and second, it is hard to make sure that farmers who buy the seeds once do not then collect and use the seeds produced by the plants next year instead of purchasing fresh seeds from the company. This meant that there was little incentive for any company to develop such seeds since it could not make a profit selling it. Although society as a whole gains considerably from the availability of HYV seeds through higher output, and so on. private benefit to the companies innovating the seeds is low. It is a typical example of how private returns to innovators may often be low compared to societal benefits. In this instance, the lead was taken by multilateral agencies such as the Consultative Group for International Agricultural Research (CGIAR),[2] in developing and disseminating information regarding these seeds.

Policies for Successful Knowledge Management

Acquiring Knowledge

Whereas standard KM is related to managing knowledge that is either already available or can be created within the company, in the context of human development the approach needs to be modified, in particular about the public good nature of such knowledge. The existing reality is that generating knowledge through research and development (R&D) is an expensive process and, therefore, it is done primarily by developed countries. Also, such solutions are usually not readily applicable in the context of developing countries such as India. Therefore, the government needs to have its own approach to this problem, which are as follows:

1. To the extent possible encourage the inflow of new technologies. Crucial determinants in this regard are trade and investment as well as industrial policies that the government undertakes. Internationally the role that foreign direct investment (FDI) plays in transferring knowledge is well documented.
2. Encourage the creation of indigenous technologies that are more appropriate for India. Although the central research laboratories have had considerable success they need to be revamped to meet the challenges of the knowledge economy. Spending on R&D needs to be increased as promised by the President of India from the current rate of 0.75 per cent to a target of 2 per cent, in the latest Science and Technology Policy, 2003. Also better utilization of existing resources needs to be made.
3. Universities and other educational institutions are key resources towards the generation of knowledge. Adequate incentives need to be put in place to encourage research activities.
4. Encourage more R&D by private sources, through suitable incentives, such as tax breaks, with adequate monitoring such that incentives are not abused, as is often the case in the current system.

Absorbing Knowledge

Considerable technical knowledge, as well as information on health, education, and so on, is already public knowledge. For instance, anything published in a scientific journal can be accessed by one and all with the help of internet from anywhere, anytime. However, such knowledge also needs to be utilized to have any value. The following policies have been shown to have worked across a number of countries:

1. Recent global experience shows that encouraging education, particularly that of girls and other disadvantaged groups (such as minorities) in the population, can have a tremendous impact on human development. It can also facilitate the dissemination of knowledge as women's power in the household increases with education, and they have a say in the family's health and educational matters.
2. Encouraging lifelong education through continuous training and skill maintenance and upgradation can significantly increase the ability to absorb new knowledge. Also technical education needs to be encouraged.
3. Overall, the best way to ensure that best practices get implemented is through publicity campaigns. This cannot be a one-shot attempt; the government needs to put in place infrastructure that is capable of disseminating such information to the public. No other authority has the trust or credibility to deliver such information to the public. For instance, the Green Revolution could not have happened without a concerted effort to disseminate information regarding HYV seeds to the farmers. For an impact on human development, such dissemination has to be a continuous process.

Communicating Knowledge

Another key role of the government is to act as a facilitator in the dissemination of knowledge. In other words, it needs to take the initiative in creation and adoption of new knowledge as well as in the dissemination of the same, and at the same time encourage dissemination among the people as well. Given the large size and diversity and the lack of adequate communication channels, it may not be enough if the government is the only player. Again recent evidence shows the power of social networks in disseminating knowledge effectively. When one person learns about a new agricultural technique and finds it profitable to adopt it, then he shares it with his peer group. Such spreading of knowledge within the community depends crucially on the availability of the means of communications. For instance, if a village functions as an isolated island then all knowledge available to its villagers remains confined to the village whereas if villages were connected to other villages through telecommunications then the knowledge can spread through informal networks without any direct intervention of the government. In this context, the government needs to play a leading role in closing the 'digital divide', which is defined as certain groups in the population (primarily urban and educated) having access to the latest telecommunications technologies (mobile phones, internet, and so on) whereas the rest of the population does not enjoy similar access. Given the role played by private players in the adoption of mobile phones across India, the government needs to put in place regulations, standards and incentives for them to establish their networks in rural low-income areas as well. Where such approaches fail, the government needs to take the initiative in rural electrification and connection of telephones, in closing the digital divide.

Knowledge Management in a Company

Knowledge management is the process through which organizations generate value from their knowledge-based assets. Information technology (IT) is usually the major enabler for implementing KM in companies. In addition, in order to implement KM, a company needs to consider leadership, culture and measurement issues. Knowledge-based assets are broadly classified into two types: explicit and tacit. Explicit knowledge includes all information that can be documented. Examples of explicit knowledge include business plans, white papers, technical reports, patents, demand forecasts, market analysis and customer and competitor information. Tacit knowledge is that knowledge which cannot be documented and resides primarily with the employees concerned.

Implementation of KM

Two issues that need to be considered while implementing KM are (*a*) cultural and employee issues and (*b*) technology. Without the active participation of employees, a KM programme would be difficult to initiate and maintain. In many organizations, employees are valued for their expertise and their knowledge of markets, customers, suppliers and processes. This knowledge helps generate value for the company. If employees are asked to share these very knowledge-based assets, which make them valuable to the company, they may resent it. This resentment often translates into a failure of the KM programme. Therefore, it is important to set up adequate incentives for employees to share knowledge-based assets, while implementing KM. Second, technology is an enabler but technology alone is not enough. Different ways in which technology is used to implement KM include knowledge repositories, communities of practice, expert locator systems, chat forums and bulletin boards.

Knowledge-Based Assets

Companies today are generating a lot of data as a part of their daily operations. Much of this information may not be timely or accurate. It is a problem to isolate knowledge-based assets from the enormous amount of data. Knowledge-based assets are those which would help managers make good decisions. For converting information into knowledge-based assets, it is important that information be presented to employees in such a form that it can be easily analyzed and acted upon.

Knowledge-based assets take many forms. These include information about the external business environment, internal business processes and customers. A large amount of information about the external environment is important to make decisions at the strategic, tactical and operational levels. Information about internal business processes includes their standard operating procedures (SOPs), that is, the set of actions necessary to maintain processes at the current desired quality level. Knowledge about customers is a key input for maintaining profitability of companies. Customer preferences and buying patterns need to be monitored. Analyzing customer data and acting upon it will help in creating customer loyalty and generating repeat purchases from customers. Customer relationship management (CRM) initiatives in companies are already doing this but there could be a need to have tighter integration between CRM initiatives and KM.

The aforementioned issues outlined in relation to companies are similar to what the governments are likely to face when they try to manage knowledge in a better way. For instance, participants and stakeholders may be extremely reluctant to share their knowledge, since, as it has been famously said, 'knowledge is power'. Also, the choice of a standard platform for sharing of knowledge is an issue for governments as well. As in the case of companies, governments also systematically collect enormous volumes of data regarding its customers/citizens. A successful KM system has to distinguish between information and knowledge. Finally, information regarding needs of citizens (customers) and satisfaction levels is critical towards successful delivery of public services.

Phases of KM Implementation

The typically four phases of KM implementation are as follows:

1. Infrastructure evaluation: The idea is not to build something completely alien but to augment what already exists. Therefore, there is a need to first take stock of what the existing knowledge-sharing system is. There is also a need to align this system with the goals or objectives set for the KM programme. The government cannot do all the things in one go and, therefore, it must prioritize. Is AIDS a major concern or Malaria? In the short run, the approaches may be very different for the two diseases.

2. Knowledge management system analysis, design and development: Several decisions need to be taken at this stage, such as whether a proprietary system is appropriate or a public one with access available to all. This will dictate the selection of appropriate technology, for example, intranet versus internet. A knowledge audit for ascertaining which documents to look into, who has the relevant knowledge and how easily it can be shared can be a useful step. A critical component is also selecting the right team of people who are sufficiently committed and have the expertise to ensure success of the system. Finally, there is the actual designing of the system that needs to be optimized for performance and scalability as well as interoperability.

3. Deployment: It is strongly suggested to have a pilot testing first and then incrementally proceed in implementing the system in phases. Phases with the highest payoffs should be taken up first in order to convert more employees to the virtues of the system. Here, considerable attention needs to be paid to setting up a leadership structure and reward system for compliance.

4. Metrics for evaluation: Finally, once the system is in place and has been allowed to operate for a while to overcome the teething troubles, it needs to be evaluated for its impact. A KM system is not a static object but needs to be continuously updated and upgraded for continued impact.

Learning from Past Experiences

In this section, a few examples of implementations of KM for human development are presented in the case study format. Common problems that are likely to arise in most cases are also discuseed.

Likely Problems

Seven likely problems are highlighted here.

First, KM systems in companies are primarily using information and communication technologies (ICT). As mentioned earlier, one of the constraints faced by India as well as other developing countries is the lack of ICT infrastructure including low penetration levels of computers and internet. On the positive side, the situation is changing fast. For instance, under the recently launched National e-Governance Plan (NEGP), there is a provision for setting up 100,000 village-level kiosks having access to the internet. These kiosks will be primarily for governance purposes but they can also be converted into other uses. Similarly, certain state governments, such as Andhra Pradesh, are in the midst of setting up optical fibre networks for broadband access to all the villages. Nevertheless, the existing 'digital divide' is a serious problem. Availability and reliability of electricity in most villages in India is problematic; telephone lines also do not exist in many places. Some progress, although, has been made on setting up wide-area networks (WANs) through wireless technologies. Therefore, providing access to internet at the village level is going to be a challenge. The cost of equipment is an issue given the low purchasing power of residents in villages. As such, an individual access model does not seem feasible; a community access model via kiosks is definitely an option. Success of the kiosk model will depend on developing applications that people are willing to pay for, since the NEGP is primarily a PPP (public–private partnership) model with individual entrepreneurs setting up and running the kiosks. Sustainability and scalability of the system will depend on its adoption by the villagers.

Second, given the existence of the large digital divide, in the short run a more feasible option would be to avoid dissemination through ICT but use a more direct approach such as the one taken by the Honey Bee Network (Box 24.4), whereby villagers are approached directly at village fairs, and so on. Such an approach, being labour intensive, can only be undertaken with the help and cooperation of other stakeholders such as local government bodies and NGOs operating in the area.

Third, the government is likely to face the same problem as is faced by a large and diverse organization, that is, conflicting goals, interests and biases. In a country as large and diverse as India, there cannot be a single solution; one has to look at a multitude of solutions. A great deal of care has to be taken to customize solutions for local needs, and obey local customs and conventions. Many initiatives have failed in the past due to the reluctance of the stakeholders to accept them. The only way to avoid such failures is to demonstrate effectiveness very clearly and also not offend local conventions. In other words, local differences matter and in a country like India they matter more.

Fourth, local languages and communications tend to be different across India. Any KM process that the government undertakes must explicitly take this into account (again, see the case studies below). Although the content may be developed in English, it needs to be translated into local languages, be easily comprehensible to people with fairly low levels of formal education, and preferably use of audio–video should be made to illustrate the point. Local content, that is, information on local events, and so on, can make such a system popular and easily accessible to the users. Also, the extent to which such a system can be combined with other systems that have been widely accepted (such as e-governance initiatives like e-Seva in Hyderabad) should be explored.

Fifth, another common problem faced by companies (see earlier) is how to set up an incentive system that adequately rewards contributors who share their knowledge. This is likely to be an order of magnitude greater when there are different agencies involved, each with their own goals and agendas. This is a part of a broader issue. Whereas companies are dealing with their own employees who are easier to control either by fiat (order) or by incentives, at the societal level where contributors are organizations (NGOs, and so on), government ministries and multilateral agencies, co-ordination among them is going to be an enormous problem. Earlier advice for companies to go in for an incremental approach in implementing KM, therefore, assumes added significance in this context.

Sixth, given that the impact of KM is hard to measure in companies, it is likely to be even harder at the societal level. However, measurement is essential to find out if there has been an impact at all and also to correct any discrepancies in the approach. Since not even the most optimistic proponents of KM will argue that all things will fall into place at the first attempt, a continuous iterative process is required to improve its impact. Particular attention needs to be paid to see that this system does not benefit primarily the well-to-do in villages (for instance, it is commonly accepted that the primary beneficiaries of the Green Revolution at least in its early days were rich landowners). Therefore, constant monitoring of the gains is required.

Seventh, another problem that is likely to exacerbate in the coming years is the issue of intellectual property. For public information, for example, information on healthcare, such issues do not arise. However, if an innovation has been developed by some villagers then they should be compensated for their efforts and others should be encouraged to follow suit. This is extremely difficult to do at the national level. Recognition alone may not be enough (peer recognition is usually a driving force in corporate initiatives on KM). Whether everything is for free on the web, for instance, or portions of the initiative are available for a fee or paid service has to be decided on. Given reluctance of early adopters to any new system, it might be advisable to start out with a free service and later switch the more successful portions of the system to a paid service, once their benefits have been demonstrated.

Case Studies

Several cases are mentioned in Boxes 24.1–24.4, which give concrete examples of KM for human development in practice and also highlight some of the issues raised earlier in the chapter. Box 24.1 discusses the implementation of KM at the World Bank. The bank, through its developmental work in a multitude of countries as an advisor and a lender, comes across diverse practices and is uniquely positioned in terms of providing this information. Most of their initiatives are on the web and are freely available. However, they are available only in English and other major languages like Spanish and French. This initiative has been very successful with widespread adoption by practitioners across the world. Box 24.2 mentions the case of a website that was primarily developed as a portal for all kinds of developmental information as a one-stop shop. Again all information is free and maintained by a non-profit organization. This website has also enjoyed considerable success. Both these cases illustrate that such initiatives can potentially have a large impact, if implemented correctly. Box 24.3 discusses the experience of United Nations Developmental Programme (UNDP) in India, in terms of creating an online portal (which they call Solutions Exchange). This brings together both practitioners on the ground as well as experts in their respective areas such as health and closes the knowledge gap. Finally, Box 24.4 discusses the story of the Honey Bee Network for harnessing grass-roots innovation. This is perhaps the most relevant model for replication in the Indian context. It uses several local languages, lot of audio-visual elements, and so on to make dissemination easier and rewards the innovator by having his picture and short biography on the website. Attempts are being made to generate revenue from royalty on these innovations. It is also unique in terms of its approach, which is direct to the village and bypasses intermediaries. Together, the case studies shown here display a wide spectrum of different approaches adopted to harness the power of knowledge for human development.

Box 24.1   Knowledge Management at the World Bank

Recently a World Bank task team leader in the Republic of Yemen urgently needed to respond to a client about setting up management information systems in an education ministry. Not so long ago, such a request would have had to wait until the team leader returned to headquarters, where he could consult with colleagues and perhaps search libraries and databases for the answer. Using the bank's knowledge management system, however, the team leader simply contacted the education advisory service in the Bank's Human Development Network, which, in collaboration with the relevant community of practice, ascertained that there was similar and relevant experience in Kenya. The information was dispatched to Yemen, enabling the team leader to respond to the client within 48 hours, rather than weeks later.

An Indonesian official needed to know the international experience on private sector involvement in vocational training. Again through the help of the Human Development Network, the relevant bank task team leader was quickly able to provide the official a comprehensive analysis, performed jointly with the United Nations Development Organization. He was even able to suggest some potential partners, identified through the International Finance Corporation, a bank affiliate.

Launched in October 1996, the World Bank's knowledge management system seeks to make the Bank a clearinghouse for knowledge about development—not just a corporate memory bank of best practices but also a collector and disseminator of the best development knowledge from outside organizations. By 2000, according to plan, relevant parts of the system will be made externally accessible, so that clients, partners and stakeholders around the world can have access to the bank's know-how. Now moving ahead rapidly on a broad front, the bank's sectoral networks are leading the effort through the following activities:

1. Building communities of practice;
2. Developing an online knowledge base;
3. Establishing help desks and advisory services;
4. Building a directory of expertise;
5. Making key statistics available;
6. Providing access to transaction information;
7. Providing space for professional conversation; and
8. Establishing external access and outreach to clients, partners and stakeholders.

Knowledge management is expected to change the way the World Bank operates internally and to transform its relationships with all those it deals with on the outside.

Source: World Bank 1998.

Box 24.2   Sharing Knowledge at OneWorld Online

OneWorld Online (www.oneworld.org) is an electronic gateway for the public to the issues of sustainable development. It draws on the websites of over 250 partner organizations spanning government departments, research institutes, NGOs, news services and international agencies. Among them are the European Centre for Development Policy Management (the Netherlands), the Institute for Development Studies (United Kingdom), the International Institute for Sustainable Development (Canada), the Centre for Science and Environment (India) and the Inter Press Service (Italy). These resources sum to a virtual library on development and global justice issues, encompassing more than 70,000 articles in six languages. Unlike in a bibliographic database, however, the documents are available in full text form and are free for anyone to read.

The partners of OneWorld Online came together because internet users are generally looking for knowledge about a development theme, not about this or that organization. Thus, packaging the materials of these various organizations under topic headings makes them much more readily available. The headings include guides to key development themes, think-tanks for professionals, news from a global perspective, educational resources, radio programming and training opportunities. The service is proving very popular: the website receives more than 4 million hits a month from more than 120 countries on average, 60 of them in the developing world.

Owned by a charity and run by a team of 15 people based near Oxford, in the United Kingdom, OneWorld Online is establishing additional editorial centres in the Netherlands, India, Africa and Central America. These are intended to provide a genuinely 'one world' perspective, especially through the use of languages other than English. They also work to support local NGOs in maximizing the internet's potential as a tool for development.

A central feature of OneWorld Online's website is a specialized search engine dedicated solely to sustainable development. This offers the user a way to avoid the needle-in-a-haystack approach of all-purpose search engines. Users of the OneWorld search engine know that the domain searched contains only relevant material of known date and provenance.

Source: World Bank 1998.

Box 24.3   Knowledge Sharing at UNDP India

Solution Exchange is a web based IT effort of the United Nations Team in India. It includes eight Communities of Practice. A Community of Practice is a group of people who are connected electronically and work together to create improvements in a particular area of interest. The eight Communities of Practice include Decentralization, Education, Environment, AIDS, Food and Nutrition Security, Gender, Health (Maternal and Child Health, Communicable Diseases) and Poverty (Microfinance). Members of any particular Community of Practice include government officials at the centre, state and district levels, members of NGOs involved in development, financing agencies in microfinance and companies serving the rural market and having a development agenda.

The Decentralization Community is one such Community of Practice established with the aim of helping *panchayats* and municipal bodies at the village level carry out effective self governance. The primary method of communication among members of the Decentralization Community is through email. A member posts a query for the entire group. Other members of the group respond to the query within a stipulated time frame. Then a consolidated response to the query is prepared by the moderator of the group. The consolidated response summarizes all discussions related to the query. This is then emailed to all members of the group. Two examples of such queries are as follows. The first query related to whether governance at the village level would become more effective if gender issues are considered and a higher percentage of women become part of the governing process. The second query relates to developing a model accounting system for *Panchayati Raj* Institutions so that the *Gram Panchayat* can function as a local self-government.

Source: UNDP, India.

Box 24.4 The Honey Bee Network

In order to document, share and widely use innovations occurring at the village level the Honey Bee Network and Multimedia Database was set up by Anil Gupta of IIM, Ahmedabad. A systematic set of steps is followed right from the point of recognizing the innovation to sharing its benefits with others. These include first scouting the innovation and evaluating its potential for improving the quality of life at the village level. The second step is to accurately document the innovation. A multimedia database is used for this purpose. The various media include text, sound and film. The next step is to disseminate the innovation as widely as possible, especially in neighbouring and far- off villages, where the innovation will be most useful. The last step is to compensate and reward the innovator.

As a part of the dissemination process, the Honey Bee Newsletter is published in six local languages. It describes the various innovations and how they can prove useful in the rural environment. By publishing the newsletter in local languages, it is ensured that the innovations described are widely shared. The database has been developed in three languages, English, French and Gujarati. At present there are over a thousand innovations catalogued and the innovations are categorized. A brief description of the innovator and the innovation is provided. On moving to the next screen a detailed description of how the innovation works is provided. This is also depicted in a film along with appropriate commentary because the visual effect is always much stronger. This helps significantly in disseminating the innovation. The database has been displayed in the local markets, village fairs and on individual trips covering many villages. When displaying the innovations at the villages, the participants watching are encouraged to volunteer their own innovations, which may not yet be documented. Some innovations found using this process have since been added to the database.

In 1993, a voluntary organization, SRISTI, was set up to strengthen the Honey Bee Network and Multimedia Database. Indian Institute of Management (IIM), Ahmedabad has also played a vital role in developing the network and database. In 1997 the Gujarat government set up a fund, the Gujarat Grassroots Innovation Augmentation Network (GIAN), to help in dissemination and wider adoption of the innovations.

One outstanding issue relates to intellectual property rights (IPR) concerns arising out of the innovations. The innovator should benefit from his innovation as it improves the quality of life at the village level. Also, an innovation soon becomes community knowledge and it should not happen that an external firm or individual patents the innovation and takes advantage. To avoid this problem, a registration system for databases such as Honey Bee could be set up. This would ensure that all innovations catalogued in the database are protected. To make this happen the Honey Bee database could be sent to all patent offices.

The Honey Bee Network and Multimedia Database is a good example of how KM is being used for development. Explicit and tacit knowledge of innovators is first being very well captured in the Multimedia Database. Once this has been done, the innovations are being disseminated so that other people in villages can use these innovations to their advantage. In this way, the knowledge that has been captured is being used to help other villagers. This process of knowledge capture and dissemination also encourages other innovators to contribute their innovations to the database and thus the KM programme is sustained.

Source: Gupta et al. (2000).

Conclusions

The recognition that knowledge is important for growth and human development is a relatively recent phenomenon. Most national governments have woken up to the challenge and have responded with various levels of success. The lead, however, has been taken by multilateral agencies and other non-profit organizations. The Government of India is keenly aware of the opportunities as well as the challenges of the knowledge-based economy. This chapter shows reasons why knowledge, particularly that pertaining to human development, is unlikely to be developed or disseminated by private players. Therefore, the lead has to be taken by governments, multilateral agencies and non-profit organizations in this regard. This chapter has also discussed the issues that are likely to be faced, together with several instances where KM initiatives have succeeded in various measures, in achieving human development. The road ahead is unknown but it is the belief of the authors that, given the large potential benefit associated with a knowledge economy, the government needs to design a policy framework for implementation. The chapter has suggested that an incremental approach should be adopted coupled with steady monitoring of progress so that changes are made in the approach accordingly.

Notes

1. For instance see *The World Is Flat* by Friedman (2005).
2. Consultative Group for International Agricultural Research is an international organization funded by developed and developing countries, as well as international and non-profit organizations. It funds 16 agricultural research centres across the world and was in the vanguard of developing new seeds and techniques instrumental in the Green Revolution. Most benefit cost analyses show that the returns on investment far exceed the amount spent by CGIAR.

Bibliography

Friedman, Thomas L. 2005. *The World Is Flat: A Brief History of the Twenty-first Century.* New York: Farar, Strauss and Giroux.
Gupta, Anil K., Brij Kothari and Kirit Patil. 2000. 'Knowledge Networks for Recognizing, Respecting and Rewarding Grassroots Innovation, in Information and Communication Technology', in S. Bhatnagar and R. Schware (eds), *Development: Cases from India*, pp. 300–24. New Delhi: Sage.
Malhotra, Y. 2003. *Measuring Knowledge Assets of a Nation: Knowledge Systems for Development*, UN Keynote Paper, mimeo.
Tiwana, A. 2002. *The Knowledge Management Toolkit: Orchestrating IT, Strategy and Knowledge Platforms*, 2nd edn. New York: Pearson Education.
World Bank. 1998. *World Development Report—Knowledge and Development.* Washington, DC: Oxford University Press.

25   Knowledge Management as a Change Driver

SANJAY DHAR

Introduction

One of the underpinnings of a developed society is equal opportunities to all. Equal opportunities to every one would imply equitable access to resources, enforcement of common rules and transparency in the management of institutions.

Deviations from this ideal are observed in all the three dimensions. It is a common experience to find

1. Distortions in the control of resources;
2. Inconsistencies in the interpretation of rules—sometimes the rules themselves have a bias in favour of the powerful elite and
3. Deliberate opacity in the running of institutions.

These tendencies lead to a large underclass of people not getting their fair share in a social order that works in favour of the powerful elite. In order to make corrections the social order is disturbed every now and then with revolutions in various forms, political revolutions like the French Revolution and the various wars of independence from colonial powers or the communist revolutions sparked by Marxism. The revolutions of the past were about a better control and redistribution of physical resources and power. In the 21st century the critical resource is going to be 'knowledge'.

Knowledge can be used to effect the re-alignment of social forces in a manner so as to make the world relatively more just and humane. Ensuring effective sharing and use of knowledge can be used as a means of approaching the ideal of a society of equal opportunities.

Knowledge Asymmetry and Inequity

One of the reasons for a large mass of the population not being able to achieve their potential is the knowledge asymmetry[1] that exists in society. Some of the ways in which knowledge gaps become the foundations of developmental gaps by inhibiting developmental processes are given here.

Asymmetry in the Domain of Institutional Support and Rights

The intended beneficiaries of developmental support are unaware of their rights and proper processes to get support that would enable them to come out of inequitable commercial relationships and transactions. The inability of the poor to access the developmental credit schemes is one of the manifestations of this knowledge gap. Corruption in the implementation of schemes intended to benefit the underclass is another outcome of this asymmetry, since the underclass does not know what is being reported as benefits provided to them.

Asymmetry in the Domain of Economic Systems

The producers of economically valuable goods are disconnected from their markets leading to the intermediaries taking away a disproportionate fraction of the difference between the cost of production and the final price paid by the consumer. A large number of people in the agricultural and cottage industries sectors suffer from this knowledge gap.

Asymmetry in the Domain of Change Management

There is inability of the developmental agencies to understand the specific support that would help their targets to achieve a better quality of life and the most effective process to provide that support. Another manifestation of this asymmetry is that targets of development programmes themselves are unaware of how successful change management occurs in their own context. Difficulties faced by many well-meaning development agencies and NGOs to make a significant self-sustaining impact in their area of work are examples of this knowledge gap. Sometimes the difficulty is because the agencies do not know specific practices that will make their projects successful. At other times their efforts are undone by the lack of corresponding effort by the target population because the intended beneficiaries do not know how to help themselves—even when people in their own social context have managed to overcome similar situations about which they are not consciously aware of.

Asymmetry in the Domain of Management of Intellectual Property

There is inability of the underclass to get rightful returns on their knowledge due to lack of information on how to protect their intellectual property rights (IPR). The recent upsurge in interest on protection of 'traditional knowledge' is a reaction to this knowledge inequity.

It is not to argue that all inequities in society are due to knowledge gaps alone or that removing these knowledge gaps will automatically remove all the inequities. There definitely are other asymmetries of power in society, but removing the knowledge asymmetry between the haves and have-nots will provide a voice and opportunities to the underclass that will make interventions in other aspects more effective.

Knowledge management (KM) can be used as a means of reducing this knowledge asymmetry by ensuring effective flow of relevant knowledge in support of the change processes for social development. Some of the aspects that KM can support are as follows:

1. Using KM processes as a means of strengthening the move towards greater transparency in the working of institutions.
2. Using KM processes to provide market information and opportunities to the underclass.
3. Using KM for effective change management. Ensuring effective knowledge transfers between development agencies to enhance efficiency of the development processes, and using knowledge creation processes to transform local knowledge about overcoming development problems from tacit knowledge held within a few successful people to explicit knowledge shared within the target community.
4. Using KM processes to enable the underclass to benefit from their own collective knowledge through better documentation and management of intellectual property.

In this chapter these four areas of application of KM shall be used as prongs of a concerted strategy to use knowledge as a means of social change. The chapter will explore the application of KM in institutions of social development like the World Bank, NGOs, and so on, application of affirmative inquiry as a means of social development, and use of knowledge-sharing practices to derive greater transparency in government and public institutions. It would also explore how KM is being used by business to create spirals of economic growth for the underclass of society.

The terms of reference of the National Knowledge Commission (NKC) of India are an articulation of the same intent. As per Government Notification of 13 June 2005, the Terms of Reference of NKC are as follows:

1. Build excellence in the educational system to meet the knowledge challenges of the 21st century and increase India's competitive advantage in fields of knowledge.
2. Promote creation of knowledge in science and technology laboratories.
3. Improve the management of institutions engaged in IPR.
4. Promote knowledge applications in agriculture and industry.
5. Promote the use of knowledge capabilities in making the government an effective, transparent and accountable service provider to the citizen and promote widespread sharing of knowledge to maximize public benefit.

Applications of Knowledge Management Processes

Transparency in the Working of Institutions

The greater the access of citizens to information about their rights and working of public institutions is, the greater will be the responsiveness of the government to community needs. Alternatively, greater the restrictions that are placed on access, greater will be the feelings of 'powerlessness' and 'alienation'. Without information, people cannot adequately exercise their rights as citizens or make informed choices.

Even the World Bank affirms, 'Corruption is the single greatest obstacle to economic and social development. It undermines development by distorting the rule of law and weakening the institutional foundation on which economic growth depends.'[2] Opacity in the running of public institutions is one of the greatest enablers of corruption.

The Right to Information (RTI) Act is the most revolutionary Act of Legislature in the recent history of India. The power of this Act is essentially in empowering the common man to get greater transparency in the working of public institutions. Ever since its introduction, it has been used with dramatic impact by a large number of people to shift the power balance simply by shifting the information asymmetry between the executors of welfare measures and their intended beneficiaries who were not getting their due rights. The presence of hype campaigns by national news channels using the RTI Act to expose corruption and in many cases getting inequities set right with the use of this Act is proof of both the power of this Act and the power of sharing success stories to inspire more people to actively seek a more transparent world. Right to information campaigner, Arvind Kejriwal, is one of two South Asian winners of the prestigious Ramon Magsaysay Awards for 2006. He was also cited for 'empowering New Delhi's the poorest citizens to fight corruption'.[3] Knowledge management for development can tap information in the domain of public documents to provide agencies fighting for the rights of the underclass the means to use the system to make improvements rather than forcing them to go beyond the system or having to create a completely new infrastructure to provide people the means of development. Although the Act has come as a powerful tool in the hands of common citizens, knowledge about the subtle nuances of how to use the Act and overcome bureaucratic blocking tactics is still evolving. It would benefit significantly from dissemination of actual experiences of getting results from the application of this Act. Possible applications of KM in this direction are

1. knowledge sharing through portals and communities about application of the RTI and other such Acts to bring about greater transparency and accountability in public institutions;
2. using mining techniques, to identify patterns in effective actions for enforcing greater accountability; and
3. providing forums for informed dialogue on specific areas of concern that could be a significant input for the policy makers.

Market Information and Opportunities

The e-choupals[4] pioneered by Imperial Tobacco Company (ITC) are an example of the transformative power of such an infrastructure. E-choupal delivers real-time information and customized knowledge to improve the farmer's decision-making ability, thereby improving alignment of farm output with market demands and securing better quality, productivity and improved price discovery. The model helps aggregate demand in the nature of a virtual producers' cooperative, in the process facilitating access to higher-quality farm inputs at lower costs for the farmer. The e-choupal initiative also creates a direct marketing channel and eliminates wasteful intermediation and multiple handling, thus reducing transaction costs and making logistics efficient. The e-choupal project is already benefiting over 3.5 million farmers. Over the next decade, the e-choupal network will cover over 100,000 villages, representing one-sixth of rural India, and create more than 10 million e-farmers. The site also provides farmers with specialized knowledge for customizing their produce for specific consumer segments. The new storage and handling system preserves the identity of different varieties right through the 'farm-gate to dinner-plate' supply chain, encouraging the farmers to raise their quality standards and attract higher prices.

Indian Farmers Fertiliser Cooperative Ltd., known popularly as IFFCO, has launched an information kiosk project called Kisan Choupal to provide information services to farmers regarding various aspects of crops, pesticides, fertilizers, and so on. Possible applications of KM in this area are the following:

1. Using knowledge portals for creating virtual markets with large geographic spread.
2. Providing knowledge about institutional support and other consultancy through the portals.
3. Accelerating the formation of co-operatives and consolidation of individual economic players into larger groups to increase their bargaining power. The costs of cooperation and synchronizing action in real time are significantly lowered by the use of portals. What is needed is support in terms of community building in the economic domains for concerted action.
4. Tracking patterns in economic activity through the portals would be a useful input to policy makers on what really happens on the ground.

Effective Change Management

This approach to removing knowledge asymmetries has two aspects.

Ensuring Knowledge Transfers for Development Agencies to Enhance Efficiency of the Developmental Processes

Development is a practice, and people involved in various roles in the development process are a community. So it is natural that the 'community of practice', that is, becoming a significant social structure in business organizations for KM, would be an equally powerful structure in the development agencies like the World Bank. In fact, there has been a significant shift in the working of the World Bank over the years. It now looks upon itself as a change agent for development primarily on the basis of knowledge about development that it can share with different countries. The mission statement of the World Bank reflects this focus on knowledge by aiming 'to fight poverty with passion and professionalism for lasting results, and to help people help themselves and their environment by providing resources, sharing knowledge, building capacity and forging partnerships in the public and private sectors'. The Knowledge for Development Program[5] of the bank is an assertion of this philosophy. The World Bank has also used KM as a major process of improving its internal efficiency.

Sharing knowledge will increase speed (faster cycle times), improve the quality of service, increase innovation (testing new approaches) and reduce costs (eliminate unnecessary processes). Lending alone cannot reduce poverty. Knowledge sharing brings new actors to the stage and provides global access to development know-how, which could change the poverty equation.

'Knowledge Management for Organizational Capacity' is an initiative of the World Bank aiming to enhance the capacity of development-oriented organizations in World Bank client countries to achieve greater impact through the application of KM tools and practices. The programme includes a range of activities from informal advisory support to formal training and deeper technical assistance.

The Knowledge Bank page has been established as a repository for some of the key documents related to the World Bank's 'Knowledge Bank' strategy. These documents describe the main KM activities of the World Bank over the past decade, since the launch of the strategy in 1996. The Global Development Learning Network (GDLN) is a global partnership of learning centres (GDLN affiliates) that offer the use of advanced information and communication technologies (ICT) to connect people working in development around the world. By applying tools and services developed in the field of distance learning—learning that takes place when participants in an event are separated by space and time—GDLN affiliates enable organizations, teams and individuals around the world to communicate, share knowledge and learn from each others' experiences in a timely and cost-effective manner.

What the bank is trying to achieve through this approach is to sustain communities of practice on different development practices across the globe both within the bank through thematic groups and also by providing linkages to external agencies. The process used by the World Bank is a good template for bringing in efficiency in the development processes using KM that can be replicated by other development agencies, especially the government.

Enhancing Self-efficacy

Development cannot be sustainable without the targets of development efforts themselves taking charge of the development process. External agencies like the state and non-profit organizations essentially leverage this drive for development by providing an enabling infrastructure and helping them ride over obstacles they would not be able to cross without support. Pure aid is doomed to failure as a development vehicle, and the record of aid programmes is ample proof of that. However, one critical success factor for sustained development of any individual or group is a strong belief that they can succeed. Self-efficacy[6] is a necessary condition for people to take charge of their own development processes. A strong sense of efficacy enhances human accomplishment and personal well-being in many ways. People with high assurance in their capabilities approach difficult tasks as challenges to be mastered rather than as threats to be avoided. Such an efficacious outlook fosters intrinsic interest and deep engrossment in activities. They set themselves challenging goals and maintain strong commitment to them. They heighten and sustain their efforts in the face of failure. One of the ways of creating and strengthening self-beliefs of efficacy is through the vicarious experiences provided by social models. Seeing people similar to oneself succeed by sustained effort raises observers' beliefs that they too possess the capabilities to succeed.

Sharing success stories along with contextual information is a means of sharing success factors and through an iterative process brings the tacit knowledge of how to succeed in a particular context progressively into the explicit domain where it is amenable to wider sharing. This would involve a process of dialogue to bring the implicit value systems and beliefs to the surface and provide solutions rooted in the context rather than imposed from a different worldview.

Similar principles would apply to the work of development agencies too. They could use a process of actively collecting and disseminating stories of success. These stories can be used as sources of reinforcement for improving the self-efficacy of the target communities for development efforts across the world.

Through nearly a decade of fieldwork in five African countries, International Institute of Sustainable Development (IISD)[7] has developed a sustainable livelihoods model that builds on local strengths by identifying and reinforcing adaptive strategies that local people often develop to maintain their livelihoods in adverse circumstances.

The appreciative approach involves collaborative inquiry, based on interviews and affirmative questioning, to collect and celebrate good news stories of a community—those stories that enhance cultural identity, spirit and vision. Appreciative inquiry[8] is a way of seeing that is selectively attentive to—and affirming of—the best and highest qualities in a system, a situation or another human being. It involves an appreciation for the mystery of being and a reverence for life. Local people can use their understanding of 'the best of what is' to construct a vision of what their community might be if they identify their strengths, and then improve or intensify them. They achieve this goal by creating provocative propositions that challenge them to move ahead by understanding and building on their current achievements. Provocative propositions are realistic dreams; they empower a community to reach for something better, but base that empowerment on an understanding of what gives them life now.

Practitioners of AI believe that this approach is true to human nature because it integrates different ways of knowing. Appreciative inquiry allows room for emotional response as well as intellectual analysis—room for imagination as well as rational thought. Story-telling as a KM tool also taps into this human characteristic.

Leveraging Knowledge to Protect Intellectual Property Rights of the Underclass

In recent years, interest has been increasing in the 'traditional knowledge' of developing countries realizing that the indigenous people have been having such knowledge for a long time. This interest has given rise to a need for concerted efforts to protect this knowledge from being usurped by organizations from developed countries for patenting and commercialization. They rediscover such knowledge through modern scientific methods. Attempts made recently to patent the medicinal properties of *neem* and *haldi* in the West exemplify the need to protect rights of the underclass over their knowledge. The debate and intense jockeying over IPR in international affairs is an indicator of the importance of this issue. The issue of providing the underclass a fair share of the benefits of their knowledge is not limited to just traditional knowledge. It has significant applications in the area of crafts and local innovations carried out within small communities by people who do not have the resources available to leverage their knowledge by licensing or mass manufacturing, but whose ideas could be taken up by some organization with large resources to gain significant financial advantage. Some of the applications of KM in this domain are as follows:

1. Developing a knowledge bank of indigenous knowledge.
2. Ensuring widespread dissemination of local traditional knowledge to facilitate discovery of related knowledge that can then be used to develop further intellectual capital.
3. Using a knowledge portal as a means for local innovators to share their innovations for application and refinement.
4. Reduce re-invention of the wheel in technological innovations that help the underclass by networking among agencies working in this domain.

Developing a Framework of KM for Social Development

Different measures for removing the knowledge asymmetry are not mutually exclusive and together they form a comprehensive framework for using KM as a tool for accelerating the development process. However, for this strategy to have significant impact, it would need an institutionalizing framework for combining the three thrust areas of effective knowledge transfers between development practitioners, strengthening transparency in the working of institutions and empowering the underclass with knowledge.

Five elements of such a knowledge-based strategy of development are described below.

Developmental Portal

The portal provides a gateway to all the development practitioners for accessing and sharing knowledge about work being done for social development. The portal would provide

1. a platform for different communities of practice to share practices and knowledge resources within their domains of activity, for example, all groups working with street children;
2. a starting point for identifying institutional resources available for development practitioners, for example the schemes of the Government of India, international development agencies like the World Bank, United Nations Development Programme (UNDP); and
3. a channel for reporting the activities and successes of development initiatives to bring about greater transparency in the working of development institutions, especially how public funds are being used. Provisions of the RTI Act could be used to keep the portal updated with information about what was planned and what was actually executed.

Institutional Forum

The forum will facilitate sharing of examples of success and failure of different social development initiatives. Some of the forums could be as follows:

1. A government–industry interface on sustainable development. Increasing relevance of corporate social responsibility (CSR) makes such an institution more viable now.
2. An inter-agency forum on transfer of best practices within the government sector. This would help transfer of best practices between states and between different departments. An assessment framework for comparative efficiency linked with resource allocations would give such a forum greater value.
3. A public–government interface for taking feedback from the public at large about the direction and efficiency of development efforts, and identifying areas for the public at large to contribute.

Social Infrastructure

Social infrastructure will be facilitated by grass-roots knowledge brokers who would provide facilitation for KM processes within the communities of intended beneficiaries of the development processes. Such knowledge facilitators and champions have been very useful in industry, and the e-choupals have demonstrated how the knowledge broker's role can be made a means of employment in addition to being a change agent. For knowledge sharing to be a social activity, the basic social unit, a village in rural areas or a *mohalla* in urban areas, has to be involved in it.

Technological Infrastructure

Technological infrastructure enables village-level access to the knowledge portal and means of benefiting from knowledge of markets for their products. This would mean access to the internet at the village level through kiosks or community cyber cafes.

Institutional Mechanism

The fifth element would be an institutional mechanism for the protection of intellectual property of local innovators. This could be facilitated by an e-market for ideas mediated through a portal, a developmental equivalent of e-bay. This marketplace would need the active support of public and government institutions that can provide safeguards for local innovators and copyrights for creative work of local artisans. Copyrights are a potential of great economic gain in a crafts-rich country like India.

Tying up different prongs together in a KM strategy would provide reinforcing cycles of application of knowledge and leveraging, thus creating a momentum of small wins that translate into bigger wins. Elements of such a strategy are already in place, and there are examples of many initiatives succeeding on these principles. What is needed is an overarching framework for connecting these different elements together to provide mutual reinforcement. This requires a greater degree of collaboration on knowledge sharing among different institutions through electronic means like a portal as well as forums for physical interaction. Some of the policy implications of this strategy are as follows:

1. To centralize registration of NGOs and make certain knowledge sharing through a portal mandatory for further assistance. This would not be difficult, since aid-giving agencies anyway ask for reports on the projects funded partially or completely by them. However, what is proposed here is to use experiences as means of social learning and not limit them to assessment of agencies.
2. Creating knowledge brokers in every village and small urban units, who are well-versed in different development initiatives and the use of ICT to facilitate using of the knowledge portal. Major existing development schemes that have grassroots-level roles for facilitators could convert some key roles into knowledge brokers.
3. Issue guidelines to government agencies for 'duty to publish' information that may be relevant input for practitioners involved in development work.

4. Regular review within similar clusters and incentives for sharing and absorption of best practices within private and government development agencies making it a part of their assessment in order to create a knowledge pull for sharing of best practices, thereby enhancing the efficiency of the development process as a whole.
5. Development of guidelines for providing copyrights to local innovators and craftsmen through agencies like the Khadi and Village Industries Commission, local NGOs and e-enabling these processes so that knowledge brokers can manage the process on behalf of the local innovators.

Conclusions

Knowledge management practices and processes being used extensively in the industry can be utilized to bring in similar increase in efficiency in development activities by removing inequities based on knowledge asymmetries. A KM system would help to leverage the impact of positive experiences and use them to reinforce cycles of inspired development, with each success inspiring many more in quick succession by spreading the stories quickly. Managing social development is essentially a process of managing change and one of the ways of managing change is to quickly shift the momentum in favour of the desired change. Knowledge management provides the means to build that momentum. Margaret Mead is quoted to have said, 'Never doubt that a small group of committed individuals can change the world. Indeed, it's the only thing that ever has.' What KM can do is provide these individuals a means of magnifying their voice, and others a means of hearing it and acting on it.

Notes

1. In economics, information asymmetry occurs when one party to a transaction has more or better information than the other party. George A. Akerlof of University of California at Berkeley, A. Michael Spence of Stanford University and Joseph E. Stiglitz of Columbia University jointly got the 2001 Nobel Prize in economic sciences for their contributions to the analyses of markets with asymmetric information. Information asymmetry models assume that at least one party to a transaction has relevant information whereas the other(s) do not. A related construct that has been used in this paper is knowledge asymmetry.
2. Website of the World Bank: http://go.worldbank.org/K6AEEPROC0. The World Bank has published a number of working papers on the impact of corruption and remedial measures, which can be accessed from its website.
3. The complete quotation can be accessed at the website of the Ramon Magsaysay Foundation at http://www.rmaf.org.ph/index.php?task=4&year=2000.
4. ITC's e-choupal has been a revolution in the use of ICT to bring about economic change in rural India, and the model has been taken up by many other organizations. The ITC portal http://www.itcportal.com/ provides extensive information on e-choupal.
5. The World Bank has described how KM can be used as a key driver of the development agenda. The website of the bank http://www.worldbank.org/ is a very good reference point to explore different options of using KM for development. A related website which specifically focuses on Knowledge Managemnt for Development is www.km4dev.org
6. Self-efficacy is a concept that has been extensively studied in the context of learning and motivation. In this paper the concept has been related to appreciative inquiry in the context of development work by highlighting the importance of providing concrete reinforcement for initiatives. http://www.des.emory.edu/mfp/BanEncy.html is a good starting point for exploring the concept.

7. The International Institute of Sustainable Development has used appreciative inquiry as a means of building capacity of networks of NGOs. Similar initiatives have been taken by other institutes and organizations. http://www.iisd.org/ai/ provides more details on the work done by this organization using AI for developmental projects.

8. D.L. Cooperrider and S. Srivastva originally gave the concept of appreciative inquiry (AI) in 1987 and since then it has been increasingly used as a new form of action research by Organization Development practitioners. AI involves, in a central way, the art and practice of asking questions that strengthen a system's capacity to apprehend, anticipate and heighten positive potential. It centrally involves the mobilization of inquiry through the crafting of the 'unconditional positive question' often involving hundreds or sometimes thousands of people. In this paper AI has been explored as an externalization process for knowledge of success factors. http://appreciativeinquiry.case.edu/intro/whatisai.cfm provides more details on this concept.

26 A Digital Ecosystem Model for Competitive Agriculture in the Knowledge Economy

RUNA SARKAR AND JAYANTA CHATTERJEE

Introduction

Information and communication technologies (ICT) are generating changes in firms, markets, and economies in the developed and developing world. Whether to a large or small extent, they are present and advancing in every area of economic, social and political activity. Due to the networking possibilities they enable, ICTs reduce transaction costs changing the structure of markets and institutions, resulting in an immediate increase in the potential value of human capital. Further they embody enormous knowledge and can serve to empower people at community and national levels.

The adoption and development of ICTs takes place through specific initiatives led by communities, development agencies, donors and business organizations. As it requires local knowledge, literacy, skills development, technical capability and effort, it can be a challenge to implement a diffused network of local innovation systems, networked only through top-down *krishi vigyan kendras* (KVKs). It is estimated that there are over 104 million farm families spread over more than 590 rural districts and 6 lakh villages (Rai 2006). The digital ecosystem (DE) is one approach through which diffusion and use of ICT can be made self-sustaining and self-enabling even in the rural sector despite technological and literacy barriers. A digital business ecosystem (DBE) is an ICT-enabling technology for business networks based on a dynamic and amorphous interaction among a multiplicity of small entities to support knowledge sharing, establishment of global value chains and developing new business models.

Agricultural and food security policy makers clearly see the need for knowledge connectivity from academic/research institutes to villages and then onto the world to close the loop so that the 'best' practices can enhance India's agricultural efficiency, create the 'next' practices and create new avenues for rural livelihood. There is a national agenda for creating a 'knowledge centre' in every village. But the 'soft side' of this challenge needs more attention. There is no concerted effort to create a national agricultural knowledge repository in digital form which is alive and is nurtured daily through feeding, weeding and pruning—or enriched by interactive usage. Numerous good knowledge nuggets remain at local level as unstructured information or tacit knowledge. Moreover, agriculture is among the most complex commercial systems requiring inputs from myriad sources relating to soil, water, environment, goods, assets and labour markets.

This chapter documents the authors' experience of being involved in developing and implementing a DE for knowledge diffusion in rural India where sustainability of the initiative is wrought with challenges due to language and literacy barriers, resource scarcity, dominance of top-down solutions and limited existence of successful participative business models. A DE for agriculture offers farmers from less-developed and remote areas opportunities to participate in the global economy, resulting in dynamic knowledge sharing and global cooperation among the farmers and the world community fostering local economic growth. Co-creation and self-management of digital contents to support agriculture and rural livelihood development activities would result in access to the right kind of information at the right time, resulting in inclusive growth as well as competitive agriculture. It also facilitates two-way interactions among the farmers and agricultural scientists which is critical for further technological progress in agriculture, whether with respect to innovation or technology adoption. Given that agriculture—India's largest private enterprise—still sustains about 72 per cent of the population and contributes to 22 per cent of the gross domestic product (GDP), even the smallest improvement in agricultural productivity can have a large impact on national well-being. Moreover, agriculture has already reached the limits of land and water; thus future increases in food production must exploit biological yields on existing land (World Bank 1997). Thus, further technological breakthroughs (beyond the green revolution) and their dissemination are the need of the hour. In this backdrop, developing the soft side of knowledge diffusion and taking advantage of the multiplying effect of networks through a DE is a significant step in improving national competitiveness.

A Pathway to Information Design for Knowledge Diffusion in Rural India

Ensuring a thriving agricultural economy is critical for India's global competitiveness to be 'inclusive'. A globally competitive Indian economy must be based on knowledge-driven transformation of Indian agriculture because in many ways Indian agriculture has already reached the physical limits of land and water. This necessitates the response of cropping patterns in hinterlands of India to global commodity markets in real time. All these mean quick dissemination of technical information from the agricultural research system to the farmers. The one-way route of conventional agricultural extension system needs rapid transformation to a 'real-time and adaptive' knowledge exchange network. This network needs to build real-time feedback routes from the 'fields to the laboratory' and derive necessary traction from other industrial and business knowledge management (KM) technologies and processes like user-to-user exchange, expert-to-expert exchange and KM-oriented standards for information storage, retrieval and aggregation with analytics. In this section are reported initial empirical findings from one such collaborative project called the 'Digital Ecosystem for Agriculture and Rural Livelihood' (www.dealindia.org). The DE entails a series of inter-connected and intra-dependent digital platforms, created at key institutional levels (international, national and local/community) augmented by technical (ICT) and social networking processes that help break down barriers to both horizontal and vertical knowledge. India is behind most developed nations, even behind its smaller neighbours in Asia, in terms of almost all the rural economy efficiency and yield measures. It also has one of the longest distribution chains for most rural produce. While reasons for this inefficiency are many, researchers (Singh 2002; Bhatnagar and Schware 2000; Kaushik and Singh 2004) have pointed out information asymmetry and lack of rapid knowledge diffusion as prominent root causes. Information and communication Tchnologiese is viewed as a powerful tool to reduce asymmetries and promote knowledge diffusion. However, the cost and challenges of the ICT inter-connection for rural India coupled with the high cost to develop and maintain digital resources by governmental extension services and other content providers in this do-main impede progress. Moreover, public extension system requires a paradigm shift from top-down, blanket dissemination of technological packages, towards providing producers with the knowledge and understanding with which they solve their own location-specific problems. Continuous two-way inter-action among the farmers and agricultural scientists is the most critical missing component of agricultural extension. Moreover, while large landholders find it easy to access better information and can employ more competitive agricultural practices, marginal landholders lose out in the process due to inefficient and insufficient extension services. Table 26.1 represents a quick caricature of some of the gaps in such services.

Table 26.1 **Typical Contrasts in Agricultural Conditions for Extension Agents, Large Land Holders and Marginal Farmers**

Factor	Extension demo-units	Large farms	Marginal farms
Topography	Flat or sometimes terraced	Flat or sometimes terraced	Often undulating and sloping
Soils	Deep, fertile, no constraints	Deep, fertile, no constraints	Shallow, infertile, often severe constraints
Hazards	Nil/few	Few, usually controllable	More common: floods, drought, animal grazing
Irrigation	Usually available	Usually available	Often non-existent
Diseases, Pests, Weeds	Controlled	Controlled	Crops vulnerable to infestation
Production stability	High	Moderate to high	Low
Farming systems	Simple	Simple	Complex
Use of purchased inputs	Very high	High	Low

Source: Adapted from Das (2006).

Thus, unless there is a mechanism by which the small and marginal farmer can convey his needs to the extension counter and there is adequate perception of their circumstances, there appears no way to improve his competitiveness. Limitations of the physical face-to-face transfer of technology (ToT) model, however, remains a challenge for the public and private extension systems as there are at least 400,000 medium and large villages spread over the subcontinent that need to be reached. With the avail-ability of telephone and internet, it is now possible to bridge this gap to quite a large extent but only if an appropriate mix of technologies can deliver 'dynamic content' in response to 'user pull'. Unless the content is problem-solving oriented to help farmers to take risks in venturing out to crop diversification or adopt novel processes, the ToT cannot make adequate impact on alleviating rural poverty through im-proved competitiveness.

Agricultural Ecosystem

An agricultural ecosystem is a unique and reasonably stable dynamic arrangement of farm enterprises that households manage in response to the physical, biological and socio-economic environments. There could be several interacting subsystems within this large ecosystem such as the ones at the regional level, and equally relevant non-agricultural systems such as the market system and the rural credit system. Agricultural subsystems include the crop ecosystem, animal ecosystem, and soil, weed and insect ecosystems, some of which are co-dependent. Thus, both farm-related circumstances such as weather conditions, type of soil and stage of incidence or intensity of weeds, and socio-economic circumstances such as availability and nature of credit, cost of agricultural inputs, price of end products, farmers personal goals and resources, feed into the agricultural ecosystem. An ideal knowledge ecosystem for agriculture would be able to capture all these intricacies and build a large knowledge-sharing database to ensure that the implicit knowledge or experience of individual farmers is shared with many others without necessitating the re-invention of the wheel over geographically or temporally separated regions.

Implementation

Figure 26.1 presents the information flow diagram for rural development activities. It is obvious that an ontology-driven semantic interoperability through this maze can effectively network the different actors, while they pursue their micro-objectives. Given this network, successful implementation of a knowledge system required development of digital content from the tacit knowledge bases of KVKs, which are the agricultural extension counters of the Government of India and other frontline entities through multiple media like landline phone, mobile phone, audio/video recording and digitization of paper documents. There was a need to develop a common ontology, a semantic interoperability that facilitates knowledge storage, retrieval and exchange within the network among the various stakeholders so that a knowledge ecosystem can develop. This required open content and open source optimization so that the technology tools are affordable and remain available while evolving. To bridge the language and education divide, 'citizen interfaces' to the extensive knowledge base were required. These could be iconic, graphical and symbolic user interfaces (that relate to the ontology) for rural citizens' ease of access. Technology application included touch screen, text to speech, screen reader, visualization and animation, interactive voice response system computer-telephony integration and application of wireless data services like MMS. Digital content architecture and tools for easy telephone, mobile data and FM radio-based interactivity and back-end integration of such transactions into the knowledge base were also developed.

Partnerships were created with existing tele-centres in rural institutes, village schools and KVKs. These had an inherent advantage that an existing physical infrastructure only has to be extended and some of the ICT-relevant training can be cost-effectively integrated into the mainstream curriculum of these institutions. This partnership has successfully worked in our Digital Mandi Project (www.digitalmandi.net). Several brainstorming sessions of the stakeholders in the Digital Mandi Project generated a conceptual architecture of the desired knowledge-net. This is shown in Figure 26.2.

It was clear that to acquire the characteristics of a self-managed ecosystem in this knowledge-net, digital contents created in various forms by the stakeholders needed 'interoperability'. Interoperability

Figure 26.1   Typical Flow of Information among Rural Development Agencies

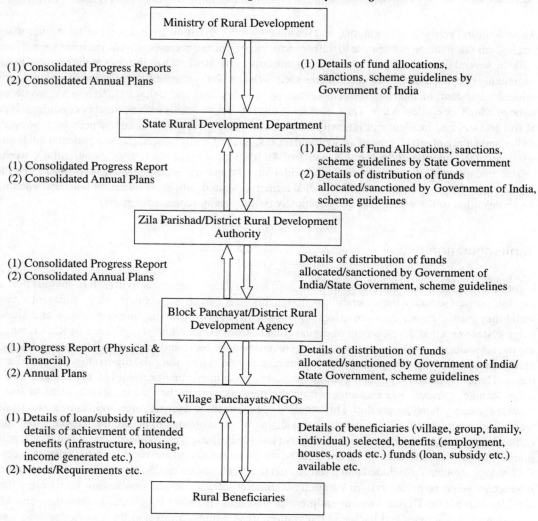

Source: CRISP group, National Informatics Centre New Delhi.

provides potential for automation and systemic self-management. Initial experiments across the digital repositories of the stakeholders in the project showed that syntactic interoperability can be achieved for transfer, exchange, mediation and integration of content by adopting compatible forms of encoding and access protocols and design guidelines. Identification and naming schemes are important at this stage for pulling together related information.

Figure 26.2   Conceptual Architecture of Knowledge-Net

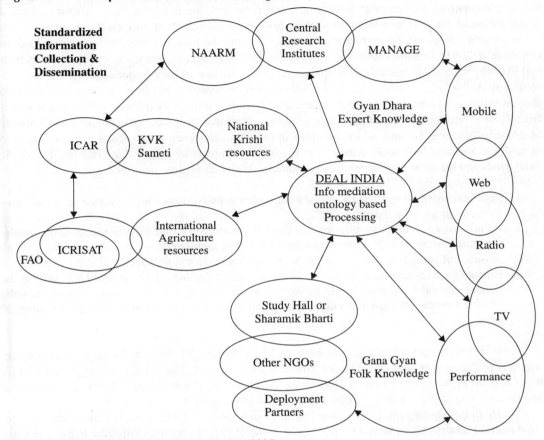

Source: Adapted from Chatterjee and Prabhakar (2005).

Lessons

While implementing the Digital Mandi Project, the existence of several barriers to information access were validated, which have often been reported in literature (see Kralisch and Mandl 2006, for example). These constraints included physical, economic, intellectual or technological barriers that impede rural user participation in activities that add to the digital knowledge repository. The architects and system designers did not actively impose the barriers but they crept in through their lack of action or lack of understanding of the critical user conditions. Such critical user conditions may arise due to particular demographic, geographic, cultural, social, psychological, economic or other factors. Although issues related to information system usability such as ease of use, usefulness (Davis 1989), decision effectiveness, user response, user satisfaction (Doll and Torkzadeh 1988) and many other aspects of usability have been studied in great detail, interactions with focus groups at various agricultural market places around Lucknow–Kanpur showed the need for a more detailed study with a localized set of priorities.

A general framework for web design, keeping in mind the human–computer interaction theories (Pirolli et al. 2001), website usability principles (Huang 2001), information intensity paradigm (Palmer and Griffith 1998) and e-customization models, is already in place and is assumed to sufficiently address the question of defining broad guidelines for designing any successful website. It was, therefore, assumed that a website with relatively high level of accurate, up-to-date and pertinent content, deployed in a user-friendly way, customized to particular user groups, and tailored to specific geographical needs should be universally successful and, hence, accepted in India too. However, it was found that challenges to agricultural and rural livelihood website usability for rural India arose mainly due to the highly specific local needs and the great diversity in local conditions. Major challenges identified were

1. Poor literacy rate—low use of textual information in daily life and high reliance on verbal communication for knowledge transfer.
2. Remote village locations—physical distances compounding problems of dependence on middlemen and a nexus of exploitation through information asymmetry.
3. Absence of content in vernacular languages (both a cause and an effect).
4. Unavailability of economic, low-cost solutions—any technology solution aimed at benefiting the masses in rural India must be affordable and low cost so that the perceived economic benefits of such an endeavour are much more than the cost of switching over to a different technological solution.

Another lesson, related to the sustainability of the DE in the agricultural and rural livelihood space, was drawn. The project soon revealed that without a self-managed, evolving ecosystem like knowledge repository, where users can co-create content and the content can be so 'tagged' that it can be re-called and re-used in multiple context, the editorial overhead remains high and expensive.

The finding from the initial research at Digital Mandi showed that the presence of a number of desired features in any ICT system design for rural India leads to higher user satisfaction. Such features are broadly aimed at satisfying one or the other of the following immediate user objectives:

1. Ease of access
2. Up-to-date content
3. Layout, design, consistent themes
4. Easy navigation
5. Higher interactivity
6. Access through multiple media (particularly voice)
7. Higher use of non-textual information
8. Language options
9. Lower cost of transaction

Since most of the farmers are quasi-literate, content in textual form becomes a challenge, especially at content creation stage. Content in audio form is often the only way that can be operated. Apart from its ease in creation, it has other advantages as well—it is more natural, there is a personal touch making it more acceptable to both the creator and the listener, and community 'viewing' (or in this case listening)

Figure 26.3   Iconic Login in the Web Interface of Digital Mandi

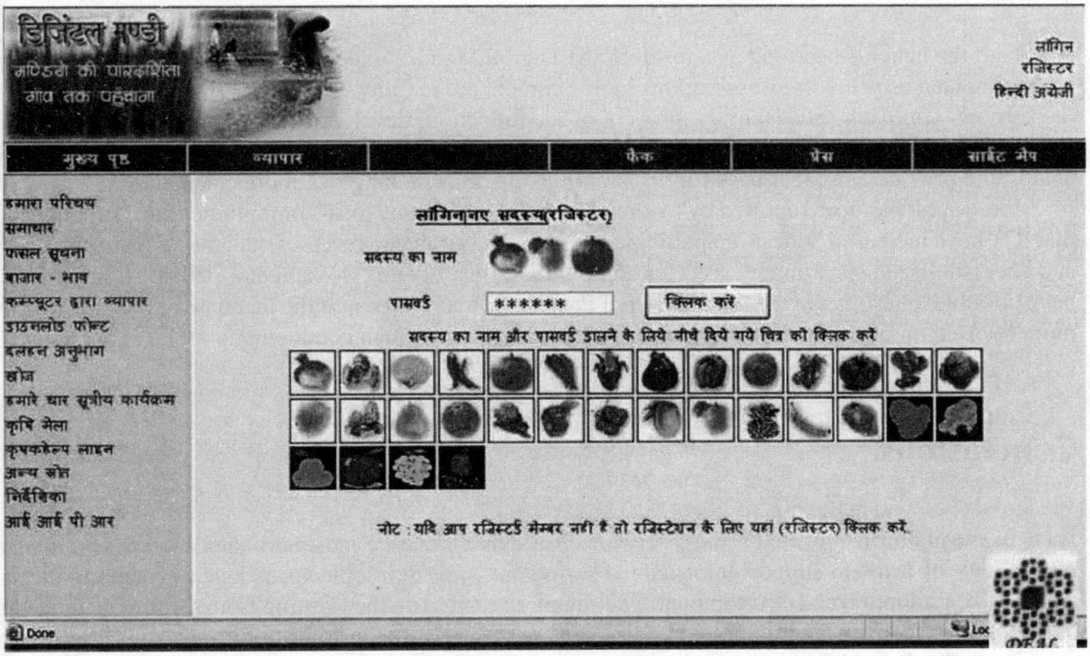

Source: http://opaals.iitk.ac.in/content/embed.jsp?url=iconlogin1.html

is easier. But indexing and search of audio content poses problems and requires manual intervention. Figure 26.3 gives a sample page depicting the user interface addressing some of these issues. The user IDs are iconic, and so are the passwords. In other words, the alphabet consists of images of fruits and vegetables and the user can 'spell' his/her user name and password with this alphabet. That is, a user can choose a tomato with two onions and a potato as the 'name' of the user and another such combination as a password.

A computer-based platform appears difficult to maintain for various reasons. Apart from the cost of the computer, due to erratic power situation, one needs to think of back-up power sources like batteries, un-interrupted power supplies and generating sets, making the whole solution quite untenable. A mobile device, like a phone or a PDA, appears to be the most workable delivery platform.

The Digital Mandi Project thus revealed that ICT tools and technologies could make knowledge and field experiences (in the form of digital content) widely available. Ethnographic observation guided design principles, which improved access and acceptance by rural citizens. But the maintenance, dynamic update and enhancement of the digital content needed regular editorial intervention, and the process of finding and assembling information remained largely a manual task. It was clear that to acquire the characteristics of a self-managed ecosystem in the knowledge-net, the digital contents created in various forms by the stakeholders needed interoperability which would lead to automation and systemic self-management. While initial experiments showed that such syntactic interoperability can be achieved and enforced in a corporate extranet, prevalent socio-technical diversities and existence of a multiplicity of hardware/software in the network pose problems in the domain of agriculture and rural livelihood.

Benefits

Although the benefits accruing as a result of the Digital Mandi Project have not been formally studied or documented as yet, some observations in this context are in order. First, it was quite evident that the 'ecosystem' approach speeds up the process of identification, development and uptake of innovation. Second, rural entrepreneurs benefited because the DE helped to improve access to markets or supply chains and provide a broader base for decision-making, thus making risk more calculable.

Moreover, it has been reported by several researchers that many local communities have experienced that ICT have increased bottom-up participation in the governance processes, and may expand the reach and accessibility of government services and public infrastructure (Dossani et al. 2005). It has not yet been possible to test this in the Digital Mandi Project, primarily because the mandate of the project was more focused on creating a self-sustaining ICT platform rather than conducting a social experiment.

Conclusions

A DBE, as a platform to foster business networks based on a dynamic and amorphous interaction among a multiplicity of firms to support knowledge sharing and skill development, is a self-sustaining mechanism of ICT adoption and development. This chapter reported on the learning from using semantic web technologies to construct agricultural portals to address the need for customization and localization at the rural level. The Digital Ecosystem for Agriculture and Rural Livelihood (DEAL) project is an ambitious web-based initiative at co-ordinating back-end infrastructure, media technology and knowledge bases to make agricultural content easily accessible through multiple channels in rural India. It attempts to overcome language and literacy barriers to knowledge networking and dissipation by the development of iconic, symbolic and visual overlays on knowledge maps. Existing KVKs serve as nodes and catalysts for knowledge-driven self-generative socio-economic development to nurture grass-roots innovation in rural livelihood models. By activating and/or strengthening knowledge, skill, technology and market links, thereby increasing returns on investment for farmers, such a DBE would be instrumental in preserving and nurturing the wisdom of the farmers while improving agricultural competitiveness at the same time.

References

Bhatnagar, S. and R. Schware. 2000 *Information and Communication Technology in Development, Cases from India*. New Delhi: Sage Publications.

Chatterjee, J. and T.V. Prabhakar. 2005. 'On to Action—Building a Digital Ecosystem for Knowledge Diffusion in Rural India', *Proceedings of the 2005 International Conference on Knowledge Management*, North Carolina, USA , available at http://emandi.mla.iitk.ac.in/deal/other/deal_paper.doc

Das, P. 2006. 'Converting Agro-ecosystem Information for Technology Assessment, and Refinement and Demonstration of Agriculture Technology', presented at Zonal Coordinating Unit, PAU, Ludhiana, 13 July.

Davis, F. 1989. 'Perceived Usefulness, Perceived Ease of Use and User Acceptance of Information Technology', *MIS Quarterly*, 13(3): 319–40.

Doll, W. and J. Torkzadeh. 1988. 'The Measurement of End-User Computing Satisfaction', *MIS Quarterly*, 6(2): 259–73.

Dossani, R., D.C. Misra and R. Jhaveri.2005. *Enabling ICT for Rural India*. Asia Pacific Research Center, Stanford University and National Informatics Center. Available online at http://iisdb.stanford.edu/pubs/20972/ICT_full_Oct05.pdf#search=%22ict%20governance%20india%20rural%22, accessed on 30 September 2006.

Huang, W. 2001. 'Using Information Technology to Enhance Communications among Agribusiness Organizations', IAMA World Food and Agribusiness Symposium, 25–27 June 2001, Sydney, NSW, Australia.

Kaushik, P.D. and N. Singh. 2004. 'Information Technology and Broad-based Development: Preliminary Lessons from North India', *World Development*, 32(4): 591–607.

Kralisch, A. and T. Mandl. 2006. 'Barriers to Information Access across Languages on the Internet: Network and Language Effects', in *Proceedings of the 39th Hawaii International Conference on Systems Science* (HICSS-39, 2006), 4–7 January 2006, Kauai, Hawwaii.

Palmer J.W. and D.A. Griffith. 1998. 'Information Intensity: A Paradigm for Understanding Web Site Design', *Journal of Marketing Theory & Practice*, 6(1), 38–42.

Pirolli, P., S.K. Card, and M. Van der Wege. 2001. 'Visual Information Foraging in a Focus+Context Visualization', *Proceedings of the SIGHI Conference on Human Factors in Computing Systems*, pp. 506–13, 31 March to 5 April, Seattle.

Rai, M. 2006. 'Foundation of National Strategy', *The Hindu Survey of Indian Agriculture*, Chennai.

Singh, N. 2002. 'Information Technology as an Engine of Broad Based Growth in India', in P. Banarjee and F.J. Richter (eds), *The Information Economy in India*, pp. 24–57. London: Palgrave/Macmillan.

World Bank. 1997. 'Rural Development: "*From Vision to Action*"', Environmentally and Socially Sustainable Development Studies and Monographs Series No. 12. Washington, DC: The International Bank for Reconstruction and Development.

27 Development Leadership in a Knowledge Economy

NAGENDRA P. SINGH

Introduction

New economy of this century has begun to witness volatile and turbulent nature of competitiveness. One can notice people walking on the tight rope in order to compete with and excel others. Passers-by in the crowd are no longer silent spectators of the past. Anybody can pick up an idea and set the agenda of their choice with a creative mindset. Thus, those currently ahead may be left behind and laggards of the present may win the race. Creativity and innovation is the essence of today's razor edge competition. Experimentation and adventure is the fulcrum of today's business game. Brooders and cautious players are likely to sink in their dilemma unless they learn to resolve the dilemmas and take risks.

This chapter describes the new age of development leadership that is not alien to business growth trend. However, it may appear far away from capitalistic frame of mind due to development concerns of the society and the State. Development leadership seems to emerge as a strong alternative for sustainable growth and equity with appropriate blend of the two. Eventually, it is technology and innovation that can bring out the blend and a balance of the two. Business leadership, seemingly apathetic to social problems, has begun looking at social concerns whereas development leaders of traditional socialistic mindset have begun paying attention to the global business call.

Emergence of Knowledge Economy

Knowledge Leaders

The trend of making new technology out of old stuff, by changing labels, bottles and packaging, has lasted long enough; that was the early trend in the modern economy. Thus, the famous saying 'American innovates, Japanese imitates, European trades, rest of the world consumes...' used to be the epitome of old belief expressed through proverbial jokes. Today, it appears that it is likely to reverse very soon. Therefore, tomorrow's age would not be merely a scene of our wishful thinking. It could become a reality in which 'Indian innovates, European and American trades, rest of the world consumes'. Imitators would have to take a back seat since there is not going to be time for them to imitate, excepting a few innovative imitators.

The recurring theme on global competition is undergoing a major shift in thinking as to what constitutes resources in the economy. Traditional economists' categorization of resources into land, labour and capital has been superseded by 'knowledge' as the prime resource. As a consequence of this change, there is increased interest in human resource management, human capital and the problem of attracting and retaining good knowledge workers. A new environment needs to be created for knowledge workers where competitiveness gives rise to collaboration instead of conflict. It is possible to inculcate those values and ethos that do not break social fibre in order to survive in the knowledge economy which is a product of the global market economy.

Thus, the issue of competition assumes critical significance in the emerging knowledge economy. For nations to succeed as global players, they need knowledge leaders. Innovators are in demand in every field, not in science and technology alone. Ironically, most of us are guided by the economics of competitive living that is opposed to social cohesion and integrated development. A change in mindset is called for. Education policy, therefore, has a major role to play.

Knowledge Workers

The following dilemmas need to be examined and resolved. The question is who will do it and at what level?

1. Whether to create jobs to combat the growing unemployment or inject right social values through a new education order?
2. Whether to create appropriate governance and civic society through social innovators or march ahead in the race of market economy?
3. Whether to build a knowledge economy that creates a fierce competition with individualized urge for excellence or inject a sense of collective social responsibility, and a value of collaboration and networking?
4. Whether to create a class of business leadership like an infectious virus of knowledge economy who wish to demand attention and gratification thereby taking the society for granted or who blend a sense of equity and social responsibility along with business growth through social innovations?.

Knowledge workers are a species different from others. Their nature and attributes add to the complexities of managing the process wherever they dominate. Academic institutions with strong technical bias are a classic example. Scientific institutions, research laboratories, apex councils of business and industry, therefore, have different management concerns. It is believed that higher the degree of technology-centric process and predominance of knowledge workers, greater is the degree of management complexities. Authority variable has three critical issues in such a situation:

1. Knowledge and technical expertise influence the work flow system. It is knowledge expertise that matters in gaining respect in the work system, not the position and structural status. Therefore, command for compliance by those who do not have enough expertise-based influence over others remains oblivious and redundant.

2. Powers and authority-driven traditional structure always clash with techno-centric management process structure.
   The classic example is that of a recent clash between the medical fraternity and the Central government with special reference to a particular institute.

3. Centrality of role and relationship is also important for knowledge workers since they believe that they know more than others for what they are expected to deliver. They work under three assumptions: (*i*) They know that others know less than them. (*ii*) They know the science of everything. (*iii*) They cannot accept others who know less than them.

This framework generates competition amongt the knowledge workers. It is the institutions' climate that gives rise to the sense of competitiveness. In order to survive in the competitive environment, they need to innovate. It is a different issue whether they really innovate or imitate. In the recent past, such a trend of imitating in lieu of innovating has escalated. Competition becomes unfair and the scenario becomes so confusing and dysfunctional that policy makers fail to decide when or where to press the button.

We are entering into a dynamic and new kind of economy that is termed the knowledge economy. It is an economy based not just on the old industrial norms but on new kinds of knowledge, new kinds of technology and the application of those kinds of technologies.

The minimum that can be done to stay ahead of others in such an economy is to keep investing in the knowledge sector. Education has to be the most significant sector where we need to pay attention in order to remain at the cutting edge. It is aggressive investment that is needed in education. That has not happened so far. Although many private players have emerged, unfortunately they have not come up because of the design of the policy but by default. Hence, there are too many problems relating to the entry of the private sector.

Education Policy for the New Order

The unending search for competitive advantage in the global knowledge economy has forced policy makers to examine the complexities of the inevitable that are emerging. The compartmentalized policy has to meet its end. We may not be able to carry on with the hitherto called modern education policy which directs all of us to jobs and careers alone. The new policy should focus on integrating the youth to face the challenges with faith, character and confidence that the society is likely to be confronted with. How do we connect the policy with civil society—issues of inequality emerging from the digital divide leading to knowledge divide? Many such policies are segmented and, as such, non-convergent.

Let us take the example of increased global outsourcing opportunities in the information technology (IT) sector. It has created huge job opportunities for Indians within the country and abroad. In order to meet such a demand for jobs, we should have put in place appropriate initiatives in the education policy. Not much was done as a policy, however. But, the market did something. A large number of poor-quality tutorial shops for teaching English came up. Business process outsourcing (BPO) employed young pass-outs of such schools and undergraduates from public schools, paid them well, but the flipside is that they promoted consumerism. This has already created a new social problem and education disorder. The mindset of the youth has changed and now they want to grab jobs at an early age in order to become consumers of the market economy. There is marked reluctance to pursue higher education and unwillingness to learn job-related skills. The kinds of jobs they are taking up do not shape careers but they do create socio-psychological problems.

Students who studied in schools run by the government fell back in the race for jobs in the BPO sector because of their poor language competence. States like West Bengal, Bihar and Orissa have launched aggressive campaigns to teach English to all the rural and urban youth to enable them to benefit from the job potential of BPOs and the glamorized IT sector.

Only a few decades back, the youth in India craved to get into the knowledge-driven science and technology fields. It was considered highly prestigious to be scientists, engineers and doctors. Recent statistics of Delhi University tell a different story. The IT sector and BPOs have changed the pattern of preferences of students. The youth are now attracted to the easier and faster way to earn big bucks without having to toil for acquiring knowledge.

These developments raise certain questions.

1. Do we want knowledge workers of the kind referred to earlier to be created in the society?
2. Is this the kind of policy we want to pursue for developing our future generations?
3. Do we want to cater to the superfluous market demands or do we want to create a strong and stable knowledge base for our youth?

While we may aspire to develop a knowledge economy, we are not innovating new ideas here. We are simply catering to the innovations that suit the US market system.

A recent study conducted by a Mumbai-based consulting firm, published in a local magazine, revealed that 40 per cent employees of 10 BPO firms had got into serious health problems and 21 per cent had got into illicit relationships, causing new kinds of problems for the society.

For education policy makers, the challenge is to not get locked in individual issues and, instead, rise above the tendency to compartmentalize policy. We must fully recognize the connections that link together various public policies that have an impact on learners of all ages. We must be externally focused and alert to positive initiatives and developments that are taking place in other policy areas. In short, we must have the larger picture of the society in view all the time in the process of transformation.

Challenges of Development Leadership

Leadership has limited options in today's context. Policy makers must see such possibilities through innovative education policy, blending equity and growth, and adding creativity, tolerance, appreciation of diversity and social skills.

For policy makers outside the education sector, who may be tempted to view education in purely economic terms, the challenge is to recognize that the primary purpose of education is to provide everyone with the opportunity to achieve their fullest potential, both as individuals and as members of society.

We may be living in a knowledge society but it is not knowledge workers alone who contribute to society or are entitled to its benefits. The leadership has to ensure that all the people have access to opportunities, they reap the benefits, and the benefits are fairly shared.

Today, information can be gathered and diffused on a global scale, bringing with it countless opportunities. But there are also fears and frustrations, as many people are apprehensive that they are being left behind.

Someone put it emphatically that

> ... in the wake of the painful series of dot.com collapses and the plummeting share prices of many leading technology corporations, it has become all too clear that technology alone will not suffice to ensure economic success. The true source of competitiveness and the key to improving human welfare is to succeed in the 21st century global economy. (Anonymous, Infosys Leadership Seminar held at Mysore, 28 August 2007)

Let us take an example from the corporate world, from the famous experience of Ford. He had the power to serve the leadership and the stockholders from whom he derived financial resources, but he failed in competition to serve the customers. Meanwhile, the company was obliged to retain many employees and ease the burden of dealers to whom it had made commitments. The $250 million budget and the vast resources of a major international company were powerful forces, but not so powerful as to make up for the failure to interest the customers. Innovation was lacking. Similarly, development leaders talk about beneficiaries and partners in development who are poor, deprived and disadvantaged groups, and constitute a large majority. They are the customers of their innovations. Not serving their interests will lead to failure.

Often, new political or business leadership brings about drastic re-organization. However, the re-organization soon flounders in the wake of resistance of employees and society in general. Some companies periodically go through drastic re-organizations. They act on the assumption that any change is good, mistaking temporary increases in productivity for long-term gain. They do not recognize that the underlying resistance of employees is increased by such re-organizations. States' failure to address the above problem would dethrone them from power. It is time the leadership demonstrated integrated development rather than showing fast economic growth without much development. There is hardly any alternative but to focus on collective benefit of society at large instead of driving the policy through pockets of growth that have already created social and economic imbalances.

Appendix: Towards Knowledge Society— A Discussion

> For countries in the vanguard of the world economy, the balance between knowledge and resources has shifted so far towards the former that knowledge has become perhaps the most important factor determining the standard of living—more than land, than tools, than labour. Today's most technologically advanced economies are truly knowledge based.... The need for developing countries to increase their capacity to use knowledge cannot be overstated (World Bank 1998: 16).

This appendix sums up the discussion that took place at the International Management Institute (IMI), New Delhi on 11 October 2006 among Professor Ashoka Chandra, Principal Advisor and Professor, IMI; Professor Subhash Sharma, Dean, Indian Business Academy (IBA), Bangalore and Greater Noida; Professor Vidhu Shekhar Jha, Professor, Corporate Strategy & Operations Management, IMI and Ms. Divya Kirti Gupta, Assistant Professor, Indian Business Academy (IBA), Greater Noida, on the emergence of knowledge economy and knowledge society, and its implications for society, individuals and organizations.

Professor Ashoka Chandra initiated the discussion with the definition of knowledge economy and knowledge society, its possible shape and configuration and the issue of 'values' that shall emerge in due course of time, and the expectations that individuals and society as a whole shall have in such an economy.

Professor Subhash Sharma enunciated a new vision of society in knowledge economy that he earlier suggested in his book, *Western Windows Eastern Doors* (2006). He indicated that the 'view of life' in a knowledge society would be *'eco-sattvik'*, that is, a state in which *'sattvik guna'* gets coupled with the 'ecological world view' thereby representing the transcendental approach. Derived from the word *'sattava'* (essence), *sattvik* means pure/spiritual and *guna* means 'substance-attitudes' (Sharma 2006). The nature of knowledge society would be 'harmonic' and leadership would be 'divine-democratic' type representing enlightened dimension of leadership. He further suggested the idea of 'sacro-scientific' approach to the development of 'sacro-civic' society. In a knowledge society there would be a need to develop sacro-scientific temper in order to address the question of values that scientific temper tends to ignore.

Professor Subhash Sharma was of the view that creating a new society with these characteristics is possible in a knowledge economy because a knowledge economy, by virtue of its nature and in comparison to the industrial economy, shall have high non-polluting elements in it. Moreover, creating such a society shall be 'development' in true sense of the term leading to 'holistic development' and 'all inclusive growth' as well as development of 'sacro-scientific' temper on the part of the citizens.

It is worth mentioning here what Sood (2002) has said about the preliminary experience of rural connectivity projects in different parts of rural India. He concludes that non-elite, rural, artisan and *Adivasi* communities of South Asia do not, and will not, use information and communication in the same way as industrialized nations do elsewhere in the world. Therefore, Sood emphasizes that far from replicating the online behaviour of highly connected and cosmopolitan societies in North America, Europe or SouthEast Asia, digital development in India warrants the design of products, services, and technologies that solve local problems and ameliorate local socio-economic conditions.

According to Professor Subhash Sharma, one element that shall play a crucial role in developing the 'sacro-civic' and 'sacro-scientific' society shall be good governance. Professor Sharma opined that organizations, in order to have good governance, would try to balance competition, conscience and consciousness. He suggested the need to balance market values, social values and spiritual values to develop a sacro-civic society and to create new types of corporates wherein there is a balance between profit, social responsibility and good governance. His model of the balance between market, society and self is presented in Figure A1.1.

Figure A1.1   Harmony Circle for Balancing Market Values, Social values and Spiritual Values

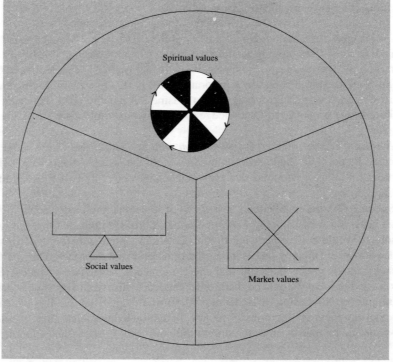

Source: Sharma 2006: 168.

Professor Sharma suggested that in a knowledge economy a new balance would be needed between market potentiality of knowledge, social development dimension of knowledge and its spiritual development potentiality. Hence, the knowledge economy should be evaluated not only from the perspective of its contribution to wealth generation but also from social and spiritual development angles. Hence in the knowledge society, knowledge would be respected not only for its commercial value or wealth generation capacity but also for its potentiality for social and spiritual advancement taking us in the direction of sacro-civic and sacro-scientific society.

Professor Ashoka Chandra looked at the concepts of knowledge economy and knowledge society from a different perspective. Instead of looking at it in terms of arriving at an ideal state of social existence, he focused on the attributes/characteristics/behaviours/things that shall be valued in a knowledge society. He tried to explore as to what shall be held as 'values' and 'disvalues' in a knowledge economy.

Professor Ashoka Chandra proposed that the first thing of great importance in a knowledge economy is 'knowledge' itself. He was of the view that knowledge, by virtue of its own merits, shall be preferred and valued, and shall have an edge over other things. The importance of knowledge has been re-iterated by many experts and authors in recent times. But Professor Chandra emphasized that knowledge shall be valued in a knowledge society beyond its immediate usage. It shall have importance due to the new vistas that it shall open for the mankind and may lead to holistic development.

Professor Chandra and Professor Sharma agreed that if knowledge defines the course of society in the future, 'creativity' shall be valued since creation of new knowledge shall be important in an economy based on knowledge. Creative people shall be in high demand and organizations and society shall invest in training people to be creative. In this scenario, the education system may undergo changes in the future for promoting creativity. In this context, the work of Perkinson (2003) may be referred, who has mentioned about the four pillars of knowledge society—economic and institutional regime, educated and skilled population, information infrastructure and innovation system of firms. Here, it is worth noting that all the four pillars shall be directly affected by not just the type of education system but also the level of education of the masses. Further, it was felt that knowledge creation takes place on the existing base of knowledge. The sharing of knowledge shall also be valued and shall take place not only for democratic reasons alone but also for building up of further knowledge.

The discussion also dwelt on the behaviour of people in respect of the need to disseminate information or knowledge. It was broadly agreed that it is certainly not for creating impact alone or benefiting people, it is also for enlightenment of masses that we need to share knowledge. Knowledge sharing has liberation potentiality. *Ya vidya sa vimuktaye*— it is knowledge that liberates. In a knowledge economy, the liberation potentiality of knowledge shall be an important value as knowledge would be widely available. Cyber revolution has already facilitated this process as it makes information and knowledge widely available to every section of society. Hence, it helps in liberation from domination.

Ms Divya Kirti Gupta stated that often it becomes almost impossible for an individual to hold back a newly created idea or knowledge. A probable reason for this is that creation of new knowledge brings with it a sense of accomplishment leading to a feeling of completeness, fullness and happiness, and the person looks forward to sharing his/her joy with other people. It was also the opinion of Professor Chandra, Professor Sharma and Professor Jha that the joy of novel creation makes sharing of knowledge possible.

Professor Chandra also raised the issue of 'hierarchy' in a knowledge society. It was deliberated that presently hierarchy is in terms of money, power, and so on, but in a knowledge society hierarchy shall get shaped by ideas. It was felt that in a knowledge society, those ideas that help in enlarging people's understanding of self and universe would be valued.

It was also felt that 'democratic set-up' shall be valued in a knowledge economy, which would include transparency, openness and fairness. The issue of 'fairness' was also discussed.

It was suggested by Professor Jha that fairness may be looked at from the perspective of 'justice and accessibility to knowledge', which may lead to a new definition of citizenship. In a knowledge economy accessibility to knowledge shall be taken and accepted as a fundamental right in the same manner as right to speech. It was also indicated that in a knowledge economy, the right to knowledge shall have to be considered equal to the right to salvation, and to have a share in the benefits accruing from knowledge shall also be considered important.

Further, it was suggested by Professor Chandra that the knowledge economy may also create a need to re-define property rights because knowledge cannot be appropriated. So, the need to transcend intellectual property rights (IPR) may also arise in the knowledge society. There was a consensus that property appropriation shall be disvalued in the knowledge economy.

Discussions as mentioned earlier also indicated that 'education of the masses' shall become a value in a knowledge economy and 'sacredness of knowledge' shall also be highly valued.

It was felt that as society is making a shift towards knowledge economy, some 'new collective values' would emerge; they shall be different from the values of economy based on agriculture or industries.

The discussion also dwelt on the 'leadership' that should emerge in the process. Leaders having 'enlightened collective interest' in mind shall be crucial for the growth and sustenance of the knowledge society. A new power framework, based on the importance of knowledge, would also emerge in the knowledge economy.

References

Perkinson, R. 2003. 'Planning Ahead for Knowledge Societies: "A Perfect Storm" for Global Higher Education'. Available online at http://www2.ifc.org/edinvest/doc/EdIndiaSpeechContentRFPApr03.pdf (downloaded on 09.12.2006).

Sood, A.D. 2002. 'Towards a Knowledge Society'. Available online at http://www.indiatogether.org/opinions/ictdiary.htm (downloaded on 05.01.2007).

Sharma, Subhash. 2006. *Management in New Age: Western Windows Eastern Doors*, 2nd edn. New Delhi: New Age International Publishers.

World Bank. 1998. *World Development Report*. Washington D.C.: World Bank.

About the Editors and Contributors

The Editors

Ashoka Chandra, Scientist, Technologist, Educationist, Human Resource Planner and Administrator

Ashoka Chandra is the Chair Professor, Ministry of IT Chair in Knowledge Economy; Chairman, Government of India Initiative on 'Competitiveness in Knowledge Economy'; and Chairman, National Institute of Technology, Patna. He was also the Special Secretary, Government of India, Ministry of Human Resource Development between June 1999 and June 2002.

Professor Ashoka Chandra headed the entire tecnical education system in the country, including IITs, IIMs, technological universities, all engineering colleges and polytechnics, institutions of management education, pharmacy, planning and architecture and applied arts for over a decade. He was also responsible for setting up the statutory All India Council for Technical Education.

M.K. Khanijo, Senior Advisor and Research Consultant

With about 50 years experience of teaching, research, consultancy, training, seminars, etc., in industry, educational institutions and research organizations, M.K. Khanijo developed, organized and taught in numerous training programmes, including international programmes and PG Diploma/Master's Degree Programmes on Human Resource Planning and Development for international participants. The Master's Programme was run with the affiliation of GGSIP University. He also has experience in developing and supervising research/consultancy/training activities, institutional networking and institutional development.

He is also in the process of setting up a Centre for Social Sector Governance for developing research and training programmes on issues relating to education, health, training and employment and participation in governance; and a A Centre for Management of Innovation and Technology for developing research and training on issues relating to development, application and assimilation of technology, working of R&D institutions, and analysis of science and technology policies.

The Contributors

Arindam Banik, Professor, International Management Institute, New Delhi

Surinder Batra, Professor, Institute of Management Technology, Ghaziabad

Savita Bhat, Ph.D. Scholar, IIT-Bombay, Mumbai

Pradip K. Bhaumik, Professor, International Management Institute, New Delhi

Ashoka Chandra, Principal Advisor and Professor, International Management Institute, New Delhi

Jayanta Chatterjee, Professor, IIT, Kanpur

Arundhati Chattopadhyay, Deputy Director, National Productivity Council, New Delhi

Sanjay Dhar, Faculty Member, Management Training Institute, Steel Authority of India Ltd, Ranchi

Divya Kirti Gupta, Assistant Professor, Indian Business Academy, Noida

Abid Hussain, Former Member, Planning Commission, Government of India

Vidhu Shekhar Jha, Professor, International Management Institute, New Delhi

Himanshu Joshi, Lecturer, International Management Institute, New Delhi

M.D.G. Koreth, Chairman, ACORD, New Delhi

T.S. Krishna Murthy, Former Chief Election Commissioner of India

G.S. Krishnan, Director, National Productivity Council, New Delhi

Naresh Kumar, Head, R&D Planning, Council of Scientific & Industrial Research, New Delhi

Niraj Kumar, Professor and Project Director, IMTT, Indian Institute of Foreign Trade, New Delhi

Vinod Kumar, Professor, IIT-Roorkee

Siddharth Mahajan, Associate Professor, International Management Institute, New Delhi

M.S. Mathews, Chairman, Board of Governance; Professor, IIT-Madras, Chennai

Vinay K. Nangia, Professor, IIT-Roorkee

K. Narayanan, Professor, IIT-Bombay, Mumbai

Ravi Prakash, Dean, Research & Consultancy Division, Birla Institute of Technology and Science, Pilani, Rajasthan

Prema Rajagopalan, Associate Professor, IIT-Madras, Chennai

K. Sankaran, Professor, International Management Institute, New Delhi

K.K. Sarkar, Secretary General, Indian Council of Small Industries, Kolkata

Mainak Sarkar, Assistant Professor, International Management Institute, New Delhi

Runa Sarkar, Assistant Professor, IIT-Kanpur

A.K. Sengupta, Professor, International Management Institute, New Delhi

Rajeeva Ratna Shah, Member Secretary, Planning Commission, Government of India

Subhash Sharma, Dean, Indian Business Academy (IBA), Bangalore

Nagendra P. Singh, Chairman, Asian Society of Entrepreneurship Education and Development (ASEED) and Director General, International Institute of Development Management Technology (IDMAT), New Delhi

U.S. Singh, Deputy Director General, National Productivity Council, New Delhi

Arun P. Sinha, Professor of Management, IME Department, IIT-Kanpur

Harsha Sinvhal, Professor, IIT-Roorkee

Index